Educating All Students in the Mainstream of Regular Education

Educating All Students in the Mainstream of Regular Education

edited by

Susan Stainback, Ed.D.
College of Education
University of Northern Iowa
Cedar Falls

William Stainback, Ed.D.
College of Education
University of Northern Iowa
Cedar Falls

Marsha Forest, Ed.D.
Center for Integrated Education
Frontier College
Toronto, Ontario

Baltimore · London · Toronto · Sydney

Paul H. Brookes Publishing Co.
Post Office Box 10624
Baltimore, Maryland 21285-0624

Typeset by The Composing Room of Michigan, Inc., Grand Rapids, Michigan.
Manufactured in the United States of America by
The Maple Press Company, York, Pennsylvania.

Library of Congress Cataloging-in-Publication Data

Educating all students in the mainstream of regular education / edited by Susan Stainback, William Stainback, Marsha Forest.
p. cm.
Bibliography: p.
Includes index.
ISBN 1-55766-022-0
1. Special education—United States. 2. Mainstreaming in education—United States. I. Stainback, Susan Bray. II. Stainback, William C. III. Forest, Marsha.
LC3981.E36 1989
371.9′046′0973—dc20 89-32596
CIP

Contents

Contributors

Douglas Biklen, Ph.D.
Division of Special Education and Rehabilitation
Syracuse University
805 South Crouse Avenue
Syracuse, NY 13244-2280

Katherine D. Bishop, M.A.
Doctoral Student
School of Education
California State University, Los Angeles
5151 State University Drive
Los Angeles, CA 90032

Gary Bunch, Ph.D.
Professor
York University
Downsview, Ontario M3J 1P3
CANADA

Sandra L. Christenson, Ph.D.
Assistant Professor
Educational Psychology
University of Minnesota
350 Elliott Hall
75 East River Road
Minneapolis, MN 55455

Jennifer Coots, M.A.
Doctoral Student
School of Education
California State University, Los Angeles
5151 State University Drive
Los Angeles, CA 90032

Mary A. Falvey, Ph.D.
Professor
School of Education
California State University, Los Angeles
5151 State University Drive
Los Angeles, CA 90032

George Flynn, M.Ed.
Director of Education
Waterloo Region Roman Catholic Separate School Board
91 Moore Avenue
Kitchener, Ontario N2H 3S4
CANADA

Marsha Forest, Ed.D.
Educational Consultant and Advisor
Frontier College, Canada
35 Jackes Avenue
Toronto, Ontario M4T 1E2
CANADA

Alan Gartner, Ph.D.
Professor and Director
Office of Sponsored Research
City University of New York
33 West 42nd Street
New York, NY 10036

Marquita Grenot-Scheyer, M.A.
Doctoral Student
School of Education
California State University, Los Angeles
5151 State University Drive
Los Angeles, CA 90032

Berj Harootunian, Ph.D.
Professor of Education
Division for the Study of Teaching
Syracuse University
Syracuse, NY 13244-2280

Peter Knoblock, Ph.D.
Professor of Special Education
Division of Special Education and Rehabilitation
Syracuse University
Syracuse, NY 13244-2280

Bernie Kowalczyk-McPhee, M.Ed.
Assistant Superintendent
Student Services
Waterloo Region Roman Catholic Separate School Board
91 Moore Avenue
Kitchener, Ontario N2H 3S4
CANADA

Dorothy Kerzner Lipsky, Ph.D.
Administrator, Bellmore
New York Public Schools
Research Scientist, City University of New York
33 West 42nd Street
New York, NY 10036

Evelyn Lusthaus, Ed.D.
Associate Professor
Faculty of Education
McGill University
Montreal, Quebec
CANADA

Jack Pearpoint, B.A.
President
Frontier College
35 Jackes Avenue
Toronto, Ontario M4T 1E2
CANADA

James G. Shriner, M.S.
Graduate Fellow
Educational Psychology
University of Minnesota
350 Elliott Hall
75 East River Road
Minneapolis, MN 55455

Robert Slavin, Ph.D.
Director
Elementary School Program
Center for Research on Elementary and Middle Schools
The Johns Hopkins University
3505 North Charles Street
Baltimore, MD 21218

Judith A. Snow, M.A.
Special Advisor
The Canadian Association for Community Living
Kinsman Building
York University
4700 Keele Street
Downsview, Ontario M3J 1P3
CANADA

Susan Stainback, Ed.D.
Professor
University of Northern Iowa
Cedar Falls, IA 50614

William Stainback, Ed.D.
Professor
University of Northern Iowa
Cedar Falls, IA 50614

Cindy F. Strully, M.A.
Inservice Coordinator
Community Living Alternatives
2460 West 26th Street
Suite 460 - C
Denver, CO 80211

Jeffrey L. Strully, Ed.D.
Executive Director
Association for Retarded Citizens in Colorado
1600 Sherman Street
Suite 750
Denver, CO 80203

Jacqueline S. Thousand, Ph.D.
Assistant Professor
University of Vermont
Center for Developmental Disabilities
499C Waterman Building
Burlington, VT 05405

Richard A. Villa, Ed.D.
Winooski School District
Director of Pupil Personnel Services
80 Normand Street
Winooski, VT 05404

Margaret C. Wang, Ph.D.
Temple University Center for Research in Human Development and Education
9th Floor, Ritter Hall Annex
Philadelphia, PA 19122

James E. Ysseldyke, Ph.D.
Professor
Educational Psychology
University of Minnesota
350 Elliott Hall
75 East River Road
Minneapolis, MN 55455

Preface

This book addresses approaches for merging or integrating special and regular education and for educating all students in the mainstream of regular education as a regular, normal, and expected practice. It also stresses the importance of regarding all students as unique and whole individuals. The book does *not* encourage strategies that espouse integrated services but result in continued segregation on a psychological, if not physical, level of students, staff, and/or resources. For instance, it does not suggest ways for separate groups of special and regular educators to team up, coordinate, or renegotiate their roles to meet the needs of "special" students in regular education classrooms. Likewise, this book does not propose a reorganization of a still separate, "special" education system into fewer categories of deviance into which some students would be so labeled. It *does* suggest strategies that can be used to achieve integration, oneness, belonging, and an egalitarian, quality system of education for all students and teachers. The book is based on the premise that students cannot be truly integrated and become one with each other unless the teachers, resources, and the systems of special and regular education are likewise integrated.

Educating All Students is divided into six major sections. Part I comprises an introduction and historical overview of educational integration (Chapter 1) and a rationale for merging the special and regular systems of education as a way of achieving both quality and equality in the schools (Chapter 2).

Part II contains examples and discussions of three situations in which a school system (Chapter 3), a classroom (Chapter 4), and a family (Chapter 5) are actively involved in promoting integration and equality.

Part III's four chapters focus on organizational considerations and strategies for enhancing both quality and equality in heterogeneous, integrated schools. Included are organizational steps for integration (Chapter 6), beliefs and practices that promote successful heterogeneous schools (Chapter 7), school administration and financial programs to promote integration (Chapter 8), and ways to facilitate the merger of integration through personnel preparation (Chapter 9).

Part IV discusses educational practices that can be used in integrated classroom settings to meet diverse student needs. General classroom organization and arrangement (Chapter 10), curriculum design and adaptations (Chapter 11), assessment procedures (Chapter 12), instructional adaptations (Chapter 13), and educational management (Chapter 14) are included.

To complement school and classroom integration strategies and practices, Part V includes a discussion of and strategies for broadening integration and equality beyond the schools through family participation (Chapter 15) and community participation (Chapter 16).

Part VI, the final section, addresses concerns relevant to the education of students in integrated schools and classrooms. The emphases are on achieving equality for all students (Chapter 17), promoting a quality education for all students (Chapter 18), and focusing on concerns regarding the implementation of a merged or unified system of education (Chapter 19).

Throughout the text, Points to Ponder are included for the reader's contemplation. It should be noted that all Points to Ponder that were not referenced were written by the editors.

Educating All Students in the Mainstream of Regular Education

PART I

Overview

CHAPTER 1

Introduction and Historical Background

William Stainback, Susan Stainback, and Gary Bunch

INTRODUCTION

A growing number of parents and educators are beginning to advocate that *all* students be integrated into the mainstream of regular education, including those who have traditionally been labeled severely and profoundly handicapped (e.g., Gartner & Lipsky, 1987; Ruttiman & Forest, 1986; Stainback & Stainback, 1987; Strully, 1986; Wellington County Roman Catholic Separate School Board, 1984). These advocates essentially believe that it is time to stop developing criteria for who does or does not belong in the mainstream, and that the spotlight should be turned instead toward increasing the capabilities of the regular education mainstream to meet the unique needs of *all* students.

For a number of reasons, this movement has gained momentum in a number of countries, including the United States and Canada, the two countries the authors in this book represent. One reason frequently cited is the benefits to the students. It has been found that, given proper guidance, students can learn in integrated settings to understand, respect, be sensitive to, and grow comfortable with the individual differences and similarities among their peers (McHale & Simeonsson, 1980; Voeltz, 1980, 1982). It has also been shown that students can learn to interact, communicate, develop friendships, work together, and assist one another based on their individual strengths and needs (Forest, 1987; Stainback & Stainback, 1988; Strully, 1986). Recent research and experience have furthermore demonstrated that, when given individualized, adaptive, and cooperative learning programs, all students can be provided an opportunity to achieve their potential in integrated settings (Berres & Knoblock, 1987; Certo, Haring, & York, 1984; Madden & Slavin, 1983; Stainback & Stainback, 1985).

Another, and perhaps more powerful, reason for educating all students in regular education is the ill effects of segregation and separation in our schools. The civil rights movement has made both Americans and Canadians more sensitive to these effects. As Chief Justice Earl Warren stated in the landmark 1954 *Brown v. Board of Education* decision, separateness in education can

> generate a feeling of inferiority as to [children's] status in the community that may affect their hearts and minds in a way unlikely ever to be undone. This sense of inferiority . . . affects the motivation of a child to learn . . . [and] has a tendency to retard . . . educational and mental development. (p. 493)

A third reason for educating all students in regular education is that it is simply the morally and ethically right thing to do.

Point to Ponder

The chief advocate for the defense in the 1954 *Brown v. Board of Education* decision, John W. Davis, argued that if segregation for black children was unconstitutional, surely it will be found that segregation of children defined as disabled is also unacceptable. (Gilhool, 1976)

In the final analysis it is a moral or value issue. As Biklen noted in 1985:

> Science cannot offer a yes or no decision on integration. An analogy may make the point clearer. At the time of the American Civil War, should Abraham Lincoln have asked to see the scientific evidence on the benefits of ending slavery? Should he have consulted with "the experts," perhaps a sociologist, an economist, a political scientist? Of course not. Slavery is not now and was not then an issue for science. It is a moral issue. But, just for a moment, suppose that an economist had been able to demonstrate that Blacks would suffer economically, as would the entire South, from emancipation. Would that justify keeping slavery? And suppose a political scientist had argued that Blacks had no experience with democracy, they were not ready for it. Would that have justified extending slavery? Or imagine that a sociologist could have advised Lincoln against abolishing slavery on the grounds that it would destroy the basic social structure of Southern plantations, towns, and cities. From a racist perspective, all of the arguments might have seemed "true." But could they really justify slavery? Of course not. Slavery has no justification. (pp. 16–17)

Those parents, professionals, politicians, and community members who are working for the integration of all students into regular education have made a value judgment that integrated education is the best and most humane way to proceed. From their perspective, the point just made about slavery applies also to current segregationist practices in Canada and the United States. If we want an integrated society in which all persons are considered of equal worth and as having equal rights, segregation in the schools cannot be justified. That is, no defensible excuses or rationales can be offered, and no amount of scientific research can be conducted that will in the final analysis justify segregation. Segregation has no justification; it is simply unfair and morally wrong to segregate any students, including those defined as disabled, from the mainstream of regular education. If we accept this viewpoint, our job as educators is *not* to conduct research on whether educating all students in regular education is a good idea. Instead, as Kendall (1971) encouraged educators some time ago, "We must . . . consider some solutions, some of the directions for action which can be taken now and not have to wait till tomorrow" (p. 20). This book examines ways to provide an appropriate and effective education for every student within the mainstream of regular education. The remainder of this first chapter presents historical background information as a prelude to this discussion.

INTEGRATING OUR SCHOOLS—A HISTORICAL OVERVIEW

"For practically all of the history of civilization, education has been for the elite, and educational practices have reflected an elitist orientation" (Blankenship & Lilly, 1981). There have been, however, persistent attempts throughout history to include all students in the mainstream of education. Until approximately 1800 in North America, the great majority of students considered disabled learners were not deemed worthy of education at all. Throughout the 19th century and much of the 20th, there followed a lengthy period of institutionalized, segregated education. Recent years have witnessed a movement toward mainstreamed education for many previously segregated learners, a movement sometimes slow and hesitant, but always progressive. Now, as we approach the year 2000, the goal of universal mainstream education is potentially within our grasp, although upward progress has been hard won. The following pages review the path this climb has taken in the North American context.

Early Years of Education

For most students considered poor, minority, and/or disabled in North America, the first hurdle was merely to receive an education; integration into the mainstream of education would come much later. As early as 1779 a plan for the first state supported school system was proposed by Thomas Jefferson to help provide the poor of Virginia an education. Unfortunately, at this time the plan was rejected. As stated by Rippa: "Indeed, in a society of class distinctions, the failure of the plan was undoubtedly caused by the refusal of well-to-do citizens to pay taxes for the education of the poor" (Sigmon, 1983, p. 5).

In Canada, movement toward publicly funded education for all followed the U.S. example, but at a later date, due to a variety of cultural, demographic, and economic factors. However, approximately a century after Jefferson's early endeavor, the efforts of educational leaders such as Horace Mann in the United States and Egerton Ryerson in upper Canada, coupled with the massive influx of immigrants during the late 1800s and early 1900s who needed to be "Americanized" or "Canadianized," persuaded the affluent that the education of the "lower" classes was in their best interest. As a result, publicly supported education was adopted, and all states and provinces, except Quebec and Newfoundland, passed compulsory education attendance laws between 1842 and 1918 (Quebec and Newfoundland both followed suit in 1942).

All was not positive, however. When blacks and native Americans were educated, they were educated in a separate system of education. Similarly, students identified as disabled were, for the most part, excluded from the public schools. Tracking by academic ability also became popular in schools. Children who were poor and disadvantaged were relegated routinely to lower nonacademic tracks. Exceptions for early school leaving, primarily affecting children from the lower socioeconomic groups, were made. All of this worked against achieving a truly integrated, mainstreamed education for all students.

Educating Students with Disabilities

Benjamin Rush, an American physician, was one of the first North Americans to introduce the concept of educating persons with disabilities. But whereas Rush put forward the idea in the late 1700s, it was not until 1817 that the first such educational program was established by Thomas Gallaudet at the American Asylum for the Education and Instruction of the Deaf and Dumb in Connecticut. Other U.S. and Canadian programs for educating students with various disabilities were established soon afterwards. For example, the New England Asylum for the Education of the Blind was founded in 1829 in Watertown,

Massachusetts, and the Experiential School for Teaching and Training Idiotic Children was founded in 1846 in Barre, Massachusetts. In Canada a short-lived school for deaf children was opened by Ronald McDonald in Champlain, Quebec, in 1931. More permanent schools were opened in Montreal by the Catholic Church in 1848 (for boys) and 1851 (for girls). The first Canadian school specifically for students designated as mentally handicapped was established on the grounds of a government institution for "feeble-minded" adults and children in Orillia, Ontario, in 1888. It should be emphasized, however, that not all students with disabilities were receiving an education by this time. Those who did, often received it in asylums or government- or church-supported institutions. (It was not until the mid-1800s that Samuel Howe advocated for the education of *all* children, an idea that, as discussed later in this chapter, did not reach fruition until over a century later with the passage of PL 94-142 in the United States and a variety of provincially based laws and initiatives in Canada.)

But even with the passage of compulsory attendance laws in the early 1900s, many children with disabilities continued to be excluded from the public schools. As noted by Sigmon (1983), "almost all children who were wheelchair-bound, not toilet trained, or considered ineducable were excluded because of the problems that schooling them would entail" (p. 3). Further, for those who were allowed to attend the schools, exclusion from regular classes was affected by "a movement for the establishment of special classes. Special classes came about, not for humanitarian reasons but because such children were unwanted in the regular public school classroom. Feelings against . . . placing them in regular classrooms, were strong" (Chaves, 1977, p. 30). This is not meant to imply that individuals who have worked in special classes and special education throughout history have not had humanitarian motives.

Teachers in regular classrooms perceived educators working in special education classes as having special training and/or a special capacity for the work. They were a breed apart, and it was inappropriate to expect teachers lacking such training and inclination to participate in educating students in wheelchairs and/or students who had difficulty learning academics. This type of defensive and rejective reasoning led to the creation of what might be termed "little red schoolhouses for students considered exceptional" within regular school buildings. Students and teachers were "in" a regular school, but in many ways were not an accepted part of it. As special classes increased in number, attitudes among "regular" and "special" educators and evolving administrative models for segregated education ensured that regular and special education developed on parallel, rather than converging, lines.

While special classes and special day schools began to gain momentum in the early 1900s, educational programs in asylums and residential institutions for students with disabilities remained a dominant growing and expanding force in educating students labeled as special until the mid 1900s. It was not until the 1950s and 1960s that special classes in public schools became the preferred educational delivery system for most students with disabilities; however, residential institutions and special schools remained the norm for educating students who were blind, deaf, and physically handicapped. Whereas the situation was improving for some students with disabilities over time, students considered severely or profoundly developmentally handicapped were generally still denied educational services of any type, and resided

Point to Ponder

A person classified as disabled recently recounted his school years in special education classes:

> We were isolated. Symbolically—and appropriate to the prevailing attitudes—the "handicapped and retarded" classrooms were tucked away in the corner of the school basement. Our only activity with the other children was the weekly school assembly. We never participated in any school program. We watched. Although the school lunchroom was also in the basement, we ate lunch in our classrooms. During fire drills, we did not leave the building (were we expendable? . . .). We stood in the hallway outside of our classroom, watching the others file past . . . looking and being looked at.
>
> Summing it up, the only contact we had with the "normal" children was visual. We stared at each other. On those occasions, I can report my own feelings: embarrassment. Given the loud, clear message that was daily being delivered to them, I feel quite confident that I can also report their feelings: YECH! We, the children in the "handicapped" class, were internalizing the "yech" message—plus a couple of others. We were in school because children go to school, but we were outcasts, with no future and no expectation of one. I, for one, certainly never contemplated my future. I could not even picture one, much less dream about it. (Massachusetts Advocacy Center, 1987, pp. 4–5)

primarily in the back wards of large state and provincial institutions. Contributing to the lack of social and educational change for many was a common public perception that people with disabilities possessed criminal tendencies because of their genetic makeup (Davies, 1930). Progress was hard won in the face of widespread public prejudice that many individuals identified as disabled had no place in ordinary school and community life.

Civil Rights and Public Education

In the 1950s and 60s, after the country had recovered from the hardships of a severe depression and two world wars, there developed an increased recognition and respect for the human dignity of all citizens regardless of their individual differences. There was a powerful momentum away from more segregated options for the education of minority students. In the most notable early landmark of this era, the earlier-mentioned 1954 *Brown v. Board of Education* decision, Chief Justice Warren ruled that "separate is not equal." While this had an almost immediate impact in breaking down the exclusionary policies toward blacks and other racial and ethnic minorities, it also led the way toward increased study of exclusionary policies for students with disabilities in later decades. Although, due to differences in population makeup and historical antecedents, Canadian school systems had developed largely without the racial segregation systems of the United States, the winds of change leading to scrutiny of exclusionary policies for specified groups of students were felt in Canada as well.

It was during the 1950s and 1960s in the United States that parents of students with disabilities organized (e.g., National Association for Retarded Citizens) and initiated advocacy activities for educating their children, and that the federal government funded legislation supporting increased education for students considered disadvantaged, low income, and/or handicapped. For example, Congress established the National Cooperative Educational Research Program of 1957, which gave priority to studying students labeled as mentally retarded; it provided funds in 1958, 1961, and 1963 to prepare teachers for students with handicaps; and it passed the Elementary and Secondary Education Act (ESEA) of 1965, allocating federal support for the schools and establishing the Head Start program, which emphasized serving disadvantaged students from low-income families. The ESEA was amended in 1969 to also support programs for students considered gifted and talented. Thus, during the 50s and 60s, the educational needs of disabled students experienced considerable growth in support and resources. A group of leaders including Burton Blatt (1969), Lloyd Dunn (1968), Gunnar Dybwad (1964), Issac Goldberg (1958), Nicholas Hobbs (1966), Stephen Lilly (1970), Maynard Reynolds (1962), and Wolf Wolfensberger (1972) had begun advocating for the rights of students with disabilities to learn in more normalized school environments with their peers. The restrictions imposed by segregated settings such as institutions, special schools, and special classes were being viewed for the first time on a fairly widespread basis as inappropriate and inimical.

Organization and support at the parent and government levels emerged more slowly in Canada. Little development occurred in the 1950s other than an expansion and elaboration of the segregated model of education. The constitutional setup in Canada places control of elementary and secondary education in the hands of the provinces; there is no effective federal power or commitment to education at these levels. As a result, the Canadian parliament cannot act on a national basis in education. Parental and educational advocacy groups thus work at the provincial level in Canada in a fashion determined by local needs and resources.

Nonetheless, decisive movement toward challenging the segregated model of education occurred in Canada in the 1960s. Parents and some professionals began advocating for the rights of children with disabilities. The Canadian Association for the Mentally Retarded (now the Canadian Association for Community Living) established provincial chapters and a national presence. There was also movement toward forming a national parents' association in learning disabilities. Local parents' associations for children with auditory difficulties were also established. As well, during the 1960s in a number of provinces, educational programs for children identified as retarded were transferred from under parents' groups to local public education systems. Here and there, across the country, children were being moved from educationally isolated situations toward the mainstream educational community. Such occurrences were few and the progress was unmarked by most educators, but it was nonetheless significant.

An important milestone in the provision of free and appropriate education for all children was reached in Nova Scotia in 1969. In that year, mandatory legislation was passed and school boards were required to provide schooling for children with disabilities as well as for nonhandicapped children. The effect of the legislation was reduced somewhat by an exclusionary clause that could be invoked in instances of extreme behavioral problems. However, this legislation forecast the passing of a series of mandatory education laws across North America.

Education in the Least Restrictive Environment

While support and resource growth in education characterized the 1950s and 1960s in both the United States and Canada, it was not until the 1970s that the natural sequel to the 1954 *Brown v. Board of Education* decision (Warren, 1954) for students with disabilities began to be widely enacted in the United States. Court decisions in Pennsylvania and the District of Columbia, in 1971 and 1972, respectively, established the right of all children labeled as mentally retarded to a free and appropriate education. This made it much more difficult for students with disabilities to be excluded from the public schools and denied an education. In 1973 the Rehabilitation Act, Section 504, and later amendments guaranteed the rights of persons with handicaps in employment and in educational institutions that receive federal monies. Subsequently, due to pressure by parents, courts, and legislatures, PL 94-142 (Education for All Handicapped Children Act) was passed in 1975 and enacted in 1978. This law stipulates that *no* child, regardless of disability, can be denied an appropriate public education in the least restrictive environment. It thus extended the right to a free public education to all children, to be offered in the least segregated arrangement possible. Spurred by the passage of PL 94-142, all states by 1976 had passed laws subsidizing public school programs for students with disabilities. In addition, several national associations for regular educators passed resolutions in support of mainstreaming; and many states began requiring regular class teachers to take coursework to prepare them for mainstreaming. Also about this time, a number of people, most notably Norris Haring, Lou Brown, Wayne Sailor, Doug Guess, and William and Diane Bricker, began strongly advocating for the education of students with severe and profound disabilities in regular neighborhood public schools. In 1979, The Association for Persons with Severe Handicaps (TASH) adopted a resolution calling for the education of all students with severe disabilities in regular neighborhood schools with their nonhandicapped peers. A few years later, the National Society for Children and Adults with Autism adopted a similar resolution calling for the termination of segregated placements.

Parallel action occurred in Canada in both the legislative and public community arenas. In 1971 the province of Saskatchewan passed legislation mandating appropriate education in the least restrictive environment for students with handicaps. Manitoba followed in 1976 with mandatory legislation, as did Newfoundland and Quebec in 1979, and Ontario, Canada's most populous province, in 1980. The details of the legislation differ from province to province. Saskatchewan, for example, was the sole province with a least restrictive environment clause. The effect of the laws, however, has been to stimulate activity in integration and to encourage attempts to integrate children previously considered only for segregated placement. Karagianis and Nesbit (1980) described the national public policy scene as fluid, but documented a bias to least restrictive placement.

From the 1950s through the 1970s, Canada did not develop the mandating of services through court decisions to the same degree as did the United States. Legal examination of the issue of segregation-integration was rare. A limited number of cases did arise, however, causing ripples in the Canadian special education scene. In 1978, in Alberta, a province yet without mandatory legislation, the parents of Shelley Carriere, an 11-year-old girl with multiple handicaps, challenged the Lamont County Board of Education's exclusion of Shelley from her local school system. The board had invoked an exclusionary clause in Alberta's education act. The Supreme Court of Alberta overruled the exclusionary clause and directed Lamont County to provide education for

Shelley. The manner in which the education was to be provided was not detailed in the judgment (Bunch, 1984).

Also during the 1970s, public pressure for the integration of children with severe and profound disabilities increased. The CELDIC Report (Commission on Emotional and Learning Disorders in Children, 1970) began the decade with the recommendation that "because of the negative effects of separate education facilities, educational authorities [should] minimize the isolation of children with emotional and learning disorders and plan programs for them that as far as possible retain children within the regular school curricula and activities" (p. 400). Shortly thereafter, Kendall (1971), a leading Canadian educator, cast another stone into the pool of complacent acceptance of continued segregation of many children.

> I believe that in an ideal educational system there would be no need for special education. We wouldn't need to single out particular children for special treatment, for each child would be on an individualized program. Above all, we wouldn't exclude children from school, or put them into inferior educational settings, simply because they didn't fit the system. It would be possible for each child to progress at the rate that was right for him and most important of all, each one of us, children as well as adults, would accept and respect the wide range of individual differences that inevitably occurs in any population. (p. 19)

A third source of ripples, this time with effects on the international scene, was the publication of Wolfensberger's (1972) *Principle of Normalization in Human Services* in Toronto at the National Institute on Mental Retardation. This principle and the subsequent modifications that focused more on social image enhancement or social valorization (Wolfensberger, 1984) have played a profound role in reducing segregationist practices.

Despite this early flurry of activities and publications from respected professionals, no one voice or set of voices cried loudly and continuously for the complete integration of all children defined as disabled with their nondisabled peers. Parents' associations were vocal, but primarily on the issue of integration for children considered to have moderate disabilities. Here and there isolated parents pushed the cause of their son or daughter with severe or profound disabilities. Receptive educators responded on a case by case basis. However, the voices of advocates in the United States were heard in Canada as well, and parents, educators, and other professionals were questioning segregated placements.

Also during the 1960s and 70s, increasing numbers of people across North America began to question the utility and to cite the detrimental effects of special education classifications and labeling practices. As a result, there was much discussion and at

Point to Ponder

The process toward integration has followed a well-worn path traveled by several generations of people classified as disabled in nearly the same sequence of graduated steps experienced by several generations of black students. The process seems to have been: identify, categorize, separate, equalize, integrate. The process for blacks was called desegregation; for people with disabilities it is called integration. (Sailor & Guess, 1983)

least some movement away from using handicapping categories or labels and toward simply addressing individual differences among students (Lilly, 1979).

Education of All Students in Regular Education

By the late 1970s and early 1980s, those students considered more mildly or moderately handicapped began to be integrated into regular class placements on at least a part-time basis, and many students who had not been served in the past (those considered severely/profoundly handicapped) increasingly began to receive educational services in regular neighborhood schools with involvement in regular school environments such as the cafeteria, playground, library, halls, buses, and rest rooms (Biklen, 1985; Certo et al., 1984; Knoblock, 1982; Lusthaus, 1988; Stainback & Stainback, 1985).

In 1986, the United States Office of Special Education and Rehabilitation Services in the U.S. Department of Education, issued the "Regular Education Initiative" (Will, 1986). The purpose was to find ways to serve students classified as having mild and moderate disabilities in regular classrooms by encouraging special education and other special programs to form a partnership with regular education. Margaret Wang, Jack Birch, and Maynard Reynolds, among others, have been strong supporters of the initiative (Reynolds & Birch, 1988; Wang, Reynolds, & Walberg, 1987).

By the mid to late 1980s there also was greater attention and recognition of the need to educate all students, not just those labeled mildly and moderately handicapped, in the mainstream of regular education (Berres & Knoblock, 1987; Biklen, 1985; Forest, 1987; Knoblock, 1982; Pugach, 1988; Sapon-Shevin, Pugach, & Lilly, 1987; Stainback & Stainback, 1987; Strully, 1986). At about the same time, as a means to accomplish this, it was proposed to merge special and regular education into a single comprehensive regular education system (Gartner & Lipsky, 1987; Stainback & Stainback, 1984; York & Vandercook, 1988). Also during this time, in both Canada and the United States, advocacy for and experimentation with actually integrating students with severe and profound disabilities into regular classrooms on a part- or full-time basis was begun (Biklen, 1988; Forest, 1987; Knoblock, 1982; Stainback & Stainback, 1988; Strully & Strully, 1985; Thousand & Villa, 1988). A number of school boards in Ontario and Quebec have carried this practice past the experimental level, establishing it as boardwide policy. In 1988, The Association for Persons with Severe Handicaps adopted a resolution that calls for the education of students classified as having severe and profound disabilities in regular education.

Despite the steady trend throughout North American history toward including all students into the mainstream of regular education (Reynolds & Birch, 1982), there have also been attempts to slow, stop, and even reverse this trend. Such attempts to impede inclusion policies are evident even today. For instance, despite mandates for placement of students in least restrictive educational environments, some states and provinces have shown no progress in this area, and some have actually increased restrictive, segregated placements. Likewise, some states have made more rigid their categorical teacher certification, and some organizations and states have proposed the reinstitution of segregated schools for students with disabilities (see Gartner & Lipsky, 1987). Also, some scholars and researchers have argued against the integration movement (Braaten, Kauffman, Braaten, Polsgrove, & Nelson, 1988; Hallahan, Keller, Mc-

Point to Ponder

On the floor of the United States Congress, former Senator Lowell Weicker stated:

> Authorities on disability have often said, and I have quoted them on this floor before, that the history of society's formal methods of dealing with people with disabilities can be summed up in two words: segregation and inequality. Psychologist Kenneth Clark, whose testimony about the damaging effects of segregation provided pivotal evidence in the landmark case of *Brown v. Board of Education*, has stated that "segregation is the way in which a society tells a group of human beings that they are inferior to other groups of human beings in the society." As a society, we have treated people with disabilities as inferiors and have made them unwelcome in many activities and opportunities generally available to other Americans. (Senator Lowell Weicker, 1988, p. 1)

Kinney, Lloyd, & Bryan, 1988; Kauffman, Gerber, & Semmel, 1988; Lieberman, 1988). However, as in the past, such arguments have done little to slow the overall recognition and trend toward achieving a mainstreamed education.

Future Needs

The development of education in North America has come a long way in the quest to end segregation in schools. It is time, however, to reexamine these gains to determine how to further assure equality of rights and opportunity for all students in the educational mainstream. In particular, society must continue to work toward the desegregation of students considered handicapped, disabled, or exceptional. As noted by Ted Kennedy, Jr. (1986), it is those individuals defined as disabled that constitute the "last bastion of segregation" (p. 6). If this segregation can be broken down within the public school system and all students educated in the mainstream of regular education, we will be well on the way to breaking down segregation in society in general.

CONCLUSION

This historical review has indicated that society is gradually moving away from the segregationist practices of the past and toward providing all students an equal opportunity to have their educational needs met within the mainstream of regular education. A major barrier to this goal, and one that is being recognized increasingly, is the continued operation of the dual systems of special and regular education (Gartner & Lipsky, 1987; Stainback & Stainback, 1984). The next chapter examines in depth the rationale for merging special and regular education.

REFERENCES

Berres, M., & Knoblock, P. (1987). *Program models for mainstreaming.* Rockville, MD: Aspen Publishing.

Biklen, D. (Ed.). (1985). *The complete school: Integrating special and regular education.* New York: Columbia University, Teacher's College Press.

Biklen, D. (Producer). (1988). *Regular Lives* [Video]. Washington, DC: State of the Art.

Blankenship, C., & Lilly, S. (1981). *Mainstream-*

ing students with learning and behavior problems. New York: Holt, Rinehart & Winston.

Blatt, B. (1969). *Exodus from pandemonium*. Boston: Allyn & Bacon.

Braaten, S., Kauffman, J., Braaten, B., Polsgrove, L., & Nelson, M. (1988). The regular education initiative: Patent medicine for behavioral disorders. *Exceptional Children, 55*, 21–29.

Bunch, G.O. (1984). Special education in Canada: An overview. In D.D. Hammill, N.R. Bartel, & G.O. Bunch (Eds.), *Teaching children with learning and behavior problems* (2d ed.) (pp. 1–27). Toronto, Ont.: Allyn & Bacon.

Certo, N., Haring, N., & York, R. (Eds.). (1984). *Public school integration of severely handicapped students*. Baltimore: Paul H. Brookes Publishing Co.

Chaves, I.M. (1977). Historical overview of special education in the United States. In P. Bates, T.L. West, & R.B. Schmerl (Eds.), *Mainstreaming: Problems, potentials, and perspectives* (pp. 25–41). Minneapolis: National Support Systems Project.

Commission on Emotional and Learning Disorders in Children (CELDIC). (1970). *One million children*. Toronto, Ont.: Crainford.

Davies, S.P. (1930). *Social control of the mentally deficient*. New York: Thomas Y. Crowell Co.

Dunn, L.M. (1968). Special education for the mildly retarded—Is much of it justifiable? *Exceptional Children, 35*, 5–22.

Dybwad, G. (1964). *Challenges in mental retardation*. New York: Columbia University Press.

Forest, M. (1987). Start with the right attitude. *Entourage, 2*, 11–13.

Forest, M., & Lusthaus, E. (1987). The kaleidoscope: A challenge to the cascade. In M. Forest (Ed.), *More education integration* (pp. 1–16). Toronto, Ont.: G. Allan Roeher Institute.

Gartner, A., & Lipsky, D. (1987). Beyond special education. *Harvard Educational Review, 57*, 367–395.

Gilhool, T. (1986). Changing public policies: Roots and forces. In M. Reynolds (Ed.), *Mainstreaming: Origins and implications* (pp. 8–13). Reston, VA: Council for Exceptional Children.

Goldberg, I., & Cruickshank, W.M. (1958). The trainable but noneducable: Whose responsibility? *National Education Association Journal, 47*, 622.

Hallahan, D., Keller, C., McKinney, J., Lloyd, J., & Bryan, T. (1988). Examining the research base of the regular education initiative: Efficacy studies and the adaptive learning environments model. *Journal of Learning Disabilities, 21*(1), 29–35.

Hobbs, N. (1966). Helping the disturbed child: Psychological and ecological strategies. *American Psychologist, 21*, 1105–1115.

Jacobs, J. (1986). *Educating students with severe handicaps in the regular education program, all day, every day*. Paper presented to the 1986 annual conference of the Association for Persons with Severe Handicaps, San Francisco.

Karagianis, L.D., & Nesbit, W.C. (1980, Summer). Special education: Pubic policy in Canada. *Education Canada*, 5–29.

Kauffman, J., Gerber, M., & Semmel, M. (1988). Arguable assumptions underlying the regular education initiative. *Journal of Learning Disabilities, 21*(1), 6–11.

Kendall, D. (1971). Towards integration. *Special Education in Canada, 45*, 19–34.

Kennedy, T. (1986, Nov. 23). Our right to independence. *Parade Magazine*, pp. 4–7.

Knoblock, P. (1982). *Teaching and mainstreaming autistic children*. Denver: Love Publishing Co.

Lieberman, L. (1988). *Preserving special education for those who need it*. Newtonville, MA: GloWorm Publications.

Lilly, S. (1970). Special education: A tempest in a teapot. *Exceptional Children, 32*, 43–49.

Lilly, S. (1979). *Children with exceptional needs*. New York: Holt, Rinehart & Winston.

Lusthaus, E. (1988). Education integration . . . letting our children go. *Journal of The Association for the Severely Handicapped, 14*, 6–7.

Madden, N., & Slavin, R. (1983). Mainstreaming students with mild handicaps: Academic and social outcomes. *Review of Educational Research, 53*, 519–659.

Massachusetts Advocacy Center. (1987). *Out of the mainstream*. Boston: Author.

McHale, S.M., & Simeonsson, R.J. (1980). Effects of interaction on nonhandicapped children's attitudes toward autistic children. *American Journal of Mental Deficiency, 85*, 18–24.

Pugach, M. (1988, May-June). Special education as a constraint on teacher education reform. *Journal of Teacher Education*, 52–59.

Reynolds, M. (1962). Framework for considering some issues in special education. *Exceptional Children, 28*, 367–370.

Reynolds, M., & Birch, J. (1982). *Teaching exceptional children in all America's schools* (2d ed.). Reston, VA: Council for Exceptional Children.

Reynolds, M.C., & Birch, J.W. (1988). *Adaptive mainstreaming*. New York: Longman.

Ruttiman, A. & Forest, M. (1986). With a little help from my friends: The integration facilitator at work. *Entourage, 1*, 24–33.

Sailor, W., & Guess, D. (1983). *Severely handicapped students: An instructional design*. Boston: Houghton Mifflin Co.

Sapon-Shevin, M., Pugach, M., & Lilly, S. (1987, November). *Moving toward merger: Implications for general and special education*. Paper presented at the Tenth Annual TED Conference, Arlington, VA.

Senator Lowell Weicker on the Americans with Disabilities Act. (1988, July). *D.C. Update*, p. 1.

Sigmon, S. (1983). The history and future of educational segregation. *Journal for Special Educators, 19*, 1–13.

Stainback, S., & Stainback, W. (1985). Integration of students with severe handicaps into regular schools. Reston, VA: Council for Exceptional Children.

Stainback, S., & Stainback, W. (1988). Educating students with severe disabilities in regular classes. *Teaching Exceptional Children, 21*, 16–19.

Stainback, W., & Stainback, S. (1984). A rationale for the merger of special and regular education. *Exceptional Children, 51*, 102–111.

Stainback, W., & Stainback, S. (1987). Educating all students in regular education. *Association for Severely Handicapped Newsletter, 13*(4), 1, 7.

Strully, J. (1986). *Our children and the regular education classroom: Or why settle for anything less than the best?* Paper presented to the 1986 annual conference of the Association for Persons with Severe Handicaps, San Francisco.

Strully, J., & Strully, C. (1985). Teach your children. *Canadian Journal on Mental Retardation, 35*(4), 3–11.

Thousand, J., & Villa, R. (1988). Enhancing educational success through collaboration. *IMPACT, 1*, 14.

Voeltz, L.M. (1980). Children's attitudes toward handicapped peers. *American Journal of Mental Deficiency, 84*, 455–464.

Voeltz, L.M. (1982). Effects of structured interactions with severely handicapped peers on children's attitudes. *American Journal of Mental Deficiency, 86*, 380–390.

Wang, M.C., Reynolds, M.C., & Walberg, H.J. (1987). *Handbook of special education research and practice*. Oxford, England: Pergamon.

Warren, E. (1954). Brown v. Board of Education of Topeka, 347 U.S. 483, 493.

Wellington County Roman Catholic Separate School Board. (1984). *Integrating Education for All*. Guelph, Ont.: Author.

Will, M. (1986). *Educating students with learning problems—A shared responsibility*. Washington, DC: U.S. Department of Education, Office of Special Education and Rehabilitation Services.

Wolfensberger, W. (1972). *The Principle of Normalization in Human Services*. Toronto, Ont.: National Institute on Mental Retardation.

Wolfensberger, W. (1984). Social role valorization: A proposed new term for the principle of normalization. *Mental Retardation, 21*(6), 234–239.

York, J., & Vandercook, T. (1988). Feature issue on integrated education. *IMPACT, 1*, 1–3.

CHAPTER 2

A Rationale for the Merger of Regular and Special Education

William Stainback, Susan Stainback, and Gary Bunch

Although special education is technically a subsystem of regular education, a dual system of education has, in effect, been in operation, each with its own pupils, teachers, supervisory staff, and funding system. While there have been attempts in recent years to reduce the sharp dichotomy between special and regular education (e.g., mainstreaming, integration), the dual system basically remains intact. There are still special and regular school personnel, students, and funding. Unfortunately, significant numbers of educators, conditioned by their training and experience, do not question the continuance of this dual system.

RATIONALE FOR MERGER

However, maintaining these two systems is, in the view of the authors, unfair. As Chief Justice Earl Warren ruled in the 1954 *Brown v. Board of Education* decision, separateness in education is inherently unequal. By assigning some students to "special" education, we physically separate them from their peers. Others, although mainstreamed, carry with them the label "special" and are separated psychologically both in their own minds and in the minds of their teachers from their "regular" peers.

One way to solve the problems created by maintaining two education systems would be to merge special and regular education into one unified system of regular education structured to meet the unique needs of all students. Merger involves the incorporation of all the resources and services (e.g., funding, curriculum, personnel) from both regular and special education into a single regular educational system. This chapter presents a rationale for merging regular and special education.

The rationale is based on several major premises. First is that the *instructional needs of students do not warrant the operation of a dual system*. Second, *maintaining a dual system is inefficient*. And third, *the dual system fosters an inappropriate and unfair attitude* about the education of students classified as having disabilities. Each of these premises is discussed in detail in the pages following.

Premise #1: Instructional Needs Do Not Warrant Dual System

"Special" and "Regular" Students: A Fallacy There are not two distinct types of students—"special" and "regular." According to Sarason (1982), many of us in education have erred in our conceptualization that there are at least two kinds of students —the normal and abnormal. All students differ along continuums of intellectual, physical, and psychological characteristics. Individual differences are universal; thus, the study of deviant people is really a study of all humankind (Telford & Sawrey, 1981).

The idea that some students are distinctly different from the "normal" population of students and are therefore abnormal or "special" has been justified on the basis that some students deviate to an extreme from the "norm" or "average" on one or more characteristics (Hallahan & Kauffman, 1982). Designation of what is extreme has been cited for a wide range of characteristics deemed pertinent to educational success, from achievement and intellect to emotional, auditory, and visual attributes. Arbitrary cutoff points have been set on scales measuring these various attributes.

However, regardless of any designated cutoffs, all students still differ to varying degrees from one another along the same continuums of differences. The designation of arbitrary cutoffs does not make students any more different between the special and regular groups than within these groups. This may be one reason why so many researchers have resorted to complex clusters and interactions of behaviors in their definitions and sophisticated statistical analyses in their attempts to differentiate "special" students from those who are "normal" or "regular." As noted by Algozzine and Ysseldyke (1983), when these definitions and "statistical concoctions are deemed most impressive, they have included every imaginable human characteristic and scores on a myriad of tests" (p. 246). However, these sophisticated definitions and analyses have not proven of significant utility to teachers charged with educating students with differing abilities and characteristics

In short, there are not—as implied by a dual system—two distinctly different types of students, "special" and "regular." Rather, all students are unique individuals, each with his or her own set of physical, intellectual, and psychological characteristics.

Individualized Services There is no separate group of students requiring special individualized services to meet their instructional needs. Special education, and the dual system, is largely based on the assumption that there is a particular group of students who need individualized educational programs tailored to their unique needs and characteristics. Such a position is educationally discriminatory. As previously noted, all students are unique individuals, and their individual differences influence their instructional needs (Blankenship & Lilly, 1981). Thus, individualized educational programming and services are important for all students and, as stated by Jordan (1980), there is nothing to warrant individualized programming as a privilege provided only to students labeled "exceptional." Tailor-made instructional programs should be provided all students, whether considered bright, handicapped, minority, or average (Ellis, 1980; Shane, 1979). Acceptance of this point signifies acceptance of a major argument for a unified system of education.

Instructional Methods A logical extension of the preceding point is that there are not two discrete sets of instructional methods—one set for use with "special" students and another for use with "regular" students. In the interest of clarification, the term *instructional methods* requires definition. As used here, it refers to basic instructional processes, such as the develop-

Point to Ponder

To achieve true equality in our schools, all children—not just selected categories of students—need educational programs that meet their unique needs. (Sapon-Shevin, 1987)

ment of behavioral objectives, curricular-based assessment procedures, task analysis, the arrangement of antecedents and consequences, and/or open education/discovery learning methods. While such methods need to be tailored to individual characteristics and needs, few, if any, can be clearly dichotomized into those applicable only for "special" students or only for "regular" students. As stated by Gardner (1977), "There are no unique methods for use with . . . [students labeled exceptional] that differ in kind from those used with normal children" (p. 74). Fortunately, the longstanding assumption that there are two methodologies or psychologies of learning—one for "special" people and one for "regular" people—is beginning to erode (Bogdan & Taylor, 1976; Sarason, 1982). It is being replaced with the view that the actual teaching strategies used with any child are but a part of the continually changing pattern of services provided in response to the individual and changing needs of the child.

The notion that special methods, materials, and programs are needed for some students is an outgrowth of the belief that there are at least two kinds of people and two psychologies of learning: the psychology of the "normal" child and the psychology of the "special" child. Sarason (1982) explains why this conception is invalid.

> Let me illustrate the "two psychologies" because it is so basic to comprehending how in schools two cultures [i.e., special and regular] developed, were sustained, and for several decades began to approximate each other in size, costs, and influence. If a child has an IQ of 100 and is discovered to have strangled to death a neighbor's cat, no one would say that it was done *because* the child had an IQ of 100; i.e., the IQ of 100 is *not* the etiological agent without which the behavior would not have occurred. However, if the child has an IQ of 50, many people would "explain" the behavior in terms of the low IQ. There are, then, two psychologies: one for "us" and one for "them," and, therefore, unless you know "their" psychology, you cannot be helpful to them, *nor should you be expected to deal with such children.* There was (and there still is) little or nothing in the preparation of the regular classroom teacher and "regular" school administrators to make them feel competent to understand and/or to teach children with a label denoting specialness. On the contrary, their training emphasized the need for two cultures in the school: the regular and the special. The two cultures in the school have mirrored the same two cultures in schools of education. (p. 237)

While basic instructional methods are emphasized here, later in this chapter a discussion is offered of why a dual system is not necessary to offer instruction in what some people consider "unique" curricular areas such as self-care/community living skills, braille, sign language, mobility or orientation, and speechreading.

When viewed through the preceding perspective, the instructional needs of students do not warrant the operation of a dual system. On the contrary, these needs support the merger of the two systems into a comprehensive, unified system designed to meet the unique needs of every student.

Premise #2: Dual System Is Inefficient

The second premise on which the rationale for merger is based centers on inefficiency of operation. Maintaining two systems is inefficient for a number of reasons.

Classification The dual system creates an unnecessary and expensive need to classify students. This is because it becomes necessary with a dual system to determine who belongs in which system. Considerable time, money, and effort are currently expended to determine who is "regular" and who is "special" and into what "type" or category of exceptionality each "special" student fits. This continues to be done in spite of the fact that a combination of professional opinion and research indicates that classification is often done unreliably, that it stereotypes students, and that it is of little instructional value (Gardner, 1982).

While most of the criticisms, research, and recommendations related to classification practices have been directed toward the "soft" categories (e.g., learning disabilities), there is little evidence that classification of students with severe limitations in intellectual ability, vision, hearing, or movement of body parts is educationally useful for comprehensive education planning. A student who has little or no vision, for example, is a whole human being with many intellectual, social, psychological, and physical characteristics. An *educational* classification according to one or a few characteristics is minimally useful in planning a total educational program. Similarly, while it may be worthwhile from a medical perspective to classify students as having Down syndrome or autism, there is little educational value to such classifications. The educational needs of students classified as having Down syndrome or autism can be distorted when students are not viewed individually and as whole persons. In short, there is much more to a child classified as autistic than the characteristics that define him or her as having autism, particularly, in educational terms.

It should be stressed that the issue is *not* whether there are people who are deaf, blind, have cerebral palsy, Down syndrome, autism, and the like. There obviously are, and such categories may be of major benefit from a medical research standpoint or for other reasons. The issue is whether educators should approach and educate children according to a categorical affiliation (e.g., normal, blind, retarded, behaviorally disordered) or whether they should approach and educate all students as individuals and whole persons. As soon as educators approach students as individuals and

Point to Ponder

In a merged system, a particular characteristic such as visual ability, for example, would be viewed as only one of numerous characteristics of a student. This characteristic, along with the other characteristics of a student, may assist educators in selecting supplemental instruction or types of materials (e.g., braille readers) that could help foster the student's educational achievements. However, it would not become the overriding focus of a student's education (e.g., the view that a blind student should receive an "education for the blind").

whole persons and get to know them personally, the category to which they belong becomes irrelevant for instructional purposes, since they learn about their interests, hearing and visual capabilities, learning rate, and other physical, psychological, and intellectual characteristics. As a consequence, educators can plan an educational program for the whole child and avoid the trap of focusing primarily on one or two dimensions of a person (e.g., blindness), which is fostered in the disabilities approach to education.

Competition and Duplication The dual system has fostered competition and, in some cases, unnecessary duplication, rather than cooperation among professionals. Educators should share their expertise and pool their resources to obtain maximal "mileage" from their instructional efforts. However, the dual system approach has interfered with such cooperative efforts. As Lortie (1978) has explained:

> The historical separation of special and regular educators has taken its toll in the relations between them; shared viewpoints and mutual understanding, it appears, are not the rule. Educators outside special education are often perceived as either indifferent to, or even prejudiced against, the needs of children considered handicapped. Special educators, on the other hand, sometimes project the attitudes of an embattled group with its "them versus us" mentality. (p. 236)

This breakdown of professional relationships, and the resulting inefficiency, occurs on multiple levels. On an educational research level, the special/regular education dichotomy often interferes with widespread use of research findings, since potentially useful information may be overlooked by special or regular educators because of its affiliation with the other system. In addition, colleges and universities often organize parallel special and regular education departments and programs to prepare teachers. This inefficiency also occurs in direct service programs. At the local, state, and federal levels there are generally divisions or offices of special and regular education that tend not to cooperate or share in the use of personnel, materials, equipment, or in the development and operation of accounting, monitoring, and funding mechanisms.

While there has been much talk recently about collaboration and cooperation between special and regular educators, there is often little opportunity for this to occur. For example, it is typical practice for special educators to meet and talk about mainstreaming, cooperation, and collaboration in their segregated, special education conferences, while regular educators meet in their regular education conferences to talk about issues of concern to them. Although there is growing recognition of this separateness in areas such as conferences, segregation of special and regular educators continues to constitute the norm.

Such divisions and poor professional relationships not only reduce the potential benefits of pooling expertise and resources, but also encourage detrimental, counterproductive advocacy attempts. Factions within education, perpetuated by the dual system, limit the advocacy potential for the education of all students, leading to competition rather than cooperation between the groups. As pointed out by Moran (1983), when interest groups are divided, all lose in the long run. By joining forces in a unified educational system, a larger, more powerful working and lobbying group could be organized. In short, a dual system creates artificial barriers between people and divides resources, personnel, and advocacy potential.

Eligibility by Category In the dual system, eligibility for instructional and related services is based on category affiliation, which interferes with attention being

Point to Ponder

As increasing numbers of children are included in the mainstream of regular education, there will be a demise of the "two-box" theory of education, that is, the view that there are two kinds of children (exceptional and normal) and two kinds of education (special education for the "exceptional" children and regular education for the "normal" children). (Reynolds & Birch, 1988)

given to the specific learning needs and interests of each student. In the dual system, an elaborate procedure for classifying/categorizing students is used to determine who is and who is not eligible for a variety of educational and related services. Services such as occupational therapy, instruction in community-referenced skills, social interaction skills, and creative thinking; access to instructional materials such as large print, talking, or braille books; and adapted seating or communication devices are generally determined on the basis of the category to which a student is assigned.

However, these categories often do not reflect the specific educational needs and interests of students in relation to such services. For example, some students categorized as visually handicapped may not need large print books, whereas others who are not labeled visually impaired and thus are ineligible for large print books could benefit from their use. Similarly, not all students labeled behaviorally disordered may need self-control training, whereas some students not so labeled may need self-control training as part of their educational experience. Such categories—perpetuated by the dual system—actually interfere with providing some students with the services they require to progress toward their individual educational goals. Eligibility for educational and related services, as pointed out by Gardner (1977), should be based on the abilities, interests, and needs of each student as they relate to instructional options and services, rather than on the student's inclusion in a categorical group.

Point to Ponder

Reducing the categories to which we assign students is really *not* the answer to the problems involved in classifying and labeling children. When we divide students into those who are gifted or normal, or those with mild or severe disabilities, or even students with "special" versus "regular" needs, we are only assigning students to broad categories as opposed to specific categories (e.g., students with retardation, behavioral disorders.) Stereotyping and other problems associated with classifying and labeling children are as severe with broad as with specific categories. The best way to solve the problems associated with classifying and labeling children is to simply stop classifying and labeling students and instead approach each child as a unique individual with his or her set of physical, intellectual, and psychological characteristics.

In regard to eligibility, it should be noted that some professionals have argued that categorization of students is essential to make them eligible for special assistance. However, as noted by Telford and Sawrey (1981), people in need of assistance can be given help without categorization. All human beings in need of assistance *should* be entitled to assistance, whether or not they fall within prescribed categorical limits. Providing special assistance only to special categories of people results in the multiplication of categories and assignment of people to these groups, rather than focusing on their circumstances and needs.

Eligibility criteria should exist only if some people are entitled to assistance and others are not. However, in education, all students are (or should be) entitled to assistance if they need it. The only criteria should be that their assessment profile indicates that they need assistance. For instance, if a student needs assistance because of a letter reversal problem, the student should receive the best assistance available regardless of whether the criteria for inclusion in a categorical group are met. To do otherwise is to blatantly discriminate against some students.

Curricular Options The dual system unnecessarily reduces the range of curricular options available to students. In the dual system, a number of curricular offerings have generally been designated as the domain of either special or regular education. For example, most regular education students are not provided access to social interaction skill training or instruction in creative thinking, whereas special education students do not always have access to many regular education curricular offerings such as typing or band. Although there has been an increasing involvement of special education students in regular education course offerings, there does not appear to be a reciprocal trend to involve regular education students in special education offerings. Furthermore, duplication of offerings in the basic skill areas such as mathematics and reading unnecessarily drains resources. By consolidating all curricular offerings into one unified system, all students could be provided a broader range of curricular options with less wasted effort.

Moreover, with consolidation, the individual needs of students would have a better chance of being accommodated. Not only would all students be provided more diverse curricular options, but also selection of learning experiences could be based more directly on what each student needs, rather than on category affiliation. For example, if a student's assessment profile indicated a need for rudimentary language development and/or functional self-care skills, the student could be included in age-appropriate experiences or activities that are designed to teach those skills without the necessity of the student being labeled. Similarly, if a student needed front row seating or instruction in speechreading to comprehend what the teachers were saying, the student could receive it. In short, by consolidating all curricular offerings into one unified system, each student would have access to any of the classes, individualized tutoring, support personnel, and material adaptations now offered in special and regular education.

The "Deviant" Label The dual system requires students to fit into the available regular education program or be labeled as deviant. With the dual system, if a student exhibits learning or behavior characteristics that do not match the demands of the regular education program, the student is typically referred for assessment and, in many cases, is labeled "deviant," "different," "special," or "exceptional." Once labeled, an attempt is then made to provide the student an appropriate program through special education in the regular classroom, resource room, or special class. The premise is that the student does not fit the program and should change to a "special" program, rather than that the regular program should be modified or adjusted to meet the needs of the student. In addition this system does not allow for addressing the unique learning needs and characteristics of the large numbers of nonlabeled students who can adjust only marginally to the demands of the regular program. An underlying tenet of North American education is that the education program should fit the needs of the student rather than that the student should fit the needs of the education program. Yet the dual system inherently contradicts this basic tenet; the student must fit the regular program or be labeled deviant or special. A single integrated system could alleviate this contradiction. By uniting in their advocacy attempts and pooling their resources, special and regular educators could pave the way for modifications and adjustments to be made in regular education to meet the unique learning needs and characteristics of all students. As noted by Reynolds and Birch (1982), for years the rhetoric of both regular and special educators has centered on adapting instruction to the individual needs of all students. Merger could set the stage for achievement of that goal.

The "Real" World The dual system does not adequately prepare students to live and work in natural "real-life" community settings. When students grow up and leave school, there is no "regular" and no "special" world. For the most part, such a division exists only within our schools. There are no regular and special grocery stores, banks, churches, restaurants, and the like. Similarly, there are no regular and special waiters in restaurants or tellers in banks. Our schools have created an artificial environment that does not exist outside in the real world. This can cause unnecessary problems for students in special education, who must undergo the strain of a transition from an artificial, special world within the schools to the real, "regular" world outside. In a merged, unified comprehensive education service delivery system, all students will have an opportunity to learn about and understand how to live in the "real" world throughout their school years with "regular" peers with whom they will need to coexist in postschool situations.

Premise #3: Dual System Fosters Inappropriate Attitude

The third and final major premise on which merger is based is that the dual system fosters an inappropriate and unfair attitude about the education of students classified as having disabilities.

The Charitable Attitude Unfortunately, because students defined as having disabilities were denied an education for many decades, it is now viewed as something special or extraordinary to provide

Point to Ponder

Sarason and Doris (1979) have argued that

> the presence of special education programs as options effectively short circuits the development of alternative solutions based in general education. (p. 385)

Point to Ponder

A student classified as having a disability and segregated throughout her school years recently stated

> I graduated . . . completely unprepared for the *real world.* So I just stayed in the house all day, a shut-in believing a job was out of the question. . . . Believe me, a segregated environment just will not do as preparation for an integrated life . . . (Massachusetts Advocacy Center, 1987, p. 4)

them an education. This notion is perpetuated by the operation of a dual system. As a result, students with disabilities continue to be viewed as special charity cases who are *given* "special" education programs and services because of their needy or "special" condition.

In a merged system, all students would be provided the opportunity to receive an education geared to their capabilities and needs as a regular, normal, and expected practice. This is important, since equality suffers when the education of some students is viewed as special, different, and charitylike, while the education of others is viewed as regular, normal, and expected. As noted by Biklen (1985): "Until accommodation for the disabled is seen as regular, normal and expected, it will be seen instead as special. As long as it is special, it will be, by definition, unequal" (p. 176).

In conclusion, it is inefficient to operate two systems. This inefficiency, coupled with the lack of need for two systems and the charitylike attitude it fosters, supports the merger of special and regular education. Table 1 presents a summary and comparison of the characteristics of the current dual system and the proposed unified system. The rationale for merger is based on the more advantageous characteristics of the unified system as compared to the dual system.

DISCUSSION OF MERGER

In summary, as stated in 1984 by Stainback and Stainback:

> Dichotomizing students into two basic types (special and regular), maintaining a dual system of education, separate professional organizations, separate personnel preparation programs, and separate funding patterns does very little to foster the values inherent in the mainstreaming and integration movement of the past decade. In essence, during the past decade we have been attempting to integrate students while separating them into two kinds of learners and without integrating programs, personnel and resources.
>
> The issue is not whether there are differences among students. There obviously are differences, even extreme differences. . . . However, this should not be used as a justification to label, segregate, or maintain a dual system of education. With careful planning, it should be possible to meet the unique needs of all students within one unified system of education—a system that does not deny differences, but rather a system that recognizes, celebrates and accommodates for differences. (p. 10)

The possibility of merging special and regular education into one unified system has been fermenting for several years. Gilhool (1976) alluded to the possibility of merger when he noted:

> We are approaching the day when, for each child, the law will require that the schooling fit the child, his needs, his capacities, and his

> wishes; not the child fit the school. Thus, special education may become general and general education, special. (p. 13)

Meyen (1978) stated that the most significant change that could occur in the future would be for public education to individualize instruction and "to eliminate the dichotomy between serving exceptional and nonexceptional students" (p. 53). A review of the history of special education indicates that the trend is in the direction of eventually eliminating the dichotomy. This has been reflected in the past several decades by the emergence of concepts such as deinstitutionalization, normalization, integration, mainstreaming, and zero rejection. Reynolds and Birch (1982) have pointed out that "the whole history of education for . . . students [labeled special] can be told in terms of one steady trend that can be described as progressive inclusion" (p. 27). At

Table 1. Comparison of dual and unified systems

Concern	Dual system	Unified system
1. Student characteristics	Dichotomizes student into special and regular on the basis of perceived "normal" or "deviant" characteristics	Recognizes continuum among all students of intellectual, physical, and psychological characteristics
2. Individualization	Stresses individualization for students labeled special	Stresses individualizaton for all students
3. Instructional strategies	Seeks to use special strategies for special students	Selects from range of available strategies according to each student's learning needs
4. Type of educational services	Eligibility generally based on category affiliation	Eligibility based on each student's individual learning needs
5. Diagnostics	Large expenditures on identification of categorical affiliation	Emphasis on identifying the specific instructional needs of all students
6. Professional relationships	Establishes artificial barriers among educators that promote competition and alienation	Promotes cooperation through sharing resources, expertise, and advocacy responsibilities
7. Curriculum	Options available to each student are limited by categorical affiliation	All options available to every student as needed
8. Focus	Student must fit regular education program or be referred to special education	Regular education program is adjusted to meet all students' needs
9. The "real" world	Some students educated in an artificial special world	All students educated in mainstream of regular education
10. Attitude	Some students given an education as a special or charitylike favor	All students given an education as a regular, normal, and expected practice

Point to Ponder

Hopefully, by the year 2000 there will be no more special education but only an educational system that serves all children. . . . *We create our tomorrows by what we dream today.* (Forest, 1985, p. 40)

this point in the progressive inclusion trend, it is time to stop developing criteria for who does or does not belong in the mainstream and instead turn the spotlight to increasing the capabilities of the mainstream to meet the needs of all students.

Reform of general education will not be accomplished quickly or easily. Regular education has a history of being reluctant to meet the needs of all students. That is the primary reason special education was developed in the first place. Furthermore, as Deno (1978) stated, categorization is

> deeply entrenched in the social commitments of categorically defined special-interest advocacy groups; in the structure of health, education, and welfare programs at direct service levels; in the staffing of teacher training institutions; in other professional training programs; and in general public thinking. (p. 39)

Despite these realities, there is a need to move toward merger to whatever degree possible. A dual system of education can serve to legitimize exclusion of some students from regular education, reduce opportunity for equal participation by other students, and sanction other forms of discrimination. As Hobbs (1980) noted, by placing a person in a separate category or system of education, it becomes possible to treat the person in ways that would not be tolerated were he or she a fully accepted member of the "normal" or "regular" group. Thus, it is important to explore, suggest, and attempt change.

This position is not advocated without the recognition that achievement of a unified system will require concentrated and sustained thought and effort. It will not be simple to change established systems of service delivery, funding, assessment, and staffing, to name only a few major areas. Similarly, it will not be simple to alter established attitudes regarding the worth of each child, nor beliefs concerning what range of students a teacher should be asked to educate. However, a growing number of teachers, parents, administrators, researchers, and others firmly believe that the thought and effort required are necessary and are in the long-term best interest of all students.

The remaining chapters of this book offer practical strategies for achieving merger and educating all students in the mainstream of regular education.

REFERENCES

Algozzine, B., & Ysseldyke, J. (1983). Learning disabilities as a subset of school failure: The oversophistication of a concept. *Exceptional Children, 50,* 242–246.

Biklen, D. (1985). (Ed.). *The complete school: Integrating special and regular education.* New York: Columbia University, Teacher's College Press.

Blankenship, C., & Lilly, S. (1981). *Mainstreaming students with learning and behavior problems.* New York: Holt, Rinehart & Winston.

Bogdan, R., & Taylor, S. (1976). The judged, not the judges: An insider's view of mental retardation. *American Psychologist, 31,* 47–52.

Deno, E. (1978). *Educating children with emotional, learning, and behavior problems.* Minneapolis: University of Minnesota, College of Education, National Support Systems Project.

Ellis, J. (1980). Individualized education in the 1980's. *Serrculator, 9,* 7–8.

Forest, M. (1985). Education update. *Canadian Journal on Mental Retardation, 35,* 37–40.

Forest, M., & Lusthaus, E. (1987). The kaleidoscope: A challenge to the cascade. In M. Forest (Ed.), *More education integration* (pp. 1–16). Toronto, Ont.: G. Allan Roeher Institute.

Gardner, W. (1977). *Learning and behavior characteristics of exceptional children and youth.* Boston: Allyn & Bacon.

Gardner, W. (1982). Why do we persist? *Education and Treatment of Children, 5,* 369–378.

Gilhool, T. (1976). Changing public policies: Roots and forces. In M. Reynolds (Ed.), *Mainstreaming: Origins and implications* (pp. 8–13). Reston, VA: Council for Exceptional Children.

Hallahan, D., & Kauffman, J. (1982). *Exceptional Children.* Englewood Cliffs, NJ: Prentice-Hall.

Hobbs, N. (1980). An ecologically oriented service-based system for the classification of handicapped children. In E. Salzinger, J. Antrobus, & R. Glick (Eds.), *The ecosystem of the "risk" child* (pp. 271–290). New York: Academic Press.

Jordan, K.F. (1980). Individual plans for all children. *Serrculator, 9,* 7–8.

Lortie, D. (1978). Some reflections on renegotiation. In M. Reynolds (Ed.), *Futures of education for exceptional students* (pp. 235–244). Reston, VA: Council for Exceptional Children.

Massachusetts Advocacy Center. (1987). *Out of the mainstream.* Boston: Author.

Meyen, E. (1978). An introductory prospective. In E. Meyen (Ed.), *Exceptional children and youth* (pp. 2–84). Denver: Love Publishing Co.

Moran, M. (1983). Inventing a future for special education: A cautionary tale. *Journal for Special Educators, 19,* 28–36.

Reynolds, M., & Birch, J. (1982). *Teaching exceptional children in all America's schools* (2d ed.). Reston, VA: Council for Exceptional Children.

Reynolds, M., & Birch, J. (1988). *Adaptive mainstreaming.* New York: Longman.

Sarason, S. (1982). *The culture of the school and the problem of change.* Boston: Allyn & Bacon.

Sarason, S., & Doris, J. (1979). *Educational handicap, public policy, and social history.* New York: Free Press.

Shane, H. (1979). Forecast for the 80's.*Today's Education, 68,* 62–65.

Sapon-Shevin, M. (1987). Giftedness as a social construct. *Teachers College Record, 89,* 39–53.

Stainback, S., & Stainback, W. (1988). *Merging regular and special education.* Paper presented in Merging Course at Syracuse University, Syracuse, NY.

Stainback, W., & Stainback, S. (1984). A rationale for the merger of special and regular education. *Exceptional Children, 51,* 102–111.

Telford, C., & Sawrey, J. (1981). *The exceptional individual* (4th ed.). Englewood Cliffs, NJ: Prentice-Hall.

Warren, E. (1954). *Brown v. Board of Education of Topeka,* 347 U.S. 483, 493.

PART II

Educational Equality in Practice

CHAPTER 3

A School System in Transition

George Flynn and Bernie Kowalczyk-McPhee

Robert Muller, assistant secretary-general of the United Nations, said in a speech to the 1985 convention of the National Congress of Education Advisors:

> Beyond the turmoil, the divisions and perplexities of our time, humanity is slowly but surely finding the ways, . . . new codes of behaviour which will encompass all races, nations, religions and ideologies. It is the formulation of these new ethics which will be the great challenge for the new generation. (p. 4)

One application of these new ethics—that is, the new standard of conduct and moral judgment—currently being formulated relates to how educational systems respond to the diverse needs of young people in an effective and equitable manner.

This chapter addresses this issue by discussing how Ontario's Waterloo Region Roman Catholic Separate School Board (WRRCSSB) is being restructured so that all young people, regardless of the nature of their educational and related needs, may feel that they truly belong. In essence, the aim is for all students to be not just placed or tolerated in ordinary or regular schools but to become part of the very fabric of schools and classrooms.

This new moral framework for educational decisionmaking suggests alternatives for school systems and schools that are founded on a cooperative ethic. However, despite the strength of the values and ethics involved, the weight of past practices and the difficulties professionals face in changing these practices—as so well described in the literature—greatly increase this challenge.

QUALITY EDUCATION FOR ALL STUDENTS

Special education was developed over a century ago as a means to provide more suitable programs for children and young adults who could not succeed in the regular program as it was structured. Special education was an outgrowth of a "do-gooder" mind-set, in that professionals dealing with students defined as having disabilities felt sorry for them and so decided to establish special programs for them. From being a subsystem of regular education, special education grew to become a system parallel to regular education, with its own teacher training courses, support systems, administrative system, funding, and literature. Professionals and students exposed to special education are reaching a point, however, at which the "recipe" knowledge (pedagogical, clinical, psychological) offered them appears dissatisfying; they object to the fact that they are often asked to accept as unproblematic what are, in reality, debatable notions and concepts. Professionals are thus recognizing a need to acquire wider social, historical, and political perspectives on the policies, practices, and processes of special education.

It is important to note that special education was developed to deal with children and young adults who were categorized out of the ordinary educational system offered the majority of students. This fact takes on additional significance when one realizes that in our modern society, which still demands qualifications and credentials acquired through the education system, to be excluded from the "ordinary" system is the ultimate in nonachievement. Occupational success, social mobility, privilege, and advancement are legitimated by the education system, and those who receive a special rather than an ordinary education have, by virtue of their position in society, largely been denied these rewards. To be excluded from an ordinary education career and placed in a special education system probably means the person is destined for a "special" life-style and special employment.

Special education is unique in another way. The people who are involved in special education have the power to mystify others. This might be described as the "white coat" image of special educators. The special training, the special equipment, the special tests, the children with "special" needs, all of these circumstances have allowed special education to acquire a mystical image, which has reinforced the separation of the special from the ordinary. These circumstances also make it more difficult to alter special education, especially if the change entails bringing special and ordinary education together.

Special education has, in effect, acted as a safety valve for ordinary education, in that certain students could legally be excluded and placed in a separate system. This separate system has been legitimated by categorization and more recently by applying to these students a more general categorization called "special needs." This points up a concern regarding the possibility of any real change in special education. In spite of much new legislation throughout much of the world relating to special education, it may be that, unfortunately, only the terminology, forms, and ideologies of the system are changing, with the basic functions remaining the same. The trustees and staff of the WRRCSSB firmly resolved that special education would not be allowed to continue, even in a different form, as a permanent subsystem of the ordinary education system. The goal was to achieve one remodeled, ordinary system in which all children and young adults, regardless of their abilities or disabilities, would be ac-

Point to Ponder

It is illogical to state that *some* children (e.g., those labeled "disabled") have unique needs that must be met. *All* children have unique needs that must be met. Thus, the public schools should be held accountable to meeting the unique needs of *all* students, rather than those of any one category of students. There simply are no children in the public schools whose unique needs should not be met.

commodated and provided every opportunity to reach their full potential.

INTEGRATION IN THE SCHOOL SYSTEM

Integration has been something of a slogan word, with much advocacy occurring in its behalf without the benefit of sound reasoning. Integration issues are the prime focus of debate in special education today, as a result of several factors. Foremost are the following:

Pupils' needs are not being met as well as they might be or should be under the prevailing arrangements.

There is a reaction against segregation and a corresponding movement toward integration.

New concepts of handicap are emerging that see handicaps less in terms of individual characteristics and more in terms of the learning environments.

There is a reaction against categories and labeling and the segregative mechanisms associated with them.

There is a move away from formal identification by means of a label and the emergence of the need for greater flexibility in provision of services in the ordinary school.

The concept of the ordinary school has changed, and it is now legitimate to have wider expectations of it.

There is a growing and continuing concern for human rights.

There is increasing pressure from parents who are active, knowledgeable, and determined.

Most significantly, perhaps, is the record of highly successful efforts in the integration movement that seem to show that not only is it possible but highly desirable for all students to be educated in integrated classrooms and schools.

For the authors' purposes within the Waterloo Catholic School System, *integration* is defined as a process by which something is made whole—uniting different parts in a totality. This sense of *integration* is already common to some fields of study—for example, in electronics with the integrated circuit or in psychology with personality theory. But the meaning shifts when *integration* is used in connection with ethnic minorities or students considered disabled. Here the emphasis is on the part. One is led to believe that one is doing something to the part—to the ethnic minority or to the students labeled as disabled—as though it is the part's problem that it is not now part of the whole. This may be true even though the "whole" may have so far successfully rejected or resisted the inclusion of the part. In the authors' view, integration is a process whereby an ordinary school and a segregated group interact to form a new educational whole. Integration is a means and not an end in itself. All students need not only integration but also quality education. For the reasons indicated in this and earlier chapters of this book, it is the author's opinion that quality education can only occur in integrated, ordinary schools.

This definition of quality education is intended to allow and make available typical conditions of school life for all children and young adults (and now with lifelong learning, adults as well), regardless of their abilities or disabilities, however these may be defined. It is imperative that special education labels, images, attitudes, and symbols be discarded, because they are negative and stand in the way of providing an ordinary school life for all children and young people.

The model now being developed within the WRCSSB is based on the kind of thinking outlined in a 1984 article in *Exceptional Children* by William and Susan Stainback, in which they stated:

> Dichotomizing students into two basic types (special and regular), maintaining a dual system of education, separate professional organizations, separate personnel preparation programs, and separate funding patterns does very little to foster the values inherent in the mainstreaming and integration movement of the past decade. . . .
>
> The issue is not whether there are differences among students. There obviously are differences, even extreme differences. . . . However, this should not be used as a justification to label, segregate, or maintain a dual system of education. With careful planning, it should be possible to meet the unique needs of all students within one unified system of education—a system that does not deny differences, but rather a system that recognizes and accommodates for differences. (p. 109)

WHY THE WATERLOO SYSTEM IS BEING CHANGED

Integration of instructional programs with options for all students is the goal of all educational programs and services in the WRCSSB. While this aim may not be reached "tomorrow," it is the intent of the school board to create organizational structures over the next 5 years to ensure that the goal becomes a reality.

For this goal to be explicit and operational, it must be understood and supported by the total system, that is, trustees, senior administration, principals, teachers, teacher aides, secretaries, clerical staff, and custodians. Too frequently, new initiatives are implemented and passively sabotaged by staff who are unaware of the initiative's goal or purpose.

The WRCSSB has historically been viewed as a longstanding promoter of integration, with well-established special education supports before this service was mandated by legislation. Most schools in the system had a special education teacher so that students requiring supports were frequently provided a totally different program in the special education room. The responsibilities of a special education teacher were perceived as being significantly different and challenging, so that these individuals were provided an allowance on top of the teacher's regular salary.

But whereas it was commonly perceived that the system supported integration, a closer examination reveals this to be a fallacy. Children who were presented as being autistic, behaviorally disturbed, or intellectually handicapped were isolated into specialized environments in the belief that they could not benefit from regular education. The schools where segregated programs existed were supervised by the superintendent of special education, and program development for these classes occurred on an individual, isolated basis. These schools had their own budget and operated without integration of budget or staff/curriculum development with regular educational programs. The special education programs expanded significantly over the years, and changes were made in the delivery of special education services so that they complemented the regular educational program; however, the majority of special education programs were still delivered in a system parallel to the regular education program.

When the present director of education assumed his position in 1985, he inherited an organizational structure that supported a parallel system of education but espoused integration. It quickly became evident that integrating a school system required a new organizational structure, participation, trust, ownership, and commitment by all to the unification goal so that the system could withstand challenge and not opt out or revert to the segregated, self-contained special class system. This lack of equal educational opportunity had resulted in the reorganization of a centralized system to a more decentralized system. While the parallel centralized system was viewed as being economically efficient, it was not in the best interests of educating all students in integrated classrooms and schools. If all students are expected to live, work, and play in the real world, it is the school's responsibility to teach them in real environments, beginning at an early age.

IMPETUS FOR CHANGE

A series of factors and events caused the WRRCSSB to alter its model of delivery.

First was the realization by a number of staff and parents that philosophically the WRRCSSB did not support the concept of a parallel system and segregated classes. There was a sense that a mutation of the original special education model was all that had really occurred to date. Small advocacy groups consisting of teachers and parents gathered to discuss how to stop further mutation. Within the system there were a number of examples where total integration occurred at the grassroots level in spite of the administration. For instance, a student who was identified as having autistic tendencies was totally integrated at her local high school. This occurred because of advocacy on the part of the parents and support by the school administration and staff, in spite of the lack of services and hesitation on the part of senior administration and the student's previous teachers.

The second major event was the earlier-mentioned appointment of a new director of education in 1985. This individual, who was known for his strong advocacy of integration, immediately set in motion the wheels of change. He organized a committee chaired by the special education consultant to conduct a study of the existing service delivery system as viewed by school staffs.

The third event occurred when the director of education and a high school senior administrator were approached by an advocacy group of school and central office staff who were concerned about a totally segregated class of male and female adolescents with challenging needs. This class was located in St. Jerome's High School, an all boys high school, and little meaningful integration was occurring. The advocacy group was led by the special education consultant, the principal of St. Jerome's, and the chaplain. Their mission was to promote the integration of all students at the high school. Subsequently, a proposal was developed outlining a 5-year plan for total integration. This plan (discussed in more detail later in the chapter) is now well ahead of schedule.

Fourth, the special education advisory committee, a powerful committee in the school system, was beginning to express a number of concerns about the apparent incongruence between the system's philosophy of integration and the actual delivery of service to students. Parents who were members of SEAC and who had children in the system were very cooperative, but were active proponents of change. As a result, there was a tremendous declaration of support for the position that all students regardless of need should be served in integrated classrooms and schools.

The fifth factor was a new organizational plan by the director. This plan shifted portfolios and administrators, placing greater emphasis on schools and principals as main leaders and change agents. In an unprecedented move, three assistant superintendents were hired, and superintendents were made totally responsible for the budgets and goals of the schools assigned to them (this is discussed more later in the chapter).

Sixth, under the director's supervision, a 3-year inservice plan for teachers was embarked upon. The training focused on developing the skills of teachers so that they looked at the whole child and learned to adapt the instructional program to meet the needs of the child, rather than adapting the child to meet the needs of the program. This approach aided in problem solving relating to student learning and behaviors.

CHANGING THE SCHOOL SYSTEM

To integrate a school system, all individuals belonging to that system or culture must share a clear vision of the purposes of and beliefs inherent to the system.

The *purpose* of delivering an integrated instructional program in the WRRCSSB is to attempt to meet the individual learning styles and needs of *all* students. This requires the school system to offer a variety of options within the educational programs and services provided all students. The educational programs, while being comprehensive, must be flexible and differentiated so that all students have an equal opportunity to learn.

To *deliver* an integrated program, it is imperative that all individuals involved with students be invited "to come to the table." Schools must therefore plan to actively coordinate with parents, community agencies, and school staffs when developing programs and services for individual children. The role of the senior administration is to develop a framework from which all planning occurs.

For an organization, such as the WRRCSSB, to operate in the best interests of all students, its services and programs must be based on a major *set of beliefs* that everyone within the system understands and adheres to. These beliefs form the philosophical foundation upon which all programs and services are built. These beliefs have major implications for the allocation of personnel, equipment, materials, physical space, and resources, in addition to determining the relationship the school system has with other organizations (Community and Social Services, and Health) and agencies. A school system cannot espouse integration without the school culture acting on those beliefs, as delineated next.

WRRCSSB Beliefs

The following beliefs are at the core of the WRRCSSB plan:

1. That all children belong regardless of abilities or disabilities.
2. That all children are entitled to a quality education.
3. That all children should work and play with their peers in their home school.
4. That only one quality system of education should exist, not a regular system of education and a special system of education.
5. That all necessary support services such as support facilitators, transportation, and speech and language therapy be available so that a quality education program exists for all students.
6. That the system is viewed as K–12/OAC (kindergarten to the end of secondary school) for all students.

7. That a comprehensive but flexible system of programs and services be provided for all students at their home school.
8. That all students receive individualized programming as needed and that the program be designed for the student and not the student for the program.
9. That parents be involved throughout their child's career in the school system, including assessment and programming phases. Parents must feel welcome and be seen as an integral part of the entire process.

A Sociology of Acceptance

The WRRCSSB has gone beyond just unifying and restructuring the system to accommodate all students within one system. It has also developed what Bogdan and Taylor (1987) call a sociology of acceptance. This notion is in contrast to that of a sociology of exclusion. Bogdan and Taylor state:

> An accepting relationship is one between a person with a deviant attribute and another person, which is of long duration and characterized by closeness and affection and in which the deviant attribute does not have a stigmatizing, or morally discrediting, character. Accepting relationships are not based on a denial of difference, but rather on the absence of impugning the different person's moral character because of the variations.
>
> The sociology of acceptance is directed towards understanding not only how people with deviant attributes come to be accepted in personal relations, but also in groups, organizations, communities, and society. Rather than focusing on how human service agencies serve as mechanisms of social control and create deviance by socializing people into deviant roles, the sociology of acceptance reflects on incidents where human service programs integrate people who might otherwise be isolated, excluded or segregated from typical people. (p. 36)

The notion of acceptance and affection is a powerful one, and recognition of it is perhaps the only way that the special education empire will be finally dismantled. When professionals witness real and lasting acceptance and affection between and among persons with so-called deviant attributes and other persons throughout the system, they are forced to question the underlying and firmly entrenched functions and purposes of special education. The degree of acceptance and affection that can be witnessed throughout the system between persons with varying abilities and disabilities has helped to promote lasting change, leading to a unified system.

CRITICAL ELEMENTS IN SYSTEM CHANGE

A number of management/organizational elements have been found to facilitate the goal of changing the Waterloo Catholic school system to reflect the beliefs and values inherent in an integrated education of quality and equality for all students.

Alignment/Agreement

Kiefer and Stroh (1987) define *alignment* as the condition wherein people operate freely and fully as part of a larger whole. Such a condition is created when people see their organization's purpose as an extension of their personal purposes. People who are aligned identify with the organization and consciously assume responsibility for its success. There is natural support for each other stemming from the recognition that each person is a part of the same whole. Clarity of purpose and vision helps to catalyze alignment; people in an aligned organization pull in the same direction.

Alignment is not the same as agreement. People who agree are saying simply that they share the same ideas. Agreement deals with the mechanics of goals and objectives, while alignment deals with the more inspirational aspects of organizational purpose and vision. People in an organization who are aligned are more likely to keep their agreements because of their deeply felt personal commitment to a common purpose. People in unaligned organizations tend to break agreements more easily because of an identification with self-interest. Alignment development is a primary strategy, because once people are aligned, it is easier for them to make and keep agreements necessary to achieve their purpose.

Since ours is a Catholic system, alignment development may have been easier to achieve because the employees share a common faith and value system. Again, clarity of purpose and vision, tied directly to the Catholic value system, has markedly hastened alignment accompanied by sound strategic planning.

One way alignment was achieved was the inclusion in the WRRCSSB strategic plan of two professional development days. All 1,600 employees in the system—teachers, custodians, secretaries, child care workers—were invited to attend. The intended message of these staff development days was that a new community is being built in which everyone's contribution is valued, recognizing that the level of responsibility varies greatly across the system. As administrators in the system, the authors want people to feel equally valued and respected because they are people first, and also because they belong to the system and are an important part of the integration movement. The professional development days were very successful and brought a degree of alignment to the purpose and visions of this system not previously dreamed possible.

Personal Responsibility and Empowerment

People in organizations generally feel that either they can or cannot make a difference in the organization. If they feel they cannot make a difference, they see themselves as victims of external forces beyond their control. At the individual level, such persons feel controlled by their boss; at the department level they feel manipulated by other departments; at the organizational level they feel victim to competition, to regulations, or to the economy. This powerless point of view pervades the organization and easily becomes a self-fulfilling prophecy.

On the other hand, some organizations recognize that personal power is a critical factor in personal satisfaction and organizational effectiveness. The Waterloo Catholic school system relies heavily on staffpersons at all levels to make meaningful contributions to organizational results. People are encouraged to exert influence over both the problems and solutions in their lives and to establish new opportunities. People who feel responsible in this way are enabled to assume some control over external forces, rather than feel powerless before them. Mistakes, instead of being viewed as failures, are seen as learning opportunities. Outside forces, the boss, the organization, the environment, are seen as potential partners, as opposed to obstacles to the creative process.

It is important to value personal power because when people are fundamentally committed to the same direction (alignment), the enhancement in their individual power increases the total power of the organization. By contrast, in unaligned organizations, increasing personal power tends to increase organizational conflict.

Within the WRRCSSB, the authors have found it important to use every opportunity to remind people that personal power is a creative force for the organization, provided that the system maintains alignment. It is amazing how many successes can be achieved when aligned people are given personal power.

System Structure

It is a well-known fact that good initiatives die if the structures are not in place to facilitate them. Vision, alignment, and personal power are quickly dissipated in a poorly designed organizational structure. In contrast, well-designed structures, policies, and procedures allow the individual energies developed by alignment and personal power to translate effectively into collective results. Inspired, high-performing organizations evolve organizational structures appropriate to their purpose and visions.

The WRRCSSB looks at the organization as a complex, whole system. As mentioned previously, a proposal for organizational redesign was developed. The proposal called for the creation of five divisions, each headed by a superintendent. Each division was given responsibility for setting and controlling its own budget, with the assistance of a central accounting department. Each division also set its own goals and objectives in accordance with the organization's purpose and visions, and these were reviewed by the administrative council. This strategy lent personal power to the divisions, and the creativity and energy of each division enhanced the overall organization.

The intent of the organizational redesign was to decentralize authority and responsibility and to place as many people as feasible as close to the action in the schools as possible. At the same time, principals and support staff were brought more directly into the collaborative decision-making process. These actions have engendered greater understanding of the decision-making process throughout the system and have increased alignment to the purpose and vision of the system as a whole.

Integration of Intuition and Reason

Traditionally in education it seems that everything has had to be rationally analyzed to be accepted. We know now, however, that rational analysis alone cannot cope with the magnitude of existing complexity and change. Difficult decisions are often made in a complex and changing environment, demanding the use of intuition, which can gain access to information not usually available to the rational mind and process it in an inductive, nonlinear way. At the same time, reason helps reinforce or test intuitive conclusions.

Intuition plays a vital role in creating the organization's vision, in developing alignment, and in planning organizational design. Organizations with a clear sense of underlying purpose are that much more likely to have a captivating, workable vision for the future. Intuition helps to mediate and define this purpose and foresight. Most of one's conclusions are, afterall, intuitive until tested by reason. Once tested by reason and if reinforced by a rational analysis, the basis for the decision can then be communicated clearly and confidently to others.

The author's purpose has been to teach people and work with them collaboratively to build a new organization, as opposed to simply teaching people to cope with the old one. In the process, individuals have created a vision that has led to the discovery of a common purpose, which in turn, has aligned them to the organization and what it stands for. More than anything else, spirit enables people and organizations to produce results in ways consistent with their most deeply held values. It is gratifying for the authors that throughout this period of change, a spirit of enthusiasm has infused the system's activities. The authors have become committed to achieving the highest potential in themselves and others. This commitment is seen as vital to realizing the potential and greatness of any organization.

Imaging the Future

Organizations are social units, deliberately constructed and reconstructed to achieve specific goals. As these goals or the context within which they must be achieved change, the structure of an organization must be critically reexamined.

After much consultation, study, and reflection, the WRRCSSB has defined a desired future state for the organization. Arriving at this definition is important, because the organization's success in creating future images, which is a major responsibility of professionals in the system, is dependent on its ability to conceptualize that desired future state. Part of strategic planning involves strategic assessment—environmental scanning, imaging of future options, and policy and program assessment. At the same time, congruence throughout the system must be maintained. Figure 1 is a rather simplistic but effective schematic for achieving an effective organizational framework and also for maintaining congruence.

As the desired future state changes, an organization's goals change. And when goals change, people in the organization are asked to think and behave differently in at least some areas. The authors have found it useful to thoroughly instruct staff in the new elements of organizational design including informing them of how decisions are made and who will be affected, clarifying what new tasks they will be asked to perform, what structures will have to be modified or changed, how this will affect personnel policies and procedures, and how information about these changes will be made known throughout the organization.

The desired future state in the WRRCSSB is to have one remodeled system where everyone belongs, where all are accepted naturally, with affection, and where

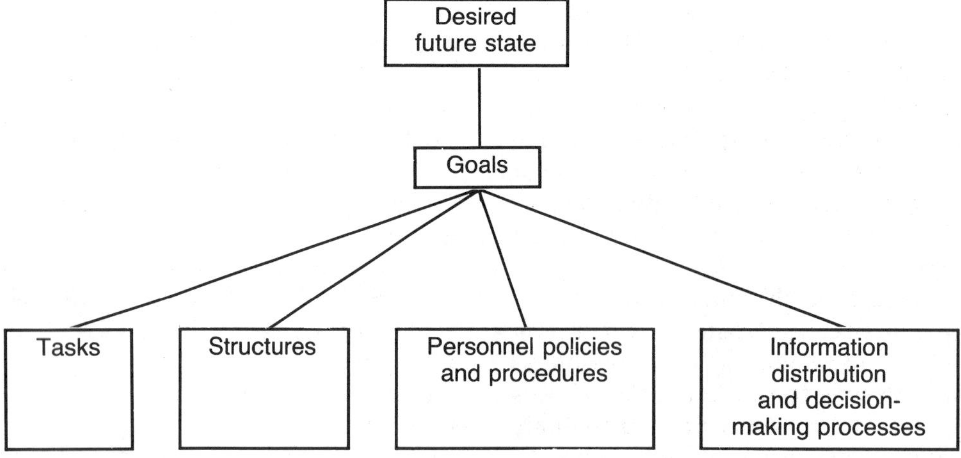

Figure 1. Elements of organizational design.

the quality of education is the highest possible.

WRRCSSB CASE HISTORIES—INTEGRATION IN ACTION

The following two case examples demonstrate acceptance and affection at work within the unified school system.

Case Example—T.D.

T.D. is a 17-year-old boy who was born with Down syndrome. T.D. came to St. Jerome's High School with the label "trainable retarded." In his first year at St. Jerome's he was given a full course load of history, mathematics, physical education, drama, instrumental music, religion, and English. His work placement was in the school library. One lunch hour T.D.'s usual lunch friend was absent and so T.D. walked up to the table where the football team ate. Approaching the biggest football player, he asked, "Can I eat with you guys?" An over 6-foot-tall player stood up, carried a chair over for T.D., and put it on his immediate left. As a result of the peer support system and the level of commitment between students that this event generated, T.D. is genuinely a part of school events.

T.D.'s integration at St. Jerome's is particularly gratifying for his parents. "He's really learning, and getting an academic challenge for the first time in his life," says his mother. At last he is being treated "like a young man." He identifies with the boys at St. Jerome's and his behavior is much more appropriate for his age. Like many people with Down syndrome, T.D. was an extremely affectionate child and people were inclined to play with him and baby him. "I think he was trained to be retarded," observes his mother, recalling the years he spent in special classrooms. The companionship of his adolescent peers who take him to football games, to movies, to dances, and regularly visit him after school by telephone has overcome that tendency.

Case Example–E.P.

E.P. is a beautiful 23-year-old young woman with bright blue eyes and blond hair. She is currently employed at the WRRCSS board office in a clerical position and is doing exceptionally well. E.P. attended St. Mary's High School for 5 years and was the first student labeled autistic to attend one of our secondary schools. She is a special person who taught staff and students that we all belong. During her elementary years, when she was in segregated classes, E.P.'s self-abusive behavior was intense and disruptive. When E.P. entered the ninth grade, the idea of putting her in regular classes seemed totally unrealistic to her teachers—they were afraid. But with the support of her parents, peers, and teachers, E.P. blossomed into an independent student. She became one of the kids, she carried a comb in her knee socks like the other students, and swore when she thought adults were not present. She participated in extracurricular activities and was the team manager of the girls volleyball team.

It is reassuring to see the effect on all students of students formerly classified as "different." It was arranged that each "special" student would be provided a support circle of friends to meet his or her needs during school time—taking them to class, lunch, and so forth. These support circles have spilled over into other areas. For example, T.D.'s mother telephoned in shock because a fellow student in T.D.'s mathematics class had asked her son to join the other guys on the weekend. This was his first call, ever, from a friend. From that point on T.D.'s social calendar blossomed. For E.P.'s part, she brought one of her peer support friends home, and now that friend is her sister-in-law.

The support circles have been a major factor in the success of the program at both schools. They have reached out to T.D. and E.P. and in the process have learned about themselves. These young people are an energetic group that never asked why but always replied, "Sure, why not?"

DESIRED REALITY

The ideal reality that the authors would envision for the WRRCSSB is for *all* children and young adults to truly belong, and to feel deeply that they belong. These authors firmly believe that *all* children and young adults can learn and that they have a right to be fully integrated with each other (belong) and to be successful (learn). This vision helps explain the system's purpose and has led to the establishment of certain goals. It is important to recognize that goals established without purpose tend to allow hidden conflict about organizational direction and rationale to go unresolved. Placing primary importance on purpose naturally clarifies basic direction and allows people to concentrate on this purpose, without being sidetracked into debate about specific goals.

A description of educational purpose is contained in an article by Alan Gartner and Dorothy Lipsky (1987), entitled "Beyond Special Education: Toward a Quality System for All Students." They stated:

> There is an alternative to separate systems: a merged or unitary system. The conception of a unitary system requires a "paradigm shift," a fundamental change in the way we think about differences among people, in the ways we choose to organize schools for their education, and in how we view the purpose of that education. It rejects the bimodal division of handicapped and nonhandicapped students, and recognizes that individuals vary—that single-characteristic definitions fail to capture the complexity of people. Moreover, it rejects the belief, common to all human services work that incorporates a medical or deviancy model, that the problem lies in the individual and the resolution lies in one or another treatment modality. The unitary system, in contrast, requires adaptations in society and in education, not solely in the individual.
>
> In a unified system no longer would there be a need to approach differences in human capabilities or characteristics as disabilities on which to base categorical groupings. In a merged system an individual difference in visual ability, for example, could be viewed as only one of numerous characteristics of a student, rather than the overriding educational focus of a student's life. . . . It would not dictate differential placement and treatment according to a categorical affiliation which is often inherent in the disabilities approach to education.
>
> In a merged or unitary system, effective practices in classrooms and schools would characterize education for all students. No longer would there be an education system that focuses on the limitations of "handicapped" students, a teacher's incapacity to teach students because of a lack of special credentials, or instruction that is determined by the label attached to students. Nor would blame be placed on students or on family characteristics. Rather, the focus would be on effective instruction for all students based on the belief that substantial student improvements occur when teachers accept the responsibility for the performance of all their students and when they structure their classrooms so that student success is a primary product of the interaction that takes place there. (p. 388)

As the basis for sound strategic planning, the WRRCSSB has developed certain short- and long-term initiatives. For example, for the next school year, these are among the goals that have been set:

1. To continue the restructuring process in the Waterloo system until we have one

unified system to which *all* children and young adults will have equal access and equal opportunity for success in education

2. To continue the work of the committee on race and ethnic relations to develop policy and guidelines that will ensure that *all* children and young adults have equal access and equal opportunity for success in education
3. To continue the work of the committee on parent-teacher partnerships to develop policy and guidelines that will ensure that all children and young adults, regardless of the level of privilege their families enjoy, have equal access and equal opportunity for success in education

The aim has been to bring a degree of congruence to the system so that each of these goals is not seen as a separate entity but as part of an integrated whole. The overriding motivation for this work has been the concept of justice for all, flavored by a sincere, deep respect for all that is human.

CONCLUSION

The Waterloo Region Roman Catholic Separate School Board (WRRCSSB) has come a long way toward achieving its desired future state, that is, a single unified organizational structure that serves all children and young people. The task now is to continue to scan the environment and to explore future options for strengthening this new community.

REFERENCES

Bogdan, R., & Taylor, S. (1987). *Toward a sociology of acceptance: The other side of the study of deviance.* Syracuse, NY: Syracuse University, Center on Human Policy.

Gartner, A., & Lipsky, D. (1987). Beyond special education: Toward a quality system for all students. *Harvard Educational Review, 57* (4), 367–395.

Kiefer, C.F., & Stroh, P. (1987). A new paradigm for developing organizations. Unpublished manuscript.

Muller, R. (1985, November). *The need for global education.* Paper presented at the meeting of the National Congress of Education Advisors, St. Louis.

Stainback, W., & Stainback, S. (1984). A rationale for the merger of special and regular education. *Exceptional Children, 51,* 102–111.

CHAPTER 4

Promoting Educational Equality for All Students

Circles and Maps

Marsha Forest and Evelyn Lusthaus

Mr. and Mrs. Russell and their two children, May and Jennifer, walk to school down the street from their apartment to register for school in an ordinary fashion. They are welcomed like any other parents of neighborhood children.

No big deal, one is apt to say. These authors agree. But the big deal is that May, now 11 years old, has been out of the mainstream of regular education since kindergarten, attending segregated schools and classes for children labeled as mentally handicapped. The school staff tell the parents that they are delighted to have both children in their school and that they will need to work together to meet their children's needs.

This is an example of what occurs under a system of educational equality, in which all students are treated as integral parts of the regular educational mainstream. In such a system, all children are welcomed and provided the support they need in their neighborhood schools, where they attend ordinary classrooms with students their own age. These schools operate on the belief that all children belong and are equally accepted. Their focus is on ordinary classrooms, which they strive to make into communities in which all children can grow, learn, and contribute.

This chapter describes such a vision of educational equality. It also outlines in detail two practices currently used in some schools to assist students needing support to be incorporated into the educational mainstream.

Point to Ponder

Some children obviously will need support and assistance to make it in the mainstream. When required, those students who need it should receive the best assistance available, regardless of their label—disabled or nondisabled.

INTEGRATION: A PROCESS FOR EDUCATION EQUALITY

What is integration? Integration, both in education and in society in general, is the process of people coming together to achieve the objective of living together in a harmonious whole, each one an integral part. In the *Random House College Dictionary*, *integration* means:

1. the act or an instance of combining into an integral whole
2. behavior in harmony with the environment
3. the organization of the constituent elements of the personality into a coordinated, harmonious whole
4. one unified system.

The key words here indicating the purpose of integration are to achieve an "integral whole," "harmonious whole," and "unified system."

The concept of an integral and harmonious whole in education can be illustrated by the imagery of the kaleidoscope. The concept and image are of a circle–full, complete, inclusive. It is not a box, a cascade, a rectangle, or a linear continuum of services. Like the kaleidoscope, regular education as a unified system for *all* students is an ever-changing panorama of color and design, in which bits and pieces of everything–all colors, shapes, and sizes—exist in an integrated whole. Every kaleidoscope has a handpiece. Twist it and one gets another color, another design, another look. The kaleidoscope is a wonder and mystery to all who hold it up to the sunlight and see that the whole is far more beautiful than the sum of the parts.

Regular education for all students means creating a community in which each person belongs. It is first and foremost a social ethic of acceptance of diversity, followed by common sense curriculum planning.

QUALITY EDUCATION FOR ALL CHILDREN

In school systems that use the kaleidoscope image of education, all children–with their unique backgrounds, gifts, and special needs—learn together in regular classrooms, in neighborhood schools, with the supports required. In these school systems, a pattern of procedures is beginning to emerge. These include:

1. All children in the community are welcomed into their local school.
2. If a child lives in the community, the parent registers the child in the local school.
3. All children begin school in an ordinary classroom with children their own age.
4. The school arranges meetings to discuss how best to meet the needs of the children, and of the teachers who need extra help or assistance.

In Canada, community and school support for educating all students in regular education is being demonstrated in pockets nationwide. In the Northwest Territories and throughout the province of New Brunswick, a policy of full inclusion has been adopted. Harvey Malmberg, deputy minister of education in New Brunswick, explains his province's direction:

> The education system must approach all students according to their educational needs, not according to their labels. A student is a student first! Several years will be required to reach our new goal of full integration for all students, but with persistence and patience we will eventually get there (1987).

Other examples of systems that are committed to regular education for all students

Point to Ponder

Separation is repugnant to our constitutional tradition. Integration is a central constitutional value—not integration that denies difference but, rather, integration that accommodates difference, that appreciates it and celebrates it. (Gilhool, 1976, p. 8)

include several major separate school boards in Ontario. Most notable are the Hamilton Wentworth Separate School Board, the Wellington Separate School Board, and the Waterloo Region Separate School Board. These boards state simply and emphatically: "*Each belongs.*"

ASSUMPTIONS FOR EDUCATIONAL EQUALITY

Regular education for all is based on several simple but deep assumptions about people and learning. These are discussed in the paragraphs following.

1. *Each child has the right to belong.* Every child needs to be welcomed as a full member of his or her neighborhood school and community. This welcome should be taken for granted by any child, including those defined as having the most severe and profound disabilities. When a child has very challenging needs, or requires support, the onus should be on the school environment to problem-solve and make adaptations—the goal is to make the child a belonging member, not to prepare the child to "fit in" or "get ready."

When a child is considered a full member of the class, this does not mean that he or she must sit in one classroom all day. The child may certainly be in other places for parts of the day—for activities, for work, for learning in other classrooms, and in other school and nonschool environments. Being a full member means that every child can automatically go to school and become a member of a regular class, just like everyone else. The word *belonging* is the key.

One often hears, "Oh, but you couldn't mean integration for *those* kids. . . ." The authors' response is, "Yes, we believe the criteria for membership into the regular class and the community at large is *breathing*. Come to talk with students, parents, and staff, to share in a vision of what a good school looks like."

In both the United States and Canada, it is against the law to segregate students based on race, sex, or color. Hopefully, in the near future, it also will be against the law to segregate on the basis of handicapping conditions and their concomitant labels.

2. *To grow and develop, each child needs relationships with peers who have diverse skills.* Children's cognitive growth and social development is optimized when they feel they belong and have relationships with others, especially *friends.* When schools provide an opportunity for students with diverse needs and abilities to learn among their friends, they are taking a common-sense approach. Does it make sense to group four children together who have difficulties speaking and expect them to learn to speak, even with speech therapy? Does a child learn better to lift her head by headlifting exercises in the "special" room or by being in a regular class with friends, where there are exciting people and things to look at when her head is lifted?

As educators, we need to shift our thinking dramatically about the gains that can occur as a result of relationships among children with differing characteristics and skills. For decades, the myth has pervaded that "regular" students will not want to be friends with students who traditionally have been in special education. This myth comes from us adults, perhaps because we had no relationships with such children when we were in school; they were all in segregated schools, segregated classes, or not in schools at all.

The approach advocated here is to encourage friendships and "being together." Peer buddies, peer helpers, and special tutors are all fine in their place, but the point is that all children, regardless of their individual differences, have so much to offer each other that real, true friendships can and do exist.

3. *Schools should strive to be communities that value diversity.* All children can benefit from a classroom environment that has a rich diversity of class members, since this adds greater depth and meaning to school and life. Educating all students in regular education provides the opportunity to teach the worth of each individual. To teach the value of diversity, it *must* be recognized that all children, regardless of differences, should be included in heterogeneous class arrangements.

Because everyone has a contribution to make and has unique strengths and gifts, all children are "gifted." Regular education for all presents the chance to teach our children that all are gifted in one way or another, and to build bridges between children who have not had the chance to know each other and learn from one another.

By welcoming children who have been left out, we change the system. When teachers learn to adapt and individualize, it helps everyone, importing a new sense of belonging among all students. Father Pat Mackan (1988), a noted Canadian educator, emphasizes that when "regular" students see the children who have been left out accepted and welcomed, they experience a deep strengthening of their own sense of security—they know that they, too, are welcomed, and are not at risk of losing their place.

4. *People need to dream and to express what they hope for the future.* Because it is easy to be bound by what is "realistic" or current standard practice, people need to take the time to dream and to develop new visions and new pictures. Parents, teachers, administrators, and students all can benefit from dreaming, and from breaking through the existing boundaries of what is thought possible. To make dreams happen, we need teamwork, cooperation, brainstorming, problem solving, imagination, and the will to learn more and to pioneer new frontiers.

CIRCLES OF FRIENDS: A NETWORK OF SUPPORT

Students themselves are a major underutilized resource in schools today. Yet as a resource, students are plentiful, energetic, inexpensive, and the heart of schools. When students have been included in the integration process, solutions have been found that were never anticipated, and energy has been tapped that is a source of wonder to all involved. The assumption underlying the students' involvement is that it is a valid and vital educational experience for students to participate in planning their own lives and also in helping others.

Many students who traditionally have been in special education have few or no friends. For many, paid service providers are their primary daily "outside" contact. Most of us, when asked what is most important in our own lives, would answer, "our family, our loved ones, our friends." For many of us, friends are a natural part of our lives, something taken for granted. It would be hard to imagine living alone without them, without the telephone ringing, the get-togethers, the tennis games, the dinners out. Yet for many children this support has not been available.

Often, we educators have directed too much attention to developing interventions for skill acquisition, maintenance, and generalization, and have lost sight of the most important aspect of the child's life—his or her social, emotional, and spiritual life. While academic and/or daily life skills and competencies are significant, educators need to focus their creativity not only on designing programs and curriculum but on encouraging and nurturing relationships.

One way to build relationships among regular students and those who have been integrated is through "circles of friends" (Snow & Forest, 1987). In this process, an exercise is conducted with regular students which helps to sensitize them and identify those who are most willing to get involved in the lives of the integrated students. This is not a "special friends project" or a "buddy system" for "unfortunate" students, or a chance for students to do a good deed for the day. The "circle of friends" is a network that allows for the genuine involvement of children in a friendship, caring, and support role with their peers. As one school principal said recently, "If I hadn't seen it with my own eyes, I truly wouldn't believe it. The children are at the heart of the process and it works."

Building "circles of friends" and involving children means sharing *power* or decision making with them and giving up the authoritarian and patriarchal system so inherent in most schools. It means permitting children to help decide what is needed for themselves and their peers and how it can be achieved in school. A special education consultant telephoned the authors recently and was appalled that the children were involved in school program decision making. "But who's in control? Who's in charge?" she asked. "Control is shared," was the reply. Following are two case studies demonstrating what can be accomplished with a "circle of friends" approach.

A Circle for May: Case Study #1

In September, a few days before May Russell would be attending her new seventh grade classroom, an integration consultant visited the class to speak with the students. She asked them the following series of questions. The students' actual responses are included here, too.

Consultant (C)—"Hi, I've come to talk to you about May who is coming to your class next week. You met her last week when she visited with her mother. For years May has gone to a segregated school or been in a self-contained life skills class. What does that mean?"

Students (S)—
"Places for retarded people"
"Schools for kids who are really bad"
"Like the one near my house where all the wheelchairs go"

C—"Well, May is coming here and I'll tell you a secret. Everyone is really scared. Her mother and father are scared, Mr. Gorman [teacher] is scared. Mr. Cullen [principal] is scared. I'm scared. Why do you think all of us are so scared?"

S—
"You all think we'll be mean to her."
"You think we'll tease her and be mean to her."
"You think she'll be left out."

C—"There are some things we don't want you to do when she arrives. What do you think these are?"

S—
"Don't treat her like a baby."
"Don't pity her."
"Don't ignore her."
"Don't feel sorry for her."

C—"Why are we doing this? Why is May coming to this class?

S—
"Why not? She's our age, she should be here."
"How would you feel if you were 12 and never were with kids your own age?"
"It's dumb for her not to be here."
"She needs friends."
"She needs a boy friend."

C—"What do you think we want you to do?"

S—
"Treat her like one of us."
"Make her feel welcome."
"Help her make friends."
"Help her with her work."
"Call her and invite her to our parties."

C—"I want to switch gears for a few minutes and ask you to all do an exercise with me called "circle of friends." I do this very same thing with teachers and parents and I think you are all grown up enough to handle it."

(The consultant handed out a sheet with four concentric circles on it. After the first circle, each circle was a little larger and farther away from the center of the page where a stick person was drawn.)

C—"There are four circles. On each circle you are to list people you know. I want you to think about whom you would put in your first circle. These are the people closest to you, the people you really love. You can do this privately or in pairs, and you can tell us or keep it private."

(The consultant filled in her own circles on the chalkboard while the students did theirs at their seats. When finished, the facilitator shared her circles and then asked for volunteers to share theirs.)

S—"OK. In my first circle I put in my mom, my dad, Matt who is my best friend, and Stacey—that's my Mom's best friend and she often helps me when I have a problem."

C—"Why did you put those people in your first circle?"

S—"They are people I feel close to. I love them."

C—"What do you do with the people in circle one?"

S—"I share my secrets, I can be myself, I go to them when I'm hurt, I trust them, I love them."

C—"Now let's do circle two—these are people you really like but not enough to put in circle one."

S—"I put in my dog and my two best friends Tim and Todd, and my teacher Mr. Gorman.

I put them in because I can do everything with them and we have fun together and we visit a lot."

C—"The third circle is groups of people you like or people you do things with, like Scouts, swimming, hockey, etc."

S—"I have lots—I'm in Boy Scouts, my church, my Sunday school, this class, my street hockey group, and my family is like a group."

C—"The last circle is for people you pay to be in your lives, like your doctor, dentist, and so on."

S—"I put in my doctor and my eye glass doctor, that's all."

C—"Now I want you to think about a person's circle. Here's a fantasy person named Sebastian. He's your age (12) and his circles look like this. He only has his Mom in circle one and the rest of his circles are empty except for circle four, which is filled with doctors, social workers, therapists, etc. Think hard for a few minutes because this is real serious. How would you feel if your life looked like Sebastian's?"

(This is a list of responses from the seventh grade students in the brainstorming session.)
S—"Lonely, depressed, unwanted, terrible, disgusted, like what's the use of living, I'd want to commit suicide, like dying, awful, crazy, hurt, nobody cares, angry, furious, mad."

C—"How do you think you'd act?"

S—(Again, a list of responses from the brainstorming.) "I'd hide and keep my head down all day, I'd hit people, I'd cry all day, I'd hate everyone, I'd kill myself, I'd want to kill others, I'd steal, I'd curse and spit, I'd fight."

C—"Ok, I want to wind this up for today and I'll be back in a few weeks to see what's happening. Remember, I came and we started talking about May who will be in your class soon. Well, right now her life looks a bit like Sebastian's imaginary circle. So why did I do all this?"

S—"To help us understand about all the new kids who are coming into our classes—about how they must feel."

C—"What I'd like is for a group of you to act as a welcome committee and another group to act as a telephone crew. I want a phone caller for each day of the week. Do you think that's a good idea?"

S—"Wow, yeah—what a neat idea!"

C—"Remember, friends don't develop overnight. This is just the start. Not all of you will be May's friends—though all of you can be "friendly." My dream and hope is that out of this great class May will have at least six friends who will do things with her in school and most of all after school and on weekends. This won't happen fast, but I bet it will happen. Who wants to help?"

It never fails that when the "circle of friends" is done correctly and sensitively, almost everyone wants to get involved. The facilitator turns the process over to the classroom teacher who takes ownership and continues selecting a small group of students to be in the new student's circle. No credits are given—it is all voluntary.

One mistake educators have made in the past is to "plunk" into a classroom a child who is in need of support, and attach a teacher-maid (teacher-aide) to shadow the child. This creates dependency and what Doug Biklen (1985) so aptly calls "the island in the mainstream" (p. 18).

Circle building is intended to make the implicit become explicit. It legitimizes the students' and teachers' fears, questions, and anxieties. It also provides the opportunity to say that it is okay to be different; that as human beings we all have similar needs, but we all come in unique packages.

Circles must be informal, flexible, and open. They must not be turned into behavior-management teams, teaching assistants, or disciplinary bodies. They are circles of friends. Tutors can become friends, but peer tutors are not the friendship circle. Because friends, especially when young, change and come and go, friendship circles must be given time and nourishment. Above all, they must not be made into something they are not. Circles should meet regularly (i.e., once a week) and be facilitated by a warm and caring teacher who will promote the reciprocal nature of real friendship.

Amy: Case Study #2—A Friend's Perception

Amy is a beautiful redheaded seventh grader who got involved in May's circle. After 8 months' involvement with Amy, her teacher, Kerry Gorman, talked to her and recorded the conversation. Their conversation has profound implications for all of us as educators, parents, and citizens.

Mr. G—"Amy, when you think back to September, can you remember why you got involved in May's circle?"

Amy—"The idea excited me. I came to see what May could really do. I stayed [in the circle] all year because when I look back at May then and now I can see what we've all done."

Mr. G—"What do you see?"

Amy—"I now see May as my friend—as one of us. I think she is really very smart but I didn't know that at first cause she had been in the "retarded" room and acted real weird. I learned she has real feelings and that she feels real bad when people tease her—it hurts her, but now she can come to her friends—to us."

Mr. G—"Sometimes she has hurt you a lot. How do you deal with that?"

Amy—I talk to my other friends and then I tell May, "I don't appreciate it when you do that. Don't expect to have me or anyone else as a friend if you act like that!"

Mr. G—"Where do we go from here?"

Amy–"Well, of course keeping May as my friend. I think when I'm older I'd like to do what Judith Snow and Marsha Forest do—help get kids learning together and being friends."

Mr. G—"What do you think of the integration at our school?"

Amy—"I love it! I've learned more this year that I have any other year—its been something that really hits you and gets you. I heard Father Pat Mackan speak at church last week and I understood what he was saying about community and learning. Yeah, I love integration and I love May and all the others in our circle."

Mr. G—"What do you really think you did with May?"

Amy—"I think we made her feel she belongs and she really does belong now. She feels human. Before she was always by herself or with a teacher or adult. Now she has us to play with. She has friends."

Mr. G—"What else has being in the circle given you?"

Amy—"It has given me a whole new way of looking at things—how lucky I am—that all my life I've had friends and I took it for granted. It makes me feel better about everything I can do. When I see May work so hard I really admire her, and I'm thankful I'm her friend and she's my friend."

Mr. G—"Have you seen any differences in the class this year?"

Amy—"Yes! Everyone is more open. You are great, Mr. Gorman, and if you can help May then you can help and listen to all of us. Everyone seems more open and willing to care more this year."

Keep in mind that Amy is 12 years old. She has had no trouble with the concept of integration and neither have any of the children involved in friendship circles that have been built during the past 5 years. Integration is an adult problem. As stated earlier, it is we ourselves who are afraid of people who have traditionally been in special education, because most of us went to segregated schools and have lived in segregated communities all our lives. It is hoped that children in the schools today—the adults of the next decade—will be open and can help in the quest to build loving, integrated communities.

MAPS: DEVELOPING A SCHOOL PROGRAM

Equally important as building a caring community through friendship is the task of planning the day-to-day program. MAPS, short for McGill *action planning system* (Lusthaus & Forest, 1987) is a systems approach to help team members plan for the integration of new students into regular age-appropriate classrooms. The planning meeting involves the student himself or herself (when appropriate), the parents (and other family members), professionals who know the student, and, most important members of the student's circle of friends.

Including the family as primary players in the MAPS process is extremely important and cannot be compromised. Family members are key because they know most about the child; they have a sense of history that no one else realizes. They have been with their child since birth, and often have persevered through years of struggle trying to get the services they need. During the planning process, when parents have an opportunity to share their child's history, the other members of the MAPS team gain new insights into the family's perspective. In many cases, they hear for the first time the family's dreams and hopes for the future, as well as the family's fears and deep concerns.

Most families need support from others around them to express what they hope for their children. They, too, need a circle of support. The MAPS process should provide a beginning framework of support and strength to the family, as others listen to what they say and work throughout the MAPS session to make plans based on this interaction.

The inclusion of students is also a key element in the MAPS process. The point of the exercise is to devise an effective action plan for the student being integrated. Students often understand the necessary ingredients of such a plan far better than adults, and unless some young people are present, it is impossible to get the same results.

To illustrate MAPS, this chapter once again focuses on May, whose friendship circle, built during the first weeks of school, was described in the previous pages. May's "regular education" teacher said that he was willing to welcome May into his class with no assistance for a few weeks, to get to know her and to see what she could do. He was worried and skeptical, but willing to try. A month later, when the initial MAPS meeting was held, the class and May had gotten to know each other.

The Initial MAPS Meeting

Included in the MAPS meeting were: May, May's mother, May's sister Jennifer, Mr. Gorman (seventh grade teacher), Mrs. George (special education teacher), Mr. Cullen (school principal), the MAPS facilitator (Marsha Forest), the MAPS illustrator/recorder (David Hasbury), and May's seventh grade circle of friends (Stacey, Becky, Amy, Fatima, Tina, Kelly, and Pam).

The first part of the meeting focused on seven key questions that are the heart of the MAPS planning process. Following are these questions, along with a discussion and actual responses for each.

1. *What is May's history?* This important first question is meant to give everyone present a picture of what has happened in May's life. May's mother was asked to summarize the key milestones that have had an impact on the life of the family and have affected the school situation. For example, in May's story we found out that May was born 6 weeks early and had major surgery within 24 hours of birth. She began an infant stimulation program at 6 weeks of age and has continued her education from then on. From ages 2½ to 11, she attended segregated schools and classes until September 1987, when she became a full member of grade seven at St. Francis School.

2. *What is your dream for May (assuming no money restraints, etc.)?* Parents of children defined as having disabilities often have lost their ability to dream for their child and have stopped asking themselves what they really hope and wish for him or her. Including this question in the meeting helps to restore the dream and impresses upon parents the need to articulate a vision of the future based on what they really want, not simply what they think they can get. The following were answers from the group:

Dreams for May:

To be out on her own and have a place of her own
To share a life with her friends
To achieve in school
To go places
To have independence with friends
To be self-supporting
To be free to choose friends
To have friends—have lots of roommates
To have a good education
To have a good job
To have self-respect
To have happiness
To take a trip to Hawaii
To figure things out on her own
To take singing and dancing lessons
To play baseball
To learn computers
To get married
To play in a band with Jennifer

May's dream for herself is the following (her speech is not perfectly clear, but her friends acted as interpreters for Marsha if Marsha couldn't understand).

Marsha: May, what is your dream when you grow up?
May: I want to get married.
Marsha: What else do you want when you grow up?
May: I want to have my own baby named Joey.
Marsha: Anything else?
May: Yeah—a job with a computer; also buzz around.
Marsha: Where are you going to live?
May: On a farm. Fantastic!

3. *What is your nightmare?* The nightmare makes explicit the fears for their child that are in the parents' hearts. The nightmare for May was that she would face rejection from the community; be pigeonholed into a sheltered workshop; be taken advantage of sexually; be ostracized from others because of her disability; and live in fear of being sent to an institution.

4. *Who is May?* The next question is meant to begin a general brainstorming session on who May is, with no holds barred. The facilitator asks everyone to go around the circle and provide words until they run out of words and all thoughts are exhausted. These are the answers to May's *Who* question:

Stubborn
Confident
She has style
Enthusiastic
Active
Good memory
Sharing
Determined
Spontaneous
Friendly
Tries
Independent
Loving
Smart
Character
Fun
Emotional
Actress
Friend
Shy
Willing
Sensitive
Helpful
Hyper
Lovable
Kind
Bossy
Cute
Hard worker
Giggler
Caring
Bugger
Joker
Moody
Expressive
Talker
Likes to do things

To find out more about May, everyone also said what they thought May liked:

To demonstrate what she can do
Stickers
To be around friends
Sports
To make people laugh
Laughing
To be involved in games
Reading
Computers
Food
Working hard
TV
To be on her own
People
Meeting people
Music
Boys
Helping people

Point to Ponder

To provide children every opportunity to learn and be happy, contributing members of society, we must learn not to underestimate them—we must believe in them and help them believe in themselves. Thus, we need to stop labeling some children as retarded, disordered, disabled, or handicapped. We must believe that all children have abilities and gifts and can contribute to society.

Dancing
Eating
Singing
Her teacher
Horseback riding
Superstars
To help people when they are scared
To be part of a group

The preceding exercise helped to provide a picture of a real person named May who, like everybody else, is unique and different from anybody else.

5. *What are May's strengths, gifts, and talents?* Often educators, and parents too, have come to focus on a person's perceived weaknesses. This question turns the table to the positives. Parents generally love to hear good things about their children. Here's how May's group characterized her strengths:

Independent
Caring
Likes helping
Outgoing
Has a good memory
Talkative
Determined
Helpful
Stubborn
Strong
Smart
Generous
Sees people for who they are

6. *What are May's needs?* Needs can be found in many areas—social, emotional, physical, spiritual, academic, and so on. Here is the list that May's MAPS team generated when asked to say what she needs most:

Friends
Love and caring from her family and friends
A good education—to be challenged and have a challenging program
Extra help from teachers to accomplish her goals
To communicate more clearly
An exercise and nutrition program
To drink water (4 cups a day) at school
To develop more leisure activities and sports interests
Awareness of her body and how she presents herself
To learn to accept help more
People to teach her more things
To be more understanding of her friends and their problems
To be more patient
To get medical attention for her feet
To do more reading

7. *What would an ideal day for May look like? What do we need to do to make this ideal real?* To many educators, May is still a child who should be segregated in a school or class for students labeled as mentally handicapped. To Principal Brian Cullen and his staff at St. Francis school and

to May's seventh grade teacher, Keri Gorman, however, May is a spunky 12-year-old who is rightly in grade seven with her peers.

With fear, trembling, and excitement and with a TEAM approach (MAPS) that involved other students in the process, a plan emerged for May's day. Much to the surprise of everyone involved, the team concluded that her day should look almost identical to that of the rest of the seventh grade. Step by step, the team analyzed the timetable, asking at each point: Does it make sense for May to be doing this activity? Does any modification need to be made? If yes, who needs to provide extra assistance? (teacher? assistant? peer tutor? high school helper? etc.).

Here is the timetable for grade seven in Mr. Gorman's room:

8:30AM–9:00AM Students "hang out" in the yard and are in room by 9:00 sharp. Announcements, prayers, and so forth.
9:00–9:25 Physical Education. The class is working on basketball review and drill.
9:25–9:50 Religion, Unit 7–"Who do you say that I am?" The class is continuing discussion on who people think we are and who we really are.
9:50—10:30 French Conversation.
10:30–10:45 Recess.
10:45–11:45 Science Unit—"Characteristics of Living Things." The class is studying behavior adaptation in birds of North America.
11:45AM—1:00PM Lunch
1:00–2:30 Language. The class is reading *The Hobbit* and working on recapping and on predicting what comes next in the story. Students do individual reading at this time for spelling and grammar.
2:30–3:45 Mathematics. The class is studying improper fractions and mixed forms; individualized math programs are common.
(The language period is on rotation with other subject areas: geography, history, and art. There is also a music and guidance period once a week.)

May now follows the general pattern of all the students, with modifications as necessary. For example, in language arts, May listens to the story, takes part in the discussion as well as she can, and is expected to copy the notes from the board or borrow notes from a friend. She writes in her journal along with the others and asks for help when needed from other students or teacher.

May has several individual periods of speech with the speech therapist during the week in the school library. These focus on conversational forms.

In math, May is working on an individualized program, designed for her by the "special" education teacher, called "Money Use and the Calculator." She is learning to do problem-solving with real money and using her own small calculator.

In history and geography, May is part of a small group project in all the subject areas and is expected to do some part of each project and follow through on all assignments. She is learning to do research with the others in the school library.

In summary, May is doing what no one thought possible. One visitor recently said, "I never thought I'd see a 12-year-old child with Down syndrome in a grade seven class with real friends and doing real school work." He and nearly everyone connected with St. Francis are pleased and surprised that May went so easily from the world of segregation and pain into the real world of learning, challenge, and excitement. When asked how she likes her new class, May beams and says, "Fantastic."

CONCLUSION

Educating all students in regular education can be achieved through the process of integration. The procedures outlined here, one for building friendship supports and the other for developing daily education programs for new students entering regular classrooms, have been found effective in facilitating the integration of new students. Although the goal is worthwhile, the process is not always easy. As noted in a letter from May's teacher (Keri Gorman, personal communication, 1987):

> "It is now Easter time. A new student arrived last week so we now have 35 students in this grade 7 class. May is fully part of my class and their circle [circle of friends] is still continuing.
>
> It has not all been sweetness and light. May has managed to hurt and anger many of the people in her circle so much so that many were ready to give up on her on several occasions. She has trouble learning that she, too, can hurt people. They share together as a group, and although some sessions have been highly charged, they have really made it work, and all their school work has improved, to boot.
>
> At the beginning of the year everyone had a tendency to mother and smother May or to be "teacher" rather than a friend. They would almost gang up on May when she did something wrong. I had to help them sort out their roles. There need to be stronger ties built outside of school . . . that's our next step.
>
> May's mother has such high hopes for the circle of friends. Will these hopes be realized? I don't know. Some may.
>
> She is thoroughly assimilated into the group, and her school work astounds me. She is doing the regular spelling tests now. She is quite slow in her other schoolwork but does what she can. She has, I believe, come a long way this year. She is part of our class.
>
> I didn't have a clue what was going to happen this year. I guess I wasn't burdened with a lot of preconceptions, nor were my students. Thus, we were able to trade ideas and thoughts back and forth. I was reasonably sure that circles were meant to be friends—that is helpers, confidants, companions and not teachers or mothers or fathers.
>
> The students have proved to be what Marsha Forest said they'd be—sources of useful and realistic ideas for the integration of everyone in our school. They have helped me and gently corrected me and the other teachers when we have not perceived what was so obvious to them as children. They have also accepted advice from me. It has been a most amazing year and a most amazing partnership!

Educating all students in regular education is controversial because it raises deeply provocative educational and social issues. At its root lies the question, What do we want our society and our communities to look like? What life do we want for ourselves and our children?

May, her friends, family, and teachers have all changed in wonderfully positive ways this year. They present one scenario for the future. They represent the part of society that is welcoming back people who have been left out for too long. They are the bridge builders to the future.

REFERENCES

Biklen, D. (1985). *Achieving the complete school.* New York: Columbia University, Teacher's College Press.

Gilhool, T. (1976). Changing public policies: Roots and forces. In M. Reynolds (Ed.), *Mainstreaming: Origins and implications* (pp. 8–13). Reston, VA: Council for Exceptional Children.

Lusthaus, E., & Forest, M. (1987). The kaleidoscope: A challenge to the cascade. In M. Forest (Ed.), *More education integration.* (pp. 1–17). Downsview, Ont.: G. Allan Roeher Institute.

Mackan, P. (1988). *Facilitating circles of friends.* Paper presented at Frontier College, Focus on Integration Conference Day, Toronto.

Snow, J., & Forest, M. (1987). Circles. In M. Forest (Ed.), *More education integration.* Downsview, Ont.: G. Allan Roeher Institute.

CHAPTER 5

Friendships as an Educational Goal

Jeffrey L. Strully and Cindy F. Strully

This chapter offers a personal perspective on the importance of friendships and integration for our children. First, however, as a background to this discussion, the chapter outlines how many of us often describe our children and dream about their futures.

DESCRIBING OUR CHILDREN

Description #1

Depending upon who is talking, we have two teenage daughters. One daughter could be described in the following ways:

15½ years old
Beautiful brown eyes and brown hair
Favorite musicians and musical groups are: Bruce Springsteen, Tiffany, U2, Bangles, and Madonna.
She will wear clothes with the following labels only: Guess® and Esprit®
Her favorite movie stars are: Rob Lowe, Matt Dillon, and Matthew Broderick.
She is a sophomore at Arapahoe High School.
She tried out for cheerleaders, but didn't like it.
She works part-time at Sound Warehouse.
She "hangs out" in shopping malls, at Burger King and 7-Eleven Food Store, the gym, and anywhere there are boys!
She spends time on the phone talking to friends.
She loves swimming and getting a tan.
She loves to decorate her room, including the ceiling, with posters.
Friends are very important to her.
Extracurricula activities have included signs and posters, gourmet cooking, Girl Scouts, and the high school newspaper.
She is caring, bright, and very typical.
When you ask her friends to describe her, they say:
Happy, exciting, pretty, silly, normal, wonderful, intriguing, engaging, unique, fun, enjoyable, stubborn, great, laughable, caring, annoying, energetic, picky, fickle, affectionate, pushy, lovable, decisive, sensitive, strong-willed, temperamental, spontaneous, diplomatic, terrific.

Desirable Future Hardly a day goes by without our thinking about the kind of future we would like for our daughter. Our dreams for her are much like those outlined by her friends, including, in their own words:

Living with someone who cares about her
Doing something during the day that she likes to do
Having lots of friends to do things with

Living in her own condo
Having an active life
Being around people who want to be with her
Having friends over every day to do "stuff" with
Being happy
Going to college
Modeling for a fashion magazine
Working in a job that she likes and that makes money

Description #2

Our other daughter, also 15½ years old, has been described in the following ways:

Severely/profoundly mentally retarded
Hearing impaired
Visually impaired
Has cerebral palsy
Myoclonic seizures
Does not chew her food and sometimes chokes
Is not toilet trained
No verbal communication
No reliable gestural communication
If given the chance, will self-stimulate, mainly hand-in-eye and hand-in-mouth
If given a developmental checklist, would "top out" at 17–24 months
Loves Fisher-Price® toys
Loves music—"Row, Row, Row Your Boat"; "Three Blind Mice"; "London Bridge"

Desirable Future Thinking about a desirable future for our second daughter is more difficult for most people. They might dream about her future in the following ways:

Group home with six or eight other people
Sheltered workshop–day activity center
Special Olympics
Volunteers to "work" with her
Need for programming
Group field trips
Friends to be with her who are just "like" her

WHO ARE THESE CHILDREN?

The two girls just described, *are the same person*, our daughter Shawntell.

What Is Most Important in Life?

When thinking about desirable futures for people, we need to think about issues such as: "how we generally think about people's lives; how we describe people; and what we dream for our sons/daughters or the people we serve."

We hope that Shawntell's future will be filled with excitement and that she will enjoy her life to the fullest. This includes, as noted earlier, our hope that she will have an opportunity to live in her own place with people she wants to live with, to work at a job that she likes and that pays well, to be an active community member, to play and so-

Point to Ponder

It cannot be denied that some people are different. But it should be denied that *only* some people are different. All people are unique and different. That is, we are all alike in that we are all different from each other. Thus, it makes little sense to talk about the child who is different—who is not different?

cialize in her community, and, most of all, to be surrounded by a group of friends who want to be with her because they enjoy her and she enjoys them—people to hang out with, people to help her when she needs it; people that she can lend a hand to also; in short, people who care about her.

There are a number of skills in which Shawntell needs to show improvement—toilet training, eating properly, verbal communication, and walking stability. However, despite our active efforts to help her in these areas, whether Shawntell achieves such skills during her lifetime is not what concerns us most as parents. It is that there will be no one in our daughter's life who wants to be with her; that there will only be paid human service workers who come and go; that professionals who do not know our daughter will be making decisions about her future; that people will not spend the time to get to know Shawntell; that she will be isolated, lonely, and without friends.

Given these realistic concerns, what can parents, educators, and others do to help children develop friendships? How can we help ensure that our daughter and many other children with a "handicapped" label will have a circle of friends over the long haul?

Developing friendships is not something that comes easily or naturally to most of us, children or adults. Most people simply have trouble connecting with other people. The schools, for their part, pay little attention to the social and educational value of friendships. Yet, it is our friendships and relationships that are our only real hope, our guideline to being true members of our community. It is friendships that protect us from vulnerability and ensure that our lives are rich and full. However, the lives of people who are labeled as mentally retarded, developmentally disabled, or whatever, seem to be filled with loneliness and isolation, that is, with few, if any, friends. This is something that all of us must work to change.

FRIENDSHIPS: ISSUES TO CONSIDER

Having spent the last 10 years addressing this concern for our daughter as well as many other children, the following issues continually seem to surface:

1. People need to share ordinary places with ordinary people for relationships to develop
2. People need to work on developing relationships. This includes parents, educators, adult human service workers, citizens, and students.
3. People need to see the gifts, talents, and contributions that each person can make, and use those to help develop relationships.
4. Friendships come and go: they change; are unpredictable; are "loose" and hard to get your hands around.
5. Friendships are two-way streets—both parties must give and take in the relationship.
6. Friendships are freely given. People are not paid to be with you; they are not getting extra credit for a project; they are not getting a Girl Scout badge or the Mother Teresa Humanitarian Award of the Year. Friendships are not the same as peer tutors, special buddies, helpers, and the like—this is not to say that such forms of assistance are not good ideas under certain conditions; however, they are not friendships.
7. Friends come in a variety of different packages. While we are talking primarily about people with "labels" coming together with people without "la-

bels," this does not preclude friendship between people who are "labeled."

8. Most people are interested in having many different friends from many different "walks of life" in their lives, including friends currently labeled.

Developing friendships in school for all children is one of the most important things that we as parents and educators can do. Whether getting together means, for example, going out after school for an ice cream cone, hanging out in the school yard and talking, visiting a friend in his or her home or having someone over to your house, the schools need to help foster opportunities for friendships between and among people with varying abilities and characteristics. The following is a list of specific and general suggestions for nurturing friendships among all students:

All children must attend their neighborhood school.

All children must be a part of the regular education program.

All children must ride their regular school bus.

All children must be included in the "associational life" of school (this includes the Friday night dance or pep rally, the Saturday morning baseball game, the clubs, and the yearbook).

The concept of special education (irregular education), as opposed to regular education must be eliminated in favor simply of education for all children.

Schools must be inclusive, not exclusive, communities. They must "invite" people in and welcome them to their unique environment.

Parents must encourage and demand, if necessary, that schools facilitate children learning to play and work together in integrated classrooms.

Educators must learn to embrace and support the work that needs to take place in order for friendships to blossom.

All children, whether labeled as disabled or nondisabled, must be involved in helping friendships to develop.

Children need to be introduced to one another by other friends and interested others such as support facilitators. (The role of support facilitators is described in Chapter 6.)

Facilitation of relationships may need to take place in the beginning or even over time for relationships to develop.

It is important to clarify what we mean here by the words *integration and community*. *Integration* does not mean a special education self-contained classroom with opportunities to be with nonlabeled children only for recess, art, music, lunch, and the like. It does not mean bringing nonlabeled children into a special education class and working on a project. *Integration* means the process of making whole, of bringing together all children and having all children learn all that they are capable of being. It means helping all people (youth and adults) to recognize and

Point to Ponder

The ultimate rationale for quality education of students in an integrated setting is not based on research, law or pedagogy, but on values. "What kinds of people are we? What kind of society do we wish to develop? What values do we honor?" (Gartner & Lipsky, 1987, p. 389)

appreciate the unique gifts that each of us has.

Community is a concept that for the most part has not been experienced by people who are labeled. There is a difference between being in a community of services with professionals and being in a community of citizens. We need to work toward the day when churches, neighborhoods, and schools will become places that are inclusive and respectful of differences among everyone, rather than fearful and ignorant. Embracing differences rather than avoiding differences is what community is all about.

All of which is easier said then done. How do we accomplish this for our children or the children/youth we serve? The following case example of our daughter illustrates some of the measures that parents and educators can take to facilitate friendships for their children.

SHAWNTELL'S STORY

Two years ago, our family moved from Louisville, KY, to Littleton, CO. The move was difficult for all of us. After 7 years enjoying life in Kentucky, it was hard to distance ourselves from friends and others we had come to count on. Our daughter Shawntell, who was 14 when we moved, had made close friends that she hated to leave—Tanya, Wendy, Jacenta, Stacy, and Regina. However, we were convinced that even though it would be a difficult transition for Shawntell, there would be people in our new community who would come to know and want to spend time with her. The challenge was to use the community structures (i.e., schools, churches) to help facilitate these relationships. It would require us as parents to work together with educators to create a desirable future for Shawntell. In other words, it meant sharing our "dream" with all of these people.

The most important first step was obtaining access for Shawntell to attend eighth grade at her regular neighborhood school (Powell Middle School), to ride the regular bus, and to be involved in afterschool activities. For this to take place, we had to work with the school to negotiate an agreement that Shawntell would not be a "part" of the special education class, but a regular eighth grade student. Although this sounds easy, it was indeed challenging to refocus a school in an educational system that had a history of segregating children into self-contained special education classes.

Our first year was a hectic one. Shawntell was new to the other kids and they were new to her. What society calls "typical" kids are in truth generally deprived in their experiences—for instance, they have not had the opportunity to interact and to get to know children such as Shawntell. When Shawntell arrived in their class they did not understand why she was there or what she was doing among them. Slowly, however, interactions took place that could be built on.

School personnel did their best to introduce Shawntell to other students in the school. This was not always easy, however, because it seemed that adults—aides, teachers, therapists—were always hovering around Shawntell. Kids will not get to know someone when they are surrounded by adults. This is especially true for teenagers, who generally are not thrilled with any adult! This was a lesson in sensitivity that school personnel had to learn.

Another critical challenge was convincing the adults involved with Shawntell that friendships with the "regular" students were both possible and important to work on. If the adults did not have the "right" mind-set (i.e., values and beliefs), it would be difficult, if not impossible, for Shawntell to develop friendships. However, a number of relationships did form in school. Oppor-

Point to Ponder

Sometimes people in schools need others from the outside to help them consider issues or to say the same things that local parents and/or educators would. An outside expert can often contribute elements of objectivity and credibility that make the difference in a student's future. (Strully & Strully, 1985)

tunities were provided both during the day as well as after school. Kids started to include Shawntell in after-school activities such as Girl Scouts, the school newspaper, and gourmet cooking.

We arranged for a number of outside consultants to help the personnel at Powell Middle School consider ways to include Shawntell in school life. Although progress was made gradually throughout the year, it would be incorrect to state that Shawntell had any real friends at year's end. She had people to spend time with, "helpers" in school, and others whom she knew, but no real friends.

The next year, Shawntell was to attend Arapahoe High School. During that summer, my wife and I decided to hire a "guide"—a "bridge builder"—to life at Arapahoe High School. We hired Dede Schum. Dede was a graduating senior, a Miss Colorado Teen with a 3.9 grade point average, and she was a cheerleader. Bright, attractive, and energetic, she was the perfect person to introduce Shawntell to life at Arapahoe High School. She saw endless possibilities and opportunities for Shawntell, whom she regarded as a person almost her own age with lots of similar interests, desires, and likes and dislikes.

It was Dede's "job" to introduce Shawntell to as many people as she could at Arapahoe High and to ease the transition to high school. That summer was filled with wonderful opportunities for social connections. On a number of occasions, Dede invited other Powell eighth graders, as well as undergraduates from Arapahoe High, over to her house to spend time with and get to know Shawntell.

At the same time, Arapahoe High School hired Pat Osbon to be a support facilitator. She had a natural ability with teenagers and was a great asset for Shawntell.

When the year began, Pat and other school officials had lots to learn about Shawntell. One early problem was that of balancing Shawntell's educational program with our desire that every opportunity be exploited in school to help Shawntell develop valuable relationships with people. We shared with Pat and other staff our "dream" for Shawntell, as well as specific strategies and ideas on how to include Shawntell with the other kids—we provided information, articles, and the like. We also brought in other outside experts to provide enlightenment on how best to maximize opportunities for Shawntell, and gave Pat the chance to observe similar students in other schools. Pat, too, came to understand that having a staffperson in the school to work on friendships is an absolute necessity, and that it was her role to help introduce Shawntell to people—to connect her to people and then to let things happen naturally. However, Pat never was completely removed from Shawntell's situation—available as needed to assist the support group of friends, and to help promote their relationships with Shawntell.

As a result of Pat's, Dede's, and other people's efforts, Shawntell now has a group of 15 girls who spend time with her. These girls initially had a free period available, or they received community service credit for helping Shawntell (all Arapahoe High School students must have community service credits), or they had formerly been involved with Shawntell at Powell, or they were impressed with the seniors' efforts to assist Shawntell and wanted to get involved also. The common bond, of course, was their personal interest in Shawntell.

The support group of girls planned weekly meetings to talk about issues such as: how to include Shawntell, whether Shawntell would like telephone calls, whether she would like to go to the baseball or basketball game, or to the movies, or to lunch/dinner. Pat helped to facilitate these meetings, but she gave the girls the responsibility to plan ways to include Shawntell and to overcome any barriers (i.e., money handling, transportation).

The more the girls spent time with Shawntell, not only in school but at home meeting with us, the more they got to know Shawntell as a person, as someone who enjoyed many of the activities they do—listening to favorite musical performers, collecting their tapes, horseback riding, swimming, going to the movies, going out to eat pizza, shopping at the malls, and going to baseball games, to name a few. Soon Shawntell was included in these activities, as well as school functions such as class meetings, car washes, and parties. Things did not always work out perfectly—nothing ever does—but Shawntell's social life started to return to where it was prior to leaving Kentucky! People started to "see" Shawntell as a $15\frac{1}{2}$ year old with similar needs and interests. She was no longer a handicapped child, but a teenager who attended Arapahoe High School and had the same problems they did—boys, their hair, parents, money, and all the rest.

Recently, we invited the 15 girls to Shawntell's personal planning session for the future. We asked them questions such as: Who is Shawntell? What are your dreams for Shawntell? What are your nightmares? What are her needs? What are her gifts/talents? What can we do to make her life and yours richer? The girls had wonderful ideas on how to spend time and what to do. Things are looking up for Shawntell. Our second summer, Shawntell spent a great deal of time having fun with Erin, Lori, Karen, Judy, Roxanne, and Heather. She does not yet have the close friendships she had in Louisville. She still misses Tanya, but now new people—seniors, juniors, sophomores as well as freshmen—are starting to get to know and appreciate being with her. Shawntell has a wonderful gift for attracting teenagers who are very different from each other—those with "punk" clothes and hairstyles, as well as "preppy" kids, the prom queen, honor students, and also one student who was having trouble with attendance. Bringing such diverse students together has helped them all find ways to appreciate each other.

IMPORTANT THEMES IN MAKING FRIENDSHIPS

Our experience in helping to promote meaningful relationships for Shawntell leads us to make the following suggestions for parents and educators:

Believing that friendships are possible and that people do want to get to know and spend time with your child or the people you serve is important.

It takes effort to make friendships happen. There will be mistakes and ups and downs when working with teenagers, especially freshmen. Planning is sometimes difficult with this group.

For friendships to happen, you must identify places that allow opportunities for people to be together—whether in regular education classes, at home, after school, or in the community. The more chances that a child has to be together with people, the greater probability that true friendships will form.

Get adults out of the way and let kids get to know one another.

Utilize adults to facilitate friendships forming only when needed and only for the amount of time required.

Ask, ask, ask. Sometimes simply asking people to get to know another person is a real start.

Understand the power of letting kids problem solve and think about creative solutions. Let them come up with ideas; intervene only when needed or to provide the initial direction or focus.

Help people understand the similarities of all people. People need to have a common bond, whether that is popular music, or shopping for clothes, or eating pizza, or hanging out in the mall, or riding horses. The issue is to find what people like to do and use that to link them with one another.

Do not place demands on people, especially teenagers, that they cannot live with. Take people at their "face value" and move them forward.

The ultimate salesperson is Shawntell (i.e., the focal person). Most kids are good at selling themselves to other kids. Let them do it!

Appreciate that creating friendships for the focal person has at least an equal benefit for the nonlabeled kids.

WHY IS IT WORTH THE EFFORT?

As this chapter has already emphasized, all people's futures are linked not to just what they know (i.e., their competency) but to the people in their lives. Shawntell will learn whatever she is capable of learning; however, learning skills is only part of the picture. The other part, which in our opinion is even more important, is her need to be surrounded by people who want to be in her life—people who will ensure not only her actual protection but her inclusion in the community. As her parents, we will stand by Shawntell for the remainder of our lives, but our role as parents should change. For Shawntell to be an active member of her community, both during her school years and afterward, she will need to get to know and incorporate other people into her life.

It should be reemphasized that so-called typical people have at least as much to learn from Shawntell as she does from them. Shawntell is as much a teacher as she is a learner. The same is true for all people who have been labeled. Unfortunately, many so-called typical citizens, including researchers and professional educators, have not taken the time to learn from people who have been labeled in our society.

Dede Schum's comments about Shawntell are a testament to the extent that an individual with "special needs" can enrich the life of a "normal" student. Now at the University of Colorado at Boulder, Dede writes, calls, and visits regularly with Shawntell, and treats her on the same level as any other friend. Dede has stated that she believes Shawntell has given her more than she herself has given Shawntell. She appreciates Shawntell's unconditional acceptance of people, and her natural abilities to be free, to be open, and to be happy. Dede says that Shawntell has changed her life! It is exciting to see someone with Dede's "gifts" and special qualities appreciate the gifts that Shawntell has to offer. Dede's one concern for Shawntell is that people will not take enough time to get to know Shawntell; that they will take a quick glance and miss a wonderful opportunity to get to know someone as exciting and rewarding as Shawntell. Our schools and families have a responsibility to help people with diverse characteristics get to know one another.

FINAL THOUGHTS

Developing friendships at any age is something that all of us need to work on. There is no one way to go about developing friendships; there are no books (including this one) with quick and easy answers.

Of course, there are paths that one can take to make the travel easier. Family life is one of them. Children need to grow up in a family—not in a group home, residential child care facility, or institution—to learn the give and take of relationships. Of course, like friends, families have strengths and weaknesses too. Children also need to go to school in their own neighborhood, to attend classes with typical kids their own age, and to be involved with kids in activities outside of school on weekends and in the evening. Adults should not interfere with kids getting to know each other, but at the same time should understand that some kids may need help in being introduced to others, in sharing their gifts with them, and in making connections. That is a major role of the support facilitator (Pat) and a peer guide (Dede). Such a facilitator needs to know when to help out, when to get out of the way, and when to offer a friendly suggestion. This is a difficult task and one that is not generally taught—but should be a goal of—university programs.

For parents, the issue of friendships can be problematic, even frightening. Parents need to recognize that working on friendships takes time. And they need to relay to other students and adults the message that friendships are critical in their children's lives. Many parents think that if only their child receives another hour of speech therapy or of individualized instruction, they will get what they need. Sometimes parents even feel guilty if their children are not receiving instruction that one professional or another has told them is needed in a self-contained special education class. However, the issues of friendship and quality education are not mutually exclusive. Parents should not be placed in an either/or situation of being forced to choose one over the other. In fact, it is impossible to have a quality education without having friendships; and friendships will go a long way toward ensuring a quality education. It should be remembered that it is possible to offer both within the framework of a regular education.

For some children and parents, the promise of the future will take some getting used to. For the formerly "special" student, being part of a regular education class, being just another student, will entail some limitations and difficulties. For instance, it may mean standing outside in the rain waiting for the school bus instead of staying in your home until the special van beeps its horn. For parents, it means picking up and taking kids all over to meet friends, attend parties, go swimming, or go to the gym. It means sending your kids out with their friends to concerts, parties, and malls. It means making sure that your child dresses "correctly," that he or she has the "right" possessions, that his or her room looks the way other kids' rooms look. Other potential by-products include soft drinks, loud music, and lots of kids talking in the bedroom with the door closed, kids making telephone calls, and strange hairdos. *It means struggling with issues of life, not issues of disability!*

Friendships are indeed at the heart of what we all need for one another. It is our friendships that enable us to be active and protected community members. Friendships help ensure that being a part of the community, rather than just being in the community, is a reality for everyone!

REFERENCES

Gartner, A., & Lipsky, D. (1987). Beyond special education: Toward a quality system for all students. *Harvard Educational Review, 57*, 367–395.

Strully, J., & Strully, C. (1985). Teach your children. *Canadian Journal of Mental Retardation, 35*(4), 3–11.

PART III

Strategies to Promote Merger

CHAPTER 6

Practical Organizational Strategies

William Stainback and Susan Stainback

Educators throughout the nation are beginning to experiment with ways to educate all students in regular education. As a result, a number of organizational strategies for doing so are beginning to emerge.

This chapter summarizes some of these strategies (for review purposes, each subhead in the chapter outlines a strategy). The strategies are based on: a) participating with, observing, and interviewing school personnel and students in integrated schools and classrooms, b) telephone conversations about the topic with school personnel from several locations in the United States and Canada where students with diverse backgrounds and characteristics are being educated together, and c) a review of the professional literature and videotapes on the topic (e.g., Biklen, 1988; Forest, 1987; Gartner & Lipsky, 1987; Knoblock, 1982; Stainback & Stainback, 1987, 1988; Strully, 1987).

STRATEGIES FOR INTEGRATION

Promote Understanding, Acceptance, and Support

A strong commitment of school personnel and parents to the goal of educating all students in regular classes is critical to achieving success. Once a commitment by one or several people in a school community has been made, they can help persuade others of the advantages. This can occur in a number of different ways. For example, the authors have seen a parent gain the support of a teacher, and then the two of them have approached the principal and other school personnel. In another situation, a principal took the idea to his faculty and from there, a task force and integration plan developed. In still another setting, a university instructor enlisted the support of a local school acquaintance, followed by several teachers, the school principal, and eventually the entire school faculty. In most instances, an inservice preparation session(s) for teachers, administrators, and/or parents was held at which someone experienced in integration practices discussed the reasons for integration and provided initial suggestions for how it might be accomplished. Videotapes depicting successful regular class integration have been particularly effective in showing that there are major positive benefits for all involved. But whatever the chain of events, success is unlikely unless an understanding is gained of the potential advantages for all students participating in the educational mainstream and unless key school personnel and parents demonstrate acceptance, support, and commitment.

A commitment on the part of the regular classroom teacher accepting a new student(s) is essential. The teacher must be willing to take responsibility as the key educator in charge of the new student's behavior and achievements. The teacher must agree to accept the new student as an equal and vital classroom participant, beyond simply allowing him or her to attend the class. To facilitate this, any specialist or aide who enters the regular class with the new student(s) should be prepared to help the regular class teacher integrate the student and assist in the education of all students in the class, as opposed to the specialist being responsible for teaching the new student in an isolated corner of the classroom.

A recommended way to gain the regular class teacher's commitment is for those who advocate for integration to talk with the teacher informally. The authors have found that informal, casual conversations about the reasons for integration and how it might be accomplished can be an excellent follow-up to any formal meetings. In addition to meetings prior to integration, meetings should also occur after the new student has been in class for several weeks, since it is only then that the teacher really knows what his or her feelings are and can formulate questions that need answering. It is important that all meetings, whether formal or informal, focus on solutions and not drift toward a discussion of problems only.

Not everyone in an entire school or school district has to be committed before getting started. If only a few people in one school are committed, a small pilot or demonstration project can be launched while efforts are continuing to promote wider understanding, acceptance, and support. In fact, a small, successful demonstration project that encourages school personnel, parents, and community leaders to visit can be very helpful in promoting widespread acceptance and support.

Integrate Students, Personnel, and Resources

It is imperative that all students have friends and educational experiences that meet their needs in regular education and this may not happen if we fail to integrate in the resources and personnel that can help make it happen. Where integration has been most successful, personnel and resources from special education, in addition to the former "special" students themselves, have been integrated into regular classes and regular education (Stainback & Stainback, 1988). Even when an initial, small demonstration project is organized in which only a few students are integrated into regular education, it is still important to integrate, proportionally, personnel and resources from special education into regular education to assist in handling the extra work. If this is not done, the quality of services all students receive in regular education potentially could be jeopardized. Regular educators need the resources now in special education to help them individualize and adapt instruction to diverse student needs in regular education classes.

It should be noted that one major advantage of integrating all the students from any one special education class into regular education, rather than only one or two students, is that the special education teacher and the teacher's aide(s) in the special class are freed up and can be integrated into regular education to serve as team teachers, support facilitators and/or consultants. When only one or two students from a special class are integrated into regular classes, this usually means that the special class teacher must remain in the special class to teach the students who were left behind, or try to serve the dual roles of a support facilitator in regular education and a special class teacher. This dual role is almost impossible to fulfill.

Integrate Only One or a Few Students into a Single Class

It is important to avoid concentrating large numbers of former "special education" students into one or several regular education classes. Only one student (or no more than a few) should be integrated into any single class whenever possible, to avoid the potential for developing segregated clusters or pockets of former "special education" students within regular education classrooms. Thus, the students, personnel, and resources from special education should be integrated across regular education classes, rather than being concentrated in a few classes.

Develop Support Networks

Because of the diversity of student needs in integrated regular classes and schools, it is sometimes necessary to develop support networks for teachers and students needing assistance.

One way to provide a network of support has been described as a "circle of friends" (Forest, 1987; see also Chapter 4, in this volume). Teachers and other school personnel can encourage a circle of friends for new students being integrated into regular classes by demonstrating acceptance and support of the new student(s) themselves and by organizing buddy systems, tutors, special friends, and cooperative learning goals and activities (see Chapter 10). Teachers also can ask the students already in the class how they all (teacher included) might be a friend to and help any new student(s) feel welcomed, learn classroom routines and rules, and become an integral part of the classroom activities and programs.

For any new student being integrated into regular classes, having a friend or friends in the class to provide encouragement, support, and/or assistance, when needed, is critical. The development of friends can help a new student be successful and feel more secure and welcome in the regular classroom. It should be stressed that, along with encouraging others to be friends with a new student, the new student is also encouraged to be a friend and to help other students. This prevents the new student always being the recipient of assistance. Friendships can and should involve reciprocal giving, although a new student may require greater support initially.

Teacher and/or student assistance teams (TSAT) are another way to provide support for students and/or teachers in regular education classes. Such teams also can be conceptualized as "circles of friends." Support teams involve a group of people coming together to brainstorm, problem solve, and exchange ideas, methods, techniques, and activities directed at assisting a teacher and/or student requiring help. The team might include two or more people such as students, administrators, parents, classroom teachers, aides, school psychologists, speech and hearing specialists, and/or learning and behavior consultants.

Along with the student who needs assistance, including on the team the classmates or peers of the student needing assistance can be very helpful. Classmates can provide many practical suggestions regarding how the student can become integrally involved in regular class activities and be made to feel welcome and secure in the classroom. With the assistance of school personnel, these students often are able to mobilize a circle of peers or friends in the regular classroom around the student needing assistance. They also can suggest practical ways that such a student can help other students. It bears reemphasizing that it should never be a one-way street, with one student always the recipient of help. A student who is the recipient of help in one situation may be on another team or the same team at another point in time that is involved in assisting someone else. All students should be involved in helping each other rather than always focusing on so-called nonhandicapped students helping those who are classified as having disabilities.

A major advantage of involving the student's peers on the team is that they are in the regular classroom every day and are readily available to provide friendly and accepting overtures and assistance and encouragement. Unless they are involved on the team they may not formulate clearly in their own minds what is needed and/or never think about the specifics of how they could help. There is probably nothing more important than involving students on the team and encouraging them to be friends and provide assistance, when necessary.

Generally, the regular classroom teacher or the student needing assistance is the leader or center of the team. The team is responsible for providing ideas and support when the teacher or student is unsure of what to do. The team makes as many helpful suggestions as possible and, in some cases, becomes involved in assisting in implementing the suggestions.

The TSAT is *not* intended to function as a special education referral system and is *not* a multidisciplinary assessment and placement committee. It is a teacher and student support system to serve teachers and students in the regular education classroom who require encouragement and/or assistance.

Designate a Person to Serve as a Support Facilitator

A number of schools have begun to designate a person to serve as a support facilitator. Support facilitators have been found to enhance the success of efforts to educate all students in regular education (Forest, 1987).

One source for support facilitators is former special educators. As noted by Annmarie Ruttiman, who served as one of the first support facilitators, it requires someone who "is open, flexible, willing to take risks, work hard, accept failure and try again. . . ." (Ruttiman & Forest, 1986, p. 26). The support facilitator needs experiences in and knowledge of regular classroom curriculum, methodology, and programs. He or she also needs to have the ability to listen to and gain an understanding of what support regular classroom teachers and students experiencing difficulties believe they need. As Johnson, Pugach, and Hammittee (1988) and Pugach (1988) have pointed out, former

Point to Ponder

We need to develop in our regular education schools and classrooms a sense of community; a belief that everyone belongs, is welcomed, and has gifts and talents to offer. (Forest, 1987)

special educators working in regular classes must be careful not to assume that they know more about regular classroom problems than regular class teachers and students in regular classrooms.

A support facilitator can assume a number of responsibilities. He or she generally encourages or formally organizes support networks such as those previously described. A major aim of the support facilitator is to encourage natural networks of support. Particular emphasis is placed on promoting peer friendship development, wherein students want to and learn how to assist each other. Cues as to how such friendships might be encouraged can be found in Chapters 4 and 5.

The support facilitator also will need to function as a resource locator, since a classroom teacher cannot be expected to have expertise in every possible assessment, curricular, or behavior management area needed by all students in a heterogeneous classroom. This role may involve locating appropriate material, equipment, or specialists, consultants, teachers, and other school personnel who have expertise in a particular area(s) needed by a classroom teacher and/or student. For example, if a student needs instruction in braille and/or mobility and orientation, a support facilitator can help the teacher locate the appropriate specialist to provide assistance. Likewise, as a resource locator, the support facilitator can assist in the recruitment and organization of classroom assistants or helpers such as peer tutors, paraprofessionals, and volunteers.

Support facilitators also can provide direct help as team teachers. They can assist classroom teachers in adapting and individualizing instruction to meet the unique needs of all class members. In addition, as team teachers, the support facilitators can offer students direct support or instruction for such things as understanding and communicating with peers and teachers, completing assignments, developing positive social and friendship behaviors, learning bus schedules and routines, understanding and dealing with individual differences, and/or learning to support and assist others. As the student(s) needing support adjust to the school environment and the school environment is adjusted to meet his or her needs, the facilitator's support is gradually faded. As noted by Kathy East, a support facilitator, the most difficult task of the job is backing out of the situation once one begins experiencing success. This involves recognizing the point at which all of one's efforts begin to pay off and the teacher and student(s) no longer intensively need one's support and assistance (K. East, personal communication, May 2, 1988). The facilitator literally wants to work himself or herself out of a job by encouraging natural networks of friendships and support in regular classes.

When facilitators were first used in the schools, they were employed to work only with students classified as having disabilities. They often shadowed these students in regular class and school settings. This tended to draw attention to these students, setting them apart from their peers and interfering with the development of natural support networks or friendships because of the omnipresent facilitator. That is, since the student needing assistance always had an adult to assist him or her, natural peer support networks and friendships seldom developed, even when they were encouraged or facilitated by the teacher or support facilitator. Thus, in recent years, as team teachers, support facilitators have served a broader role, helping all students, disabled or not, who are having difficulty in educational tasks and/or in gaining peer acceptance. They also are sensitive about when to help any particular student and

Point to Ponder

Few people, including those classified as disabled, want to be in a mainstream that does not meet their needs or does not make them feel welcome and secure. Thus, it is essential that we make the mainstream flexible and sensitive to the unique needs of all students and that we foster friendships for students who lack friends in the mainstream. The importance of friendships cannot be overestimated. All young people have a better chance for success when they have friends to provide encouragement and support.

when to encourage and allow natural peer supports and friendships an opportunity to develop. It is crucial that support facilitators not provide support when it is not needed or be overprotective. Finally, it should be stressed that the support facilitator is the *teacher's* resource or support person and should not assume the role of the new student's personal teacher in the regular classroom.

Broaden the Regular Education Curriculum

Some students, including those with disabilities, sometimes need experiences in curriculum areas traditionally not included in regular education. Thus, the curriculum in mainstream education requires expansion to meet the needs of all students. Curriculum areas such as daily life and community living skills, competitive and supportive employment, sign language, braille, speechreading, and other similar areas need to become an inherent part of regular education.

The expertise among personnel to expand the curriculum offered in regular education is already available in the schools under the aegis of what is now "special" education. Thus, to make the regular education curriculum more comprehensive, those professionals currently in special education can join regular education and, in effect, become regular educators. They can provide consultative help to regular class teachers in their areas of expertise and/or direct instruction as team teachers within regular education to any students, disabled or nondisabled, who potentially could profit from their expertise. They also can, of course, become support facilitators.

Use Natural and Normal Opportunities for Instruction

Lunch and snack times in regular education can be used to develop eating and dining skills; bus-riding skills can be taught when students need to travel back and forth to school or in the community; braille can be taught and practiced during reading classes, and mobility skills can be taught to students who need them when they are called upon to maneuver around the regular education classroom, school building, and playground. Likewise, many community-referenced and functional skills can be taught in the community during nonschool times. For instance, one parent described how her daughter (a student with Down syndrome) gained her most valuable vocational skills in a supervised after-school and summer jobs program for teens in her community (Sylvester, 1987). Summer, weekend, and after-school jobs as natural, normal ways of developing vocational skills can work for all stu-

Point to Ponder

We do not have to choose between socialization and friendships in regular classes and a quality education in segregated special classes. We can provide a quality education in regular classes. (Strully, 1987)

dents when varying degrees of support are provided as needed.

Include All Students in Regular Education Classes

In addition to teaching community-referenced skills, braille, and the like during natural times, it also is possible for all students, including those traditionally classified as having severe or profound disabilities, to participate in a meaningful way in regular science, mathematics, geography, and similar lessons or classes in regular education. This has been the case in a number of regular classes or schools the authors have worked in or visited. For instance, during a map-reading activity, one student may be called upon to discuss the economic system of the country, another may be requested to identify a color, while another student may simply be requested to grasp and hold a corner of the map. In reading class, during oral reading activities, one student may be requested to read out loud, another to listen to a story and answer questions, another to pick out a picture that describes the story, and another to pass out reading materials to classmates. In integrated, heterogeneous classrooms, any one student's participation in a group or individualized class activity is based on that student's capabilities. Within a single mathematics class, for example, objectives may range from grasping an object or following a one-step direction to computing or analyzing a highly complex problem. When appropriately organized, regular education classes can provide a wide variety of appropriate learning opportunities and challenges for students with a broad range of learning needs, interests, and capabilities. In addition, exposure to and participation in regular education classes provide students—traditionally segregated in special classes—an opportunity to learn about and share information and experiences with their peers. This is not only functional but essential to promoting an integrated society in which students learn to live, understand, and share things in common with their fellow community members.

The regular class curriculum agenda and/or activities may not always have to be changed or modified to accommodate students classified as having severe or profound disabilities. The following case example illustrates how a student, classified as having autism and severe mental retardation, participated in a meaningful way in the normal activities of a regular sixth grade class.

Case Example: Ryan in a Regular Class When the authors observed Ryan he was 12 years old, ambulatory, and 80% to 90% toilet trained. He spoke mostly in single words but occasionally uttered phrases or partial sentences that would be understood by most people.

When Ryan was first integrated, he often did *not* participate in regular class activities and programs. For example, during the first 15 minutes of class each morning the teacher asked the class to report on a news story they had seen on television or read in the newspaper. During this time, Ryan usually walked around the classroom, turned the water on and off in the sink at the back of the room, and/or played with the light switch.

To help Ryan become more integrally involved in the class, a teacher and student assistance team recommended that his mother have him watch a television news story each night and that she coach him on one story he could share with the class. In this way, when the teacher asked for volunteers to report on a news story, Ryan would have something to say. Prompting from the teacher, classmates, and/or the support facilitator was often necessary, but Ryan gradually became an active participant in the class.

One logical question this example raises is whether what Ryan did and/or learned was functional or potentially useful to him. It was functional, in the authors' opinion, in that Ryan learned something that allowed him to participate with other students his age, which opened up opportunities for socialization and potential friendships. It also provided him an opportunity to become more aware of his environment (news stories); increase his vocabulary; learn skills in taking turns and interacting with his peers; and practice remembering, listening, and sharing ideas. These are all very functional and useful skills.

Finally, placing all students in regular classes does not mean that all students necessarily have to be engaged in the exact same activities or learning experiences all day, every day. Any student or students may be in a different activity or learning experience for part of a day, based on his or her unique interests, needs, and capabilities. For example, some students may receive instruction in a community-referenced curriculum, take an advanced college level calculus, physics, or foreign language class, or receive tutoring in braille, speech correction, or computers. Similarly, there are students who may desire intensive instruction or coaching in gymnastics, music, or art because of their unique interests or talents. As pointed out by Forest and Lusthaus in Chapter 4, when a child is a full member of regular education and regular classes, it does not mean that he or she must sit in one classroom all day long. Children certainly can be in other places for part of the day—for activities, for work, and for learning in other classrooms and other school and nonschool environments. Being in regular education means that every child can go to his or her neighborhood school and become a full member of regular education classes, just like everybody else.

View All Students as Regular Education Students Receiving a Regular Education

To facilitate the goals of a unified, comprehensive, regular education system, all students need to become an integral, natural part of regular education. In integrated schools, personnel work to view all students as regular education students deserving of an education geared to their capabilities and needs as a normal and standard practice, rather than viewing some students as "special needs" students needing "special instruction" in regular education. This is important, to avoid some students being set apart, psychologically, in the minds of their teachers and peers as "different" or as not quite belonging in regular education. It also avoids the problem, noted in Chapter 2, of some students' education being viewed as a special, charitable accommodation. For instance, if a student requires braille, sign language, or community-referenced instruction, it should be provided as a regular rather than a special practice, and he or she should be viewed as a regular rather than a "special needs" student.

Point to Ponder

The terminology used to describe students, personnel, and programs is very important. As Will (1986) stated, "the terminology we use in describing our educational system is full of the language of separation, of fragmentation, of removal" (p. 412). For example, at present, we separate and fragment students, educators, and programs by labeling some "special" and others "regular." Even when everyone is in the mainstream, separation still occurs on a psychological level in the minds of students, teachers and parents. That is, some students, teachers, and programs are viewed as regular or normal and belonging, while others are seen as special or different and therefore as not quite belonging. This works against achieving a sense of oneness or community, where everyone belongs and is a natural and integral part of the mainstream.

Identify Personnel by Areas of Instructional Expertise

Many of today's schools have "special" teachers and consultants to work with students labeled as mentally retarded, severely handicapped, or behaviorally disordered. This divides or segregates students, based on the educators designated to work with them. It also mitigates against those educators being viewed and treated as regular educators and as integral members of regular neighborhood public schools. Moreover, a title such as "special educator of students with learning disabilities or severe handicaps" does not clearly communicate the specific and functional expertise area(s) these educators have to offer students and other colleagues, that is, exactly what curricular and instructional expertise they can provide.

There are ways to rectify this situation. One can begin by modifying personnel titles or roles that designate some educators as being outsiders or different from "regular" educators and/or as only available to work with a certain category of students. More specifically, teachers, consultants, and other school personnel who have expertise in such areas as learning disabilities, behavioral disorders, severe and profound handicaps, giftedness, mental retardation, deafness, or blindness need to redefine and refocus their expertise away from *whom they can serve* and *toward what expertise they can provide* any student or colleague who requires assistance. For instance, the educator who previously defined his or her abilities as serving students labeled as behaviorally disordered should redefine his or her role as being an educator with expertise in behavior management, social skill development, and/or self-control. The focus needs to be toward more functional, curriculum-based, and instructionally relevant expertise areas including curriculum adaptations, behavior management, community-referenced daily life instruction, support facilitation, braille, mobility, and alternative communications skills.

Finally, it should be noted that regular educators now organize themselves according to instructional expertise areas (reading, mathematics, science) and/or levels of schools (preschool, elementary, secondary), as opposed to categorical groups of "deviant" students. Thus, as present-day special educators *integrate themselves* into regular education, they will need to similarly organize themselves. The importance of special education and other specialists "blending into" regular education and becoming an integral part of regular education cannot be overemphasized. School personnel have found that many students are sensitive about and embarrassed to have specialists work with them in front of their peers, especially if the specialist is known as the teacher of the "retarded," "disordered," "disturbed," or "severely disabled" (Stainback & Stainback, 1988). For this reason, it is better for the specialist to be viewed as just another "regular" educator who works with any student, disabled or not, who happens to need his or her expertise.

Promote Respect for Individual Differences

To enhance the chances of everyone being respected, accepted, and treated kindly in integrated regular classrooms and schools, many educators attempt to foster a basic understanding of and respect for individual differences and similarities among all students. The support facilitator, as discussed earlier in the chapter, often takes an active role in ensuring that this is accomplished, usually by infusing information about individual differences and similarities into the school's existing curriculum, programs, and activities. For example, information is often integrated into reading materials, health or social studies classes, and/or extracurricular activities such as assembly programs, plays, school projects, service activities, and/or clubs.

School personnel can also encourage respect for individual differences by showing respect themselves and encouraging and reinforcing it when it occurs. This can be done during natural, daily interactions in regular class, school, and nonschool settings.

While promoting an understanding of individual differences, it is essential to guard against setting up or perpetuating a "them and us" mentality. This can occur when one group is frequently being taught about another group. The recent emphasis on teaching nonhandicapped students to be sensitive toward and to develop an understanding of students with disabilities is a classic example. It sets students apart from each other and promotes a "them and us" mentality. It also can promote superiority feelings among nonhandicapped students.

Few of us would want other people studying us and receiving instructions on how to be sensitive to and understanding of us, as if we were somehow strange or different from our peers. There also is no reason to assume that *only* students considered as nonhandicapped need to learn to be sensitive to individual differences and similarities. There are students, classified as disabled, who are disrespectful of and insensitive to individual differences and who need to learn how to be more tolerant and understanding. Thus, it is important for all students, not just "nonhandicapped" students, to learn to be sensitive to and understanding of individual differences and similarities.

As an alternative to the "handicapped versus nonhandicapped" approach, we can teach *all* students together in integrated settings to be sensitive and understanding of individual differences among everyone. In this way, no one person or group is singled out as different and strange. We are all the same in that we are all different from each other. Schools and society at large are made up of people of different ethnic backgrounds, races, vision and hearing ability, intellectual

Point to Ponder

It is not a good teaching strategy to attempt to teach a value, but then implement practices directly opposed to that value. For instance, it is not logical to divide and segregate students in their school years, yet try to teach them the value of integration, respect for individual differences, and how to live and work together in an integrated society. (Sarason, 1982)

ability, and so on. This should be discussed, and respect for and acceptance of individual differences fostered among all students.

Promote the Heterogeneous Grouping of Students

We can foster an integrated education for all students in regular education by promoting the heterogeneous grouping of students of similar ages into the same school programs and activities whenever possible. For example, all students are normally together in heterogeneous groupings during the preschool years and most of the elementary grades. Thus, all students should be in the same classes during these years.

While heterogeneous educational arrangements should be encouraged whenever possible, students may still need to be homogeneously grouped—in some instances, into specific tutoring sessions, courses, or classes according to their instructional needs. This should occur, however, in normal ways for all students. For instance, as all students get older, they sometimes are homogeneously grouped by interest, abilities, and projected future goals into different classes or courses. Some students might take an advanced physics, money management, or calculus class, while others take a foreign language, typing, or computer usage class, or a class out in the community that focuses on learning community living or vocational skills. Thus, during their later school years all students might take some different classes. However, it is critical that this not be overdone (see Oakes, 1985, for the reasons why). Care also must be taken to keep such groupings flexible and fluid to avoid the development of a tracking system and to allow students to move in and out and across the groupings according to their individual needs and interests.

It should be emphasized here that because a student cannot read, multiply, or write does not necessarily preclude the functionality of and importance of him or her taking core regular education high school courses such as science, history, and literature. By allowing all students to enroll in regular education core high school classes and participate, if in only small ways, all students can profit from high school educational experiences designed to help them learn to reason, think, and learn about how society and the world operates. Likewise, by integrating students with diverse characteristics into such basic information and idea developing and sharing classes, students can swap common experiences, come to better understand what people with different perceptions think, and also learn from and interact with their peers.These are all functional and necessary skills.

Although a student may not be as intellectually astute or as physically adept as many of his or her classmates, he or she still will be expected to and have the right to vote, live and recreate in, adapt and contribute to, and understand the world around him or her. Thus, we must seriously evaluate what learning opportunities we limit some students from participating in in order to make time for them to learn such things as fluency in a job or daily activities, under the guise of providing a functional curriculum that may virtually become obsolete in the future (e.g., pumping gas, washing dishes). We must guard against educating a subgroup of students in such a way that they share few common experiences and understandings with people they are expected to live with in the community. Moreover, any student's education would be incomplete without at least providing him or her an opportunity to be introduced to materials and discussions in history, literature, music, art, and science that promote an understanding of the world, sensitivity to the human condition, and reasoning and thinking skills. It is very difficult at best to predict what the future might be for any student; thus it is a mistake, in the authors' opinion, to limit any student's education to learning only "daily life, functional" skills. For instance, it should be noted that if a class is reading the novel *Red Badge of Courage*, a student who cannot read or comprehend the novel, can still participate at least partially. For example, he or she can listen to a tape recording or be told the rudimentary elements and ideas in the story through picture cards or other means. Even a small understanding of the story can be helpful.

In short, while teaching floor sweeping, dishwashing, grocery shopping, bus riding, vocational, and other skills is important, it is essential not to overlook the other side of any person, that is, the more intellectual and human side. All students—including those traditionally classified as severely, profoundly, and multiply disabled—need to be provided *opportunities* to think, reason, and make moral and ethical decisions; to become sensitive to the needs of others; to appreciate art, music, and poetry; and to understand the world in which they live. In addition, all students need to share such common experiences together so that they can live and function together in an integrated society. When subgroups of students are provided an almost totally different curriculum throughout their school years, there is a real danger they will have little in common with each other in later life.

Promote Individualized, Cooperative, and Adaptive Instructional Practices

Many personnel in regular education already believe in and adapt instruction to the individual needs of students. However, in places where this does not occur, those individuals who believe in integrated schools need to promote individualized, adaptive, and cooperative approaches to instruction. The reason is that successful integration of diverse students into regular education is more feasible in schools and classrooms that are sensitive to individual differences.

Some procedures that have been successfully used in heterogeneous classrooms include cooperative goal structuring, which has proved effective in addressing diverse student needs in integrated classrooms and at the same time promoting socialization and friendships (Johnson & Johnson, 1981). Adaptive Learning Environments is another approach (Wang & Birch, 1984), involving evaluating and describing students by learning needs, providing individually designed educational plans, and teaching self-management skills. Another approach is peer tutoring, such as the Classwide Peer Tutoring Program described by MaHeady, Sacca, and Harper (1988). More information on such practices designed to meet the diverse educational needs of students in the mainstream of regular education is included throughout the remainder of this book.

Adopt Criterion-Based Assessments

Much educational assessment today is norm referenced, meaning that students' achievements are compared with those of their peers. These assessments are often focused toward identifying, classifying, and labeling students to determine whether they should remain in regular education or be placed in special education. There is little or no research to support the value of doing this. In addition, there is no longer any real or functional reason to engage in such assessments, if all students are to remain in regular education and be approached and educated according to their individual needs, interests, and capabilities.

To provide appropriate instruction for all students in regular education, it will be necessary to break away from assessments designed to classify or categorize students in relationship to their peers. Instead, the focus needs to be on assessments that determine the specific instructional needs of each student and how to arrange the instructional environment to maximize teaching effectiveness. Evaluating each student's ability on skills related to the curriculum to be learned (i.e., curriculum-based assessment) has begun to receive increased attention and acceptance as "a way of matching student ability to instruction" (Tucker, 1985, p. 201). Similarly, instructional assessments, designed to evaluate the nature of the instructional environment of a student, have been found to be a valuable asset in individualizing instructional programming to meet a student's unique needs (Ysseldyke & Christenson, 1986). Curriculum-based assessment paired with instructional assessment procedures can provide a means of determining appropriate instructional programming needs on a per-student basis. (The emphasis here is on approaching students as individuals and planning educational programs according to their specific characteristics and needs, *not* on the value of individual or one-to-one teaching, which is not always in the best interest of students.) More information regarding curriculum-based and instructional assessment procedures is contained in Chapter 12.

Point to Ponder

Labeling some children and segregating them has consequences for those students who remain in regular classrooms. As noted by Granger and Granger (1986):

> Every time a child is called mentally defective and sent off to the special education class . . . , the children who are left in the regular classroom receive a message: no one is above suspicion; everyone is being watched by the authorities; nonconformity is dangerous. (p. xii)

Prepare Personnel According to Instructional Expertise

Integration of students in the schools is impeded by segregating educators during their preparation. In general, personnel preparation programs separate educators into, on the one hand, those who are studying to work with students classified as nonhandicapped and, on the other hand, those preparing to work with students labeled as handicapped. This personnel division, in turn, separates students considered "normal" from those considered "handicapped" on the basis of educators prepared to work with them. As noted by Sarason (1982):

> School personnel are graduates of our colleges and universities. It is there that they learn there are at least two types of human beings and if you choose to work with one of them you render yourself *legally* and conceptually incompetent to work with the others. . . . What we see in our public schools is a mirror image of what exists in colleges and universities. (p. 258)

To facilitate the integration of all students into a regular education system designed to provide students appropriate instructional programs based on their individual needs, all school personnel need to be prepared to work with any student, regardless of categorical label assigned (normal, handicapped, gifted), who may require assistance in their particular area of expertise.

To accomplish this, current special education professors could join regular education departments in colleges and universities and become regular education professors. They could organize areas of specialization not currently available in regular education preparation programs to meet *all* students' needs, such as community-referenced instruction, support facilitation, alternative communication systems, and supported and competitive employment. As a result, school personnel who have been traditionally prepared and certified for special education careers could do as regular educators currently do. That is, they could specialize or major in instructional areas rather than specializing in categories of deviant students they can serve. Certification and job assignments for former "special" educators could be focused on specific areas of instructional expertise such as behavior management, daily life and community living, alternative communication methods, or basic supported and competitive employment. (See Chapter 9 for further details about how we might modify personnel preparation and certification practices.)

Focus Teaching Methods, Materials, and Programs toward Whoever Needs Them

While most regular education programs and materials are focused toward students who need them, nearly all materials and programs in special education are designed and developed for certain categories of students. For instance, it is not uncommon to find articles, books, or curricular materials on topics such as *Teaching Reading to Students with Learning Disabilities, Social Skill Development for Students with Special Needs, Language Development in Autistic Children,* or *Teaching Students with Severe Handicaps in Regular Schools.*

Two assumptions underlie the development of such materials and programs: first, that some students learn differently from their peers and, second, that a different set of teaching strategies applies exclusively to these categories of students even though regular students may be learning the same thing. However, these assumptions have been repeatedly recognized as invalid (Bogdan &

Taylor, 1976; Sarason, 1982; Stainback & Stainback, 1984). As stated by Gardner (1977), "There are no unique methods for use [with students classified exceptional] that differ in kind from those used with normal children" (p. 74). (For further information as to why these assumptions are invalid, see "Instructional Methods" in Chapter 2 in this volume.)

This practice also does a disservice both to the students assigned to the categories as well as to those not assigned. By developing programs and materials for categories of students, the practice of assigning negative educational categorical labels to students, which sets them apart from their peers, is perpetuated. Likewise, students not assigned categorical labels are often denied access to many worthwhile teaching strategies and programs they may need to achieve their educational goals. In addition, it works against integration when some programs, methods, and materials are designated for students classified as having disabilities and others are for nonhandicapped students. Thus, there is a need to break away from the development and design of materials and programs that promote services and strategies for categories of students. Rather, we need articles, books and programs with titles such as: *Introduction to Individual Differences, How to Teach Self-Care and Community Living Skills, Fostering the Gifts and Talents of Children, Teaching Alternatives to Severe Forms of Maladaptive Behavior, Fostering Basic Socializations and Friendships, Promoting Integration in the Schools,* or *Essentials For Understanding and Teaching Braille.* By designing and developing methods, materials, and programs such as these, whatever methods, materials, and programs are available in a school can be made accessible to any student who needs them.

Reorganize Professional Associations

The education of all students in regular education as a normal, standard, and regular practice could be enhanced by modifying the way professional associations are organized and operated. Currently, many such associations are structured to serve a designated group or category of students. Rather than setting apart a group of individuals according to a categorical label, professional organizations and journals could be reoriented toward a functional instructional programming or service needs focus. That is, they could be focused on the expertise the membership has to offer any students who need it in the schools, rather than on a deviant category of students. If, indeed, we want to encourage all students to be viewed as individuals with unique needs, interests, and capabilities rather than as members of special categorical groups, our professional organizations should reflect this position.

Point to Ponder

When we design teaching and other programs for persons with disabilities, we are unintentionally fostering segregation. It leads to people defined as disabled having their own special programs that are apart from those everyone else participates in. An alternative would be to expand, adjust, and modify regular programs to be sure they meet everyone's needs.

For example, The Association for Persons with Severe Handicaps could reorient its expertise base by calling itself The Association for Supported Education and Community Living, or The Association for Integrated School and Community Living, or another similar title. Such an emphasis would correspond with that of professional organizations such as the American Association for Occupational Therapy, the International Reading Association, or the American Speech-Language-Hearing Association, which focus on an expertise area rather than a category of students.

There is a precedent of moving away from a special subgroup categorical focus to a more functional expertise area focus. In 1985 the Canadian Association for the Mentally Retarded was renamed the Canadian Association for Community Living to reflect a more normalized and functional focus. Likewise, the *Canadian Journal on Mental Retardation* has been renamed *Entourage*.

Advocate in Normalized Ways for Needed Services

Advocacy should focus on obtaining programs and services needed to meet all students' needs in age-appropriate regular classes in regular neighborhood schools, rather than on special programs and services for special categories of students. We educators initiate the separation of students classified as having disabilities from their peers by advocating for them as a category of separate students to receive special school programs. We then try to reverse this by designing and implementing special integration projects so that they will not be regarded as a separate group of students but as regular, natural members of neighborhood schools. It would be better to work toward integration from the beginning.

Rather than advocating by categories of students for special programs, we could advocate for instruction in basic self-care/community living skills, vocational and competitive employment skills, sign language, braille, speech reading, or self-control training. That is, rather than seeking "child-in-category" funding, advocates could lobby state and federal legislators to earmark funds to facilitate research, training, and the assimilation of resources in the deficient instructional area(s). Chapter 19 contains a more detailed discussion of advocacy and funding approaches to promote the education of all students in regular education.

CONCLUSION

A number of strategies can be employed to foster the education of all students in regular education. While no one person can do all of the things that need to be done, each of us can contribute. For example, teacher trainers can help reorganize teacher preparation; parents and professionals active in educational and advocacy organizations can help reorganize these groups; and special education teachers, consultants, and administrators in the elementary and secondary schools can join regular education, become regular educators, identify themselves by their specific area(s) of instructional expertise, and provide services within regular education. By each person joining with his or her colleagues to support and foster the development of a comprehensive regular education system capable of meeting all students' needs, we can gradually change current practices and eventually reach the goal of educating all students in regular education as a normal, routine, and standard practice.

REFERENCES

Biklen, D. (1988). (Producer). *Regular lives* [video]. Washington, DC: State of the Art.

Bogdan, R., & Taylor, S. (1976). The judged, not the judges: An insider's view of mental retardation. *American Psychologist, 31,* 47–52.

Forest, M. (1987). *More education integration.* Downsview, Ont.: G. Allan Roeher Institute.

Gardner, W. (1977). *Learning and behavior characteristics of exceptional children and youth.* Boston: Allyn & Bacon.

Gartner, A., & Lipsky, D. (1987). Beyond special education: Toward one quality system for all students. *Harvard Educational Review, 57,* 367–395.

Granger, L., & Granger, B. (1986). *The magic feather.* New York: E.P. Dutton.

Johnson, L., Pugach, M., & Hammittee, D. (1988). Barriers to effective special education consultation. *Remedial and Special Education, 9,* 41–47.

Johnson, R., & Johnson, D. (1981). Building friendships between handicapped and nonhandicapped students: Effects of cooperative and individualistic instruction. *American Educational Research Journal, 18,* 415–424.

Knoblock, P. (1982). *Teaching and mainstreaming autistic children.* Denver: Love Publishing Co.

MaHeady, L., Sacca, K., & Harper, G. (1988). Classroom peer tutoring with mildly handicapped high school students. *Exceptional Children, 55,* 52–59.

Oakes, J. (1985). Keep tracking: How schools structure inequality. New Haven, CT: Yale University Press.

Pugach, M. (1988). The consulting teacher in the context of education reform. *Exceptional Children, 55,* 273–274.

Ruttiman, A., & Forest, M. (1986). With a little help from my friends: The integration facilitator at work. *Entourage, 1,* 24–33.

Sarason, S. (1982). *The culture of the school and the problem of change.* Boston: Allyn & Bacon.

Stainback, S., & Stainback, W. (1987). Educating all students in regular education. *TASH Newsletter, 13*(4), 1 & 7.

Stainback, S., & Stainback, W. (1988). Educating all students with severe disabilities in regular classes. *Teaching Exceptional Children, 21,* 16–19.

Stainback, W., & Stainback, S. (1984). A rationale for the merger of special and regular education. *Exceptional Children, 51,* 102–111.

Strully, J. (1987, October). *What's really important in life anyway? Parents sharing the vision.* Paper presented at the 14th Annual TASH Conference, Chicago.

Sylvester, D. (1987, October). *A parent's perspective.* Paper presented to Vermont's Least Restrictive Environment Conference, Burlington.

Tucker, J. (1985). Curriculum-based assessment: An introduction. *Exceptional Children, 52,* 199–204.

Wang, M., & Birch, J. (1984). Effective special education in regular class. *Exceptional Children, 50,* 391–399.

Will, M. (1986). *Educating students with learning problems—A shared responsibility.* Washington, DC: U.S. Department of Education, Office of Special Education and Rehabilitative Services.

Ysseldyke, J., & Christenson, S. (1986). *The instructional environment scale.* Austin: PRO-ED.

CHAPTER 7

Enhancing Success in Heterogeneous Schools

Jacqueline S. Thousand and Richard A. Villa

This chapter identifies and describes those practices that appear to be associated with successful schooling of students in heterogeneous groupings. Before discussing these practices, it is important to clarify what the authors view as fundamental characteristics of successful heterogeneous public schools.

CHARACTERISTICS OF SUCCESSFUL HETEROGENEOUS SCHOOLS

First, heterogeneous schools are comprehensive, in that they actualize the "zero reject" principle (Lilly, 1971) by welcoming and educating *all* students in their own "home" schools; they accommodate the unique variations in students' educational needs through responsive and fluid instructional options rather than pigeonholing students into one of several standing, standard programs (Skrtic, 1987). They also are comprehensive in that they expand the body of decision makers concerned with individual student, instructional, and organizational issues to include not just a small, select group of administrators and instructional personnel but members of the broader school and general community (e.g., parents, students, paraprofessionals, school nurses, guidance counselors, lunch room staff, community members, generic human service agency personnel, community employers). Finally, they are comprehensive in that they look beyond academic achievement as the major or sole criterion of school success and promote the mastery of social and life skills requisite to success in work, home, recreational, and community life beyond high school.

The second characteristic of successful heterogeneous schools is the great amount of effort put forth to ensure that school personnel are as effective as they can be in their instructional practices. The leaders of these schools are bent upon merging and successfully implementing exemplary educational practices from both general and special education to take advantage of the knowledge base and demonstrated benefits of both sets of practices. They do this by making available to all instructional and administrative staff timely and intensive training and supervision related to targeted practices.

This chapter provides readers with brief descriptions and specific examples of organizational and educational beliefs and practices that promote student success in

Point to Ponder

When faced with a regular education mainstreamed environment that does not meet the needs of some students, there are two basic options in regard to what can be done about it. We can either develop a separate, special environment that is more accommodating or work to change, modify, adjust, and adapt the regular mainstream environment to be sure it meets the needs of all students. Those who advocate for integrated schools choose the latter since they believe that when children of different races; religions; sexes; and intellectual, sensory, physical, and psychological characteristics are educated together in integrated schools and classrooms, there is a greater chance that, with proper guidance, they will learn how to live and work together, respect each other, and hopefully care about each other in an integrated society.

heterogeneous schools. These examples are derived from the results of research and model demonstration efforts as well as the authors' firsthand experiences in a number of Vermont schools that have made the commitment to educating *all* of their students in heterogeneous groupings.

REDEFINING SCHOOL ORGANIZATIONAL STRUCTURE

"Achievement of the goals of an organization is highly related to the structure of the organization" (Brookover et al., 1982, p. 78). Given that schools are organizations, if they are to educate all learners in heterogenous environments, their organizational structure must promote or, at the least, allow for heterogeneity.

A number of characteristics of the organizational structure of the traditional American school stand in the way of heterogeneous schooling. First, most schools continue to stratify their students into high-, medium-, and low-achieving groups through heavy reliance upon segregated or pullout special and compensatory education service delivery models, ability groupings, and tracking systems.

Second, most schools continue to rely upon a "lock-step" curriculum approach (Stainback & Stainback, 1985); that is, what students are taught is determined not by their assessed individual needs but by the grade level to which they are assigned. Students are placed in a grade according to their age and are expected to master the predetermined curriculum by the end of the school year. If they fail, they are retained, referred for special education or compensatory education services, and pulled out of the regular classroom for part or all of their day. This practice makes the goal of heterogeneous grouping of all students difficult, if not impossible.

Finally, most teachers, whether labeled regular or special educators, generally are expected to work alone. Few schools encourage or expect instructional personnel to team teach with one another; and little, if any, time is structured into the work day for collaboration or planning with others.

By contrast, schools that are educating all of their students in heterogeneous environments have attempted to eliminate these and other organizational barriers in several ways. Specifically, they have redefined professional roles; created opportunities for collaboration; and created common conceptual frameworks, knowledge, and language among school staff through inservice training.

Redefining Professional Roles and Dropping Professional Labels

"I used to think of myself as a speech and language pathologist; but now I think of myself as a teacher who happens to have training and expertise in the area of communication" (Harris, 1987). This statement was made by an educator who works in a school system in which the roles and responsibilities of regular and special education have continuously been redefined over the past 5 years. The redefinition of job functions was viewed as necessary to allow this system to shift from categorical educational programs (e.g., regular classroom, special classes, pullout services for speech and language and compensatory education services) to a single unified system where broad-based support ultimately would be available to all teachers and any of their students (Villa, 1988).

Job titles and the formal or informal role definitions that accompany them determine the way in which a staff member behaves within a school (Brookover et al., 1982). For example, the title, resource room teacher, may carry with it a set of expectations that: 1) this teacher works in a separate room, 2) students must leave the regular classroom to get this person's services, and 3) only those students identified as "special education eligible" can or will be allowed to benefit from this person's expertise. This person, however, may have a great deal of training and expertise in assessing students' strengths and needs, in task and concept analysis, in designing and implementing classroom and behavior management programs, and in other areas that, if shared with classroom teachers, might help them to maximize their responsiveness to the diverse educational needs of students.

Suppose the resource room teacher label were dropped and this person's role was redefined to be a support person who would provide technical assistance to any number of educators in the building through modeling, consultation, team teaching, and inservice training. Such a change in job definition should result in an exchange of skills, thus increasing the number of students whose needs could be met in heterogeneous classrooms. There is considerable evidence that this type of consultative, training-based intervention model is effective in maintaining students in general education settings (Idol, Paolucci-Whitcomb, & Nevin, 1986; Knight, Meyer, Paolucci-Whitcomb, Hasazi, & Nevin, 1981; Lew, Mesch, & Lates, 1982; Miller & Sabatino, 1978). The steps for implementing this so-called consulting teacher model are described by Idol et al. (1986).

The Winooski [VT] School District is an example of one system that has taken steps to redefine roles and responsibilities of school personnel to successfully educate all students in general education settings. First, a single Department of Pupil Personnel Services was created to unite guidance, health, gifted and talented, special education, compensatory education, and early childhood services and personnel. The former special education administrator directs this department and collaborates with the other administrators to jointly supervise and evaluate *all* district instructional personnel. These changes have eliminated the preexisting departmental boundaries that had administratively separated programs and have facilitated the coordination of services and sharing of professional expertise.

Second, the roles of professional and paraprofessional personnel in the new Department of Pupil Personnel Services have become primarily consultative in nature. Whereas in the past these individuals delivered services exclusively through pullout programs, they now are expected to consult and team teach with general educators. The elementary communication specialist, for example, has emerged from the resource room and now delivers speech and language instruction mainly by team teaching with regular classroom teachers.

In a final move to alter professional roles and responsibilities, the special education classes for students with moderate and severe handicaps were closed. Students who would have been in these classes now are educated in age-appropriate classrooms and in integrated community and vocational settings. The responsibility for supporting these students is distributed among a cadre of educators who collectively have skills in health, vocational, communication, counseling, and functional (i.e., domestic, community, recreational, vocational) curriculum domains, as well as in traditional areas (e.g., reading, mathematics).

Montlake, a Seattle, WA, elementary school of 243 students, provides an example of an individual school in another state that has dramatically altered the job responsibilities of its school staff to improve education for all students (Olson, 1988). Pullout programs for special instruction have been eliminated, and the librarian and former special education and compensatory education teachers now teach reading and mathematics groups along with the other teachers in a multi-aged arrangement. In the afternoon, students are regrouped by grade level, and teachers cover social studies, science, and other subject areas. According to the principal, because teachers now share students, they work more cooperatively and feel more responsible for the whole school. Moreover, discipline problems have declined, teacher morale has improved, and students' standardized test scores have increased.

By redefining instructional roles, the schools just cited have allowed for more creative use of the human resources that always were present within them. In addition, in carrying out their new job functions, educators model collaboration for their students. "The integration of professionals within a school system is a prerequisite to the successful integration of students. We cannot ask our students to do those things which we as professionals are unwilling to do" (Harris, 1987).

Point to Ponder

Too often regular educators do not attend special education conferences and activities and special educators do not attend regular education conferences and activities. Instead, we each meet in our segregated groups to discuss how we can coordinate, collaborate, and integrate together.

Creating Opportunities for Collaboration

Local schools have within them a natural and often untapped pool of experts. Each teacher's unique skills and interests may be of value to another teacher or to a broader range of students than those for whom he or she is directly responsible. A key to successfully meeting the educational needs of all students is the development of a collaborative relationship among the school staff so that expertise may be shared. "A teacher is more willing to share responsibility for a student who presents challenges when that student comes with a team to support him" (Tetreault, 1988).

Establishing a Collaborative Teaming Process In a number of Vermont schools, a problem-solving and decision-making process referred to as "collaborative teaming" is employed to promote the sharing of expertise (Thousand, Fox, Reid, Godek, & Williams, 1986). In collaborative teaming, team members work cooperatively to achieve a common, agreed-upon goal. The process involves the application of the principles of cooperative group learning, as described by Johnson and Johnson (1987b), to adult planning groups. In the words of a collaborative team member:

> We've taken the technology of cooperative group learning for kids and applied it to our adult teams. We meet as cooperative groups. Everyone shares in the common goal, that goal being the most appropriate education for the students we serve." (Cravedi-Cheng, 1987)

In a collaborative team, members perceive themselves as positively interdependent, as "sinking or swimming together." They also are expected to exhibit certain interpersonal and small-group skills that have been related to successful cooperative group work (Johnson & Johnson, 1987a). For a team to be optimally effective in planning and problem solving, its members need to learn and practice these skills, including basic group management skills that result in an organized team with an established set of expectations; leadership behaviors that help the team accomplish its tasks and maintain positive working relationships; and skills for managing conflict or creating constructive controversy.

Members of collaborative teams frequently are at different levels in terms of their competence and confidence in performing collaborative skills. However, all of these skills can be taught and learned. In some school districts, direct instruction in collaborative teaming skills has been arranged for staff. Teachers also have chosen the development of select collaborative teaming skills as annual professional growth goals.

Creating Opportunities for Teams to Meet One issue that all schools attempting to implement a collaborative teaming process must address is how the school's organizational structure can be modified to provide opportunities for staff to meet as teams. One Vermont school district (Franklin Northwest) has dealt with this issue by contracting with a permanent substitute who rotates among schools and relieves regular classroom teachers so that they may participate in meetings concerning students in their class.

Another school district in Vermont (Winooski) has instituted the practice of reserving every Friday morning for team meetings. All professional and paraprofessional support personnel (e.g., special education teachers, nurses, counselors) are expected to hold their Friday mornings open until they are notified of scheduled meeting times for students on their caseload. During the times when these individuals are not scheduled for meetings, they relieve classroom teachers so that they may attend their Friday meetings.

In this same district, it was decided that students would benefit if the junior high school content area teachers had a common daily planning period to supplement their individual planning times. This was considered a priority in the development of the master schedule for the following year. These teachers now have a structured agenda for their common planning period, which addresses a host of curricular issues and includes meetings with students, families, or pupil support staff.

Subgroups of collaborative teams also need time outside of team meetings to jointly adapt curriculum or instructional approaches for upcoming lessons, plan for team teaching activities, and modify instructional programs for individual students. Administrators need to appreciate and support this type of collaborative time by adjusting the school's schedule to accommodate these times; by setting an expectation that teachers will collaborate; and by arranging incentives and rewards for collaboration.

Including Students as Team Members In a number of successful heterogeneous schools, students have come to be seen as essential members of collaborative teams. They are recognized as the source of information in determining appropriate social integration goals to be included in the individualized education program (IEP) of their peers with identified handicapping conditions. A special education administrator who now routinely includes peers in IEP development has stated: "Although we have emphasized socialization and inclusion for years, it never really took off until we turned to the students and asked for their help. We previously were leaving out of the planning process the majority of the school's population" (DiFerdinando, 1987).

Students also have been enlisted to assist in planning for the transition of students with handicaps from more segregated to regular education settings. Recently, the entire student body of a small junior high school met with school staff in small groups to plan the transition of a student with multiple handicaps from a segregated residential facility to their seventh grade. The advice they gave was enlightening, ranging from suggestions for an augmentative communication device that they felt would best help the new student communicate his needs to the kind of notebook he should carry to "fit in" (Scagliotti, 1987).

Empowerment through Collaboration Collaborative teaming empowers teachers and students by enfranchising them through their participation in decision-making processes (Johnson & Johnson, 1987c; Slavin, 1987; Thousand et al., 1986). It facilitates the distribution of school leadership responsibilities beyond the administrative arm of the school to the broader school community. Thousand and colleagues (1986) offer an expanded description of the collaborative teaming process and strategies for implementing the process in heterogeneous schools. Readers who wish to learn more about specific collaborative skills are referred to *Joining Together: Group Theory and Group Skills* (Johnson & Johnson, 1987a).

Creating Common Conceptual Frameworks, Knowledge, and Language through Inservice Training

It has been pointed out that the way in which teachers choose to interact with students is dependent, at least in part, upon the conceptual frameworks and terms they use to think and talk about students (Smith, 1988). Smith has effectively argued that what instructional personnel need is "shared meaning"—a common knowledge base, conceptual framework, and language for communicating about students and learning. In addition, this shared meaning needs to be based upon sound theory and research. "In order to establish and maintain constructive dialogue between and among professional groups about intervention methods, we must identify and communicate the notion of best practice in intervention based on known theory" (Smith, 1988, p. 8). In short, for school personnel to be most effective in their collaborations with one another and their instruction of students, they need to share common concepts, vocabulary, and training in instructional strategies that are founded in sound research and theory.

Lyon (1988a, 1988b) has pointed out that teaching is a complex act requiring quality models and intensive guided practice and feedback across a number of teaching situations and conditions in order for teachers to translate demonstrated assessment and instructional techniques into productive, effective teaching. Lyon also discusses disturbing survey results that reveal regular and special educators' dissatisfaction with preservice training experiences. Teachers feel they have been ill-prepared to effectively adapt their own instruction to accommodate students who fail to learn from their typical "first-shot" instruction.

Taken together, Smith's and Lyon's observations point to the need for staff of heterogeneous schools to acquire the conceptual frameworks, language, and technical skills to communicate about and implement assessment, instructional, and collaborative teaming practices to enable them to respond to the unique needs of a diverse student body. If personnel in heterogeneous schools have not received this training in the past, an inservice training agenda needs to be formulated and ratified by the school community. This agenda must be thoughtfully formulated and may need to extend across several school years to ensure that teachers have the opportunity to progress from acquisition to mastery.

The authors' reading of the literature and their own personal experiences in providing inservice training to staff of schools attempting to establish more heterogeneous instructional opportunities for students has led them to identify several areas in which inservice training may be needed (Villa, Thousand, & Fox, 1988). One content area in which all school staff may need training involves collaboration (Johnson & Johnson, 1987a, 1987c; Thousand et al., 1986). As already discussed, school personnel need to become skillful in implementing a collaborative teaming model and using interpersonal and small-group skills to function optimally as collaborative team members.

A second area of training would promote knowledge and positive beliefs regarding current "best educational practices" in heterogeneous schooling. This training would examine school characteristics that general education researchers have found to be more effective than others in promoting students' learning and development (Brookover et al., 1982). It also would examine what is considered best educational practice by special education researchers (Fox et al., 1986). Armed with this information, school personnel would be equipped to articulate the demonstrated benefits of these practices and argue for the establishment and merger of exemplary practices within their school.

A third content area would cover a variety of instructional practices that enable teachers to effectively accommodate a heterogeneous group of students within general education classrooms. Training might include outcomes-based instructional models (e.g., Block & Anderson, 1975; Hunter, 1982); cooperative group learning models (e.g., Johnson, Johnson, Holubec, & Roy, 1984; Slavin, 1983); computer assisted instruction (e.g., Heerman, 1988); an assessment model that enables teachers to discuss learner characteristics and make decisions about their own instructional behavior (e.g., Lyon & Moats, in press; Lyon & Toomey, 1985); classroom management strategies (e.g., Becker, 1986); methods for teaching positive social skills and reinforcing students' use of these skills in school (e.g., Hazel, Schumaker, Sherman, & Sheldon-Wildgen, 1981; Jackson, Jackson, & Monroe, 1983); and the use of peers as tutors (e.g., Cooke et al., 1983; Good & Brophy, 1984; Pierce et al., 1984), buddies (Williams et al., 1984), and members of educational planning teams.

Finally, school supervisory personnel may need some specialized training and practice in using a clinical supervision model (e.g., Cummings, 1985). If the supervisory personnel of a school are to promote teachers' successful and continued implementation of any of the assessment and instructional strategies just mentioned, they must be skilled in observing, analyzing, and conducting conferences regarding teachers' instructional performance.

It is important to emphasize here that, whatever the training content a school's staff elects to study, the principles of effective instruction should be followed in the delivery of the content; that is, trainers need to model multiple and diverse examples of the desired knowledge or practice, provide guided practice in the application of the knowledge or practice, and arrange for coaching and feedback in the actual school situations in which the knowledge or practice is expected to be employed (Joyce & Showers, 1980).

BELIEFS

The organizational and instructional practices discussed thus far in this chapter have been found to promote student success in heterogeneous schools. However, it is the beliefs held by parents and the educational and support personnel within a school that ultimately determine whether or not *all* learners will be welcomed and successfully educated within regular education classrooms. The authors feel comfortable making this statement because of an emerging body of research (Ajzen & Fishbein, 1980; Fortini, 1987; Miller & Gibbs, 1984) in social psychology supporting a "theory of reasoned action," which relates the voluntary behaviors of adults and children to their beliefs (Ajzen & Fishbein, 1980).

According to this theory, one's personal beliefs about performing a particular voluntary behavior combined with beliefs about what others think one should do influence whether or not one actually performs the behavior (Ajzen & Fishbein, 1980). Applying the theory to the issue of heterogeneous schooling, the theory would argue that the beliefs of school personnel regarding the consequences of structuring heterogeneous learning environments combined with their perceptions of what respected colleagues, friends, or family members think should be done influence whether or not they actually create heterogeneous educational opportunities.

The following is a discussion of often-stated beliefs that, in the authors' view, are important to promulgate in the establishment of heterogeneous schools and in ensuring the success of students in those schools.

Beliefs Regarding the Value of Heterogeneous Schooling

Heterogeneity Is Possible For school personnel to enthusiastically open their doors to a more diverse student body and promote each learner's success within regular educational classrooms, it is important for them to believe or, at least temporarily suspend disbelief, that heterogeneous age-appropriate classroom environments *can* meet the unique educational needs of each student (Nevin & Thousand, 1986; Thousand, 1985). In other words, they must believe that they can do a quality job. They also need to trust that they will receive the material and human resources, technical assistance, and training to enable them to effectively do the job.

Oftentimes, school and community members take a "show me" posture; they embrace the belief that heterogeneous schooling is possible only after they have had positive firsthand experience educating a diverse group of students. Others wait to evaluate their colleagues' experiences, to

Point to Ponder

Bobby M., a 6-year-old boy with microcephaly and a visual impairment, was described by his school as a delightful and engaging child. Bobby enjoyed playing with the "nonhandicapped" children in the neighborhood. He and his friends loved to ride bikes, play games, swing, climb, and play make-believe. He attended a gymnastics class and summer camp program with his nondisabled friends.

In the fall, the public schools assigned Bobby to a segregated special education classroom. The seven other students in this class had different types of disabilities. One child was completely nonverbal, one child had a physical disability and used a wheelchair, and another child was tied into her seat some of the time, due to attention deficit problems. Bobby's neighborhood friends attended the regular kindergarten located next door to the "special" classroom. A glass door in the wall separated the students defined as disabled and nondisabled.

Bobby's parents requested that their son be integrated into the kindergarten part of the day with an aide assigned to assist the teacher. The kindergarten teacher welcomed Bobby's participation in her classroom. However, the school special education department denied the request, deciding that Bobby should remain in the segregated classroom. Bobby's neighborhood friends did not understand why he had to stay in the "handicapped room."

Bobby's parents fought for over 2 years to enforce Bobby's right to pass through the glass door and participate with his nonhandicapped peers. The school system, on the other hand, spent thousands of dollars in attorney fees in its attempt to force Bobby to remain in the isolated setting. Finally the parents prevailed in an administrative hearing conducted by the state Department of Education.

At long last, Bobby is thriving in the regular classroom. He participates in all the activities and tries very hard. The other children readily accept Bobby. When one mother asked her son about what it was like to have Bobby in the class, her son said in an exasperated tone, "Oh, Mom, it's no big deal!" (Massachusetts Advocacy Center, 1987, p. 2)

hear whether support was provided when it was needed. In either case, it is critical to create successful demonstrations of heterogeneous schooling.

Heterogeneity Is Beneficial to All Another belief held by those who support heterogeneous classroom groupings is that heterogeneous educational opportunities are beneficial to all students and school personnel. Recently, at a workshop presentation, a kindergarten teacher who has integrated a student with moderate handicaps full-time into her classroom was questioned as to why she chose to have this child in her classroom. She responded:

> I, as a teacher, have no right to limit the possible potential of this child. No one knows his limits and neither do I. I like to think of [this child] as having no limits. Anything is possible for him. I feel fortunate to have had the opportunity to grow in a new direction by having [this child] in my classroom. I am learning and adapting along with the other students, accepting and believing that everyone is special. (Donahue, 1988)

Clearly, this teacher's response reflects not only her appreciation of this student's human and educational rights but her belief that the student's presence in the classroom is beneficial, a catalyst for new learning both for herself and all of her students.

Some students, parents, and teachers highlight the positive impact of heterogeneous grouping upon the development of students' moral and ethical characters. For example, a classmate of a teenager with multiple handicaps who had recently transferred to regular junior high school classes reported, "I was scared. I didn't know what it would be like. . . . I think we learned that it's important to treat other people better. The kids don't pick on him, so they don't pick on each other" (Scagliotti, 1987). Reflecting upon this and other students' impressions of the benefits of being educated alongside someone with a significant disability, the school's principal commented, "School is an exposure experience. I think it's really healthy for kids to say they now know more about caring about other people" (Scagliotti, 1987).

A junior high school language arts teacher in this same school also has noted how heterogeneous school experiences promote students' acceptance and appreciation of human differences:

> Educating students in heterogeneous groups allows for students to recognize individual differences. It does not take away from [high-achieving] kids; it adds to their knowledge of people. The more we separate, the less recognition and acceptance of individual differences occurs among students and teachers. If we are going to separate students, we might as well go back to the labelling and name-calling that we had in the early days of special education.(Villemaire, 1987)

A final set of beliefs regarding the benefits of heterogeneous schooling concerns the students who typically would have been excluded from regular educational experiences. Students with special educational needs who have spoken out as to the positive effects of heterogeneous schooling focus on their own emotional well-being and sense of belonging. A female high school sophomore has commented, "I was in a special class. I've been in regular classes for five years. I'm more a part of the school now" (Budelmann, Farrel, Kovach, & Paige, 1987). A classmate who relies upon a wheelchair for mobility and who is educated with her peers in heterogeneous classrooms has stated: "I feel like I am a part of the school. I am aware of the things that are going on; I've gone to the school car wash and homecoming. I have friends in and out of school, and this helps me feel better about myself" (Budelmann et al., 1987). Clearly, both young women recognize their heterogeneous school experiences as a primary source of their feelings of inclusion.

Heterogeneity Enables the Attainment of the Goals of Public Education Over the past 3 years, the authors have had the opportunity to ask thousands of parents, educators, administrators, and community members the following question: "From your personal perspective, what do you believe should be the goal(s) of public education?" Regardless of the audience queried, two categories of responses have repeatedly emerged—one concerned with *independence* and the other with *positive social interdependence* within the community. When discussing independence, people talk about the school's responsibility to prepare its graduates to live, work, play, and be lifelong learners in their chosen communities. When discussing positive social interdependence, people frequently cite the schools' responsibilities for shaping attitudes and skills for "seeking, establishing, and maintaining friendships and social networks" (Harris, 1987); of "creating an atmosphere of *pride* in which students learn the values of *patience, respect, inquiry, desire,* and *excellence*" [all emphases added] (Villemaire, 1987); and of "eradicating myths and building positive images and pictures in the mind of the community" (Sylvester, 1987).

To summarize, the diverse group of people the authors have sampled seem to share in the belief that the goals of public education should be to optimize students' acquisition of attitudes and skills that enable them to: a) make decisions and choices about the quality of their lives, b) establish and maintain friendships and social networks, and c) be contributing members of society. In the authors' experience, community members, students, and school personnel who support heterogeneous schooling strongly believe that heterogeneous schools are more likely to create opportunities that will promote the attainment of these goals by all students than schools in which students are homogeneously grouped.

The beliefs just discussed have been nicely articulated by a mother of a young girl who attends the first grade of her local school. In an address to several hundred educators and school administrators she stated:

> My goals for my daughter are no different than your goals for your children or the children in your classrooms. I want her to be the best that she can be. The limitations placed on her are to be her own. I want Jennie to have every opportunity available to her. Whether she can do it or not will be up to her. But I do not want her denied anything. . . . My goal for my daughter is that someday she will be an independent, contributing member of our society. I hope that she will be able to hold down a job. I'd like to think that she could live, if not alone, in the least restrictive home option available. . . . Somewhere in her classroom today are tomorrow's future employers. Years from now, when approached to hire a person with special needs, they will remember Jennie—not as Down syndrome, not as retarded, but as a person who could assume responsibility and do a task. She may not be able to read or speak like us, but she *can* [emphasis added] assume responsibility. (Blair, 1987)

Belief Regarding the Value of Collaboration: None of Us Is as Good as All of Us

If one were to walk into a Vermont school that has committed to educating all students in regular education settings and ask the staff, "In a word, what do you believe to be the key ingredient to your success?" one would likely hear words such as "teaming," "collaboration," "cooperation," and "sharing." For a heterogeneous school to operate smoothly, school staff need to believe in the power of collaboration. School personnel who effectively collaborate will agree that each teacher, left alone, is limited in the instructional responses he or she can conceptualize or deliver. However, when school staff pool their conceptual, material, technical, and human resources, students and staff benefit from the "collective wisdom."

A rationale for collaboration has been succinctly expressed by a classroom teacher, who stated:

> We are all going in the same direction. We all have to help and cooperate with one another. As a classroom teacher, I must be open to communication; I can't have a moat around my classroom. I have to welcome resources into my room and be open and flexible. I have to seek information from others and not just wait for people to come to me. If I am not open to working with others, then the student gets cheated, and that is the person we are here to serve. (Villemaire, 1987)

A speech and language pathologist has enumerated the ways in which collaborative teaming contributes to successful heterogeneous schooling, pointing out both teacher and student benefits:

> As individuals we bring to our teams a wide range of values, experiences, training, resources, strengths, and weaknesses. We share our diversities and work toward meeting mutually defined goals. We've created an interdependence among ourselves as professionals. When we meet there is shared leadership, a division of labor, an atmosphere of trust, and effective communication. The result is a professional support network through which we meet the needs of learners and grow as professionals. (Harris, 1987)

Parents as Equal Partners In successful heterogeneous schools, parents are considered valid and valued members of the collaborative team; they are seen as active, contributing members in the educational planning process for their child. To view parents otherwise, limits the school's access to the valuable resources that parents offer in identifying their child's strengths and needs, designing realistic and effective interventions, and evaluating the outcomes of their child's education. An appreciation for parents' unique expertise is conveyed in the eloquent words of a parent: "Parents should be thought of as scholars of experience. We are in it for the distance. We see and feel the continuum. We have our doctorate in perseverance. We and the system must be in concert or the vision shrinks" (Sylvester, 1987).

Beliefs Are Infectious

It is important to point out here that not all school staff, students, parents, or community members need to believe in heterogeneous schools for them to be successful. However, there must be a group of individuals who *do* hold these views and who have the formal or informal leadership roles in the school community to demonstrate success and to influence the thinking and behaviors of others. In the words of a superintendent of a school district committed to heterogeneous schooling, "Everything in education is infectious. If you can get one teacher to support educating all learners in heterogeneous classes, then you will get others" (Cross, 1987).

SUMMARY

The organizational, instructional, and attitudinal variables presented in this and previous chapters influence the success of students and educational personnel in heterogeneous schools. The authors encourage all who are interested in or charged with the responsibility of planning for school improvement to carefully examine the practices and beliefs operating in their schools to promote or impede continued progress toward meeting the diverse needs of all students. The authors further encourage the school community to embrace the belief that there are actions that each individual can take to positively influence the learning environment of all students, for "we know that a school can change if the staff desires to improve or modify beliefs, structures, and instructional practices" (Brookover et al., 1982, p. 35). The quality of education provided to this generation of school children will be determined by the collective, responsible actions of the diverse group of educators and parents who commit to being lifelong learners and students of the promise that research, current best educational practice, and creative problem solving offers.

REFERENCES

Azjen, I., & Fishbein, M. (1980). *Understanding attitudes and predicting social behavior.* Englewood Cliffs, NJ: Prentice-Hall.

Becker, W. (1986). *Applied psychology for teachers: A behavioral cognitive approach.* Chicago: Science Research Associates.

Blair, K. (1987, October). *A parent's perspective on age appropriate placement.* Paper presented at Vermont's Least Restrictive Environment Conference, Burlington.

Block, J., & Anderson, L. (1975). *Mastery learning in classroom instruction.* New York: MacMillan.

Brookover, W., Beamer, L., Efthim, H., Hathaway, D., Lezzotte, L., Miller, S., Passalacqua, J., & Tornatzky, L. (1982). *Creating effective schools: An inservice program for enhancing school learning climate and achievement.* Holmes Beach, FL: Learning Publications.

Budelmann, L., Farrel, S., Kovach, C., & Paige, K. (1987, October). *Student perspective: Planning and achieving social integration.* Paper presented at Vermont's Least Restrictive Environment Conference, Burlington.

Cooke, N. L., Heron, T. E., & Howard, W. L. (1983). *Peer tutoring. Implementing classwide programs in the primary grades.* Columbus, OH: Special Press.

Cravedi-Cheng, L. (1987, October). *A special educator's perspective on teaming to accomplish cooperation between and among regular and special educators for the provision of services in the least restrictive environment.* Paper presented at Vermont's Least Restrictive Environment Conference, Burlington.

Cross, G., (1987, October). *A superintendent's perspective on teaming to accomplish cooperation between and among regular and special educators for the provision of services in the least restrictive environment.* Paper presented at Vermont's Least Restrictive Environment Conference, Burlington.

Cummings, C. (1985). *Peering in on peers.* Edmonds, WA: Snohomish Publishing.

DiFerdinando, R. (1987, October). *An administrator's perspective on the value of peer support networks.* Paper presented at Vermont's Least Restrictive Environment Conference, Burlington.

Donahue, S. (1988, March). *Examples of integration in Addison Northeast Supervisory Union.* Paper presented at Teaming for Creative Mainstreaming Conference, Ludlow, VT.

Fortini, M. (1987). Attitudes and behavior toward students with handicaps by their nonhandicapped peers. *American Journal of Mental Deficiency, 92,* 78–84.

Fox, W., Thousand, J., Williams, W., Fox, T., Towne, P., Reid, R., Conn-Powers, C., & Calcagni, L. (1986). *Best educational practices '86: Educating learners with severe handicaps.* (Monograph No. 6-1). Burlington: University of Vermont, Center for Developmental Disabilities.

Good, T.L., & Brophy, J.E. (1984). *Looking into classrooms* (3d ed.). New York: Harper & Row.

Harris, T., (1987, October). *A speech and language pathologist's perspective on teaming to accomplish cooperation between and among regular and special educators for the provision of services in the least restrictive environment.* Paper presented at Vermont's Least Restrictive Environment Conference, Burlington.

Hazel, J.S., Schumaker, J.B., Sherman, J.A., & Sheldon-Wildgen, J. (1981). *ASSET: A social skills program for adolescents.* Champaign, IL: Research Press.

Heerman, B. (1988). *Teaching and learning with computers.* San Francisco: Jossey-Bass.

Hunter, M. (1982). *Mastery Teaching*. El Segundo, CA: TIP Publications.

Idol, L., Paolucci-Whitcomb, P., & Nevin, A. (1986). *Collaborative consultation*. Rockville, MD: Aspen Systems.

Jackson, N.F., Jackson, D.A., & Monroe, C. (1983). *Behavioral social skill training materials—Getting along with others: Teaching social effectiveness to children*. Champaign, IL: Research Press.

Johnson, D.W., & Johnson, R. (1987a). *Joining together: Group theory and group skills* (3d ed.). Englewood Cliffs, NJ: Prentice-Hall.

Johnson, D.W., & Johnson, R. (1987b). *Learning together and alone: Cooperation, competition, and individualization* (2d ed.). Englewood Cliffs, NJ: Prentice-Hall.

Johnson, D., & Johnson, R. (1987c). Research shows the benefit of adult cooperation. *Educational Leadership, 45*(3), 27–30.

Johnson, D.W., Johnson, R., Holubec, E., & Roy, P. (1984). *Circles of learning*. Arlington, VA: Association for Supervision and Curriculum Development.

Joyce, B., & Showers, B. (1980). Improving inservice training: The messages of research. *Educational Leadership, 37*(5), 379–385.

Knight, M., Meyers, H., Paolucci-Whitcomb, P., Hasazi, S., & Nevin, A. (1981). A four year evaluation of consulting teacher services. *Behavior Disorders, 6*, 92–100.

Lew, M., Mesch, D., & Lates, B.J. (1982). The Simmons College generic consulting teacher program: A program description and data-based application. *Teacher Education and Special Educational, 5*(2), 11–16.

Lilly, M.S. (1971). A training based model for special education. *Exceptional Children, 37*, 745–749.

Lyon, R. (1988a). *What we know and don't know about learning disabilities*. Paper presented at First Vermont Symposium on Learning Disabilities, Rutland.

Lyon, R. (1988b). Addressing individual differences in the classroom: Are we up to the job? *Teacher Education and Special Education*.

Lyon, R., & Moats, L. (in press). Critical factors in the instruction of the learning disabled. *Journal of Consulting and Clinical Psychology*.

Lyon, R., & Toomey, F. (1985). Neurological, neuropsychological and cognitive-developmental approaches to learning disabilities. *Topics in Learning Disabilities*. Montpelier: Vermont Department of Education.

Massachusetts Advocacy Center. *Out of the Mainstream*. (1987). Boston: Author.

Miller, C., & Gibbs, E.D. (1984). High school students' attitudes and actions toward "slow learners." *American Journal of Mental Deficiency, 89*, 156–166.

Miller, T., & Sabatino, D. (1978). An evaluation of the teacher consultant model as an approach to mainstreaming. *Exceptional Children, 45*, 86–91.

Nevin, A., & Thousand, J. (1986). Limiting or avoiding referrals to special education. *Teacher Education and Special Education, 9*, 149–161.

Olson, L. (1988, April 13). A Seattle principal defies the conventional wisdom. *Education Week*, pp. 1, 22–23.

Pierce, M.M., Stahlbrand, K., & Armstrong, S.B. (1984). *Increasing student productivity through peer tutoring programs*. Austin: PRO-Ed.

Scagliotti, L. (1987, December 20). Helping hands: School works to overcome student's handicap. *Burlington Free Press*, Section B, 1, 10.

Skrtic, T. (1987). An organizational analysis of special education reform. *Counterpoint, 8*(2), 15–19.

Slavin, R.E. (1983). *Cooperative learning*. New York: Longman.

Slavin, R.E. (1987). Ability grouping and student achievement in elementary school: A best-evidence synthesis. *Review of Educational Research, 57*, 293–336.

Smith, C. (1988, March). What's in a word? *On our acquisition of the concept language learning disability*. Paper presented at First Vermont Symposium on Learning Disabilities, Rutland.

Stainback, S., & Stainback, W. (1985). The merger of special and regular education: Can it be done? *Exceptional Children, 51*, 517–521.

Sylvester, D. (1987, October). *A parent's perspective on transition: From high school to what?* Paper presented at Vermont's Least Restrictive Environment Conference, Burlington.

Tetreault, D. (1988, March). *The Winooski model*. Paper presented at Portsmouth School District Integration Workshop, Portsmouth, NH.

Thousand, J. (1985). *Social integration and parent involvement: Special education teacher at-*

titudes and behaviors. Unpublished doctoral dissertation, University of Vermont, Burlington.

Thousand, J., Fox, T., Reid, R., Godek, J., & Williams, W. (1986). *The homecoming model: Educating students who present intensive educational challenges within regular education environments*. (Monograph No. 7-1). Burlington: University of Vermont, Center for Developmental Disabilities.

Villa, R. (1988, January). *Full integration*. Paper presented at Administrators' Training Project Conference, Eau Claire, WI.

Villa, R., Thousand, J., & Fox, W. (1988). *The Winooski Model: A Comprehensive Model for Providing a Quality Education for all Learners with and without Handicaps within an Integrated Public School Setting*. (Paper available from Richard Villa, Winooski School District, Normand Street, Winooski, VT 05404)

Villemaire, B., (1987, October). *A regular classroom teacher's perspective on teaming to accomplish cooperation between and among regular and special educators for the provision of services in the least restrictive environment: Winooski*. Paper presented at Vermont's Least Restrictive Environment Conference, Burlington.

Williams, W., Salce Iverson, G., & Urich, C. (1984). *Promoting inschool social integration of learners with severe handicaps through peer involvement*. (Monograph No. 4-6). Burlington: University of Vermont, Center for Developmental Disabilities.

CHAPTER 8

School Administration and Financial Arrangements

Dorothy Kerzner Lipsky and Alan Gartner

The current organization of schools and the funding of services for students labeled as handicapped (as well as others called "at risk") promotes segregation and fails to assure quality. This chapter first addresses organizational practices of schools and then funding issues, keeping in mind that the two are intertwined.

SEPARATION OF HANDICAPPED AND NONHANDICAPPED STUDENTS

In 1976–77, when the first data on the implementation of PL 94-142 were collected, 67% of the students were served in general classes (that is full-time or with resource room services), 25% in special classes, and 8% in separate schools or other environments (Walker, 1987, p. 104). A decade later, with an increase of some half a million students served in special education programs, the placement percentages for the 1986–87 school year are uncannily similar to the earlier ones: 67% in general classes, 24% in special classes, and 9% in separate schools or other environments (Viadero, 1988c, p. 17). These figures considerably overstate the extent to which students receiving special education services are pulled out of their regular classes to receive these services, often losing opportunities to be educated with their peers (Allington & McGill-Franzen, 1989).

These overall figures mask a great deal of variation—between states, among categories of handicapping conditions, and over time. For example, data show that while 7 states place more than half of their students with handicaps full time in regular classes, another 10 place fewer than 10% full time in regular classes (*Tenth Annual Report*, 1988, Table BC1).

A more fine-grained analysis emphasizes this disparity. While nationally the percentage of children ages 3 to 20 labeled as handicapped and receiving special education services was 6.47% in the 1986–87 school year, among the states the range was from barely half that (3.82% in Hawaii) to nearly a half greater (9.82% in Massachusetts).

As for categories of handicapping conditions, there have been sharp changes over time, as well as continuing wide variability among states. Between 1976–77 and 1986–87, when the total special education population grew 17%, nationally those labeled as learning disabled grew 141% (*Tenth An-*

nual Report, 1988, Table 1, p. 12). Among the states there is wide variation in this category. While the national average of students labeled as learning disabled was 43% of those in special education, the range among the 50 states was from 30% to 67%, and in 30 large cities the range was from 0% to 73% (Gartner & Lipsky, 1987).

There is also wide variation in how the states serve those in differing categories. The national average among students for all handicapping conditions served full time in regular classes was 26% in 1985–86. The range among the 50 states was from 1% to 71%. For those students labeled as learning disabled, the national average was 15%, with a range from 0% to 86%. For those students labeled as speech impaired, the national average was 66% placed in regular classes, with a range from 1% to 99%. For those students labeled as mentally retarded, the national average was 3% placed in regular classes, with a range from 0% to 43%. And for students labeled as emotionally disturbed, the national average was 9% placed in regular classes, with a range from 0% to 51% (*Tenth Annual Report,* 1988, Table BC1).

These variations in the overall numbers of students labeled as handicapped, in the distribution among categories, and in placement arrangements, are a function of a number of factors. First of all, overall national policy changes have had their effects. McGill-Franzen (1987) pointed out that the increase in students identified as learning disabled nearly matched the decline in Chapter I participants over the past decade. A report prepared by the directors of special education in large cities noted that the pressure for school excellence has led to dumping of students from special education, where their scores on standardized tests are often excluded from overall district totals (*Special Education,* 1986). A 1987 study cited by the U.S. Department of Education confirms this point, concluding, "Higher standards in the name of educational reform seem to be exaggerating the tendency to refer difficult children to special education" (Viadero, 1988c, p. 17).

Faced with charges of racial discrimination in special education evaluations and placement, the National Academy of Sciences commissioned a series of studies in the late 1970s, a major conclusion of which was, "we can find little empirical justification for categorical labelling that discriminates mildly retarded children from other children receiving compensatory education" (Heller, Holtzman, & Messick, 1982, p. 87). The academy's study reiterated points made earlier by Hobbs (1975), and an ever-growing number of studies has reinforced and expanded upon this point. Specifically, there is little educational basis on which to distinguish students placed in remedial or special programs for the "mildly handicapped," that is those called learning disabled, some of those called mentally retarded, and some of those called emotionally disturbed (Algozzine & Ysseldyke, 1981; Allington, 1983; Allington & Johnston, 1986; Jenkins, Pious & Peterson, 1987; McGill-Franzen, 1987; Wang, Reynolds, & Walberg, 1987b; and Ysseldyke, 1987). And in a petulant attack on the regular education initiative, articles featured in a special issue of the *Journal of Learning Disabilities* (January 1988) offer little to defend the current segregated patterns.

Within special education, there is also the concomitant decline in those labeled as mentally retarded (by over 300,000 between 1976–77 and 1986–87) with the rise of those labeled as learning disabled. It is a form of "classification plea bargaining" (Gartner & Lipsky, 1987, p. 373), with schools responding to the claims of racial discrimination by reclassifying students into more acceptable categories. Despite this overall decline, "the figures continue to suggest an overrepresentation of black children in EMR programs, even after further implementation of PL 94-142" (Macmillan, Hendrick, & Watkins, 1988, p. 427).

Variations in state laws and regulations defining particular categories, inaccurate evaluation systems (for a summary of the extensive literature here, see Ysseldyke, 1987), and the effects of funding schemes (discussed in the following section) all contribute to these disparities in implementing a common national law.

Something of the extent to which these distinctions are carried out is illustrated in a Washington State document designed to help local districts coordinate between and among differing programs for "students with mild learning problems" (*Program Linkage*, n.d.). Following 27 pages of text distinguishing special education into Chapter I–Regular, Chapter I–Special Education, and several state Remedial Assistance Programs, a 5-page appendix further distinguishes these, plus local district remedial programs, along 24 different axes. These include: statutory authority, regulatory authority, fund source, fund driver, application procedure, fund use, supplemental versus supplantive, bases for establishing a program, building eligibility for service, permissible curriculum areas, eligible population, basis of student selection, nature of individual student needs addressed, forms of student evaluation, student records required, allowable costs, use of material and equipment, program design, instructional location, size of instructional group, annual needs assessment, monitoring and auditing, and private school involvement. All this calls to mind the characterization by Jenkins et al. (1987) of the classroom as "a rail station, with arrivals, departures, groupings and regroupings—the teacher acting as a dispatcher and students travelling to different locations" (p. 5). What is missing is instruction and learning.

ALTERNATIVES FOR ORGANIZING SERVICES

Given the variety of criticisms of the existing organization of special education services, it is not surprising that current reform activities range across a broad spectrum. Some proposals seek to bridge the gap between the two parallel systems, others attempt to blend aspects of each together, and still others call for an end to dual systems.

Bridging Parallel Systems

The current organization of special education has developed an elaborate system to

Point to Ponder

Literally billions of dollars are spent in special education each year, and hundreds of thousands of personnel are employed in special education. Could not we in the future require by law that each child be given a free and appropriate education in the mainstream of regular education and bring to bear all the resources and personnel now in special education to help make this a reality? If we did, it would be critical to include proper safeguards to be sure that all students, including those unserved or ill-served in the past, received an appropriate education and related services within regular education.

assess and classify students for the purpose of placing them in appropriate programs, broadly organized in a bimodal design of special and general education systems. Within this basic dual system approach, various efforts have been made to bridge the gap between them.

One set of activities might be described as strengthening the holding power of the general education system. This includes the development of prereferral alternatives, including providing assistance to general education teachers to strengthen and expand their skills. The most prominent of these is the "consulting teacher" model (Huefner, 1988). Proposed prior to the passage of PL 94-142, it has gained increasing attention in the past several years—for example, in a special issue of *Teacher Education and Special Education* (Blankenship & Jordan, 1985) and in the report of the National Task Force on School Consultation (Idol, 1986). This model is being used statewide in Idaho, Massachusetts, and Vermont, as well as in districts in many other states.

An interesting design with significant potential, there is not yet sufficient data to warrant wholesale adoption of the consulting teacher model, and its advocates are careful to warn of inappropriate or premature implementation (Huefner, 1988, pp. 406–410). Moreover, in the context of this chapter's argument, the model as presently conducted continues the dual system. On the other hand, its underlying principle—assisting general education teachers to enhance their ability to educate students in a mainstream setting—is a necessary part of the larger reforms the authors propose.

Mainstreaming is a frequently used term, although it does not appear in PL 94-142. It melds two concepts worth keeping separate: 1) the general stricture for placement in the least restrictive environment (LRE) and 2) activities involving a student whose basic placement is in a special education setting who spends a portion of the day in a general education ("mainstream") setting. In this latter regard, a recent ERIC search identified over 120 studies (*Research*, 1987) in which two sets of factors predominated in determining the effectiveness of "mainstreaming": 1) the adequacy of the preparation and the appropriateness of the identification of the students to be mainstreamed; and 2) the activities in the mainstreamed class, including organization of the environment, adaptation of the curriculum, and teaching strategies. The data as to the effectiveness of this type of mainstreaming are mixed: some showing positive social benefits, others both social and academic benefits, and still others no benefits (*Research*, 1987).

The most extensive study reviewing mainstreaming (Kaufman, Agard, & Semmel, 1985) was Project PRIME (Programmed Re-Entry into Mainstreamed Education). It was conducted, however, in only one state (Texas), in the 1970s before the full implementation of PL 94-142, and was limited to students labeled as mentally retarded (which in that period included a greater percentage of students receiving special education services than is currently the case). Of continuing interest, however, is the study's finding that "the unequivocal evidence that schools and teachers make critical contributions to explaining the academic and social competence of EMR and nonhandicapped elementary grade children" (pp. 406, ff.). This supports the school effectiveness studies in general education that indicate it is the classroom and school environment that make the greatest difference in accounting for achievement.

Beyond the limits in the quality of the instruction students receive in separate special education programs (Gartner & Lipsky, 1987; Lipsky & Gartner, 1989; Wang, Reynolds, & Walberg, 1987a), there are the inadequacies of the arrangements made in the general education setting. Zigmond and colleagues have conducted some of the few studies that examined the actual conditions of mainstreaming, in both the lower grades and in high schools. Their study of mainstreaming in the 38 elementary schools in Pittsburgh found that "over 90 percent of the mildly handicapped elementary students . . . were *never* assigned to regular education academic classes" (Sansone & Zigmond, 1986, p. 455; emphasis in the original). Not only were few students involved but for those who were, their participation was limited in three ways: 1) students were scheduled for fewer than the full number of periods in the week, 2) students attended several different general education classes for the same subject, and 3) students were assigned to inappropriate (by age or level) general education classes. The opportunity "to provide preparation periods for special education teachers . . . seems to be the decisive factor in these assignments" (p. 453).

In four studies involving the mainstreaming of students labeled as learning disabled in 12 high schools, few instructional differences were found when these students were mainstreamed (Zigmond, Levin, & Laurie, 1985). The major adjustment identified was the lowering of grading standards so that the students had a better opportunity to pass the course. Given the inadequacies of the adjustments made, it is not surprising that only 1.4% of the special education students in Pittsburgh returned to general education (*Special Education*, 1986, Table 13).

Beyond such flaws in implementing "mainstreaming" efforts, there is a more fundamental problem with the "cascade" or continuum concept basic to current special education practice. This concept, considered an advancement when originally introduced in the 1960s by Deno and Reynolds, has resulted both in many students being placed inappropriately at the restricted end of the continuum and too few students moving upwards (i.e., from special education to general education). While, at least in part, these may be problems of programmatic implementation, there is a more deepseated conceptual flaw in this model. Namely,

> the "most restrictive" placement did not prepare students for the "least restrictive" placements. Parents of children in institutions and special schools were often told that their children "weren't ready" to live in the community or to attend regular neighborhood schools. The irony of this situation was that segregated settings did not prepare students with disabilities to function in integrated settings. That is to say, the skills necessary to function in integrated settings, whether in a public school, a grocery store, or a restaurant, are different from those that can be taught in a segregated environment. Many students spent their entire lives "getting ready" only to leave the segregated school without the skills they really needed to make it in the general society. (Biklen, Lehr, Searl, & Taylor, 1987, p. 10)

Taylor (1988) sharpens this critique, suggesting that the very concept of least restrictive environment needs to be reconsidered. He argues for an unrestricted commitment to integration, with the intensity of services varying according to the students' needs. This formulation is in sharp contrast to the variation of the extent of "mainstreaming" in the traditional continuum model.

Blending at the Margin

Increasingly, efforts have been underway to break down the wall between the special and general education systems. That is, there are educational programs designed to serve students now in special education, those variously called mild or moderately handicapped, in a common setting with other students with learning problems, or those "at risk." Among the various efforts are those under the rubric of the "general education initiative" launched by former U.S. Department of Education Assistant Secretary Madeleine Will. In a report to the secretary of education, Ms. Will noted that the present program designs suffer from: 1) fragmented approaches ("Many students who require help and are not learning effectively fall 'through the cracks' of a program structure based on preconceived definitions of eligibility. . . ."); 2) a dual system ("The separate administrative arrangements for special programs contribute to a lack of coordination, raise questions about leadership, cloud areas of responsibility, and obscure lines of accountability within schools."); 3) stigmatization of students (producing in students "low expectations of success, failure to persist on tasks, the belief that failures are caused by personal inadequacies, and a continued failure to learn effectively"); and 4) placement decisions becoming a battleground between parents and schools. In light of such practices, the panel called for experimental programs for students with learning problems—programs that incorporate increased instructional time, support systems for teachers, empowerment of principals to control all programs and resources at the building level, and new instructional approaches that involve "shared responsibility" between general and special education (*Educating Students*, 1986, pp. 7–9).

While garnering considerable attention, few new educational initiatives as yet have been implemented in practice. Most of what can be seen is an expansion of programs for mildly learning disabled students that were established prior to the federal report. One such program is the Adaptive Learning Environments Model (ALEM), developed by Margaret Wang (Epps & Tindal, 1987; Wang & Reynolds, 1985; Wang et al., 1987a). ALEM programs are in effect in scores of schools across the country.

Another approach, developed at the University of Washington, Seattle, has been in operation since 1980. Under this approach, professionals work with local school systems to develop programs to educate students with mild handicaps in integrated classrooms. A study of one program, in the Issaquah school district, the Integrated Classroom Model (ICM), found "the integrated classroom model as a viable alternative service delivery model for students with learning disabilities, as the results are virtually indistinguishable from those of the resource room program. Any significant differences found supported the integrated model . . . " (Affleck, Madge, Adams, & Lowenbraun, 1988, pp. 345ff.). As for the general education students, "there were no distinguishable differences in achievement between these students in an ICM classroom and those in a classroom with no handicapped peers" (Affleck et al., 1988, p. 346). Furthermore, the staffing of the ICM program produces a significant cost savings (about $50,000 a year in an elementary school). Thus, the ICM program costs less than a segregated program, it fully integrates students, and produces equal learning as segregated programs.

In Olympia, WA, in Project MERGE (Maximizing Educational Remediation within General Education), students with mild handicaps are served in an integrated setting that also includes low-achieving, nonhandicapped students. While the ICM program serves students in an integrated setting with a single teacher, Project MERGE brings support staff into integrated classrooms, both to assist the regular education teacher and to work directly with students. As with the ICM program, the evaluation of Project MERGE indicates achievement benefits for students, greater integration, and cost savings. Of particular note is the inclusion of behaviorally disabled students, those generally seen as the most difficult to integrate. And, a promising note for the future, the support given in these enhanced general education classes has reduced the number of students labeled as handicapped. Indeed, the program is designed to provide assistance to all students without the requirement that they first be labelled (Wood, MacDonald, & Siegelman, 1987).

At the same time that questions are increasingly being asked about services for those labeled as mildly or moderately handicapped, concerns are being expressed about other students in "pullout" programs such as Chapter I and other remedial efforts. Of concern is the wide variety of school programs that have been created to provide special, compensatory, and/or remedial educational services for students not well served in the general education system. Despite the numerous improvements that have resulted from such efforts, they nonetheless have created large, separate, costly, and overall ineffective systems. Furthermore, they have left the mainstream largely unaffected—that is, except for having extruded from it an ever-growing group of students who do not fit an ever-narrowing standard of normalcy.

Still other alternative efforts have taken several different forms. Some are sponsored by state education departments, as those discussed in Washington State (Jenkins et al., 1987; Olson, 1988; *Program Linkage*, n.d.). Important new efforts are underway in Delaware, Iowa, and Pennsylvania. Others are the work of individual school systems, such as the Minneapolis plan, supported by the General Mills Foundation, to establish an academy that will eliminate pullout programs in serving a full cross-section of the city's pupils, K–6 (Gold, 1988). Still others are efforts at individual schools, such as the Edward Smith Elementary School in Syracuse, NY, and the Key School in Indianapolis, IN. Some researchers, approaching these issues from the perspective of remedial education programs, have called for the redesign of both remedial and special education to serve what are viewed as students with common needs (Allington, 1989; Allington & Johnston, 1986; Allington & McGill-Franzen, 1989; McGill-Franzen, 1987). Other educators have identified specific instructional strategies, such as cooperative learning, for integrating special education and remedial services within the regular program (Johnson, Johnson, Holubec, & Roy, 1984; Slavin, 1987). More recently, educators and private industry have collaborated in a number of efforts to address the role of secondary students "at risk." For example, the Council of Chief State School Officers has proposed to "guarantee" to students least likely to graduate from school access to quality education programs (*Elements*, 1987). Unlike previous efforts by governors (Honetschlager & Cohen, 1988) and the business community (*Children in Need*, 1987), the council's proposal explicitly includes students now labeled as handicapped.

A Single System

The changes described in the previous two sections, while positive, nonetheless continue to educate students with disabilities in dual systems. They represent, to one extent or another, the continuation of an old paradigm (Kuhn, 1962) regarding the nature of students and, thus, of the appropriate organization of educational programs.

It is a paradigm that

> operates to identify among persons with disabilities areas of deficits and "deviancies," as determined by the consensus of those persons who assume responsibility (and control) over their behavior, and buttressed by an array of

diagnostic instruments and surveys that depict either expected "normal" development or assumed community standards for behavior and conduct. The assumption is, of course, that once having identified the problems associated with the disability, the environment can be arranged, controlled, or otherwise manipulated to bring about the desired change in the student. This orientation, variously referred to as "prescriptive-teaching," "remedial," "let's fix it," and so on always carried with it the (at least) implicit assumption that persons with disabilities are somehow less than normal or, at its worst, "deviant." (Guess & Thompson, in press)

A dual system continues to operate despite the data indicating the lack of its effectiveness. Ysseldyke (1987) summarizes that data as follows:

> 1) There is currently no defensible psychometric methodology for differentiating students into categories. . . .
>
> 2) There is no evidence to support the contention that specific categories of students learn differently. . . .
>
> 3) The current system used by public schools to classify exceptional children does not meet the criteria of reliability, coverage, logical consistency, utility, and acceptance to users. (p. 265)

The basic assumptions underlying the present special education programs are summarized by Bogdan and Kugelmass (1984).

> 1) Disability is a condition that individuals have;
>
> 2) Disabled/typical is a useful and objective distinction;
>
> 3) Special education is a rationally conceived and coordinated system of services that help children labelled disabled;
>
> 4) Progress in the field is made by improving diagnosis, intervention, and technology. (p. 173)

Skrtic (1986) argues that the first two preceding assumptions are challenged by different understandings of disability, ones that are less rooted in biology and psychology "and derive more from sociological, political, and cultural theories of deviance, and which provide many different perspectives on virtually every aspect of special education and 'disability' . . . " (p. 6). Skrtic (1987) goes on to argue that based upon the inappropriate understandings,

> current school organization creates—and can do nothing but create—students with mild disabilities as artifacts of the system, and, furthermore, [current] efforts to reform the system—without replacing it with an entirely different configuration—do little to eliminate mild disabilities or their effects, produce even more students with mild disabilities, and create a new and largely hidden class of student casualties. (p. 3)

A different conceptualization of a single system is emerging. This formulation argues that "there are not two distinct types of students—special and regular. . . . [R]egardless of any designated cutoffs, all students still differ in varying degrees from one another along the same continuums of differences" (Stainback & Stainback, 1984, p. 102). There are two points worth emphasizing: first, that students are more alike than different; and, second, that the differences among students are not along a single axis, the old-fashioned "g" of intelligence, but that there are multiple intelligences (Gardner, 1983; Goldman & Gardner, 1989) to which schools and their organization must adapt.

While much of the criticism of the current organization of special education comes from the actual practice, increasingly there are more fundamental challenges to its basic conceptualization (Berres & Knoblock, 1987; Biklen, 1985, 1987; Biklen et al., 1987; Bogdan & Kugelmass, 1984; Gartner & Lipsky, 1987; Lipsky & Gartner, 1987, 1989; Skrtic, 1986, 1987b; Stainback & Stainback, 1984).

Some of these formulations focus on the nature of students, while others emphasize the conceptualization of special education.

Stainback and Stainback (1984) disagree with a dual system and emphasize the shared characteristics of students. They argue: 1) that there are not two distinct groups of students, regular or normal students and others who deviate from the norm, but rather that all students vary across a range of physical, intellectual, psychological, and social characteristics; and 2) that it is not only special education students who can benefit from (or indeed need) individualized services, but that all students can benefit.

The authors have pointed out that the current models reflect disdain for persons with disabilities and that only when such individuals are seen as "capable of achievement and worthy of respect" (Lipsky & Gartner, 1987, p. 69) will new, more appropriate school designs be developed. The role of persons with disabilities and the disabilities rights movement is central in both this conceptualization and its incorporation in the education of students labeled as handicapped (Fine & Asch, 1988; Funk, 1987; Gliedman & Roth, 1980; Hahn, 1987, 1989; Lipsky & Gartner, 1987, 1989).

Programs of full (or nearly so) integration are being carried out in a few states, such as Iowa, Pennsylvania, Vermont and Washington; in whole districts such as Johnson City, NY; and in individual schools in communities such as Syracuse, NY, and in the Riverview School District, PA. These and other designs are discussed elsewhere in this volume; see also the discussion in Lipsky and Gartner (1989), including Sailor's discussion of integration of students with the most severe impairments.

* * *

Shifting from the students to the characteristics of the environment and from schools to the larger society, Groce (1985) describes the community on Martha's Vineyard in the 19th century where persons who were deaf were full participants in community life as workers, friends, neighbors, and family members.

> The fact that a society could adjust to disabled individuals, rather than requiring them to do all the adjusting, as is the case in American society as a whole, raises important questions about the rights of the disabled and the responsibilities of those who are not. The Martha's Vineyard experience suggests strongly that the concept of a handicap is an arbitrary social category. And if it is a question of definition, rather than a universal given, perhaps it can be redefined, and many of the cultural preconceptions summarized in the term "handicapped," as it is now used, eliminated.
>
> The most important lesson to be learned from Martha's Vineyard is that disabled people can be full and useful members of a community if the community makes an effort to include them. (p. 108)

FUNDING PATTERNS

In the 1982–83 school year, federal, state, and local funding of special education and related services totaled $9.23 billion (*Tenth Annual Report*, 1988, Table BJ1). The federal total barely exceeds 10%, despite PL 94-142 provisions for 40% federal support.

Despite this massive national expenditure, there are no comprehensive studies of special education finances. A few U.S. Department of Education-commissioned studies have collected some data (Kakalik, Furry, Thomas, & Carney, 1981; Wright et al., 1982), and an as yet unpublished study conducted by Decision Resources Corporation is analyzing data from 60 Local Education Agencies (LEAs) and 18 State Education Agencies (SEAs). However, special education funding is a topic for the most part ignored (at least in the literature) by special educators. For example, a 391-page CEC-sponsored symposium on the future of special education contains not a single chapter on financing special education (Prehm, 1987), nor were any of the invited sessions at a 1987 CEC National Conference on the Future of Special Education on this topic.

To date, the richest body of data is available from the Collaborative Study of Children with Special Needs (Raphael, Singer, & Walker, 1985; Singer & Butler, 1987; Singer & Raphael, 1988). The study reports on a wide range of special education program factors in five city school districts (Charlotte-Mecklenburg, NC; Houston; Milwaukee; Rochester; and Santa Clara County, CA), for the period 1982–85. The study's findings confirm those of other studies that special education services overall cost about twice as much per pupil as do those for students in general education. There is a considerable range in per-pupil cost among the five sites, depending largely upon the level of teacher salaries, and at all the sites depending upon handicapping condition (from a mean expenditure of $5,414 per student who is speech impaired to $10,791 for a student who is physically or sensory impaired). The findings point out that contrary to "[t]he stereotypical view . . . that the education of a handful of severely impaired children costs huge amounts of money. . . . [i]n fact, because the most expensive students tend to be in the low prevalence groups, expenditures for these students do not dominate special education budgets" (Singer & Butler, 1987, p. 147). Of course, given the nature of the study, the generalizability of the data to the country at large is limited. Indeed, the high cost of placements for severely impaired students in private schools has led to a gubernatorially appointed work group in Massachusetts to reexamine special education funding (Viadero, 1988a, p. 12).

While the data here are extensive and suggestive, they do not address some of the fundamental policy issues, particularly the extent to which funding affects program. For example, Noel and Fuller (1985) report that identification rates are influenced by state and local expenditures; Epps and Tindal (1987) characterize this as "the yoking of funding to child counts [which] establishes a bounty system that generates an active search for students with mildly handicapping conditions. . . ." (p. 242).

Brinker and Thorpe (1985) point out that state policies affect the extent to which schools integrate students with severe disabilities. One of the drafters of PL 94-142 summarizes this issue as follows:

> Funding formulas that create incentives for more restrictive and separate class placement or that support particular configurations of services based on special education teacher allocations maintain an inflexible program structure and fail to allow models that encourage students to remain in general classrooms with resource room or individualized help. One need only examine the variation in statistics between general classroom placements at the state level and the state funding formulas to know that states that provide financial incentives for separate placements, or which traditionally have had dual systems of services, place students disproportionately in more restrictive placements. States such as New York, Illinois, Florida, Maryland, the District of Columbia, Pennsylvania, New Hampshire, and New Jersey have much higher rates of separate classroom placements for certain disability groups for these reasons. (Walker, 1987, pp. 110 ff.)

According to this report, while there are appropriate concerns regarding financial accountability, the present systems maintain "organizational patterns that may be dysfunctional to the integration of disabled

Point to Ponder

Many state departments, federal agencies, and other organizations espouse integration objectives, but their financial arrangements encourage segregation. More money is usually given for classifying, labeling, and segregating students than for providing an appropriate education to all students in integrated classrooms and schools.

children in schools" (p. 111). The author concludes, on this point, that rather than "the infinite categorization of financial supports," there needs to be "greater reliance on program monitoring and the resulting educational achievement by the student . . ." (p. 111).

The circle is then complete: separation, which is the current norm, neither is educationally sound nor essential for financial accountability.

FUNDING FOR INTEGRATION AND QUALITY

The funding designs for educational (and other human services) programs provide more than resources to support the activities. In addition, they set the parameters for the programs. For example, in the Olympia, WA, program described earlier, the power of the sustaining effort was such that the number of students "qualified" for special education was reduced and, thus, the stream of funds that supported their integration model nearly dried up. Consequently, in order to maintain the program and continue to sustain students in an integrated setting, several months of fall 1987 were spent evaluating and certifying students as "handicapped." Yet the youngsters continued to be served in the same integrated setting. While the Washington State education department cooperated in supporting integration efforts, the New York State education department refused to reimburse the New York City Public Schools for an ALEM project (which the authors initiated). They claimed, in what can only be described as a "Catch 22," that if the students could be mainstreamed full time, they were not really handicapped! (Gartner, 1986; Wang & Reynolds, 1985). But, of course, the state education department was not willing to follow that argument to its logical conclusion, namely, a single integrated system.

Not only do funds and funding patterns directly affect the organization of programs, but they become a battleground. The particular categorial divisions have become the basis for (some) parent and advocacy groups to organize, in order to protect or gain additional funds for "their" children. A notable exception to this parochialism is The Association for Persons with Severe Handicaps (TASH).

In addition, overall, the yoking of funding to the current bimodal division between special and general education leads those concerned with the special needs of students now labeled as handicapped to fear that a consequence of integration plans will be to divert funds from such students. Understandably, parents and advocates remember the pre-PL 94-142 treatment of these students, and in the light of current funding constraints fear that—as in the pre-*Mills*[1] era—they again will be at the end of the queue for funds. And, now, with the pool funds expanded for the needs of such children, it would be doubly offensive to do so.

The resource allocation question, as with the programmatic issues, then becomes one of how to assure fair treatment of all students in a new, integrated configuration. Funding schemes must be consonant with program designs; indeed, they ought to contribute to the achievement of program goals. This should be true both in the school and in the political arena. That is, the way programs are funded should encourage full integration.

CONCLUSION

The program examples cited here, and in other chapters in this volume (see also Lipsky & Gartner, 1989), while not the only ones in existence, do represent some of the major efforts currently available. They all provide integrated settings without ignoring the individual needs of students, whether labeled as handicapped or not. By providing for the individual needs of each student, a unitary system is not a dumping ground; rather, it is a refashioned mainstream.

At present, some integrated programs and some integrated schools exist, but no whole districts. Indeed, it is not unlike the situation in the reform of general education a few years ago. But as in that effort, when the late Ron Edmonds argued that if some schools could effectively educate low-income and minority students, then others—with commitment—could also do so (Edmonds, 1979b), so too, here in special education. Thomas K. Gilhool, then a lawyer at the Public Interest Law Center of Philadelphia (and now secretary of education, Commonwealth of Pennsylvania), and E. Stutman, put forward what they called the "developmental twin" argument. "If a child with a particular type of disability can be successfully integrated, with special services in a regular class or school, then why can't all children with the same type and level of disability also be integrated?" (Gilhool & Stutman, 1978). A decade after this question was posed, there are enough examples of quality and integration for the full range of students for Gilhool and Stutman's challenge to be answered with commitment and action.

[1]In *Mills v. Board of Education* (348 F. Supp. 866), the federal district court ruled that a district's financial exigencies could not be the basis for either excluding students with handicaps or for funding their needs only with what was left over.

REFERENCES

Affleck, J.Q., Madge, S., Adams, A., & Lowenbraun, S. (1988). Integrated classrooms versus resource model: Academic viability effectiveness. *Exceptional Children, 54*(4), 339–348.

Algozzine, G., & Ysseldyke, J.E. (1981). Special education services for normal students: Better safe than sorry? *Exceptional Children, 48*, 238–243.

Allington, R.L. (1983). The reading instruction provided readers of differing ability. *Elementary School Journal, 83*, 548–559.

Allington, R.L. (1989). Integrating Instruction. In D.K. Lipsky & A. Gartner (Eds.), *Beyond separate education: Quality education for all.* Baltimore: Paul H. Brookes Publishing Co.

Allington, R.L., & Johnston, P. (1986). The coordination among regular classroom reading programs and targeted support programs. In B.I. Williams, P.A. Richmond, & B.J. Mason (Eds.), *Designs for compensatory education: Conference proceedings and papers.* Washington, DC: Research and Evaluation Associates.

Allington, R.L., & McGill-Franzen, A. (1989). Different programs, indifferent instruction. In D.K. Lipsky & A. Gartner (Eds.), *Beyond separate education: Quality education for all.* Baltimore: Paul H. Brookes Publishing Co.

Berres, M.S., & Knoblock, P. (Eds.). (1987). *Program models for mainstreaming: Integrating students with moderate to severe disabilities.* Rockville, Md: Aspen Systems.

Bickel, W.E., & Bickel, D.D. (1986). Effective schools, classrooms, and institutions: Implications for special education. *Exceptional Children 52*(5), 489–500.

Biklen, D. (1985). *Achieving the complete school: Strategies for effective mainstreaming.* New York: Teachers College Press.

Biklen, D. (1987). In pursuit of integration. In M.S. Berres & P. Knoblock (Eds.), *Program models for mainstreaming: Integrating students with moderate to severe disabilities.* Rockville, MD: Aspen Systems.

Biklen, D., Lehr, S., Searl, S.J., & Taylor, S.J. (1987). *Purposeful integration . . . inherently equal.* Boston: Technical Assistance for Parent Programs.

Blankenship, C.S., & Jordan, L. (Eds.). (1985). *Teacher Education and Special Education 8* (3), (Special Issue).

Bogdan, R., & Kugelmass, J. (1984). Case studies of mainstreaming: A symbolic interactionist approach to special schooling. In L. Barton & S. Tomlinson (Eds.), *Special Education and Social Interests.* London: Croom-Helm.

Brinker, R.P., & Thorpe, M.E. (1985). Some empirically derived hypotheses about the influence of state policy on degree of integration of severely handicapped students. *Remedial and Special Education, 6,* 18–26.

Children in need: Investment strategies for the educationally disadvantaged. (1987). New York: Committee for Economic Development.

Crowner, T.T. (1985). A taxonomy of special education finance. *Exceptional Children, 51*(5), 503–508.

Edmonds, R.R. (1979a). Effective schools for the urban poor. *Educational Leadership, 3,* 15–27.

Edmonds, R.R. (1979b). Some schools work and more can. *Social Policy, 9*(5), 28–32.

Educating students with learning problems—A school responsibility. A report to the secretary. (1986). Washington, DC: U.S. Department of Education.

Elements of a model state statute to provide educational entitlements for at-risk students. (1987). Washington, DC: Council of Chief State School Officers.

Epps, S., & Tindal, G. (1987). The effectiveness of differential programming in serving students with mild handicaps: Placement options and institutional programing. In M.C. Wang, M.C. Reynolds, & H.J. Walberg (Eds.), *Handbook of special education research and practice, Vol. 1. Learner characteristics and adaptive education.* New York: Pergamon.

Fine, M., & Asch, A. (1988). Disability beyond stigma: Social interaction, discrimination, and activism. *Journal of Social Issues.*

First, J. (1987). *Special education reform.* Boston, MA: National Coalition of Advocates for Students.

Funk, R. (1987). Disability rights: From caste to class in the context of civil rights. In A. Gartner & T. Joe (Eds.), *Images of the disabled/ disabling images.* New York: Praeger.

Gardner, H. (1983). *Frames of mind: The theory of multiple intelligences.* New York: Basic Books.

Gartner, A. (1986). Disabling help: Special education at the crossroads. *Exceptional Children, 53*(1), 72–76.

Gartner, A., & Lipsky, D.K. (1987). Beyond special education: Toward a quality system for all students. *Harvard Educational Review, 57*(4), 367–395.

Gilhool, T., & Stutman, E. (1978). Integration of severely handicapped students: Toward criteria for implementing and enforcing the integration imperative of P.L. 94-142 and Section 5094. In *Criteria for evaluation of least restrictive environment provision.* Washington, DC: U.S. Department of Health, Education, & Welfare.

Gliedman, W., & Roth, W. (1980). *The unexpected minority: Handicapped children in America.* New York: Harcourt, Brace, Jovanovich.

Gold, D.L. (1988). Firm to fund model school in Minneapolis. *Education Week, 7*(24), 8.

Goldman, J., & Gardner, H. (1989). Multiple paths to educational effectiveness. In D.K. Lipsky & A. Gartner (Eds.), *Beyond separate education:*

Quality education for all. Baltimore: Paul H. Brookes Publishing.

Goodman, L. (1985). The effective schools movement and special education. *Teaching Exceptional Children, 17*, 102–105.

Groce, N.E. (1985). *Everyone spoke sign here: Hereditary deafness on Martha's Vineyard*. Cambridge: Harvard University Press.

Guess, D., & Thompson, B. (in press). Preparation of personnel to educate students with severe and multiple disabilities: A time for change? In L. Meyer, C. Peck, & L. Brown (Eds.), *Critical issues in the lives of people with severe disabilities*.

Hahn, H. (1987). Civil rights for disabled Americans: The formulation of a political agenda. In A. Gartner & T. Joe (Eds.), *Images of the disabled/disabling images*. New York: Praeger.

Hahn, H. (1989). The politics of special education. In D.K. Lipsky, & A. Gartner (Eds.) *Beyond separate education: Quality education for all*. Baltimore: Paul H. Brookes Publishing Co.

Heller, K.A., Holtzman, W.H., & Messick, S. (Eds.). (1982). *Placing children in special education: A strategy for equity*. Washington, DC: National Academy Press.

Hobbs, N. (1975). *The future of children*. San Francisco: Jossey Bass.

Honetschlager, D., & Cohen, M. (1988).The governors restructure schools. *Educational Leadership, 45*(5), 42–43.

Huefner, D.S. (1988). The counseling teacher model: Risks and opportunities. *Exceptional Children, 54*(5), 403–414.

Idol, L. (1986). *Collaborative school consultation*. Report of the National Task Force on School Consultation. Reston, VA: Council for Exceptional Children.

Jenkins, J.R., Pious, C., & Peterson, D. (1987). *Exploring the validity of a unified learning program for remedial and handicapped students*. Unpublished manuscript.

Jewell, J. (1985). One school's search for excellence. *Teaching Exceptional Children, 17*, 140–144.

Johnson, D., Johnson, R., Holubec, E., & Roy, P. (1984). *Of learning: Cooperation in the classroom*. Alexandria, VA: Association for Supervision and Curriculum Development.

Kakalik, J., Furry, W., Thomas, M.A., & Carney, M.F. (1981). *The cost of special education*. Santa Monica, CA: Rand Corp.

Kauffman, J.M., Lloyd, J.W., & McKinney, J.D. (Eds.). (1988). *Journal of Learning Disabilities, 21*(1), (Special Issue).

Kaufman, M., Agard, J.A., & Semmel, M.I. (1985). *Mainstreaming: Learners and their environments*. Cambridge, MA: Brookline Books.

Knoll, J., & Meyer, L. (N.D.). *Principles and practices for school integration of students with severe disabilities: An overview of the literature*. Syracuse, NY: Center on Human Policy.

Kuhn, T.S. (Ed.). (1962). *The structure of scientific revolutions*. Chicago: University of Chicago Press.

Lezotte, L. (1989). School improvement based on the effective schools research. In D.K. Lipsky & A. Gartner (Eds.), *Beyond separate education: Quality education for all*. Baltimore: Paul H. Brookes Publishing Co.

Lipsky, D.K., & Gartner, A. (1987). Capable of achievement and worthy of respect: Education for the handicapped as if they were full-fledged human beings. *Exceptional Children, 54*(1), 69–74.

Lipsky, D.K., & Gartner, A. (Eds.). (1989). *Beyond separate education: Quality education for all*. Baltimore: Paul H. Brookes Publishing Co.

Macmillan, D.L., Hendrick, I.G., & Watkins, A.V. (1988). Impact of *Diana, Larry P.,* and P.L. 94-142 on minority students. *Exceptional Children, 54*(5), 426–432.

McGill-Franzen, A. (1987). Failure to learn to read: Formulating a problem. *Reading Research Quarterly, 22*, 475–490.

Ninth annual report to Congress on the implementation of the Education of the Handicapped Act. (1987). Washington, DC: U.S. Department of Education.

Noel, M.M., & Fuller, B.C. (1985). The social policy construction of special education: The impact of state characteristics on identification and integration of handicapped children. *Remedial and Special Education, 6*, 27–35.

Olson, L. (1988). A Seattle principal defies the conventional wisdom. *Education Week 7*(29), 1, 22 ff.

Peterson, D., Albert, S.S., Foxworth, A.M., Cox, L.S., & Tilley, B.K. (1985). Effective schools for all students: Current efforts and future directions. *Teaching Exceptional Children, 17*, 106–110.

Prehm, H.J. (1987). *The future of special education: Proceedings of the May 1986 CEC Symposium*. Reston, VA: ERIC Clearinghouse on Handicapped and Gifted Children.

Program linkage: Coordinating programs for stu-

dents with mild learning problems. (n.d.). Olympia, WA: Office of the Superintendent of Public Instruction.

Raphael, E.S., Singer, J.D., & Walker, D.K. (1985). Per pupil expenditures on special education in three metropolitan districts. *Journal of Education Finance, 11*(1), 69–88.

Research on the effectiveness of mainstreaming. (1987). Reston, VA: ERIC Clearinghouse on Handicapped and Gifted Children.

Reynolds, M.C., & Lakin, K.C. (1987). Noncategorical special education: Models for research and practice. In M.C. Wang, M.C. Reynolds, & H.J. Walberg (Eds.), *Handbook of special education: Research and practice, Vol. 1. Learner characteristics and adaptive education.* New York: Pergamon.

Rutter, M., Maugham, B., Mortimore, P., Ouston, J., & Smith, A. (1975). *Fifteen thousand hours: Secondary schools and their effects on children.* New York: John Wiley & Sons.

Sansone, J., & Zigmond, N. (1986). Evaluating mainstreaming through an evaluation of students' schedules, *Exceptional Children, 52*(5), 452–458.

Singer, J.D., & Butler, J.A. (1987). The Education for All Handicapped Children Act: Schools as agents of social reform. *Harvard Educational Review, 57*(2), 125–152.

Singer, J.D., & Raphael, E.S. (1988). *Per pupil expenditures for special education: To whom are limited resources provided?* Final Report to the Office of Special Education. Washington, DC: U.S. Department of Education.

Skrtic, T. (1986). The crisis in special education knowledge: A perspective on perspective. *Focus on Exceptional Children, 18*(7), 1–16.

Skrtic, T. (1987a). *An organizational analysis of special education reform.* Lawrence: The University of Kansas.

Skrtic, T. (1987b). *Prenuptial agreements necessary for wedding special education and general education.* Paper presented to American Education and Research Association, Washington, DC.

Slavin, R.E. (1987). Cooperative learning and the cooperative school. *Educational Leadership* 45(1), 7–13.

Special education: Views from America's cities. (1986). Washington, DC: Council of Great City Schools.

Stainback, W., & Stainback, S. (1984). A rationale for the merger of special and regular education. *Exceptional Children, 51*(2), 102–111.

Taylor, S.J. (1982). From segregation to integration: Strategies for integrating severely handicapped students in normal school and community settings. *Journal of The Association for Persons with Severe Handicaps, 7,* 42–29.

Taylor, S.J. (1988). Caught in the continuum: A critical analysis of the principle of the least restrictive environment. *Journal of The Association for Persons with Severe Handicaps, 13,* 41–53.

Tenth Annual Report To Congress on the Implementation of the Education of the Handicapped Act. (1988). Washington, DC: U.S. Department of Education.

Viadero, D. (1988a, March 2). Massachusetts officials take aim at special education costs. *Education Week* 1, 12.

Viadero, D. (1988b, March 2). Researchers' critique escalates the debate over "regular education" for all students. *Education Week, 1,* 16.

Viadero, D. (1988c, March 2). Study documents jumps in special education enrollments. *Education Week* 1, 17.

Walker, L. (1987). Procedural rights in the wrong system: Special education is not enough. In A. Gartner & T. Joe (Eds.), *Images of the disabled/Disabling images.* New York: Praeger.

Wang, M.C., & Reynolds, M.C. (1985). Avoiding the "catch 22" in special education reform. *Exceptional Children, 51,* 497–502.

Wang, M.C., Reynolds, M.C., & Walberg, H.J. (Eds.). (1987a). *Handbook of special education: Research and practice, Vol. 1. Learning characteristics and adaptive education.* New York: Pergamon.

Wang, M.C., Reynolds, M.C., & Walberg, H.J. (1987b). *Repairing the second system for students with special needs.* Paper presented at 1987 Wingspread Conference on the Education of Children with Special Needs, Racine, WI.

Wood, S., MacDonald, M., & Siegelman, L. (1987). Seriously behaviorally disabled children in the mainstream. In M.S. Berres & P. Knoblock (Eds.), *Program models for mainstreaming: Integrating students with moderate to severe disabilities.* Rockville, MD: Aspen Systems.

Wright, A.R., Cooperstein, R., Renneker, E., & Padilla, C. (1982). *Local implementation of PL 94-142: Final report of a longitudinal study.* Menlo Park, CA: SRI International.

Ysseldyke, J.E. (1987). Classification of handicapped students. In M.C. Wang, M.C. Reynolds, & H.J. Walberg (Eds.), *Handbook of spe-*

cial education: Research and practice, Vol. 1. Learner characteristics and adaptive education. New York: Pergamon.

Zigmond, N., Levin, E., & Laurie, T.E. (1985). Managing the mainstream: An analysis of teacher attitudes and student performance in mainstream high school programs. *Journal of Learning Disabilities, 18*(9), 535–541.

CHAPTER 9

Facilitating Merger through Personnel Preparation

Susan Stainback and William Stainback

Reynolds and Birch (1982) have pointed out that "the whole history of education for exceptional students can be told in terms of one steady trend that can be described as progressive inclusion" (p. 27). Great strides in this movement have been reflected in the past several decades by the emergence of concepts such as deinstitutionalization, normalization, integration, mainstreaming, zero rejection, and delabeling. More recently, the movement has been reflected in proposals to unify or merge special and regular education (Forest, 1987; Gartner & Lipsky, 1987; Lipsky & Gartner, 1987; Stainback & Stainback, 1984, 1985, 1988; Strully, 1986). Although historical reviews of education have indicated that the trend is in the direction of eventually integrating and merging special and regular education into a single system (see Chapter 1), there is still much to accomplish.

Institutions of higher education have the opportunity to lead the way. By collaboration, which is well under way in many colleges and universities, and the integration of personnel, programs, and resources in special and regular education departments, the goal of developing a unified comprehensive regular educational system designed to meet the unique needs of all students in the elementary and secondary schools can be facilitated. That is, colleges and universities can set the stage for integrating special and regular education in the schools by merging at the higher education level.

The impact that such a change in higher education potentially could have on facilitating merger in the elementary and secondary schools has been clearly stated by Sarason (1982):

> School personnel are graduates of our colleges and universities. It is there that they learn there are at least two types of human beings and if you choose to work with one of them you render yourself *legally* and conceptually incompetent to work with the others. . . . What we see in our public schools is a mirror image of what exists in colleges and universities. (p. 258)

The primary purpose of this chapter is to suggest some steps that could be initiated in higher education to facilitate the integration or merger of special and regular education. Before doing so, however, a rationale for merger in higher education is outlined.

RATIONALE FOR MERGER IN HIGHER EDUCATION

The advantages of merging special and regular education in the elementary and secondary schools have been discussed in a number of places in the professional literature (e.g. Gartner & Lipsky, 1987; Stainback & Stainback, 1984, 1985; and throughout this book). The advantages include: 1) all students could be approached as individuals and provided educational programs and related services based on their unique educational profiles, 2) all school personnel would be brought together into a more cohesive, integrated system of education, 3) the resources and talents currently invested in the duplication of services and in classifying and labeling students could be used to help make education more adaptive, individualized, and flexible to the unique needs of all students, and 4) all students could have their educational and related needs met in the mainstream of regular education as a normal, expected and standard practice. In addition to these advantages, a number of benefits could potentially occur by merging the special and regular education fields in higher education. For instance:

1. Faculty in higher education would not be split into those concerned with preparing educators for students classified as handicapped and those concerned with preparing educators for nonhandicapped students. With the entire faculty sharing a common goal to prepare the best possible educators for all students, the diversity in expertise across faculty members could be capitalized upon to strengthen the educational preparation program offered all educators.

2. By merging in higher education, the separation of educators during their preparation into one group focused on preparing to work with so-called normal students and another group focused on preparing to work with students labeled as handicapped need not occur. This separation impedes the goals of integration in elementary and secondary schools, because it ultimately leads to some teachers being responsible for and teaching students with handicaps, while others teach nonhandicapped students. In a merged higher education system, all school personnel would be prepared to work with any students (disabled, normal, or gifted) who could benefit from their area of expertise, eliminating the unnecessary separation of students labeled handicapped and nonhandicapped based on teacher preparation.

3. Merger in higher education could set the stage for preparing all educators to approach students as individuals who require educational programs and services based on their unique needs, interests, and capabilities. At present, in a nonmerged system, educators are generally prepared to approach students on the basis of whether they are labeled as handicapped or nonhandicapped. This is an educationally unsound approach, since the presence or absence of one or more characteristics on which a handicapping label is often based has been found to be an insufficient, and sometimes not even relevant, basis on which to build an educational program (Lilly, 1979). Further, when students (or any individuals) are approached according to a categorical affiliation, whether it be handicapped/nonhandicapped, male/female, black/white, or any other categorical grouping, they are denied the individual consideration they deserve. As noted by Reynolds and Balow (1972): "In all of society there is a rising revulsion against simplistic categorization of human beings" (p. 357). A merger in higher education could lead the way in helping education to break away from this discriminatory practice.

4. Finally, as noted early in this chapter, merger in higher education could set a model for merger in the elementary and secondary schools. In general, the educational organizational arrangement learned by educators during their preparation will influence what they perceive as appropriate and what they follow when working in the education field (Sarason, 1982). Demonstrating a commitment to and the benefits of operating a single, unified, comprehensive system of education in higher education could set the stage for its implementation and maintenance in the elementary and secondary schools.

STEPS TO FACILITATE MERGER IN HIGHER EDUCATION

A number of steps could be taken to promote merger in higher education. The following is a series of steps that could be used as one approach to unify special and regular education into a single system within colleges and universities.

Step 1: Strengthen Collaborative and Cooperative Efforts

The first step toward merger would be to enhance any existing collaborative and cooperative efforts between special and regular education. This might take the form of representatives from special and regular education convening in formal and informal meetings to discuss: common concerns, problems, and goals; what content is similar and dissimilar across departments; how faculty expertise could be shared; and what joint teaching, research, and service activities might be organized. This could set the stage for merger by encouraging faculty to become more interdependent and by helping them understand and respect the contributions each could make to an integrated, merged higher education structure.

Step 2: Work to Restructure Organizational Units

Once strong collaborative efforts are established, the merger of special and regular education in higher education could be facilitated by restructuring organizational units. This could occur in a number of ways. For example, a special education department might merge with a curriculum and instruction department, or whatever regular education department seemed most appropriate and receptive. An alternative to this would be for the faculty in special education to individually join the regular education department that most closely matched their area of expertise. A special education faculty member with expertise in administration and finance, for instance, might join the educational administration department, while a special education faculty member with expertise in teaching strat-

Point to Ponder

Preparation of special education teachers creates a safety valve for universities and colleges. Given special education's existence, programs of general teacher preparation have not had to accept full responsibility for preparing prospective teachers to accommodate the range of students they will routinely encounter in integrated classrooms. (Pugach, 1988)

egies might join the curriculum and instruction department.

Another option might be to simply rename and reorganize present-day special education departments into regular education departments, such as a department of consulting and supportive services, wherein consulting personnel and support facilitators are prepared to work in integrated schools and classrooms. Consulting personnel in community-referenced instruction, alternative communication systems, supported employment, behavior management, and the like, could be prepared in such departments, along with support facilitators, with the competencies and skills necessary to serve as team teachers and to facilitate within regular education natural networks of friendships; locate resources and expertise in braille, sign language or whatever; and/or organize teacher and student assistance teams. (See Chapter 6 for more details about support facilitators.) Such departments might change the titles of their courses from, for example, "Introduction to Exceptional Children" to "Introduction to Individual Differences" or from "Curriculum Planning for Students with Severe Handicaps" to "Designing Age-Appropriate and Community-Referenced Curriculum." Courses in how to facilitate support networks to help classroom teachers and all students function and succeed in heterogeneous regular education classes would be needed, as would courses on how to collaborate with, team teach, and/or provide consultative help to students and teachers. As visualized here, prospective school personnel majoring or specializing in such areas would *not* be prepared to work with any category of students such as students with mild or severe handicaps, but instead would be prepared as regular educators to work in regular education with regular class teachers or any students, disabled or not disabled, who needed their particular expertise. In addition, the faculty as well as students in such departments would need to be viewed as regular educators and become an integral part of all regular education programs and activities.

To become an integral member of a regular education structure, faculty previously associated with special education would need to determine what area of expertise they could offer: behavior management, curricular-based assessment procedures, support facilitation, individualized and adaptive instruction, interdisciplinary teaming, alternative communication systems, community-referenced instruction, and/or supported and competitive employment. By identifying their areas of instructional expertise, faculty previously associated with special education could move away from being identified with a deviant subgroup or category of the student population. As a result, they would be in a position to prepare prospective and/or practicing school personnel in an instructional expertise area, rather than preparing school personnel to work with a category of students (e.g., mildly handicapped, severely handicapped, or gifted). Also, by organizing in this way they would be organized in the same manner as current regular educators are organized, that is, according to instructional categories.

Step 3: Reorganize Program Offerings and Content

The reorganization of program offerings and content is divided into two parts. The first is the delineation of core courses, focusing on basic content required by all school personnel, and the second is specialization courses, focusing on more advanced content in a specific instructional area.

Within an integrated regular education personnel preparation program, those bodies of knowledge and skills related to basic philosophies and processes of teaching and learning could be offered within a common professional core for all educators. That is, the best knowledge and practices from both special and regular education could be consolidated and coordinated into a basic professional core for all educators. See Table 1 for an example of what might constitute a common professional core.

Most colleges of education already require a similar professional core to the one outlined in Table 1. Thus, in most cases, it would be just a matter of representatives from regular education and what was formerly special education sitting down together to analyze the existing professional core and modifying it, where necessary, to consolidate best practices from all aspects of education.

Table 1. Common professional core of courses for all educators

Courses	Credit hours
Historical/Philosophical Foundations of Education	3
Child and Adolescent Development	3
Human Relations and Sensitivity to Human Differences	3
Classroom Organization, Management, and Motivational Strategies	3
Curriculum Design and Adaptations	3
Educational Measurement and Curricular-Based Assessment	3
Adapting Instruction to Individual Differences	3
Utilization of Audiovisual/Media/Computer Technology	3
Home, School, and Community Relations	3
Issues and Trends in Education	3
Total	30

In addition to the professional core, specialization area offerings would require consideration. Specializations (or majors) in education might include science, history, English, foreign language, reading, individualized and adaptive learning approaches, behavior management, support facilitation, community-referenced curricular content, supported/competitive employment, and/or alternative communication systems. Likewise, emphasis in early childhood, elementary, and secondary education could be delineated. This would provide preparation, certification, and job assignment in all areas of expertise needed in the schools to meet all students' instructional needs. Table 2 includes examples of courses that might be included in the curriculum for specialization in the community-reference area.

These changes in program and content offerings are needed to move away from offering majors or specializations in categories of students (e.g., students with severe disabilities). It should be stressed that, as conceptualized here, no school personnel would be prepared as special educators to work with any specific categories of stu-

Table 2. Community-referenced curricular content

Courses	Credit hours
Physical Adaptations, Accessibility, and Management Strategies	3
Ecological Assessments	3
Designing Age-Appropriate and Community-Referenced Curriculum	3
Age-Appropriate and Functional Methods and Materials	3
Building Networks of Community Support and Interdependency	3
Field Experience/Student Teaching	12
Total	27

dents. Rather, all educators would be prepared as regular education personnel to provide any student, labeled disabled or not, instruction, if needed, in whatever the educator's specialization happened to be—history, science, community-referenced curricular content, or alternative communication systems. Similarly, consulting and support facilitation personnel would be prepared to team teach and collaborate with classroom teachers in their instructional area of expertise, as opposed to a category of students.

Step 4: Coordinate with State Certification Agencies and Elementary and Secondary Schools

While universities can facilitate change and become a positive force in promoting a merged system in education, they cannot be expected to do this in isolation from other educational agencies. Close coordination with both state and local education agencies likely will be required throughout the entire process of change to successfully promote the merger of the special and regular education systems.

Coordination with state agencies involved in certification will be essential to allow school personnel to become certified to teach by successfully completing a specialization in an instructional area, as opposed to a category of students. This could be accomplished in one of two ways. First, a state certification agency might be willing to work out new certification categories that recognize personnel with expertise in areas such as alternative communication skills, community-referenced instruction, or individualized and adapted instruction. Or, second, as an interim step, a certification agency may be willing to certify personnel with an instructional expertise area under a traditional special education category. This might involve certifying a person with, for example, behavior management, social skill, and/or self control expertise in the traditional category of behavioral disorders or a person with individualized and adaptive instructional expertise in the traditional category of mild mental or learning disabilities. Likewise, some state (and federal) agencies may be willing to modify funding regulations to allow educators to work with students who demonstrate a need for certain expertise, rather than only allowing personnel to make their expertise accessible to a predefined subgroup or category of students (e.g., mildly handicapped, severely handicapped, gifted, or normal). A similar approach has been taken by the waiver system initiated by the U.S. Office of Special Education and Rehabilitative Services under the title of "the regular education initiative."

Along with certification agencies, coordination with local hiring agencies such as elementary and secondary schools will also be necessary. That is, it will be essential to work with local school agencies to initiate and define personnel roles according to instructional categories, as opposed to traditional special education categories. More and more school systems have already begun to do this; however, funding restrictions on "special education" monies have generally served as roadblocks. With the use of waivers and a reorganization of personnel roles focused on addressing the individual interests, needs, and capabilities of all students (Will, 1984; 1986), job opportunities are likely to become increasingly more available to teachers with expertise in instructional areas rather than in deviant student categories.

The four steps outlined in this section are not intended as an exhaustive treatment of everything that will need to be done or of the ways to accomplish merger. The steps simply represent one approach to facilitating merger.

DISCUSSION

An increasing number of educators are interested in exploring possible ways to move toward merging special and regular education in institutions of higher education (Brantlinger, 1988; Feden, 1987; Feden & Clabaugh, 1986; Hoover, 1987; Pugach, 1988; Sapon-Shevin, Pugach, & Lilly, 1987; Stainback & Stainback, 1989). In fact, in many colleges and universities, movement toward merger in higher education gradually has been occurring during the past decade. For instance, collaborative efforts between regular and special education, mainstreaming courses for regular education personnel, and the infusion of "special" education content into regular education courses all constitute steps in the direction of integration or merger. However, in general, except for a few isolated cases (see Feden & Clabaugh, 1986), more holistic, comprehensive integration or merger strategies in higher education have typically not been attempted.

Reorganization of personnel preparation cannot be expected to be accomplished quickly or easily. This does not mean that we should not begin working toward the goal of merging higher education personnel preparation. Barriers that confront change in higher education that need to be addressed include: a) the tradition of higher education personnel, and other educators, to think and operate in terms of categories of students; b) state certification regulations organized according to categories of students; c) hiring practices in the elementary and secondary schools arranged according to categories of students; and d) educational books and other published materials directed toward teaching categorical groups of students. These barriers stand in the way of refocusing education toward the goal of addressing the educational needs of all students based on their unique interests, needs, and capabilities. However, these barriers can be overcome. In higher education we can work to change our attitudes and recognize all students as unique individuals rather than members of a categorical group; collaborate with state and local education agencies to modify certification and hiring practices; and write and develop books and materials for prospective or practicing educators conducive to the organization and maintenance of a merged, comprehensive, unified school system. In turn, these things can make the task of developing strong merged higher education personnel preparation programs a workable reality.

A few school systems in the United States and Canada have begun experimenting with ways to merge at least some aspects of special and regular education and educate all students in regular education (Biklen, 1988; Forest, 1986; Olson, 1988; Porter, 1987; Sapon-Shevin, 1987; Strully, 1986; York, 1987). Ways to better educate all students in regular neighborhood schools and regular education also are being discussed in the professional literature (Nevin & Thousand, 1986; Skrtic, 1987; Thousand, Nevin-Parta, & Fox, 1987). It is now time to start experimenting with how to merge special and regular education in higher education in order to prepare school personnel to work within a single unified regular education system designed to meet the educational needs of all students.

As personnel in higher education, we should be ever mindful of our responsibilities and role in promoting educational change. In the words of Seymour Sarason (1982): "What we see in our public schools is a mirror image of what exists in our colleges and universities" (p. 258).

REFERENCES

Biklen, D. (Producer). (1988). *Regular lives* [Video]. Washington, DC: State of the Art.

Brantlinger, E. (1988, November). *Exploring a combined regular education teacher preparation program.* Paper presented at the Eleventh Annual TED Conference, Salt Lake City.

Feden, P. (1987, November). *Effects of merging special/elementary preservice programs.* Paper presented at Tenth Annual TED Conference, Arlington, VA.

Feden, P., & Clabaugh, G. (1986). The "new breed" educator: A rationale and program for combining elementary and special education teacher preparation. *Teacher Education and Special Education, 9,* 180–189.

Forest, M. (1986). Just one of the kids. *Entourage, 1,* 20–23.

Forest, M. (1987). Keys to integration: Common sense ideas and hard work. *Entourage, 2,* 16–20.

Gartner, A., & Lipsky, D. (1987). Beyond special education. *Harvard Educational Review, 57,* 367–395.

Hoover, J. (1987, November). *Integrative training in regular and special education.* Paper presented at Tenth Annual TED Conference, Arlington, VA.

Lilly, S. (1979). *Children with exceptional needs.* New York: Holt, Rinehart & Winston.

Lipsky, D., & Gartner, A. (1987). Capable of achievement and worthy of respect: Education for handicapped students as if they were full-fledged human beings. *Exceptional Children, 54,* 69–71.

Nevin, A., & Thousand, J. (1986). What the research says about limiting or avoiding referrals to special education. *Teacher Education and Special Education, 9,* 149–161.

Olson, L. (1988, April 13). A Seattle principal defies the conventional wisdom. *Education Week,* 1, 22–23.

Porter, G. (Producer). (1987). *A chance to belong* [Video]. Downsview, Ontario: Canadian Association for Community Living.

Pugach, M. (1988, May–June). Special education as a constraint on teacher education reform. *Journal of Teacher Education,* 52–59.

Reynolds, M., & Balow, B. (1972). Categories and variables in special education. *Exceptional Children, 38,* 357–366.

Reynolds, M., & Birch, J. (1982). *Teaching exceptional children in all America's schools.* Reston, VA: Council for Exceptional Children.

Sapon-Shevin, M. (1987, October). *Broaden the base of integration: Moving schools to comprehensive mainstreaming.* Paper presented at Fourteenth Annual TASH Conference, Chicago.

Sapon-Shevin, M., Pugach, M., & Lilly, S. (1987, November). *Moving towards merger: Implications for general and special education.* Paper presented at Tenth Annual TED Conference, Arlington, VA.

Sarason, S. (1982). *The culture of the school and the problem of change.* Boston: Allyn & Bacon.

Skrtic, T. (1987, April). *Prenuptial agreements necessary for wedding special and general education.* Paper presented at annual meeting of the American Educational Research Association, Washington, DC.

Stainback, S., & Stainback, W. (1985). The merger of special and regular education: Can it be done? *Exceptional Children, 51,* 517–521.

Stainback, S., & Stainback, W. (1988). Needed changes in strengthening regular education. In J. Graden, J. Zins, & M. Curtis (Eds.), *Alternative educational delivery systems: Enhancing instructional options for all children* (pp. 17–32). Washington, DC: National Association of School Psychologists.

Stainback, S., & Stainback, W. (1989). No more teachers of students with severe handicaps. *TASH Newsletter, 15,* 9.

Stainback, W., & Stainback, S. (1984). A rationale for the merger of special and regular education. *Exceptional Children, 51,* 102–111.

Strully, J. (1986, November). *Our children and the regular education classroom: Or why settle for anything less than the best?* Paper presented to Thirteenth annual TASH Conference, San Francisco.

Thousand, J., Nevin-Parta, A. & Fox, W. (1987). Inservice training to support the education of learners with severe handicaps in their local public schools. *Teacher Education and Special Education, 10,* 4–13.

Will, M. (1984). Let us pause and reflect—But not too long. *Exceptional Children, 51,* 11–16.

Will, M. (1986). Educating children with learning problems: A shared responsibility. *Exceptional Children, 52,* 411–415.

York, J. (1987, October). *Initiating the move from separate to regular education classes in a middle school.* Paper presented at Fourteenth annual TASH Conference, Chicago.

PART IV

Educational Practices to Meet Diverse Student Needs

CHAPTER 10

Classroom Organization for Diversity among Students

Susan Stainback, William Stainback, and Robert Slavin

Owing to the mainstreaming, integration, and merger movements, the student population in regular classrooms is becoming more heterogeneous (Forest, 1987; Stainback & Stainback, 1988; Strully & Strully, 1985). As a result, teachers are confronted with the task of adapting their classrooms to accommodate wide diversity among students in physical, intellectual, psychological, and social characteristics. Along with addressing the unique needs of a diverse class membership, the challenge to foster educational excellence for all students and the concept of the equal worth of every student are integrally involved in appropriate classroom organization.

This chapter presents suggestions to assist in organizing a classroom with heterogeneous class membership. The suggestions are based on the premise that classroom organizational strategies to allow for diversity among students should be focused toward needs reflective of the entire continuum of differences inherent within the class membership, rather than on accommodations for students considered disabled (or nondisabled). This approach recognizes that every student, regardless of label or categorical group assignment, is unique and worthy of individual consideration in regard to his or her educational needs.

PROVIDE RECOGNITION FOR GOAL ACHIEVEMENT

Within public schools today, most recognition is "norm referenced," based on competition and comparisons with a peer group (Tucker, 1985). Recognition is provided to those students who excel in performance in relation to their classmates or other school

Point to Ponder

The fruits [of integration efforts] will be poisoned if they yield merely integration into a mutual sameness; they will be enriched only if each child in all of general education is seen as special and is provided an education tailored to her/him. (Gilhool, 1976, p. 9)

members. For instance, positive attention and recognition are generally given for such accomplishments as writing the best poem, getting the highest score, winning a game, or ranking in the highest percentile range on a standardized test.

In a heterogeneous class structure, the use of such student recognition is questionable. Because of the diversity in characteristics, skills, and underlying uniqueness of each class member, each student has at his or her disposal a different set of resources to draw upon for the competition. These underlying differences in intellectual and/or other resources can make competition with peers for recognition futile for some students, regardless of the effort expended, while other students require minimal effort to receive recognition. Unfortunately, classroom recognition and success based on competition with peers can result in a lack of motivation and even a negative attitude toward learning and achievement for many students.

In a heterogeneous class arrangement, motivation and/or competition for positive attention and recognition should be focused toward *competing against one's own achievements* rather than against the achievements or performance of others (Ysseldyke & Christenson, 1986). With this approach, students can be compared with and encouraged to excel beyond their present highest achievements, rather than the achievements of others who have a different set of potential resources from which to draw.

This is not to imply that all forms of competition between peers are inappropriate. Indeed, much of the enjoyment in some school activities, games, and recreational activities is based on competition. However, competitions that allow every student the opportunity to be considered a worthwhile player, and evaluation of success based on the individual resources of each participant, should be encouraged in heterogeneous classroom settings.

FOSTER STUDENT INTERDEPENDENCE

In heterogeneous classrooms, individual students and small groups of students are often called upon to function without continuous direct teacher guidance and supervision at various times throughout the school day. Fostering interdependence can help in developing natural support networks that enable students to function without direct teacher guidance and supervision.

Natural support networks can be promoted by encouraging students to share

Point to Ponder

Nearly three quarters of a century ago, Walter Lippman wrote of his fear that norm-referenced IQ tests would be used to label some children as inferior, and consign them to a second class life.

> It is not possible, I think, to imagine a more contemptible proceeding than to confront a child with a set of puzzles, and after an hour's monkeying with them, proclaim to the child, or to his parents, that here is a C-minus individual. It would not only be a contemptible thing to do; it would be a crazy thing to do . . . (cited in Gartner & Lipsky, 1987, p. 387)

with each other and teach each other through various cooperative learning activities, buddy systems, tutoring programs, and—possibly most effectively—natural, informal friendships. When natural networks of support develop, students learn to meet the needs of one another naturally, without teacher intervention. For example, a student who has a mobility problem may receive peer assistance in exiting the school building when the fire alarm rings, and at the same time may provide comfort to a classmate confused or upset by the alarm, without the teacher directing students to help one another. Everyone requires some type of support in certain situations, and everyone likewise can provide some type of support to others. Thus, to help classrooms with heterogeneous class membership to function smoothly and to foster good citizenship values, there is a need to assist and encourage students to learn to recognize others' needs and to support each other whenever possible.

ORGANIZE FOR INDEPENDENT FUNCTIONING

In heterogeneous classrooms, teachers often assume a greater role as organizers and facilitators of learning within instructional settings, rather than attempting to function as a continuous source of direct input and supervision for students as passive receivers of information. A number of classroom procedures can be used to promote students' independent functioning. For example, presenting and/or posting a schedule of daily activities can enable students to know when and what materials need to be put away or taken out at various times throughout the day. Likewise, rules can be developed, reviewed, and posted that inform students how to independently carry out routine classroom activities such as sharpening a pencil, getting supplies, going to the restroom, or what to do when a task is completed. The use of individual daily student checklists of classroom activities and duties, or individual student folders outlining tasks to be completed and instructions, can also help to individually guide students throughout a class session or class day with minimal teacher assistance. Such procedures can be used to at least some degree with most, if not all, students if care is taken to adjust the presentation of the directions to meet individual student needs, whether in written, pictorial, or audio and/or visual tape recorded form. An example of how a tape recorder was used to help a nonfunctional reader function more independently is contained in the following case example.

Case Example: James Increases His Independence

James, a nonfunctional reader in a fourth grade classroom, has been able to develop a considerable degree of independence by using a tape recorder with personal headphones. Mrs. Harrison, one of the volunteers in his classroom, tape records directions for a series of activities for him to use throughout the day. An example of a taped sequence is as follows:

"Good morning, James. This morning you are to begin by getting out your math book and doing the multiplication exercise on page 87. When you have completed the exercise, check the answers with your pocket calculator, put your math work on my desk, and turn on your tape recorder to get further directions. Turn the recorder off now.

Now that you have finished your math assignment, you may go to the science center and work with the microscope slides. Look at the picture accompanying each slide to determine what you are looking at on the slides. You may study the slides until I call you for reading group. You may turn the recorder off now."

By using the tape recorder James can work independently without having to read directions written on the chalkboard or in a workbook. Also, if James does not listen closely or remember the directions the first time they are given, he can rewind his tape and listen again.

Many types of classroom materials and equipment are available that provide direction, support, and/or feedback to students. Computers, programmed books, calculators, and audio and/or visual tape recordings can allow students to work in small groups or individually with minimal teacher supervision and assistance. While it is essential to provide plenty of direct instruction time to students, it is also important for ample activities to be done without a great deal of teacher involvement. Otherwise, it will be difficult to maintain a classroom organizational structure that keeps a heterogeneous group of students busy and on task throughout the day.

The arrangement of a classroom into learning centers offers yet another way to organize a classroom to help teachers meet a wide range of learning needs without having to provide continuous supervision or direct instruction to all students at the same time. Learning centers are places where students can go to explore a subject area in more depth or simply to gain a different perspective. They usually contain materials, equipment, games, and other activities allowing for varying skill levels and interest related to a particular subject area, ranging from telling time to human relations. They can be constructed for a single purpose for one day only or for an ongoing semester's project. However, regardless of how the centers are constructed or used, the important point is that they can provide a means to help students work more independently at their own pace and to achieve their individual learning objectives within a heterogeneous classroom.

USE AN INTEGRATED SUPPORT SERVICES MODEL

Teachers often cannot, without the assistance of support staff, deal with the diversity and dynamic array of needs exhibited across a heterogeneous group of students. The procedure involved in the utilization of available assistance can influence the benefits derived. This section of the chapter is devoted specifically to the use of specialized support staff.

Traditionally, support staff (school psychologists; physical therapists; occupational therapists; speech correctionists; or reading, learning, and behavior experts) have concentrated their time into direct service activities. In general, specialists have taken the student(s) needing assistance to an isolated section of the classroom or school building (e.g., the resource room) to engage in intensive one-to-one or small-group activities.

Recently, there has been a shift away from this isolated service model, due to a growing recognition of its inefficiency and ineffectiveness (Sternat, Nietupski, Messina, Lyon, & Brown, 1977), and toward a more integrated service model. In the integrated model the specialist not only works with the student to evaluate needs and facilitate progress but works in natural and integrated settings (e.g., the regular classroom), in which the student is typically involved and surrounded by people with whom he or she naturally associates. This increases the chances that what is being taught can become an integral part of the student's daily curriculum and activities, which can help in the generalization and maintenance of the skills being learned.

In the integrated service model, the specialist not only provides a model for and teaches the individual student but also models for and teaches the student's teacher, peers, and friends. As a result, there is an increase in the number of individuals who can provide cues and assistance to the student(s). In this way, the activities and experiences needed by the student can be fostered not only by specialized personnel at direct service times but also by others the student is in contact with in natural environments throughout the day. An important ancillary benefit is that teachers and peers learn skills they can use with other students and friends in need of similar assistance. Thus, in the integrated service model the expertise of the specialists is readily and easily shared with a wide array of people, who in turn can share what they learn with others. The following is a case example of how a specialist working within the regular classroom can influence peers to help.

Case Example: Students Can Learn How to Help Each Other

Judy, a 14-year-old student who had for years attended segregated services for the "severely retarded," was getting accustomed to attending regular high school classes. At one point, Michelle, a fellow student of Judy's, told a teacher that Judy used the sign for wanting to go to the bathroom. When the teacher asked Michelle how she knew the sign Judy used for wanting to go to the bathroom, Michelle said that she had observed the communication specialist teaching the sign to Judy. Michelle said that she would try to get Judy to repeat the use of the sign the following day.

The focus of services also requires consideration in an integrated model of service delivery. In addition to directing service provisions toward individual students identified as requiring the services of specialized personnel, there is a trend toward expanding or broadening the specialist's focus to assist the teacher in adapting classroom procedures and activities to be responsive to the individual interests, needs, and capabilities of all class members. All students vary from one another in their visual, hearing, and motor abilities and in their reading, mathematics, self-care, and/or communication needs. Thus, all students, whether singled out for specialized services or not, benefit when more teacher/specialist instructional time is available and when a classroom is organized to be responsive to individual differences.

A word of caution about the integrated support services model. When specialists work directly with a student having learning and behavior difficulties in regular classrooms, they need to be careful not to embarrass or draw undue attention to a particular student and to his or her difficulties. Some students are very sensitive about having a specialist work with them in front of their classmates, especially if the specialist is identified as a "special" educator with expertise in helping students who are "disordered," "disturbed," or "retarded". This problem generally can be avoided if the specialist: 1) identifies himself or herself by an instructional or curricular expertise area (e.g., individualization of instruction, reading, math, community-referenced instruction), rather than by a deviant category of students, and 2) is available to help any students needing assistance rather than only those labeled as "retarded," "disordered," or "disabled."

Finally, placing emphasis on an integrated support services model does not mean that a specialist (or teacher) does not ever tutor, teach, or otherwise work with a student or small group of students in a quiet place that is not directly in the center of ongoing daily classroom activities. It may occasionally be necessary to organize a quiet place in a corner of a classroom or another school or nonschool setting to work with or counsel a child or small group of children. But this can be done in regular, normalized ways without establishing special separate classes or "therapy" rooms for the "retarded" or "disordered." It should be able to occur as a regular, normal activity for any child, classified disabled or nondisabled, who needs it, and the room or space where such activities occur should be associated with the instructional focus or function for which it is used (e.g., this space is for individualized reading, speech and language activities, or counseling and guidance).

MAKE USE OF AIDES AND VOLUNTEERS

The availability of aides and volunteers can do much to support the efforts of the classroom teacher in meeting the unique needs of students in a heterogeneous classroom. In fact, the benefits that can be gained by such aides and volunteers in the efficient organization of a classroom to meet heterogeneous needs cannot be underestimated. Along with increasing the potential for greater amounts of individual feedback and direction for students, aides and volunteers can provide a critical resource to the classroom by freeing the teacher from routine supervision and recordkeeping. As a consequence, the teacher can have more time to design and implement adaptive, flexible, and individualized programs suited to the unique needs of all students.

LOCATE INSTRUCTIONAL AND RELATED ACTIVITIES IN REGULAR SETTINGS

No classroom or school locations should be reserved as special for special groups of students. For instance, certain areas in and around a classroom or school building should not be utilized or scheduled such that they become associated with student subgroups such as "the left back corner of the room is for students who cannot read," "the left wing of the building is for students with handicaps," "the outer play field is for behaviorally disordered students," or "the rooms behind the stage are used for gifted student activities."

If, due to physical structure or equipment and material requirements, certain classroom space or school locations are reserved for specific activities, the locations should be associated with the instructional focus or function for which they are used. The reason is that in most cases it is more normalized, functional, and less stigmatizing to students to refer to locations according to their instructional focus or function, rather than associating certain locations with categories of students such as the "retarded," "disabled," or "disordered". As described by one primary aged child, the special education class is, "where kids go who don't fit with everyone else. I sure hope the teachers don't put me in there—I'll lose all my friends."

Another location concern is that students who require the expertise of specialized support personnel should receive such assistance in the natural classroom environment whenever possible, so as not to attract undue attention to them and disrupt their education. Reynolds, Wang, and Walberg (1987) have used the term *disjointed incrementalism* to refer to the discontinuities or interruptions that occur in a student's education when he or she is regularly pulled out of the regular classroom to receive needed specialized services. Another, and perhaps more basic reason—previously discussed in the section on using integrated support service models—is that when specialized services occur in the classroom, teachers, aides, peers, and others can become involved in assisting and ensuring that the instructional programming or related services provided are carried out as an integral part of the student's education throughout the day, rather than only when the student is taken to "special" and often nonnormalized locations.

ORGANIZE STUDENTS INTO LARGE AND SMALL GROUPS FOR MOST ACTIVITIES

In a heterogeneous classroom, in order to meet the individual needs of class members, individual (1:1) teaching and individual learning activities may *not* always be the most efficient or effective approaches to employ. There are advantages to teaching students in groups. Individual (i.e., single student) instructional activities by their very nature reduce the overall amount of teacher-student interaction possible, deny students peer modeling and skill-sharing opportunities, and offer fewer socialization, cooperation, and communication opportunities as compared to group instructional techniques. Individual teaching or work may be necessary for any student for certain activities and periods throughout the day, but, in general, properly organized group activities can be highly effective in meeting students' unique, personalized learning goals.

A wide variety of grouping practices can be effective (Dawson, 1987). The selection of any one is influenced by the goal(s) to be achieved, the type of activity involved, and the characteristics of the students. Within-class heterogeneous grouping arrangements, in which students are at various intellectual and achievement levels, serve many purposes. They can allow for shared responsibility among students and skill guidance and modeling in which peers learn from and help each other. In addition, heterogeneous group structuring can offset the potential stereotyping and/or stigmatization that often results when students are frequently associated with a particular ability, disability, or achievement group, and can promote better understanding of individual differences and similarities among all students.

In structuring within-class heterogeneous group activities, both the group activity and goal must be selected so as to allow each student to function as a contributing member of the group while fostering his or her needed individualized learning objectives (Slavin, Leavey, & Madden, 1984). To facilitate learning and positive peer interactions and attitudes, every student should be given the opportunity to be challenged and to be successful within the group structure.

Caution is advised in evaluating who can successfully participate in heterogeneous group activities. Unfortunately, educators sometimes determine that an activity (project or game) is too complex or difficult for some students, when it is *not*. Often the problem is educators' inability to adapt the activity through, for example, adding easier and smaller components or steps or providing extra assistance so that all students can participate fully or at least partially. On the other hand, some students are not challenged enough in traditional group projects. It is just as important that group activities be arranged so that such students can proceed as fast as they are inclined. This can be done by adding more difficult or complex activities to the project.

While heterogeneous group composition should be used whenever possible, homogeneous grouping of students based on instructional content, ability, achievement, interest, and/or other criteria may be appropriate and useful in some cases. Certain curricular activities, particularly in areas such as mathematics, are based on an understanding of a rigorous, systematic, internal organization of facts and concepts that require a background of experiences and skills in order to relate to the information presented. In such cases, homogeneous grouping of students according to achievement level, for example, may be beneficial. Also, there are times when individual teaching or learning activities may be needed or appropriate. While this section of the chapter has favored heterogeneous grouping of students whenever possible, this does not mean that homogeneous grouping of students or individual teaching or learning opportunities are never necessary nor appropriate. However, often such approaches are vastly overutilized and in most instances, students can be successful and derive major benefits from within-class heterogeneous grouping.

COOPERATIVE TEAM APPROACH

A factor to consider when students are heterogeneously grouped is the type of structure used. Some researchers recommend that, when feasible, group activities should be cooperative in nature to promote positive peer interaction, understanding, and camaraderie along with individualized success (Johnson & Johnson, 1986). Cooperative group structuring involves assigning the group a common goal in which the participating students are called upon to coordinate their skills and efforts to achieve the goal (e.g., construction of a map of the United States). Cooperative learning can be used as a method to bring students of various achievement and intellectual levels together in a positive way, while at the same time allowing each student to work at his or her own individual level and pace. Positive interaction and enhanced achievements among students are realized since, if the group's goal is to be reached, all students must coordinate their efforts to achieve the goal. On the other hand, when students are instructed to work alone for the purpose of either outperforming their peers (competition) or meeting a set criterion (individualistic learning), the initial tendency to reject some students, particularly those who have difficulty learning, is perpetuated and increased.

The Johns Hopkins University has developed a cooperative team approach that has been successfully used in many heterogeneously grouped classrooms. Called "student team-achievement divisions" (STAD), it is a method that may be useful not only in promoting student interdependence and improved achievement but also in freeing up teachers, support staff, and aides for supervision, direction, and trouble shooting.

Several definitive steps can be identified for developing and using STADs in a classroom. First, assignment to teams or divisions is based on the achievement level of each student in the subject or curricular area the team is being developed for. Students are ranked from highest to lowest in achievement and divided into four levels—high, upper middle, lower middle, low. One student from each quarter is then assigned to a division. (If a class is not divisible by four, divide the class into five levels and assign five members to a team, one from each level [or some similar modification] in order to have four to five students per team.)

Once division assignments have been made, the teacher:

1. Develops and assigns objectives or goals to each team.
2. Explains lessons, procedures, and materials to teams.
3. Provides time for team study, in which students work together to help each team member master his or her objective.
4. Supervises and assists each team.
5. Evaluates individual gains made by each team member.
6. Recognizes team success based on the composite gains of all team members toward their objectives.
7. Attaches recognition to privileges (i.e., team with greatest gains can get into line first, or all the members in teams in which everyone made gains receives a new pencil).

Team composition should be shifted frequently so that all students gain the opportunity to understand and work with a variety of their classmates. (For further information on STAD and other types of cooperative group structures that have been successfully used in heterogeneous classrooms, write or call: The Johns Hopkins Team Learning Project, Center for Research on Elementary and Middle Schools, Johns Hopkins University, 3505 N. Charles St., Baltimore, MD 21218, 301/338-8249.)

PHYSICALLY ORGANIZE THE CLASSROOM FOR DIVERSITY

The needs of every class member should be considered when organizing the physical environment. An initial step involves the selection or needed modification of classroom furniture. Characteristics of students such as their height, weight, and mobility styles will dictate the sizes, and heights of desks, chairs, chalkboards, and tables. For example, while a short student may require a desk or table closer to the floor, a tall student or students in a wheelchair may require that a table or desk be raised to achieve a comfortable working height.

Placement of furniture and assignment of students to locations in the classroom also require attention to individual needs. Aisles may need to be widened to accommodate students who lack refined motor coordination or who use wheelchairs. Similarly, students should be assigned places in the room that best meet their unique needs. Some students, for instance, may need to be assigned seats close to sources of visual and/or auditory input such as the chalkboard, tape recorder, or teacher. Also, students who speechread may need to be seated close to and/or facing the teacher during teacher-directed instruction. Students who tend to be impulsive or who lack self-control may similarly require placement close to the teacher for additional guidance or monitoring.

Other student characteristics must also be taken into account in room organization. For students who tend to be distractible, a somewhat isolated, comfortable, quiet, and relaxed area can be set up in the room to meet their needs, as well as those of class members requiring a quiet area to read or concentrate on specific assignments. Likewise, all students require, to varying degrees, room areas that allow for position changes including places for sitting, standing, or lounging on the floor. Opportunities for position changes are just as important for ambulatory students who sometimes get cramped or restless as it is for nonambulatory students who can develop contractures and pressure sores from sitting in wheelchairs for too long a time period.

Since heterogeneous classrooms have students with diverse needs and learning characteristics, such classrooms also need to be physically organized so that a variety of different types of instructional and related activities can easily occur. Classrooms that are organized, for example, to accommodate only one type of instructional format such as the lecture format are usually not very conducive to meeting diverse learning needs and styles. On the other hand, classrooms that are organized to allow for individualized and small-group activities, noisy and quiet activities, and various types of lectures, films, and discussions tend to be more accommodating. For this reason, successful heterogeneous classrooms often have furniture that can be easily arranged in different ways; carpeted and noncarpeted floor spaces; and areas that can be opened, closed, or screened off depending on the needs of the students when working on different tasks.

Thus, the diverse needs of all students must be considered in developing a physical arrangement conducive to learning. The teacher does not have to do it alone. In nearly all school districts, there are specialists in a variety of areas such as classroom management, individualized and adaptive instructional programming, and hearing and vision differences that can provide classroom teachers with ideas and cues to help make the physical organization of any classroom more accommodating to a wide range of individual differences among students.

ARRANGE FOR ACCESS TO A VARIETY OF MATERIALS AND EQUIPMENT

Materials such as worksheets, books, charts, and displays of varying instructional levels, print sizes, vocabulary difficulty, complexity, and age appropriateness may be needed when attempting to meet the instructional and related needs of a heterogeneous student group. For instance, large-print materials may be useful for students who are visually impaired or beginning readers, or any other students who for some reason need large-print materials. Some students, including those who are distractible, may need, for example, mathematics worksheets with only one or a few problems per sheet, or worksheets with heavy black lines drawn around the problems on which they are to concentrate. Similarly, instructional equipment such as braille or standard typewriters, tape recorders, and various types of computers may be useful in the classroom to meet a broad range of student needs. An audio converter computer, for instance, may be used to translate verbal directions to written form for auditorially impaired students, may provide immediate feedback and reinforcement for students who require immediate gratification to remain motivated, may be used to clarify the function and importance of the written word to the beginning reader, and/or may provide needed support to the dependent learner. Since all students have unique characteristics, a variety of instructional materials and equipment is important to any classroom, and particularly those with a heterogeneous group membership.

One approach to achieving greater variety is to set up a cooperative sharing and trading exchange with colleagues. Even potentially more effective is to develop a centralized equipment and material bank in a school in which each teacher or resource specialist can select and exchange equipment and material as needed, based on the individual instructional needs of class members. In this way certain materials and/or pieces of equipment are not bound to one classroom. For example, rather than locating all level-four reading materials in a fourth grade classroom, such materials can be used for any student who needs them, regardless of class placement. In addition, by pooling available resources, shortages of needed materials and/or equipment can be quickly spotted and duplication on a per-classroom basis is unnecessary. Also, by organizing a school bank, students can have access to materials and equipment based specifically on their needs rather than having to "make do" with predetermined materials and equipment available in a particular classroom.

ARRANGE THE CLASS SCHEDULE ACCORDING TO STUDENT NEEDS AND THE INVOLVEMENT OF SPECIALIZED INSTRUCTIONAL STAFF

A classroom schedule, while needing to work within the framework of the general school's timetable, should be developed based on the needs of the students in the class and of the specialized instructional staff involved in student and classroom activities. Students in a heterogeneously organized classroom will have varying characteristics that influence scheduling. Some students may be able to complete assignments easily and quickly, so that the teacher will need to schedule other worthwhile and challenging activities for them, if they are to be provided the opportunity to fulfill their potential to the greatest extent possible. Other students may require longer study periods in a curricular area because of a slower working pace or because they cannot concentrate for long time periods. However, it should be stressed that it is important not to just accommodate the classroom schedule to the learning characteristics of the students, but also to assist students to modify their learning characteristics when appropriate and possible. For example, for students who work at a slow speed and/or have difficulty in concentrating, the teacher may want to gradually reduce the length of some work sessions to facilitate greater speed or intensified concentration, while at the same time instructing the students in various techniques and ways to improve speed and concentration.

The involvement of specialized instructional staff in the classroom also influences the development of the classroom schedule. When planning for the involvement of other staff, not only their availability but also the scheduled activities of the student(s), teacher, and other classroom personnel must be considered. For example, specialized staff are considered most effective when they are associated with and facil-

Point to Ponder

Rather than continuing efforts to perfect a separate, segregated system, we must turn now to changing the mainstream and to make general education flexible, supple, and responsive—educating the full range of students. While some professionals in special education may prefer the shelter and opportunities of a separate setting, and other professionals in general education may resist serving "those" students, most in both systems can be mobilized for the needed changes." (Lipsky & Gartner, 1987, p. 72)

itate normally scheduled natural class activities. That is, a reading specialist would likely best be scheduled during class reading activities, a physical therapist during physical education, and a speech therapist or speechreading specialist during activities involving oral communication skills. In this way, specialized staff can work within normal classroom activities that most resemble their expertise areas, to help not only any students (disabled or nondisabled) in need of specialized assistance, but also the classroom teacher, to make the entire classroom structure more flexible and accommodating.

CONCLUSION

Simply placing students into heterogeneous class arrangements is not enough. Within these classes all students, whether considered disabled or nondisabled, should be provided educational programs geared to their unique interests, needs, and capabilities, and challenged to be the best they can be. To accomplish this, the most effective instructional practices for dealing with student diversity in a classroom must be identified and implemented in today's classrooms and schools.

REFERENCES

Dawson, M. (1987). Beyond ability grouping: A review of the effectiveness of ability grouping and its alternatives. *School Psychology Review, 16*, 348–369.

Forest, M. (1987). *More education and integration*. Downsview, Ont.: G. Allan Roeher Institute.

Gartner, A., & Lipsky, D. (1987). Beyond special education: Toward a quality system for all students. *Harvard Educational Review, 57*, 367–395.

Gilhool, T. (1976). Changing public policies: Roots and forces. In M. Reynolds (Ed.), *Mainstreaming: Origins and implications* (pp. 8–13). Reston, VA: Council for Exceptional Children.

Granger, L., & Granger, B. (1986). *The magic feather*. New York: E.P. Dutton.

Johnson, D., & Johnson, R. (1986). Mainstreaming and cooperative learning strategies. *Exceptional Children, 52*, 553–561.

Lipsky, D., & Gartner, A. (1987). Capable of achievement and worthy of respect: Education for handicapped students as if they were full-fledged human beings. *Exceptional Children, 54*, 69–74.

Reynolds, M., Wang, M., & Walberg, H. (1987). The necessary restructuring of special and regular education. *Exceptional Children, 53*, 391–398.

Slavin, R., Leavey, M., & Madden, N. (1984). Combining cooperative learning and individualized instruction. *Elementary School Journal, 84*, 410–422.

Stainback, S., & Stainback, W. (1988). Educating students with severe disabilities in regular classes. *Teaching Exceptional Children, 21*, 16–19.

Sternat, J., Nietupski, J., Messina, R., Lyon, S., & Brown, L. (1977). Occupational and physical therapy services for severely handicapped students: Toward a naturalized public school delivery model. In E. Sontag, J. Smith, & N. Certo (Eds.), *Educational programming for the severely and profoundly handicapped*. Reston, VA: Council for Exceptional Children, Division of Mental Retardation.

Strully, J., & Strully, C. (1985). Teach your children. *Canadian Journal on Mental Retardation, 35*(4), 3–11.

Tucker, J. (1985). Curriculum-based assessment: An introduction. *Exceptional Children, 52*, 199–204.

Ysseldyke, J., & Christenson, S. (1986). *The Instructional Environment Scale*. Austin: PRO-ED.

CHAPTER 11

Educational and Curricular Adaptations

Mary A. Falvey, Jennifer Coots, Katherine D. Bishop, and Marquita Grenot-Scheyer

Throughout history, the challenge to educators has been, and continues to be, the development and facilitation of curricular and instructional options allowing for the education of all students in the most appropriate and beneficial manner. This chapter discusses issues and strategies related to curricular design and adaptations that allow for *all* students to participate in the general education program. Due to the limitations of a single chapter, the authors have chosen to address some of the general strategies that have application across the majority of curriculum areas and ages. Specific examples are included for all strategies to demonstrate their application.

Previous chapters in this book have clearly established the need for the development of educational systems that include *all* students in the same educational setting. Clearly, research has demonstrated positive effects of programs that integrate students of varying abilities and characteristics (Johnson, Johnson, DeWeerdt, Lyons, & Zaidman, 1987; Rynders, Johnson, Johnson, & Schmidt, 1980; Strain, 1983; Strain & Kerr, 1981; Voeltz, 1980). There are also basic values that drive the educational system to create schools and opportunities that include *all* students. While research can assist us in creating the most effective schools and educational strategies, the decision to develop such integrated educational programs is a value decision based upon a belief in equal access and opportunity.

LOCATION OF SCHOOL ATTENDANCE

Typically, public school students in general education attend their neighborhood schools with children who live in the same neighborhood. Until recently, some students defined as disabled have had little opportunity to attend school with their neighborhood peers. Parents of such students must still in many cases argue for their son or daughter's basic right to be educated in their neighborhood school alongside their friends and peers.

Decisions to place all students in homogeneous segregated settings for their education have emphasized the differences rather than the similarities between formerly segregated students and their peers. Promoting differences in educational services only perpetuates isolation and segregation throughout the community. The service delivery model that removes students from their neighborhood schools and/or the regular education classroom for the sake of specialized services seems untenable when one considers the enormous importance of developing friendships that will lead to integration and inclusion throughout the community (see Chapter 5 in this volume).

The implications of removing students from their neighborhood are dramatic. Based upon a substantial body of research, "typical" children and adolescents are more likely to have and maintain friendships only if they have frequent opportunities to interact with others (Hartup, 1975; Howes, 1983). Interaction opportunities are generally achieved when people, particularly children, are in close proximity to one another. For many of us, friendships formed during the elementary, junior, and high school years due to close proximity and frequent interaction opportunities with peers have endured and are essential in our personal support systems as adults. In addition to developing a personal support system, numerous social skills for social competence are acquired during and throughout relational interactions. Many of us measure the quality of our lives in terms of friends and what they mean to us. Shared support and interactions with friends are essential to one's overall sense of worth, belonging, and well-being.

While educational programs must be designed to foster basic skills and academic competencies, they also should be designed such that opportunities for the development of friendships are available. For all students, the skills necessary to interact with others and "get along" in a community are acquired through interactions and relationships. Examples of such skills are initiation, thoughtful actions, positive interaction style, good listening, and sharing belongings and feelings (Asher, Oden, & Gottman, 1977). Friendships provide opportunities to develop skills that are best learned and/or best taught through the interactions that nat-

Point to Ponder

Our daughter, Shawntell, is not going to one day wake up with all of the competencies and skills that she needs in order to live independently. The reality is that we have been working on teaching Shawntell to use the bathroom for the last nine years. At this point in time, Shawntell is approximately 58% toilet trained. This is a significant increase in her accuracy, but Shawntell may never achieve complete success. The same is true for lots of other areas such as eating independently, walking, and communicating. Though Shawntell has learned important things and will continue to do so, the issue that we face is, will the skills our daughter has learned keep her in the community? The answer, we are afraid, is no!

Yet, imagine if you will, that she did achieve all of these competencies, would that make everything perfect? Again, the answer is no! One's ability to know things or master skills is not the litmus test on capability to be an active member of your community and to have friends. What matters, we believe, is trying to be the best person you can and having people accept you for who you are, with all of your strengths and weaknesses. If we can accept people for who they are and not for who we want them to be, our communities will have moved a considerable distance. In the final analysis, whether or not Shawntell obtains all the competencies and skills in the world, it really isn't all that significant. What is important is being cared about by another human being. If Shawntell is really going to be an integral member of her community, she will need to rely on her friends who want to be involved with her because they are her friends. (Strully & Strully, 1985, pp. 7–8)

urally occur when two or more people have established friendships or relationships (Howes, 1983). The frequent interaction opportunities and close proximity of neighbors attending the same school facilitates not only the development of friendships but also the chance to acquire necessary social skills. In the accompanying, "Point to Ponder," Jeffrey and Cindy Strully have demonstrated the importance to children of having friends, as well as skills and competencies.

CURRICULAR STRATEGIES AND ADAPTATIONS

The goal of educational programs is to facilitate students to "be the most they can be." This statement has been articulated in many different ways and by many sources. In the main office of a junior high school in Boulder, CO, a mission statement is posted on the bulletin board that reads: "The Burbank Junior High School mission is to assist each student in developing academically, socially, physically, emotionally and aesthetically to his/her fullest potential as an individual" (Boulder Valley School District, 1988).

Such a mission statement is synonymous with the concept of "*criterion of ultimate functioning*" (Brown, Nietupski, & Hamre-Nietupski, 1976), which stated that educational programs should be directly related to skills expected of adults. This criterion and the Burbank Junior High School's mission statement essentially challenge educators to prepare students for the "real world." Both special and regular educational systems attempt to challenge their respective students to participate together in the same world. However, in special education these educational efforts have often been provided in segregated or separated settings, which do not allow students to practice living and learning together. Duplication of educational efforts into special and regular categories is unnecessary (Stainback & Stainback, 1984). Since the goal and mission for all students is the same, providing education for all students together in integrated neighborhood schools is not only possible but preferable.

Specific services and interventions should be based upon a *student's educational need*. Unfortunately, educational interventions for students defined as disabled are often based upon their disability label rather than their educational need. For example, a student with a severe disability is generally assigned to a teacher for the "severely handicapped." This assignment may not be appropriate because it does not include: 1) identification of the students needs or 2) identification of the teacher's specific expertise. Students' overall needs must be assessed and identified before decisions about specific programs and objectives are identified. In addition, these decisions must include the most effective strategies for educating the student and meeting these objectives within the general education classroom.

There is often a mystique associated with the specialized skills and strategies of a teacher trained in special education. However, most approaches included in special education training programs are also effective for "regular" education students. By the same token, specific strategies included in general education training programs can and have been effective in teaching all children, including those assigned a disability label. For example, special educators work on promoting different skills within a similar activity for students labeled as disabled. Regular educators work on promoting different levels of information within a similar activity for students at different academic levels. In the typical elementary school classroom, students are already working on several different grade levels in, for example, reading or math. The major point is that *good teaching is good teaching, and both systems of education have much to offer each other.* Specific decisions for location, types of services, and educational programs for all students should be determined according to students' unique interests, needs, and capabilities. The teaching also should occur alongside the students' neighbors and friends. The educational goals of every student aim toward maximizing his or her potential in the vocational, recreation/leisure, domestic, and community domains of life. Within those broad domains, educational goals and achievements will vary according to each student's needs. For example, a vocational goal for one student might require that she learn to program a computer, while another student's vocational goal might be that he enter a mailing list on the same computer. Stated another way, it is not necessary for students to have the exact same goals and ability levels to be educated in the same location.

Special education services have included, by virtue of the federal mandate, *individualized* education programs (IEPs) for each student. Given that students with a disability label, like all other students, have unique and varied learning styles, strengths, and weaknesses, strategies and objectives must be individually identified. Such an approach has allowed for the determination and development of an individualized education program for a student, considering his or her strengths and weaknesses. This approach is also used in general education, not because of a federal mandate, but because it is an effective way to approach the development of the curriculum and teaching of all students. Although the specificity of such individualization may not exactly reflect the individualization efforts in special education, the basic principle is the same.

Adelman and Taylor (1983) have articulated this principle further in calling for a personalized curriculum. An individualized curriculum suggests individual placement on a standard curriculum based upon developmental status and actual achievement level. A personalized curriculum, however, takes into account noncognitive factors as well and allows for creation of curriculum and materials that may be necessary to accommodate the individuality of each student. A tremendous advantage of merging the expertise, skills, and strengths of special and regular education is the potential to develop and use personalized approaches for all students to facilitate their learning. A personalized approach to educational curriculum development also allows teachers to merge their own expertise and interests to enhance the variety of curricular options.

The personalized curriculum approach does not imply that school districts cannot or should not develop districtwide objec-

Point to Ponder

The division of students into groups and tracks assumed to ensure considerable likeness in attainment is a meat ax approach to problems requiring much more sensitive curricular and pedagogical approaches. (Goodlad, 1984)

tives. On the contrary, the approach underscores the importance of developing a well-articulated set of objectives to be taught/learned in the schools by all students, while the specific skills identified to reach the objectives would be individualized. Thus, for example, all students would be taught vocational skills, but the particular vocational skills taught may vary from student to student. Personalization would result in modifying and/or adapting the teaching methods for an individual student based upon his or her needs. Many students may benefit from systematic attention to differing individual needs. As evidenced by the growing dropout rate in many schools, education for all students must be expanded to teach students the skills that are viewed by students and adults as the most useful for ultimate functioning in their communities. Some students may claim that technical vocational skills are a priority for them, while others may perceive a need to be in advanced academic programs. All students will need to be able to access their community independently, some by driving their own cars, others by using community buses, walking, or bicycling. By adapting all educational services currently available to meet the variety of students' needs, the overall goals of education can be met most effectively.

In the past, educational systems have created arbitrary criteria for inclusion and exclusion in the various aspects of educational service delivery. For example, in the 1960s, children and adolescents often could not go to school unless they were toilet trained, could feed themselves, walk independently, talk, and so on. Since the passage of Public Law 94-142, the Education for all Handicapped Children Act, districts have adopted a zero-rejection philosophy and have therefore provided services for students who did not possess all of those skills.

Since then, educators, families, and communities have developed segregated and self-contained educational programs for these students. The students' participation in segregated programs was contingent upon the development of adaptations and modifications. It seems reasonable that the basic premise behind the *principle of partial participation* (Baumgart et al., 1982) should be used to include these same students in general education. Simply put, this principle states: It is better to at least partially participate than to be denied access to an event, activity, setting or other opportunity. This principle could assist in the development and creation of modifications and/or adaptations that would facilitate the inclusion of all students in general education. This principle does not imply the lowering of standards in a well-thought-out and relevant curriculum in general education. However, it does imply that the development or creation of adaptations be considered so that students of varying ability levels can participate and benefit from the educational programs. Some students may never acquire the skills to be independent in a task or an activity; however, teachers must encourage their participation to whatever degree possible.

Often when conceptualizing adaptations, the development and utilization of materials and devices receive the primary attention (Bishop & Falvey, 1986). Baumgart et al. (1982) have expanded the concept of adaptations to encompass:

1. Adapting skill sequences—changing the normal order of tasks (e.g., a student bypasses learning multiplication tables and switches to learning to use a calculator to solve problems)

2. Adapting rules—discarding or creating different rules to allow greater participation (e.g., allowing a student to throw a baseball while at bat during a game rather then hitting the ball)
3. Utilizing personal assistance—utilizing others to accomplish a task (e.g., using partners to complete an art project)
4. Facilitating social/attitudinal changes —creating an impact on the values, beliefs, and/or assumptions of neighborhoods, schools, and community members (e.g., supplementing the state-adopted materials to teach a social studies lesson by using materials that include role models of adults with and without disabilities)
5. Creating materials and/or devices that assist students in completing or participating in activities (e.g., a student who cannot read because of a vision impairment, uses a "talking" book or cassette tape instead of reading *Moby Dick*)

Teachers in general education make a practice of adapting materials or developing new ones to make concepts more easily understood by the students in their classes. Nonhandicapped students will benefit equally from this expanded concept of adaptations. Table 1 contains a number of examples of adaptations demonstrating how students at different age levels and with varying abilities and objectives can participate in the general education program as well as approach specific lessons. The adaptations described are similar to adaptations made by teachers every day in objectives and materials. It could truly be challenging to adapt curricular programs to meet the individual needs of an entire class of students. In all likelihood, however, groups of students will share the same objectives, so that each student in the class will not have different objectives for specific lessons. However, there are programs available that have been developed to allow for individualized instruction. The authors have observed numerous teachers who have successfully adapted instructional programs in their classrooms to accommodate students with varying abilities and characteristics, demonstrating that adaptation of curriculum for specific activities is possible.

EFFECTIVE TEACHING STRATEGIES

In addition to utilizing specific adaptations, teachers must examine specific teaching strategies to promote greater learning and participation. Recent research has focused on identifying descriptors of effective teaching strategies. These strategies provide a framework within which teachers can effectively adapt curricula to meet a wide variety of curricular needs in the regular classroom. These strategies acknowledge the fact that classrooms include students with a wide variety of individual needs, whether those students are labeled as disabled or not. The bases for effective teaching strategies as delineated by Jones, Friedman, Tinzman, and Cox (1984) are included in the following discussion.

Components of Effective Teaching Strategies

Jones et al. (1984) delineate six components of effective teaching strategies. First, teachers must provide an overview of what is to be taught, as well as cues that include cautions concerning probable errors. To do this, teachers might give verbal instructions as well as pictorial directions as to how skills can be used. Peers can assist each other in reviewing and understanding the purpose of the lesson.

Table 1. Adaptations for students with varying abilities and at different age levels

Goal	Objectives/activities	Materials/adaptation
	Age Level: Preschool	
Subject: Snack		
To eat a snack	Student 1 The student will eat a graham cracker and juice without dropping or spilling.	Graham crackers Cup Juice
	Student 2 The student will move jaw up and down after food is placed in mouth.	
Subject: Toileting		
To use the toilet appropriately	Student 1 The student will flush the toilet and pull up pants when he or she is finished.	Accessible bathroom Potty chairs
	Student 2 When placed upon the toilet, the student will urinate within 3 minutes.	
Subject: Music		
Participate in the group activity of singing	Student 1 The student will sing and do hand movements to the songs "Wheels on the bus," "Put your hands up in the air," and "I'm a little teapot" with the group.	Pictures Records or tapes Record or tapeplayers
	Student 2 The student will stay in the group area for at least one song.	
	Student 3 The student will activate tape recorder with switch.	
	Age Level: Elementary	
Subject: Art		
Design a collage	Student 1 Students with an assigned partner will complete a collage during the specified time.	Paper Objects Glue Glue brush
	Student 2 The student glues, while other student puts the objects on.	
	Student 3 The student points to desired objects; the other student glues them on.	

(continued)

Table 1. (*continued*)

Goal	Objectives/activities	Materials/adaptation
Subject: Science		
Classify vertebrates into 5 major groups	Student 1 The student will verbally identify and classify one given vertebrate into each of the five groups. Student 2 The student will identify one characteristic of given animal. Student 3 The student will classify animals using braille cards.	Actual animal Pictures Word cards Braille cards
Subject: Reading		
To read and comprehend *The Little Engine that Could*	Student 1 The student will read pages 1–11 in the book and then correctly place in order 10 sentence strips from the story. Student 2 The student will point to pictures and orally state the components of a sentence with reading group. Student 3 The student will correctly answer 10 basic questions by pointing to pictures on sentence strips with head pointer.	Story Sentence strips Sentence strips with pictures Head pointer for student as needed
Subject: Math		
To increase accuracy of computational skills	Student 1 Student will complete five 2-digit multiplication problems. Student 2 The student will use calculator to compute five 2-digit multiplication problems. Student 3 The student will operate as lesson facilitator by handing out worksheets to all students and accurately operating the timer for timed drills.	Worksheets Calculators Timer
	Age Level: Junior High	
Subject: Physical Education		
Perform the Virginia Reel	Student 1 The student will, with assigned partners, dance the Virginia Reel, following directions.	Music

(*continued*)

Table 1. *(continued)*

Goal	Objectives/activities	Materials/adaptation
	Student 2 The student will independently push his or her wheelchair the length of the line during dance.	
Subject: Typing during Computer Class		
Type a letter	Student 1 Within a given time period, the student will type a letter. Student 2 The student will type a portion of a given letter from handwritten copy. Student 3 The student will type the heading for a letter.	Standard computer with braille template or computer with voice output Typewriter with key guards to prevent hitting the wrong key
	Age Level: High School	
Subject: Career Education		
Experience working in the community	Student 1 The student will work as a clerk in the newsroom of the local paper. Student 2 The student will ride public bus independently to and from work. Student 3 The student will operate stamp machine in the subscription department.	Work permit Job coach Bus pass Adapted stamp machine
Subject: Family Living		
Use a checkbook	Student 1 The student will write checks and fill in the register appropriately, maintaining an accurate balance. Student 2 The student will sign his or her name using a signature template after the check is written and the math is completed. Student 3 The student will use a signature stamp after the check is written and the math is completed.	Signature template Signature stamp

Second, teachers must provide a readiness/preparatory set of activities that emphasizes the linking of new information to prior knowledge and the preteaching of difficult vocabulary. To apply this, a teacher might relate what is being taught today to what was taught yesterday, as well as the application of the topic, so that skills are not learned in isolation. For example, lessons on weather relate to lessons about clothing worn in different climates: "Yesterday it was cold, so we wore coats. Today it is clear, so we took our coats off."

Third, emphasis must be placed on examples and applications of concepts, principles, and vocabulary terms. This may mean that a one-to-one correspondence lesson is conducted along with putting out cartons of milk for snack time, or measurement lessons are taught while constructing a set for a drama production.

The fourth strategy identified by Jones et al. (1984) is that vocabulary learning and/or metacognitive strategies must be taught. Therefore, key sequence vocabulary for a job might be reviewed when a student goes to a job, in conjunction with a list of tasks to be done before, during, and after work. Students may also learn self-monitoring techniques to cue themselves to provide quality work.

Fifth, students must engage in guided practice and then practice independently. To do this a teacher may provide instruction for playing games on the playground, then ask students to pair up with classmates to practice the game. Finally, the teacher monitors student comprehension, then provides continuous feedback to facilitate correct learning and also provides positive reinforcement. This may require the teacher to ask questions of the group and of specific individuals or to set up problem-solving activities, watching for students to perform skills as evidence that the skill is mastered.

Jones et al. (1984) suggest that all of the preceding components must be included in any type of instruction. These strategies should be employed with whatever educational model teachers implement and with whatever curricular material is being taught in order to assist students in mastering instructional objectives.

Heterogeneously Grouped Classrooms

Another effective teaching strategy is the way in which students are grouped. The separateness of the two systems, regular and special education, often has resulted in homogeneous grouping (i.e., grouping of students by ability levels or according to whether they were labeled as disabled or nondisabled). More recently, attempts to merge special and regular education programs have resulted in *heterogeneously grouped classrooms* (i.e., classes containing students with varying abilities and characteristics). The effectiveness of the grouping seems to depend on how teaching methods are implemented. Students grouped heterogeneously with the most effective teaching strategies have specific advantages over those grouped homogeneously (e.g., acceptance of individual differences, learning a new skill such as sign language or Spanish, learning about different cultures from firsthand experiences). Therefore, based upon the benefits to be gained by students who are heterogeneously grouped, it is necessary to continue to identify those strategies that can be utilized by teachers to meet a wide variety of curricular needs in a heterogeneously organized classroom. Richer learning environments include children of varying abilities, backgrounds, and cultures. However, teachers need to provide systematic instruction and varied groupings within classrooms to be sure that all students benefit.

Cooperative Learning Strategies

Cooperative learning strategies have proven effective in assisting teachers to meet a wide variety of curricular needs while fostering positive social relationships between students of differing backgrounds and abilities (Johnson & Johnson, 1981; Johnson, Johnson, Warring, & Maruyama, 1986; Yager, Johnson, Johnson, & Snider, 1985). Traditional classroom models have focused on individualistic and/or competitive learning experiences. The skills needed to function in competitive or individually paced learning experiences may both be critical for future independent functioning. However, the ability to cooperate and collaborate with other persons is an equally essential skill that can assist in more effective interdependent functioning at school, home, and on the job. *Interdependency* is defined as teaching students to access others in supportive and/or cooperative ways in performing a task.

The procedures delineated by Johnson, Johnson, Holubec, and Roy (1984) need to be incorporated into the structuring of cooperative learning experiences. These include clearly specifying instructional objectives. Also, the assignment of students to groups and the room arrangement should be done in a manner that facilitates cooperation (e.g., include students with differing and complementary needs in groups together, place desks, chairs, and wheelchairs so that face-to-face interaction between students is promoted). Materials, tasks, goals, and roles must be assigned and structured to promote interdependence within the group while also allowing for individual accountability. The goals, criteria for success, and desired behaviors must be clearly specified, and group collaboration must be continually monitored. Initially, the skills necessary to effectively collaborate, such as "Everyone does a job" or "Giving directions without being bossy," will most likely need to be taught to group members and then continually evaluated and retaught as needed.

The cooperative structuring of activities can allow teachers the opportunity to adapt curriculum to meet a wide variety of needs, as mentioned earlier. For instance, for a spelling lesson, each student can have a different list of words, a list of words in braille, a list of learned signs, or picture communication booklet cards that they must correctly identify while the group works cooperatively to ensure that all students meet their individual objectives. As another example, students can work together on a single group report such as a shopping list reflecting the lowest overall prices on specified items found in the food section in the weekly paper. Some or all of the group can then go to the store to purchase the items on the specified list and then use the items for a classroom cooking activity or take the items home as desired. Also, in a home economics class, students could work on a group project involving varying abilities to sew; some students might sew complicated stitches using a sewing machine while others might use a needle and thread to attach a button.

Mastery Learning

Another effective teaching method involves *mastery learning strategies* or *outcomes-based educational strategies,* which combine small-group and individualized instruction. These strategies have also been effective in improving the school performance of a wide variety of students, and give teachers the tools necessary to adapt curriculum to meet a diversity of needs (Hyman & Cohen, 1979; Rubin & Spady, 1984). The steps involved in implementing mastery learning strategies include:

1. Define the specific objective for each student; note that students likely will have different objectives.
2. Teach the skill or concept in the objective.
3. Evaluate mastery of the objective using a criterion-referenced test.
4. Provide additional instruction for those who have not met the objective.
5. Retest this group.

By employing this methodology, general education teachers can teach a skill or concept to the class or a small group, then provide additional, more individualized instruction to those students who did not master the skill or objective.

Peer Instruction

Peer instruction or *tutoring* is another effective teaching strategy (Allen & Boraks, 1978; Dineen, Clark, & Risley, 1977; Kohl, Moses, & Stettner-Eaton, 1983; and McHale, Olley, Marcus, & Simeonsson, 1981). For example, a high school student could demonstrate for a peer the "cool" way to comb hair. Or a middle school student could help a peer to make a choice and play with a board game. For peer instruction to be effective, it is important that the peers volunteer to engage in the instruction, and further, that the classroom teacher monitor the instruction to determine if the instruction has occurred (Heron & Harris, 1987). As suggested by Grenot-Scheyer and Falvey (1986), caution must be used when implementing peer instruction. It is critical that all students have the opportunity to both provide and receive instruction, and that certain students are not always put in the position of being the receiver.

ROLE OF THE TEACHER

The foregoing discussion of the necessary changes in curriculum and teaching strategies that will provide the most effective educational services to all students makes apparent that the role of the teacher will change. As a result of a variety of educational reforms (Stainback & Stainback, 1984), teachers now and in the future have the opportunity to work with students who bring a diverse mixture of contributions and challenges to the classroom. Providing education for all students—including those with a variety of learning, communication, social, cultural, and physical characteristics—within regular classrooms may require different roles for teachers. The two primary methods for delivering educational services that will define the new roles are *consulting teacher* and *team teaching*. Certainly these two roles are not new to the educational system; however, they may be new for teachers who have exclusively served as "special" education teachers.

Point to Ponder

We can, whenever and wherever we choose, successfully teach all children whose schooling is of interest to us. We already know more than we need in order to do this. Whether we do it must finally depend on how we feel about the fact that we haven't done it so far. (Edmonds, 1979, p. 29)

Consultant Teacher

Classroom teachers may be assisted and supported by *consultant teachers* who bring a particular expertise to the learning. A consultant may be viewed as a teacher who has expertise in a particular area or areas. The resources used to separate students with disabilities in special education classrooms with special education teachers should be redirected to hire consultants with varying expertise. Following are examples of consultant teachers who can support the classroom teacher:

Communication consultant
Physical education consultant
Bilingual consultant
Reading consultant
Orientation and mobility consultant
Computer consultant
Augmentative communication consultant
Low-vision or braille consultant
Interaction consultant
Community-based instruction consultant

Consultant strategies can be direct or indirect for both students or teachers. For example, the computer consultant could conduct a language arts activity with a small group of elementary-aged students. Within this small group, some of the students could be working on sentence development using a keyboard, while the student with severe cerebral palsy is learning to activate and operate the computer utilizing a chin switch. In another example, the computer consultant could facilitate an interactive game on the computer among several junior high school students. For all the students, including a student labeled as autistic, this activity would provide an age-appropriate opportunity to work on initiating skills within a peer group. As a third example, the community-based instruction (CBI) consultant might provide direct instruction to students in natural community environments (Falvey, 1986). In coordination with the classroom teacher, the CBI consultant could provide instruction for a group of three students who need to learn to access and utilize their neighborhood grocery store. The consultant might assist one student to compare the value of a generic brand of laundry detergent and a higher-priced brand name detergent. With a second student, the consultant might provide a series of instructional prompts to facilitate this student to scan a row of soup cans and direct his eye gaze to the desired can. The consultant could assist a third student to respond to the natural social interactions of grocery store employees and community members. To provide a fourth example, the interaction consultant could provide specific strategies to the classroom teacher on how best to facilitate positive social interaction among the students in the classroom. As a fifth example, the augmentative communication consultant could assist a small group of students to become familiar with and respond to an electronic communication board that a peer uses to communicate. Finally, as a sixth example, the braille consultant might assist the family of a blind student to access local community resources and materials for individuals who are blind.

Team Teaching

Team teaching arrangements can be developed between the regular education teacher and the previously identified special education teacher. That is, students formerly served by the special education teacher exclusively would be assigned to regular education classrooms in natural proportions (i.e., the percentage of former "special" education students in any one classroom would reflect the percentage of such students in the general community.) A team composed of a regular educator and former "special" educator (who is now a teacher with expertise in a specific area like community-based instruction) would share curriculum and instructional responsibilities. In this way, the strengths of each teacher can be accessed by all students and the teachers themselves are able to share and learn from each other's abilities. Moreover, through teaming, teachers can provide student groupings that create the benefits of heterogeneity as described earlier. Team teachers also have the support of another professional who knows each student well and can provide specific strategies and on-the-spot assistance and problem solving.

Although the role of both special and regular educators will change to facilitate a single model of service delivery, the changes should serve to enhance each educator's expertise. The changing roles allow for support, creativity, and a variety of teaching opportunities. Most of all, the changing roles will allow for all students to receive the best education that all services and areas of expertise can provide.

SUMMARY

There are several key components to successful implementation of a single service delivery model for all students in public school settings. First, students should attend schools in their local neighborhoods in classrooms grouped according to chronological ages. Second, curricular strategies and adaptations should be planned in a manner that allows for inclusion and participation of students who have a variety of strengths and deficits. Third, effective teaching strategies such as cooperative learning and mastery learning can be utilized to enhance skill acquisition for all students. Finally, the role of the teacher must shift to accommodate the variety of students' needs and allow for a sharing of expertise and problem solving.

This is not an easy challenge. However, the concept of merging special and regular education such that all students win is extremely powerful and positive. This chapter has provided strategies that may serve as a foundation for such service delivery. It is important to note that the purpose of providing these strategies is to serve only as a reference point from which teachers and administrators can create models and strategies that truly meet the needs of all students in their communities in integrated, age appropriate, and personalized settings.

REFERENCES

Adelman, H., & Taylor, L. (1983). *Learning disabilities in perspective.* Glenview, IL: Scott, Foresman.

Allen, A.R., & Boraks, N. (1978). Peer tutoring: Putting it to the test. *Reading Teacher, 31,* 274–278.

Asher, S.R., Oden, S.L., & Gottman, J.M. (1977). Children's friendships in school settings. In L.G. Katz (Ed.), *Current topics in early childhood education,* Vol. 1 (pp. 33–61). Norwood, NJ: Ablex.

Baumgart, D., Brown, L., Pumpian, I., Nisbet, J., Ford, A., Sweet, M., Messina, R., & Schroeder, J. (1982). Principle of partial participation and individualized adaptations in educational programs for severely handicapped students.

Journal of the Association for the Severely Handicapped, 7, 17–27.

Bishop, K.D. & Falvey, M.A. (1986). Motor skills. In M.A. Falvey, *Community-based curriculum: Instructional strategies for students with severe handicaps* (pp. 139–161). Baltimore: Paul H. Brookes Publishing Co.

Brown, L., Nietupski, J., & Hamre-Nietupski, S. (1976). The criterion of ultimate functioning and public school services for severely handicapped children. In M.A. Thomas (Ed.), *Hey, don't forget about me: Education's investment in the severely, profoundly, and multiply handicapped* (pp. 2–15). Reston, VA: Council for Exceptional Children.

Dineen, J.P., Clark, H.P., & Risley, T.R. (1977). Peer tutoring among elementary students: Education benefits to the tutor. *Journal of Applied Behavior Analysis, 10,* 231–238.

Edmonds, R. (1979). Some schools work and more can. *Social Policy,* 9(2), 28–32.

Falvey, M.A. (1986). *Community-based curriculum: Instructional strategies for students with severe handicaps.* Baltimore: Paul H. Brookes Publishing Co.

Goodlad, J. (1984). *A place called school: Prospects for the future.* New York: McGraw-Hill.

Grenot-Scheyer, M., & Falvey, M.A. (1986). Integration issues and strategies. In M.A. Falvey, *Community-based curriculum: Instructional strategies for students with severe handicaps* (pp. 217–234). Baltimore: Paul H. Brookes Publishing Co.

Hartup, W.W. (1975). The origins of friendship. In M. Lewis & L.A. Rosenblum (Eds.), *Friendships and peer relations* (pp. 11–27). New York: John Wiley & Sons.

Heron, T.E., & Harris, K.C. (1987). *The educational consultant: Helping professionals, parents, and mainstreamed students.* Austin: PRO-ED.

Howes, C. (1983). Patterns of friendship. *Child development, 54,* 1041–1053.

Hyman, J.S. & Cohen, S.A. (1979). Learning for mastery: Ten conclusions after 15 years and 3,000 schools. *Educational Leadership, 27* 104–109.

Johnson, R.T., & Johnson, D.W. (1981). Building friendships between handicapped and nonhandicapped students: Effects of cooperative and individualistic instruction. *American Educational Research Journal, 18,* 415–423.

Johnson, R., Johnson, D.W., DeWeerdt, N., Lyons, V., & Zaidman, B. (1987). Integrating severely adaptively handicapped seventh grade students into constructive relationships with nonhandicapped peers in science class. *American Journal of Mental Deficiency, 87,* 611–619.

Johnson, D.W., Johnson, R.T., Holubec, E.J., & Roy, P. (1984). *Circles of learning: Cooperation in the classroom.* Alexander, VA: Association for Supervision and Curriculum Development.

Johnson, D.W., Johnson, R.T., Warring, D., & Maruyama, G. (1986). Different cooperative learning procedures and cross handicap relationships. *Exceptional Children, 53,* 247–252.

Jones, B.F., Friedman, L.B., Tinzman, M., & Cox, B.E. (1984). Guidelines for instruction: Enriched mastery learning to improve comprehension. In D.U. Levine (Ed.), *Improving student achievement through mastery learning programs* (pp. 91–153). San Francisco: Jossey-Bass.

Kohl, F.L., Moses, L.G., & Stettner-Eaton, B.A. (1983). The results of teaching fifth and sixth graders to be instructional trainers with students who are severely handicapped. *Journal of the Association of the Severely Handicapped, 8,* 32–40.

McHale, S.W., Olley, J.G., Marcus, L.M., & Simeonsson, R.J. (1981). Nonhandicapped peers as tutors for autistic children. *American Journal of Mental Deficiency, 85*(1), 18–24.

Rubin, S.E., & Spady W.G. (1984). Achieving excellence through outcome-based instructional delivery, *Educational Leadership, 41,* 37–44.

Rynders, J.E., Johnson, R.T., Johnson, D.W., & Schmidt, B. (1980). Producing positive interactions among Down syndrome and nonhandicapped students through cooperative goal structuring. *American Journal of Mental Deficiency, 85,* 268–273.

Stainback, W., & Stainback, S. (1984). A rationale for the merger of special and regular education. *Exceptional Children, 51,* 102–111.

Strain, P.S. (1983). Generalization of autistic children's social behavior change: Effects of developmentally integrated and segregated settings. *Analysis and Intervention in Developmental Disabilities, 3,* 23–34.

Strain, P.S., & Kerr, M.M. (1981). Modifying children's social withdrawal: Issues in assessment and clinical intervention. In M. Hersen, R.M. Eisler, & P.M. Miller (Eds.), *Progress in behavior modification, Vol. II (pp. 203–249).* New York: Academic Press.

Strully, J., & Strully, C. (1985). Teach your children. *Canadian Journal of Mental Retardation, 35*(4), 3–11.

Voeltz, L.M. (1980). Children's attitudes toward handicapped peers. *American Journal of Mental Deficiency, 84*, 455–464.

Yager, S., Johnson, R.T., Johnson, D.W., & Snider, B. (1985). The effects of cooperative and individualistic learning experiences on positive and negative cross-handicap relationships. *Contemporary Educational Psychology, 10*, 127–138.

CHAPTER 12

Assessment Procedures for Use in Heterogeneous Classrooms

James G. Shriner, James E. Ysseldyke, and Sandra L. Christenson

When most teachers and preservice teachers consider the term *assessment,* they tend to think about testing students. This chapter uses the word more broadly, as "the process of collecting data for the purposes of (1) specifying and verifying problems and (2) making decisions about students" (Salvia & Ysseldyke, 1988, p. 5). This definition includes the word "*purpose*"—the key component of assessment practice. Whenever one thinks about assessment, one must consider the purposes for which data are collected. In educational settings, assessment data are collected to make several different kinds of educational decisions. For example, teachers gather assessment data to aid in deciding whether to promote students, as well as the level of instruction to use with students, whether students exhibit sufficient educational difficulties to warrant referral to a specialist, whether students are making progress in their instructional programs, and so forth.

Assessment practices are a part of *all* education. Teachers use assessment information to make instructional decisions, that is, to select the materials they will use with students, to form reading groups, and to assign grades. Teachers thus gather data for the purpose of making decisions about and sometimes for students. The data collection process is called *assessment.*

This chapter first describes the kinds of procedures teachers and other school personnel use to gather assessment information, followed by an explanation of the necessary relationship between assessment and instruction. Next, the kinds of decisions school personnel make using assessment information are discussed. The majority of the chapter is then devoted to describing alternative assessment approaches: norm-referenced assessment, curriculum-based assessment, and assessment of instructional environments.

DATA COLLECTION PROCEDURES

Assessment information is collected in many different ways. Consider the myriad ways teachers use to decide whether students are learning, whether instructional programs are working, whether students ought to be referred for evaluation by specialists such as psychologists, remedial reading teachers, or speech and language pathologists. Sometimes teachers simply look at their students and keep track "in their heads" of what is going on for specific individuals. Certainly teachers learn much about individual students based simply on their daily interactions with them. When teachers gather data simply by looking at students, one usually talks about the process as one of *observation*. Sometimes observation is a formal process (the teacher or someone else watches a student or group of students and records what is observed). At other times, the observation is informal (the teacher or someone else simply makes a few notes about what a student or group of students did at a specific time).

Assessment information is also collected by means of tests. Many different kinds of formal tests are used. The reader has probably heard teachers talk about using intelligence tests (sometimes called measures of learning aptitude), achievement tests, personality tests, and so forth. Yet, there are basically two kinds of tests, norm-referenced tests and curriculum-based tests, whose terms describe competing ways in which tests are used to make decisions. (More information on these two types of tests and approaches to testing is offered later in this chapter.)

Assessment information is furthermore often collected by means of interview. People who conduct assessments often interview teachers and sometimes parents or other individuals in a student's environment. On occasion, interview strategies are the only methods that can be used to gather data. Consider, for example, instances in which the student is severely developmentally delayed, so much so that it literally is impossible to give the student a test. The assessor is restricted in data collection to observation and interview strategies. The assessor must therefore ask people who live or work with the child the kinds of behaviors the child shows.

Finally, assessment information is collected by means of searching past records, including students' cumulative files containing records of school performance, past test scores, and some health information. Assessors sometimes also review medical records or records of individual's social histories.

In effective assessment, not all data gathered relate specifically to *the child*. Rather, gathering data about the environment in which the child is expected to perform is also necessary—such as teacher expectations, the performance and behavior of other students in a room, the nature of the home environment, the instructional methodologies or strategies being used with a student, and so forth.

ASSESSMENT-INTERVENTION LINK

As has been stated, many different kinds of assessment information are gathered on and about students. Yet when all is said and done, the only valid reason for assessing a student is to make a positive difference for the student. In some way, the act of assessing a student ought to enhance his or her life. Frankly, if it is not clear just how specific data will improve a student's life, or will enrich the student's instructional experiences, then the data should not be collected. At the same time, blind programming or instruction in the absence of good comprehensive data on pupil performance is a wasted activity. The critical point to be made here is that there ought to be well-established links between assessment and intervention. "Assessment has little purpose or value unless it leads to individualized programming; programming without assessment is an imprecise and wasteful activity" (Bagnato, 1983, p. 100).

ASSESSMENT AND DECISION MAKING

Recall that one of the purposes of assessment is to make decisions about students. Basically, there are five general types of decisions that can be made: screening, referral for specific services, classification, instructional planning, and pupil progress evaluation. *Screening decisions* are made to determine if a student is significantly different in some way from his or her peers. Screening is the initial step during which students are sorted out from the general population based on some physical, academic, or behavioral characteristic. *Referral decisions* are made when a need for assistance from other personnel is suspected. Teachers often feel that a particular student may need help in some area (e.g., vision, reading) beyond what they can provide. *Classification decisions* continue the process of sorting students into groups, usually into categories of eligibility for special services. In classification, the student is sometimes labeled as exceptional—either educationally handicapped or educationally gifted.

This chapter is concerned primarily with the two remaining types of decisions, instructional planning and pupil progress evaluation. Of primary importance to these authors is assessment for *instructional planning*. Teachers need to decide what to teach (goals and objectives for students) and how to teach (methods and strategies to be used). An ongoing task for the teacher is to ascertain the extent to which students have learned what has been taught. Both the teachers' and students' time is wasted if instruction is offered on skills and material already known by the student or on tasks for which the student does not have the appropriate prerequisite skills.

Decisions about how to teach are those that focus on finding the best method of instruction for students. The best way to teach students is to rely on generally effective procedures (see the section later in this chapter, Assessing the Instructional Environment). Teachers are charged with the continuing duty of translating principles of effective instruction into daily classroom practice. Assessment for planning how to teach is done to ascertain the extent to which the teacher's specific applications of effective teaching principles are working in a particular classroom for individual students.

Finally, *pupil progress evaluation* is also important to classroom teachers. Day-to-day, week-to-week, month-to-month, and year-to-year changes in student progress indicate how that pupil is fairing in a particular educational program. Teachers gather data to decide the extent to which an instructional program is working for the student.

NORM-REFERENCED ASSESSMENT

Often the tests used to make decisions about students are norm-referenced tests, in which the current achievement or performance level of a student is compared to the achievement or performance level of his or her peers. The purpose of norm-referenced assessment is to compare, that is, to rank a student's performance in relation to a reference group of persons with similar characteristics. The rankings can be used to describe the student's current achievement or performance level in a fairly objective manner. To a limited extent, knowledge of the scores pupils earn on norm-referenced tests is helpful in instructional planning. Such knowledge helps a teacher decide what to teach. Norm-referenced assessments yield a variety of scores that can be used in the ranking process. Several types of these scores are discussed next.

Age- and Grade-Equivalent Scores

Often when norm-referenced tests are used, the student's performance is compared to other students of a particular age or grade level. The student's raw score on a test is converted to an age-equivalent or grade-equivalent score. These scores are interpreted as being like the average performance of a student of the same age or grade. For example, if Ronald obtains a grade-equivalent score of 4.3 on a spelling measure, he is said to have spelled correctly the same number of words as the average child in the 3d month of fourth grade. Similarly, a student who earns an age-equivalent score of 8-2 spelled correctly about the same number of words as a student 8 years, 2 months old.

Grade- and age-equivalent scores are not very useful and can be misleading. This is because neither score tells how many or which questions the students attempted to answer, nor how they approached the test problems. Care in using grade- and age-equivalent scores means knowing what they do and do not communicate.

Percentile Ranks

A commonly used score from norm-referenced assessment is the percentile rank, which indicates the percentage of students scoring at or below a certain raw score. Percentile ranks can refer to grade- or age-based norm groups. For example, if an 11-year-old obtains a certain raw score that converts to an age percentile rank of 50.0, the student is said to have scored as well as, or better than, 50% of the 11-year-olds who took the test. In addition, a fourth grader whose grade percentile rank on a test is determined to be 84.5, scored as well as, or better than, 84.5% of the fourth graders taking the test.

Standard Scores

Scores on norm-referenced tests often are expressed in the form of standard scores. A standard score tells how far an individual's score is from the average score. One such standard score is the Z-score (a score with an average of 0 and a standard deviation of 1).

Z-scores are sometimes transformed into other standard scores—for example, the T-score (average = 50, standard deviation = 10). Three other types of standard scores are Stanines, Normal Curve Equivalents (NCEs), and College Entrance Examination Board (CEEB) scores. All standard scores are used simply to provide teachers with an indication of how a student performed relative to others.

Kinds of Norm-Referenced Tests

Norm-referenced assessment devices include a wide variety of tests in many domains: intelligence, language, personality, adaptive behavior, and academic achievement. Classroom teachers typically use tests from the latter two domains. Only norm-referenced achievement and diagnostic tests are discussed briefly here, but the reader is referred to Salvia and Ysseldyke (1988) for a comprehensive review of norm-referenced assessment devices in all domains.

Norm-referenced tests may be either group administered (given to more than one student at a time) or individually administered (given to only one student at a time). They may be tests of a single skill area or multiple skill batteries. Figure 1 outlines the many kinds of norm-referenced tests available today. Some of these tests are screening tests; that is, they are intended to give a global estimate of student performance. Their function is to rank order students by

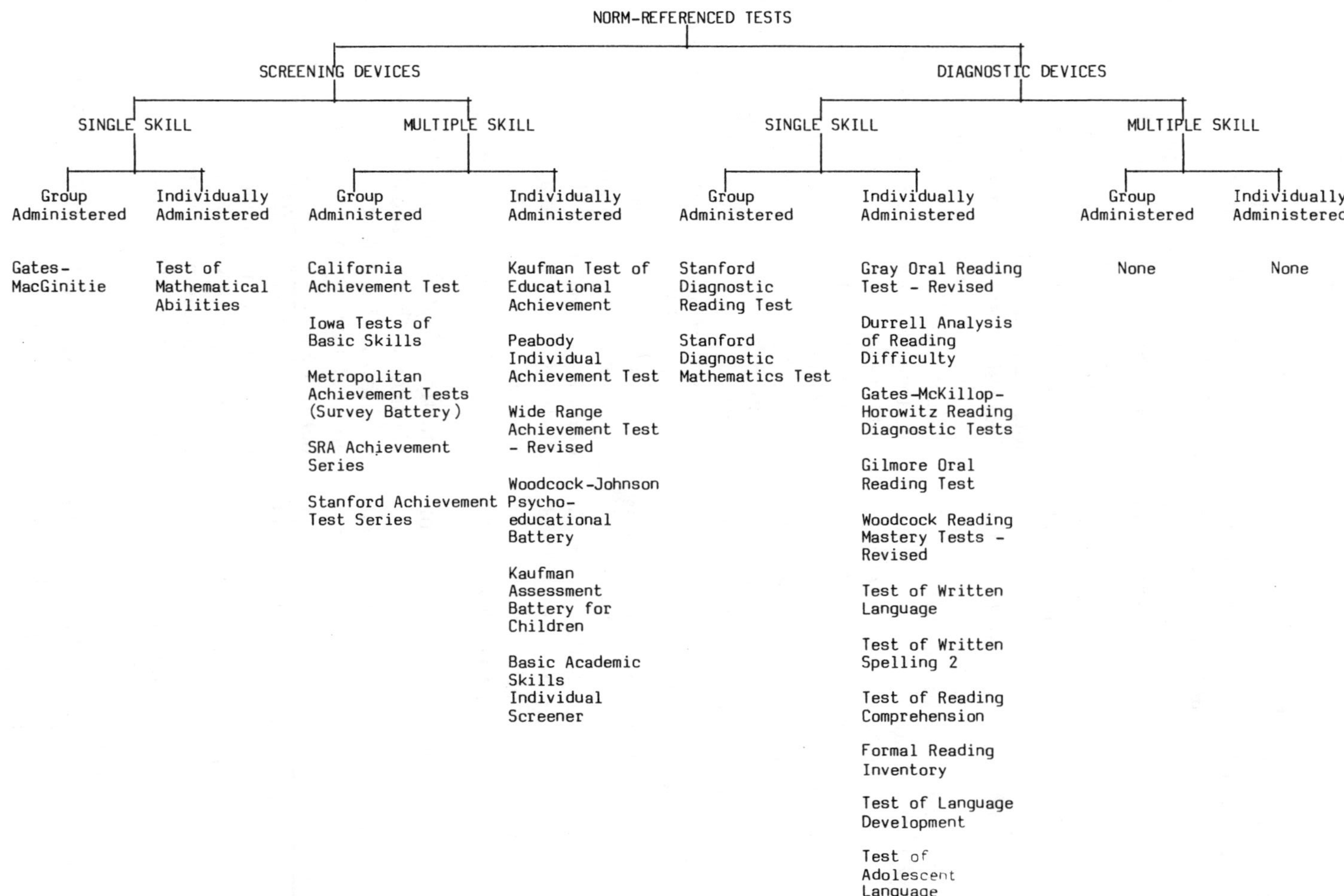

Figure 1. Norm-referenced tests. (From Salvia, J., & Ysseldyke, J.E. [1988]. *Assessment in special and remedial education* [Vol. 4]. Boston: Houghton-Mifflin; adapted by permission.)

academic performance, providing an indication of which students show low, average, or high achievement in comparison to a peer group. Other norm-referenced tests are diagnostic; that is, they are supposed to give a clearer picture of a student's academic strengths and weaknesses in a particular domain (e.g., mathematics). Below are some examples and descriptions of norm-referenced tests.

The *Iowa Tests of Basic Skills* (ITBS) (Hieronymus, Lindquist, & Hoover, 1983) is a norm-referenced, group administered, multiple skill achievement battery. It is normally given to students about once every 2 or 3 years. The complete battery has 15 subtests and measures skills for listening, vocabulary, word analysis, reading, writing, methods of study, and mathematics. The ITBS is intended for grades K–9 for the purpose of providing "information about strengths and weaknesses in the instructional program and about skills performance of individual pupils that will constitute a partial basis for making instructional decisions" (Hieronymus et al., 1983, p. 1). The ITBS is still most accurately described as a screening test, because it gives a global estimate of student skill levels and rank orders students by academic performance.

The *Peabody Individual Achievement Test* (PIAT) (Dunn & Markwardt, 1970) is a norm-referenced, individually administered test of academic achievement. It is a multiple skill screening device for students in grades K–12, and contains subtests of mathematics, reading recognition, reading comprehension, spelling, and general information. The advantage of an individually administered test is that the evaluator can gain qualitative information about the student during the testing session. Individual test administrations afford the examiner an opportunity to analyze the student's test performance much more thoroughly. Careful examination of the types of items that are difficult for the student is a most effective use of individual norm-referenced tests like the PIAT.

The ITBS and PIAT give the standard scores previously discussed. Both tests are screening tests and provide global estimates of student achievement. The *Gray Oral Reading Test–Revised* (GORT-R) (Weiderholt & Bryant, 1986) is a norm-referenced diagnostic test of reading and is designed to provide more specific information about students' abilities in a particular domain. The test's purpose is to assist in the examination of oral reading miscues and reading comprehension. As a diagnostic test, it is supposed to provide specific information about reading and, as such, yields slightly different scores than screening tests. The kinds of oral reading miscues and the number and percentage of errors are used as the bases of GORT-R scores.

In summary, norm-referenced assessment devices (screening and diagnostic) can provide the teacher with a general idea of students' performance and achievement in relation to their peers. If a new student moves into a school from another city or state, a norm-referenced test gives some indication of where the teacher should begin, possibly with more sensitive assessments of skill levels. The major function of norm-referenced tests is to rank order students by performance. Norm-referenced tests do not, however, provide sufficient information to plan instruction. In most cases, a more exact examination of student performance on individual test items is required to accurately gauge proper instructional plans.

CRITERION-REFERENCED ASSESSMENT

Seldom, if ever, does knowledge of a child's relative standing in reference to a group of his or her peers provide enough information to make sound educational decisions. Norm-referenced assessments only answer the question of student ranking. What, then, is needed to supply adequate data for other decisions? In many instances, the partial answer is criterion-referenced assessment (sometimes also called objective-referenced assessment).

Criterion-referenced assessment is not concerned with comparing students to one another, but, rather, with making judgments about students' performance in comparison to a predetermined standard. The major purpose of criterion-referenced assessment is to identify those skills that have and have not been mastered by the student. In most cases, criterion-referenced tests give more exact information about how a student performs on specific academic tasks than do norm-referenced tests.

Criterion-referenced tests give different information to the test user than do norm-referenced tests. Instead of providing grade-equivalent scores or percentile ranks, criterion-referenced tests give descriptive information such as:

Heather multiplied 2-digit numbers by 2-digit numbers without error.
Craig correctly spelled 80% of the words from Level II of the *Sprinkles Word List*.
Sylvia read 107 words per minute with 3 or fewer errors in the *HECTOR Series*, Level IV.

Criterion-referenced assessment is different from norm-referenced assessment in terms of the meaning of the scores the tests provide. Norm-referenced tests compare people to a middle point (or norm), and a person's performance is described according to how much lower or higher than the norm this score is. Criterion-referenced testing, on the other hand, provides scores relative to a standard beginning at a low end (none of the skills measured are observed) and ending at a high end (all of the skills measured are observed). A person's score on a criterion-referenced test is a comparison to a skill level, and not a comparison to other persons. Block (1971) describes ideal criterion-referenced tests when he states, "They indicate what a student has and has not learned because they are taken from a fully representative sample of skills (content and behavior), drawn from those he was expected to learn" (p. 289).

In criterion-referenced testing, there is greater concern with the issue of what to teach, along with a specific effort to link assessment to instruction. Specific items on criterion-referenced tests are often linked directly to specific instructional objectives.

The BRIGANCE® Diagnostic Inventories are an example of comprehensive criterion-referenced assessments. The BRIGANCE® consists of three batteries: the *Diagnostic Inventory of Early Development* (Brigance, 1978), the *Diagnostic Inventory of Basic Skills* (Brigance, 1977), and the *Diagnostic Inventory of Essential Skills* (Brigance, 1980). The BRIGANCE® contains over 140 specific subtests in four areas: academic readiness, reading, language arts, and mathematics. These individually administered subtests help teachers pinpoint basic skills the student has mastered. Most of the skills assessed by the BRIGANCE® are referenced to widely used commercial curricula, and it is indicated when the skills are first introduced and when they are considered mastered by the majority of students. No direct comparison to the performance of other students is made. The most useful scores given by the BRIGANCE® are really not scores per se, but, rather, a delineation of academic skills that have been mastered by the student. A teacher can use this information to write behavioral objectives and to plan instruction.

Criterion-referenced tests with limited subskill breakdown cannot provide adequately detailed information for instructional planning decisions. Also, criterion-referenced tests cannot be given repeatedly over time, since the student would most likely demonstrate altered performance because of practice on items, and because most classroom teachers simply do not have the time to devote to this endeavor.

Finally, a number of authors (e.g., Jenkins & Pany, 1978; Salvia & Ysseldyke, 1988; Shapiro & Lentz, 1986; Shriner & Salvia, 1988) warn that because most commercially available tests (norm- and criterion-referenced) are designed to reflect a wide variety of curricula, they may not adequately and accurately reflect the specific instructional content to which the student has been exposed. The noncorrespondence of test and curricular content gives misleading information about students' skill levels and instructional needs.

CURRICULUM-BASED ASSESSMENT

Curriculum-based assessment (CBA) is a generic term covering several different evaluation methods. It is a form of criterion-referenced assessment. Some authors (e.g., Gickling & Havertape, 1981) use the term *curriculum-based assessment* to describe "a procedure for determining the instructional needs of a student based upon the student's ongoing performance within existing course content" (p. CBA/R4). Deno (1986) uses the term *curriculum-based measurement* (CBM) to describe procedures developed through the Institute for Research on Learning Disabilities at the University of Minnesota. The procedures become curriculum-based when they are applied to a given curriculum. Other names for the general method include: *objective measurement, direct measurement,* and *formative evaluation* (cited in Salvia & Ysseldyke, 1988). Regardless of terminology, however, CBA procedures are a derivative of criterion-referenced testing; curriculum-based measures are used to test what has been taught in the local school curriculum.

There are almost as many variations of CBA as there are definitions. Space limitations allow only a general description of the method here; the reader is encouraged to examine texts by Deno and Mirkin (1977), Howell and Morehead (1987), and Shapiro (1987), for in-depth descriptions of CBA procedures.

Generally, all approaches to CBA have four recommended procedures in common. First, and foremost, all materials used to generate tests are drawn directly from the curriculum used by the student in the local school. Tucker (1985) has termed CBA the "ultimate 'teaching to the test' because the materials used to assess progress are always drawn directly from the course of study" (p. 200).

Second, CBA procedures can be designed to measure both student progress and student performance. Shapiro (1987) defines progress measurement as the "establishment of the individual child's actual mastery level within the curriculum in which they are being instructed" (p. 77). An important corollary to this measurement is the child's expected level of progress (mastery) at the time of the assessment. In other words, in progress measurement, one seeks to establish what the child has accomplished in the curriculum in relation to what he or she is expected to have accomplished. Deno and Mirkin (1977) provide a system for determining desired levels of progress (mastery). The average performance of a sample of the student's "average" peers can be used to describe how the student ought to be functioning within the curriculum. Deno (1985) calls this strategy "peer referencing," and suggests using the median (middle) score of a sample of 8 to 10 students as the reference. Often the curriculum publisher provides a suggested progress chart that the teacher can use as a basis for individual judgments about student achievement within the curriculum.

Also of interest to the teacher is a child's changing performance on more limited tasks within the curriculum. For example, the number of words read correctly in a 1-minute period is a performance measure of reading fluency. Performance measures are short, timed tests (most lasting 1 to 3 minutes), and indicate behavior change on individual tasks (Deno & Mirkin, 1977). Performance measurement provides information about the ongoing development of the student.

Third, the measurements (sometimes called probes) used in CBA are given on a regular and frequent basis. Deno (1985) states that curriculum-based measures must be simple and efficient so that teachers can routinely use them to monitor student achievement, and recommends that probes be given at least twice a week.

Finally, in nearly all CBA approaches, graphs are used to depict visually the data gathered on the probes. Graphing of student progress and performance is based upon time-series analysis research. Simply stated, in time-series analysis, changes in student performance are examined at fixed, constant intervals. Marston and Magnusson (1987) state that "essential to the (CBM) process is the graphing of academic or behavioral data, and the analysis of students' learning rates in response to educational intervention" (p. 7).

Given these four commonalities of CBA, a description of two variations of the method is offered here, along with explanations of why certain procedures are used. These examples are really extensions of one of the common characteristics of CBA: progress and performance measurement. The first example is an application to mathematics, demonstrating progress evaluation; and the second is a continuation of this assessment, aimed at measuring a student's performance on a more specific mathematics task.

Progress Measurement in Mathematics

Suppose a teacher wanted to use CBA with a mathematics class. The first task is to determine which skills each student in the class has mastered in order to make appropriate placements within the local school curriculum. There are two ways to do this: selecting a curriculum-based (criterion) measure and constructing a curriculum-based measure.

The first of these options is the easier. Nearly all curriculum publishers include in their tests or materials specific level criterion-referenced mastery tests that correspond to individual book chapters or book sections. Shapiro (1987) and Howell and Morehead (1987) consider the practice of selecting mastery tests that correspond to particular sections of the curriculum as reasonable, not only for the sake of expediency, but because such assessments typically provide items matching specific instructional objectives as well.

The teacher selects the mastery tests (probes) that cover a broad range of curriculum content around the student's grade placement. Then, beginning with a best estimate of the student's progress level, probes of skills are given. Successive probes are provided so long as the student reaches a predetermined mastery criterion (to be discussed later) on each test. Placement in the curriculum can be based upon the point at which the student does not attain the mastery criterion.

The highest level at which the student reaches the criterion is recorded on a progress graph. The expected level of progress, determined by the publisher's suggested level or based on the median performance of a sample of 8–10 of the student's peers on the same probes, is also recorded on the progress graph (see Figure 2). The discrepancy between the actual and expected progress of the child forms the basis for determining how much the student may need to accomplish (in terms of objectives, pages, or chapters) to catch up with his or her peers. A notable point here is that the term *progress* refers to change over time. Repeated administrations over time will indicate the pace of progress (mastery) the student is actually making.

Using the second option mentioned here, the teacher may also elect to develop probes directly from curriculum materials. First, the skills covered in the curriculum (for the purposes of this text, the authors will limit this example to a chapter within a curriculum) must be identified and sequenced with respect to difficulty. Each specific skill covered in the chapter should be included on the probe, making a rather detailed delineation of skills important.

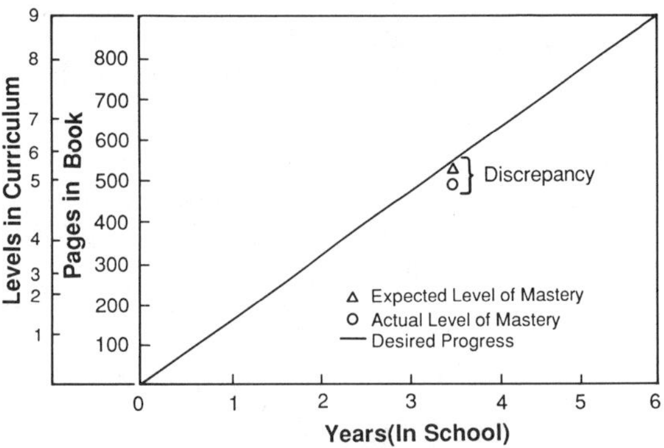

Figure 2. Sample progress graph: minor discrepancy. (From Shapiro, E.S. [1987]. *Behavioral assessment in school psychology,* p. 113. Hillsdale, NJ: Lawrence Erlbaum Associates; adapted by permission.)

Second, instructional objectives from the school district should be matched with the skills covered by the curriculum. If the district does not have predetermined objectives, an appropriate instructional objective for each listed skill should be prepared (Blankenship, 1985).

Third, test items for each objective should be prepared. CBA proponents differ on the issue of how many items are needed for each objective. Each probe should cover only a limited number of objectives, so that longer chapters may have to be assessed by more than one probe. Howell and Morehead (1987) recommend 10 items per objective. To provide a sufficiently large item pool for alternate forms of the probe, the teacher should probably expect to write at least 30 items for each objective.

Deno and Mirkin (1977) have presented an instructional sequence for elementary mathematics instruction containing 84 skills. The objective-referenced system is not tied to a specific curriculum. If an objective-referenced system is used, each specific level can be assessed by probes containing a minimum of 5 items from that level and 1 item from each of the preceding levels. No probe should be less than 25 items in total length.

After the items are written for each objective and are divided into alternate forms of each skill probe, the remaining CBA procedures are the same as though an existing mastery test from the curriculum had been selected to be used as a probe. Probes are given beginning with a best estimate of the student's mastery or progress. Successive probes are given so long as the student meets the preselected criterion for mastery. Placement in the curriculum can be based upon the point at which the student does not attain mastery. The student's present mastery level is recorded on a progress graph, as in Figure 2.

Selecting Mastery Criteria and Scoring Methods for Progress Measurement

Educators have differing opinions about the level of competence a student must demonstrate to be considered to have mastered content. Also, systems of how to score test items are open to differing opinions. The two issues need to be addressed simultaneously in CBA.

For decisions of placement within a curriculum, a criterion for successful performance is often based on the percentage of correct answers to entire problems a student gives on the tests. Frequently, the figure of 80% is used as a minimum guideline. This criterion may have to be changed based upon the type of problem the child is expected to solve.

An alternative to using correct answers to entire problems coupled with a percentage needed for mastery, is to determine the number of correct digits and incorrect digits written per minute by the student on the test. White (1986) calls these digits "movements," as does Lovitt (1981); both of these authors base their decision rules on a system of instruction called precision teaching. The use of correct and incorrect digits per minute takes into account that not all problems the student solves are of equal length and difficulty. Deno and Mirkin (1977) suggest using this system with timed probes 3 minutes in length to determine mastery within the curriculum. Table 1 contains their recommended specific rates of correct and incorrect digits per minute for three levels of competence: mastery, instructional, and frustration. The student should be placed in the curriculum at the instructional level determined by the probes.

As can be seen from the preceding discussion, a number of combinations of standards and analyses can be used in progress measurement. What is most important is that a consistent strategy be used, and that the probes accurately reflect the curriculum. Progress measurement to determine initial placement is specific to the individual student. Students are instructed on the skill(s) that the curriculum-based measures indicate as appropriate; then the probe is periodically readministered. Progress through the curriculum is monitored by probes that follow instruction on new content topics and skills.

Performance Measurement in Mathematics

Performance measurement is done to assess the student's behavior change on an individual skill. Performance measures in math-

Table 1. Placement criteria for direct assessment of mathematics

		Criterion	
		Median digits correct per minute	Median digits incorrect per minute
	Frustration	0–9	8+
Gr. 1–3	Instructional	10–19	3–7
	Mastery	20+	≤ 2
	Frustration	0–19	8+
Gr. 4+	Instructional	20–39	3–7
	Mastery	40+	≤ 2

From Deno, S.L., & Mirkin, P.K. (1977). *Data-based program modification: A manual*, p. 89. Reston, VA: Council for Exceptional Children; reprinted with permission.

ematics could include any of the basic operations, or other particular skills from the curriculum. Unlike progress measurement, where the material included on the probes changes as the student masters curriculum objectives, performance probes include problems of a constant form and level of difficulty. Performance measurement is important, because data are provided on how readily a student can handle the basic mathematics operations. It is not enough to know how to add 2 plus 3; some children who have adequate computational knowledge fail in mathematics because of slow rates (Shapiro, 1987). It is important to increase fluency and automaticity with basic calculations (Howell & Morehead, 1987).

Performance probes are typically made after the student's correct placement within the curriculum is established. Probes consist of basic skill computations commensurate with the student's current curriculum level. For example, a student at the second-grade mathematics curriculum level might be given performance probes on computation requiring addition of a 1-digit number and a 2-digit number without regrouping. A student in the fifth-grade curriculum level might be given probes of basic division facts for the 2s and 3s. Performance probes are not difficult to construct; the teacher can randomly select problems of a particular form and level of difficulty from the curriculum.

Selecting Performance Criteria and Scoring Methods for Performance Measurement

The scoring of performance probes changes as the type of problem tested changes. For simple facts and computational problems, the number of correct and incorrect problems per minute are good measures. For more complicated calculations, such as

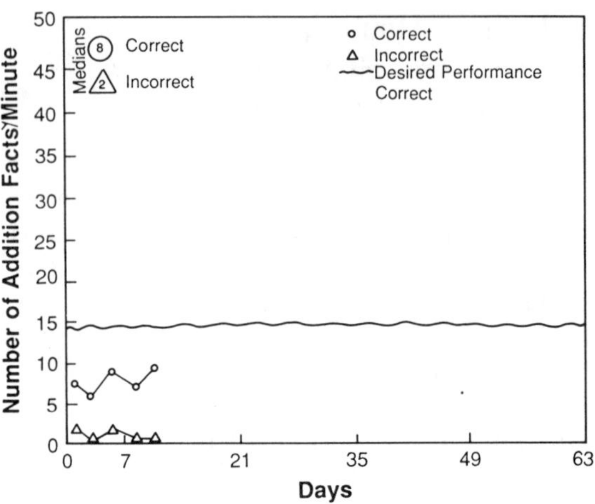

Figure 3. Sample performance graph: addition facts.

longer multiplication and division problems, the number of digits written correctly and incorrectly per minute are the preferred data to collect (Deno & Mirkin, 1977; Shapiro, 1987). Figure 3 is a typical performance graph for basic addition facts.

ORGANIZING AND USING CBA DATA

In virtually all variations of CBA, student progress and/or performance is displayed visually. There are many ways to chart and graph data, and the advantages and disadvantages of each depend on the purpose of the graph (progress versus performance) and the teacher's preference in recording data. Fuchs and Fuchs (1986), who have researched decision-making processes in curriculum-based systems, concluded that when decision rules, *including graphing of data*, are routinely applied, student achievement can be increased. Deno and Fuchs (1987) noted, however, that no clear decision of the "best" graphing system can be made.

Progress Graphs

Graphs representing progress through the curriculum are used to record the student's achievement in terms of cumulative units of the curriculum per specified unit of time. The vertical axis of a progress graph is marked off by the selected unit of the curriculum. Deno and Fuchs (1987) recommended choosing a relatively small unit of mastery such as "number of pages mastered," because students' growth can be detected more easily. Also, larger units of mastery (e.g., chapters or levels) are less likely to represent equal units of progress. (Figure 2, a progress graph, is labeled with both pages and levels as units of mastery.)

Desired progress through the curriculum is also marked on the graph. This line is sometimes called a "goal line" or an "aim line" and is determined by the long-range goal for the student. The publisher's suggested progress in the curriculum sequence is used as the basis for deciding this goal, but teachers often set differing goals for individual students.

Performance Graphs

Performance graphs visually display a child's change in behavior on a particular task or skill of a fixed difficulty level. The skill being tested is labeled on the vertical axis, and the horizontal axis denotes time. Desired performance is marked by a horizontal line representing the median performance of a sample of 8 to 10 of the student's peers on the same probes, or some other criterion for performance that the teacher believes is appropriate.

Expected and Actual Trend Lines

The expected progress lines for a progress graph connect the student's current level of mastery with the desired mastery point at the end of the current program (e.g., semester or school year). For a performance graph, the point marking the student's current performance is connected to the point marking the median performance of the student's peers or other desired performance at the end of the current program. Expected progress and performance lines indicate the trend that behavior change must take for student success (Deno & Mirkin, 1977).

Actual changes in student progress or performance are visually displayed by the use of *trend lines*. The procedure for drawing trend lines described here is based on the work of White (1972). Mirkin, Deno, et al. (1981) suggest that after 7 to 10 probes have been given, trend lines should be drawn to indicate the direction and rate of student behavior change. There are six basic steps in this procedure, as illustrated in Figure 4.

Step 1: Draw a vertical line separating the data points so that one-half are on the left of the line and one-half are on the right of the line.

Step 2: Looking at only the data points on the left half of the graph, draw another vertical line separating these points so that half are on the left and half are on the right of the second vertical line.

Step 3: Looking at only the data points on the right of the first vertical line (drawn in Step 1), repeat Step 2.

Step 4: Find the median of the lefthand data points, the median of the righthand data points, and mark them on the outer vertical lines.

Step 5: Draw a line connecting the median points marked on the outer lines. This new line is the *trend line*.

Step 6: Adjust the trend line up or down so that one-half of the data points are on or above it and one-half are on or below it. Keep the adjusted trend line parallel to the original trend line.

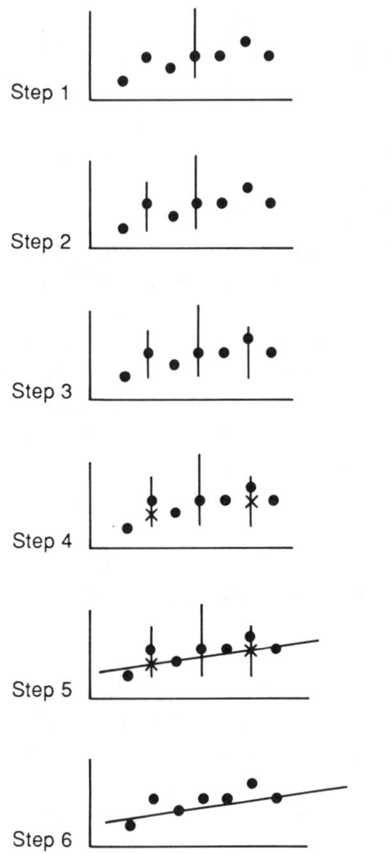

Figure 4. Six-step procedure for drawing trend lines.

MAKING DECISIONS BASED ON TREND LINES

There are two basic decision types in CBA procedures: goal-oriented decisions and treatment or program-oriented decisions (Deno & Fuchs, 1987; Marston & Magnusson, 1987). Goal-oriented decisions are based upon the relationship between a student's current mastery or performance level and the prespecified goal set for the future. Goal-oriented decisions are made by determining if the slope of the student's trend line is flatter than, equal to, or steeper than the line representing the student's expected level of performance (i.e., whether or not the student will attain the prespecified goal).

If the slope of the student's actual trend line is flatter than the expected trend line, the instructional program should probably be changed. If the actual slope is equal to or steeper than the expected trend line, the program should probably be left intact. Sometimes decisions of whether or not instructional programs need to be altered are based on the number of data points falling below the expected trend line. Deno and Fuchs (1987) note that the specific number of data points is variable, depending on how frequently probes are given. A common standard is to change instructional programs designed to increase student performance if three consecutive data points (collected on a twice-weekly basis) are below the expected trend line. Decisions to change instructional programs might also be made if student performance on the probes becomes very unstable. A high degree of variability in student performance is an indication that the teacher should analyze the current instructional program and decide if a change is warranted.

Basically, decisions based on direct measurement of student performance and interpreted systematically (i.e., slope of trend lines, number of data points below expected trend line, variability) boil down to common sense. If an instructional program is working, stick with it; if it is not, change it.

Change in instructional strategies can be adjustments in teaching procedures, in student grouping arrangements, in time allocated to instruction, in materials, or in motivational strategies. When an adjustment or change is made, a vertical line is drawn on the progress or performance graph, marking when the change occurs and labeling it with a descriptive phrase. Figure

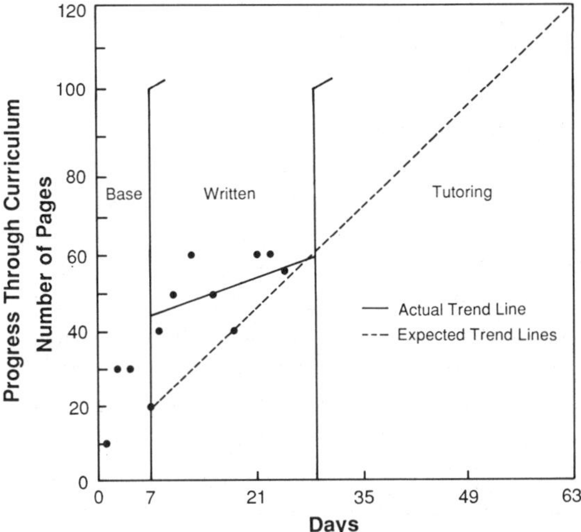

Figure 5. Progress graph: goal-oriented decision rules.

5 is a progress graph showing goal-oriented decision making and labeled instructional changes.

The other type of decision in CBA procedures is the treatment or program-oriented decision. Such decisions are based on the student's *past* progress or performance trend; the underlying objective is to increase the student's rate of behavior change and frequency of correct responses to the highest possible levels. Deno (1986) has noted that instructional plans for students are really *instructional hypotheses*. When an instructional strategy is used and CBA data are collected on changes in student behavior, the hypotheses are tested and the strategy's effectiveness is judged. Ineffective strategies produce undesirable or trivial changes in the slope of the student's performance graph, and should be changed. Effective strategies will make the slope of the trend line steeper, increase the frequency of correct responses by the student, or both. Instructional changes based on treatment-oriented decisions are recorded in the same manner as in goal-oriented decisions. The graph in Figure 6 depicts treatment or program-oriented decision strategies.

The choice between using goal-oriented and treatment-oriented decision making strategies is largely one of personal preference. Mirkin, Fuchs, Tindal, Christenson, & Deno (1981) concluded that student achievement was not differentially affected by decision type. More recently, however, Fuchs (in press) provided some evidence that student achievement was increased when teachers used goal-oriented decision strategies. Teachers also tend to believe they are more effective when they use goal-oriented decisions (Tindal, Fuchs, Christenson, Mirkin, & Deno, 1981).

Deno and Fuchs (1987) note that teachers may prefer a combination of the two data-utilization methods. Goal-oriented decision rules, indicating *when* an instructional program should be changed, coupled with treatment-oriented rules, pointing to *what* would be changed, provide a combination of information that addresses the needs of *all* students within the classroom. In this

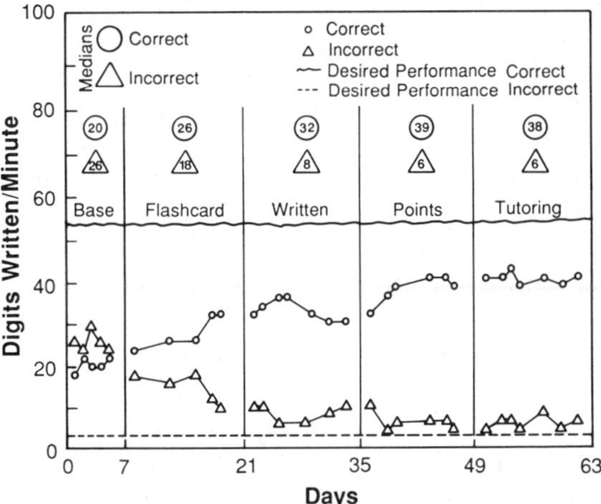

Figure 6. Performance graph: treatment-oriented decision rules. (From Shapiro, E.S. [1987]. *Behavioral assessment in school psychology,* p. 102. Hillsdale, NJ: Lawrence Erlbaum Associates; adapted by permission.)

combined system, the student's trend line is compared to the expected level of performance every time 7 to 10 data points of student performance are collected. In this way, a student's progress or performance under current instructional program conditions *and* his or her progress toward the instructional goals are simultaneously analyzed. Appropriate goal or treatment decisions can then be made. The reader is referred to Mirkin, Deno, et al. (1981) for a complete description of this approach.

CBA PROCEDURES FOR READING

Progress Measurement in Reading: Materials

The first task in progress measurement is to select the materials to be read by the student. The teacher should randomly select three reading passages from each third of every book in the reading series used in the local school. Each passage should be between 150 and 200 words in length. To save time in the long run, each selected passage should be retyped and several copies made of each one. On one of the copies, the cumulative word counts for each line should be marked in the righthand margin; this copy is for the teacher or evaluator, and the word counts will assist in scoring procedures. (To protect the copies from damage through repeated use, the teacher may wish to laminate them.)

Comprehension questions for each passage should also be written. Deno and Mirkin (1977) suggest writing who, what, when, where, why, and how questions. Hansen and Eaton (cited in Shapiro, 1987) recommend using questions of recall sequence, vocabulary, and analysis. Between five and eight questions for each passage are recommended (Shapiro, 1987).

Giving the Tests

The teacher should estimate the student's present mastery level in the curriculum as the starting point for the placement procedure. The student is asked to read each of the three passages at that level for 1 minute. The teacher records the number of correct and incorrect words *per minute* on each passage. Examples of incorrect responses are: omissions, mispronunciations, substitutions, and hesitations (of at least 4 or 5 seconds). The comprehension questions are given (orally or written) after each reading passage. The percentage of correct answers is recorded by the teacher. Passages and comprehension questions are given at successively higher (or lower) levels of the curriculum until the student's level of mastery is determined.

Determining Mastery Levels

Deno and Mirkin (1977), Lovitt and Hansen (1976), and Starlin (cited in Shapiro, 1987) each recommend slightly different criteria for mastery, instructional, and frustration levels in reading. These criteria are summarized in Table 2.

The average score (Shapiro, 1987, recommends the median) of the student across the three probes at each level of the curriculum is compared to the recommended criteria in Table 2. The student's correct placement in the curriculum is at the level where he or she matches the instructional criteria. If there is not an exact match of the criteria (e.g., correct and incorrect words match, but percentage of comprehension question does not), the oral reading rates should be used as the placement determinant. The teacher

Table 2. Placement criteria for direct reading assessment

			Criterion		
			Median words correct per minute	Median words incorrect per minute	Median comprehension (% correct)
Deno and Mirkin (1977)		Frustration	29	8+	80
	Gr. 1–3	Instructional	30–49	3–7	80
		Mastery	50+	≤ 2	80
		Frustration	49	8+	80
	Gr. 4+	Instructional	50–99	3–7	80
		Mastery	100+	2	80
Lovitt and Hansen		Instructional	45–65	4–8	50–75
(1976); Starlin (1982)		Frustration	69	11+	**Uses alterna-
		Instructional	70–149	6–10	tive proce-
		Mastery	150+	5	dure.

From Shapiro, E. S. (1987). *Behavioral assessment in school psychology*, p. 94. Hillsdale, NJ: Lawrence Erlbaum Associates; reprinted with permission.

should note the deficiency in comprehension skills and provide instruction in that area.

Graphing Actual and Expected Levels of Progress

The expected level of progress through the reading curriculum can be determined by consulting the publishers' recommended guidelines, or asking teachers to provide the expected curricular level of "average" students at the end of the current program of the school year. The expected progress is marked on a progress graph, as is the student's actual progress (see Figure 7).

Selecting Units of Mastery for Progress Goals

As mentioned earlier, a relatively small unit of mastery is recommended for progress measurement. Progress goal setting is important because it provides a guideline for student achievement, and using a small unit of mastery makes noticing student gains easier. For reading, number of pages is a good choice for unit of mastery. The progress goal is marked by the expected level of mastery at the end of the current educational program, as indicated by the publisher's guide or the teacher's alternative expectation.

Progress graphs can be made using the selected unit of mastery (pages) as the label for the vertical axis and the unit of time (weeks/months) as the label for the horizontal axis.

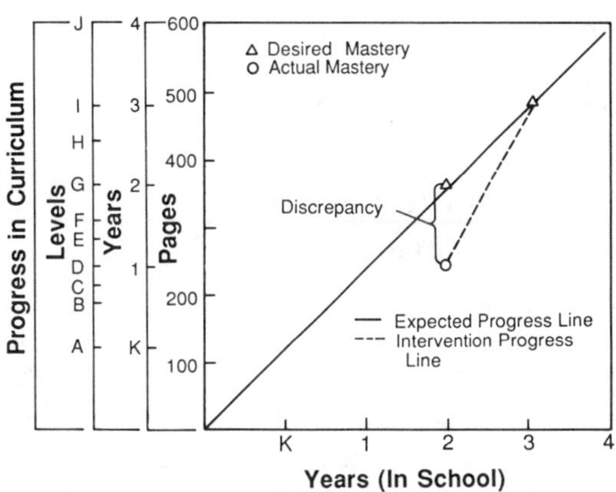

Figure 7. Sample progress graph: major discrepancy. (From Shapiro, E.S. [1987]. *Behavioral assessment in school psychology,* p. 80. Hillsdale, NJ: Lawrence Erlbaum Associates; adapted by permission.)

Performance Measurement in Reading: Materials

Performance measurement is done to assess the student's behavior change on individual skills. In the case of reading, performance measurement is typically used to judge gains in reading fluency and automaticity as measured by oral reading rates on a task of fixed difficulty. Reading passages of 150 to 200 words taken from the level of difficulty equal to the long-range goal (desired progress) level for the student are used for performance measurement. These passages are prepared as in progress measurement. Since the difficulty level of the probes used in performance measurement remains constant, several different sets of passages should be prepared so that student performance is not influenced by repeated practice on a limited number of probes.

Giving the Tests

A set of three probes of the desired progress level for the student should be selected. The student is instructed to read aloud for 1 minute from each probe. The number of correct and incorrect words per minute is recorded. The student's median performance across the three measures is noted and recorded on the graph (see Figure 8).

Determining Desired Level of Performance

A sample of 8 to 10 of the "average" students in the class are selected and given the probes at the desired level of progress. The median performance of these students for both correct and incorrect words per minute is computed and recorded on the performance graph as a horizontal line (see Figure 8).

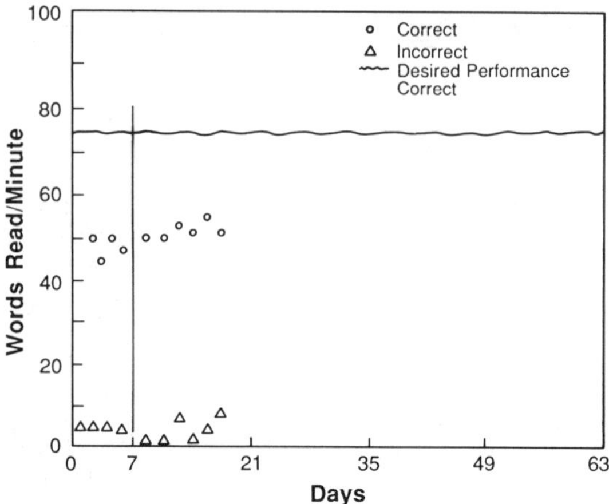

Figure 8. Sample performance graph: reading.

Interventions and Performance Measurement

The performance goals for the student are to raise the number of correct words per minute and lower the number of incorrect words per minute. When a new instructional strategy is tried (recall the discussion of decisions based on trend lines), the change is marked by a vertical line and labeled with a descriptive phrase. Performance under the new instructional strategy is then measured at least twice weekly to determine if the student is making gains toward his or her performance goals.

CURRICULUM-BASED ASSESSMENT OF SPELLING AND WRITTEN EXPRESSION

CBA can also be used for evaluation of students' spelling and written expression. The curriculum used for spelling in the local school system serves as the source of words to be used on spelling probes. The teacher should decide on a standard procedure for dictating spelling words for a probe lasting 2 minutes. White and Haring's (1980) procedure of correct letter sequences is used to score the probes. This method examines *pairs* of letters (and spaces) appearing in spelling words. Letter sequences are marked as correct or incorrect, as in Figure 9.

All other procedures (i.e., graphing, determination of expected levels of progress and performance, etc.) are only slight variations of the procedures previously described here for mathematics and reading.

Written expression is an important element of instruction for students, but often there is no formally adopted writing curriculum in the school. Some CBA proponents recommend using a "story starter" approach for CBA of written expression. In the procedure, the student is provided with an opening line of a story that matches the age and interest level of the student (e.g., "No one knew how Sheila got to the top of the hill"). They are then instructed to think about what they will write for a short time (e.g., 30 seconds), and are then given 2 or 3 minutes to write a composition. Scores are determined by counting the total number of words written correctly.

CURRICULUM-BASED ASSESSMENT-INTERVENTION LINK

Curriculum-based assessment in academic skill areas is a viable alternative to traditional assessment methods. Improved instructional planning and intervention is the bottom line of assessment. It is hard to imagine an assessment practice more closely related to the child's instruction than CBA. Decisions are made on what to teach and how to teach, and are relevant to the curriculum in which the student is taught. CBA shifts the focus of assessment from simply describing the students' characteristics to identifying the instructional needs of the student. This process is not a once-a-year, infrequent, or irregular phenomenon; determining instructional needs of students is

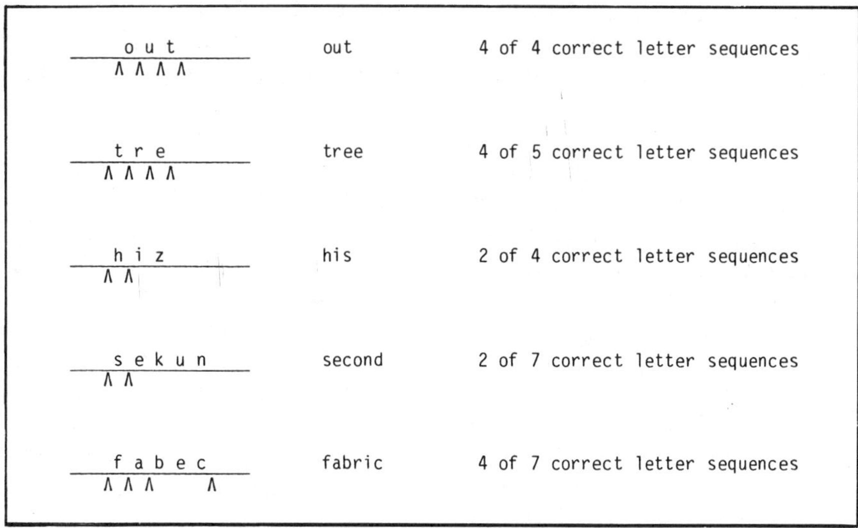

Figure 9. Scoring correct letter sequences: spelling.

the day-to-day business of teaching. Curriculum-based assessment procedures take much of the guesswork out of the practice of teaching.

ASSESSING THE INSTRUCTIONAL ENVIRONMENT

To this point, the authors have discussed methods and tools used to assess the skills, achievement, and performance *of the child*. However, assessing the student's characteristics *only* is a grave and, unfortunately, all too common mistake in education today. Christenson, Abery, and Weinberg (1986) warn that focusing on assessments that delineate within-child problems in school while ignoring consideration of factors in the ecological environment with which the child interacts is a limited, inappropriate approach to educational decision making. The environment of the home and of the school each influence student academic behavior. It is important, therefore, to broaden the scope of educational assessments to examine how home and school environmental factors affect student performance.

There is no doubt that the student's complete environment should be examined and assessed (Ysseldyke & Christenson, 1987a). Although home environmental factors have been shown to strongly influence student performance and achievement, and should ideally be considered as part of the complete assessment procedure, the focus in this chapter is on the in-school instructional environment. School classrooms are more readily accessible to teachers or other personnel for assessment purposes than is the home environment. Normally, assessment of the instructional environment is not a serious logistical concern.

Still, routine assessment of the instructional environment of students is the exception rather than the rule. This situation exists in part because the student's instructional environment is complex, and there is no quick and easy way to assess the interactions and relationships between the student and the environment in which he or she is expected to learn. The paragraphs following discuss some current and developing concepts and methods aimed at making assessment of the instructional environment a usable and productive enterprise for school personnel interested in improving instructional planning for all students in the schools.

Direct observation of the student's instructional environment is an important part of assessment practice. In the past, checklists and teacher questionnaires have been used for *indirect observation*, but often much important information is lost through this process. Direct observation emphasizes the analysis of what the student does in specific environmental conditions and how he or she interacts with the teacher and instructional tasks at hand (Shapiro, 1987).

"More than any other method, interviewing probably represents the most frequently used technique in behavioral assessment" (Shapiro, 1987, p. 44). In instructional environment assessment, interviewing of both the teacher and student is imperative, because each interacts with, and affects the behavior of, the other. Interviews afford the opportunity to collect information about the reasons for the behavior of the student or the rationale for the teacher's instructional strategies. Interviewers should be flexible in their approach and have a clear purpose in mind. Interviews often provide information not easily obtainable through other assessment strategies.

The Instructional Environment Scale (TIES) (Ysseldyke & Christenson, 1987b) is a comprehensive system geared toward examining the elements of the student's instructional environment, determining how these elements affect student performance, and using this information as a springboard for subsequent instructional planning. TIES is organized to examine 12 components of effective instruction: instructional presentation, classroom environment, teacher expectations, cognitive emphasis, motivational strategies, relevant practice, academic engaged time, informed feedback, adaptive instruction, progress evaluation, instructional planning, and student understanding.

Information about these 12 components is gathered through three main activities: classroom observation, an interview with the student, and an interview with the student's teacher. All three data-collection activities are important because the assessment of the instructional environment must be broad enough to include the student's characteristics, the teacher's instructional strategy, and the characteristics of the assigned task (Christenson & Ysseldyke, 1987b). This triangle of ecological factors defines the instructional environment for students.

Using TIES, classroom observation of the student is conducted first. Ysseldyke & Christenson (1987b) provide specific procedures for the observation, and recommend that the student be observed during the problem content area. Data from the observation are recorded in a narrative manner on the data record form.

The student interview is conducted following the observation and has two main purposes: a) to provide information on the student's perception and understanding of academic tasks; and b) to check the student success rate on assigned work. The teacher interview is conducted next to: a) provide data on those areas for which observation is inappropriate or results in incomplete information (e.g., instructional planning); and b) to understand the rationale for the teacher's instructional decisions (Ysseldyke & Christenson, 1987b, p. 12).

Following the observation and interviews, an instructional rating form is used to summarize the data in relation to each of the 12 components of effective instruction. Each component is rated on a scale of 1 to 4, with a rating of 4 corresponding to "very much like the student's instruction" and a rating of 1 corresponding to "not at all like the student's instruction." The instructional rating form also provides an opportunity to record other pertinent observations about the instructional setting, grouping arrangements, tasks, and any unusual or atypical circumstances about the observation.

The final step of the TIES procedure is to use the gathered and summarized data to pinpoint the instructional needs of the student and design interventions collaboratively with the teacher. Appropriate interventions meet student needs and are feasible for teacher implementation (Ysseldyke & Christenson, 1987a). Thus, the assessment of the total instructional environment is directly translated into instructional interventions, fulfilling the central tenet that the purpose of assessment *is* intervention.

TIES and other instructional environment assessment instruments (e.g., *Assessment of Classroom Learning Environment* [ACLE, Reynolds & Birch, 1978]) should be considered as examinations of more than just what is happening to a particular student, or of how a particular student is behaving in instructional situations. The needs assessment of instructional environments must offer a broader view of how student performance is affected by environmental variables and how those variables (student, teacher, task) *interact* with one another (Ysseldyke & Christenson, 1987a). Assessment of the instructional environment has evolved from the description of teacher and student behavior in the classroom to the analysis of the many complex interrelationships found in instructional settings.

CONCLUSION

Assessment practices in schools are changing. Until the recent past, teachers gathered data using norm-referenced tests, and, based on knowledge about a student's standing relative to others, they tried to plan instruction for the students. Sometimes the approach worked; more often it did not. Recently, assessment activities have moved closer to the arena of instruction. They have become curriculum-based, and involve direct, frequent measurement of student progress in the curriculum. Such assessment activities make it easier to plan instruction for individual students.

Until recently, those who wrote about assessment or who educated teachers only *talked* about the need to take into account the nature of students' instructional environments when making instructional decisions. At least now, there are beginning methodologies for doing so formally. Devices like TIES and ACLE can be used to gather information on the extent to which instruction is planned appropriately for the individual, the extent to which appropriate feedback procedures are being used, the extent to which instruction is presented appropriately, and so on. A combined approach in which curriculum-based strategies are paired with assessment of the instructional environment is state of the art assessment.

REFERENCES

Bagnato, S.J. (1983). Psychological and educational assessment of exceptionality. In R.M. Smith, J.T. Neisworth, & F.M. Hunt, *The exceptional child: A functional approach* (2d ed.) (pp. 100–124). New York: McGraw-Hill.

Blankenship, C.B. (1985). Using curriculum-based assessment data to make instructional decisions. *Exceptional Children, 52*, 233–238.

Block, J.H. (1971). Criterion-referenced measurement: Potential. *School Review, 79*, 289–297.

Brigance, A. (1977). *BRIGANCE® Diagnostic Inventory of Basic Skills.* North Billerica, MA: Curriculum Associates.

Brigance, A. (1978). *BRIGANCE® Diagnostic Inventory of Early Development.* North Billerica, MA: Curriculum Associates.

Brigance, A. (1980). *BRIGANCE® Diagnostic Inventory of Essential Skills.* North Billerica, MA: Curriculum Associates.

Christenson, S.C., Abery, B., & Weinberg, R.A. (1986). An alternative model for the delivery of psychology in the school community. In S.N. Elliot & J.C. Witt (Eds.), *The delivery of psychological services in schools: Concepts, processes, and issues* (pp. 349–391). Hillsdale, NJ: Lawrence Erlbaum Associates.

Christenson, S.L., & Ysseldyke, J.E. (1987). Assessing for instructional intervention: A new approach. *Topics in Learning Disabilities, 2* (4). Burlington: Vermont Department of Education.

Deno, S.L. (1985). Curriculum-based measurement: The emerging alternative. *Exceptional Children, 52*, 219–232.

Deno, S.L. (1986). Formative evaluation of individual student programs: A new role for school psychologists. *School Psychology Review, 15* (3), 358–374.

Deno, S.L., & Fuchs, L.S. (1987). Developing curriculum-based measurement systems for data-based special education problem solving. *Focus on Exceptional Children, 19*(8), 1–16.

Deno, S.L., & Mirkin, P.K. (1977). *Data-based program modification: A manual.* Reston, VA: Council for Exceptional Children.

Dunn, L.M., & Markwardt, F.C. (1970). *Peabody Individual Achievement Test.* Circle Pines, MN: American Guidance Service.

Fuchs, L.S. (in press). Effects of computer managed instruction on teacher's implementation of systematic monitoring programs and student achievement. *Journal of Educational Research.*

Fuchs, L.S., & Fuchs, D. (1986). Effects of systematic formative evaluation: A meta-analysis. *Exceptional Children, 53,* 199–208.

Gartner, A., & Lipsky, D. (1987). Beyond special education. *Harvard Educational Review, 57* (4), 367–395.

Gickling, E.E., & Havertape, J. (1981). Curriculum-based assessment. In J.A. Tucker (Ed.), *Non-test-based assessment: A training module.* Minneapolis: University of Minnesota, National School Psychology Inservice Training Network.

Hieronymus, A.N., Lindquist, E.F., & Hoover, H.D. (1983). *Iowa Tests of Basic Skills.* Chicago: Riverside.

Howell, K.W., & Morehead, M.K. (1987). Curriculum-based evaluation for special and remedial education. Columbus, OH: Charles E. Merrill.

Jenkins, J.R., & Pany, D. (1978). Standardized achievement tests: How useful for special education? *Exceptional Children, 44,* 448–453.

Lovitt, T.C. (1981). Charting academic performances of mildly handicapped youngsters. In J.M. Kaufman & D.P. Hallahan (Eds.), *Handbook of special education* (pp. 393–417). Englewood Cliffs, NJ: Prentice-Hall.

Lovitt, T.C., & Hansen, C. (1976). Round one—placing the child in the right reader. *Journal of Learning Disabilities, 9,* 347–353.

Marston, D., & Magnusson, D. (1987). Curriculum-based measurement: *An introduction.* Minneapolis: Minneapolis Public Schools.

Mirkin, P., Deno, S., Fuchs, L., Wesson, C., Tindal, G., Marston, D., & Kuehnle, K. (1981). *Procedures to develop and monitor progress on IEP goals.* Minneapolis: University of Minnesota, Institute for Research on Learning Disabilities.

Mirkin, P., Fuchs, L., Tindal, G., Christenson, S., & Deno, S. (1981). *The effect of IEP monitoring strategies on teacher behavior* (Research Report No. 62). Minneapolis: University of Minnesota, Institute for Research on Learning Disabilities.

Reynolds, M.C., & Birch, J. (1978). *Teaching exceptional children in all America's schools.* Reston, VA: Council for Exceptional Children.

Salvia, J., & Ysseldyke, J.E. (1988). *Assessment in special and remedial education* (4th ed.). Boston: Houghton Mifflin.

Shapiro, E.S. (1987). *Behavioral assessment in school psychology.* Hillsdale, NJ: Lawrence Erlbaum Associates.

Shapiro, E.S., & Lentz, F.E. (1986). Behavioral assessment of academic skills. In T. Kratochwill (Ed.), *Advances in school psychology, 5* (pp. 87–139). Hillsdale, NJ: Lawrence Erlbaum Associates.

Shriner, J.G., & Salvia, J. (1988). Chronic noncorrespondence between elementary math curricula and arithmetic tests. *Exceptional Children, 55,* 240–248.

Starlin, C.M. (1982). On reading and writing. *Iowa Monograph Series.* Des Moines, IA: Department of Public Instruction.

Tindal, G., Fuchs, L., Christenson, S., Mirkin, P., & Deno, S. (1981). *The relationship between student achievement and teacher assessment of short-or long-term goals* (Research Report No. 61). Minneapolis: University of Minnesota, Institute for Research on Learning Disabilities.

Tucker, J.A. (1985). Curriculum-based assessment: An introduction. *Exceptional Children, 52,* 199–204.

White, O.R. (1972). *A manual for the calculation and use of the median slope—A technique for progress estimation and prediction in the single case.* Working Paper No. 16, Regional Resource Center for Handicapped Children, University of Oregon, Eugene.

White, O.R. (1986). Precision teaching—precision learning. *Exceptional Children, 52,* 522–534.

White, O.R., & Haring, N.G. (1980). *Exceptional Teaching* (2d ed.). Columbus, OH: Charles E. Merrill.

Wiederholt, L., & Bryant, B. (1986). *Gray Oral Reading Test—Revised.* Austin: PRO-ED.

Ysseldyke, J.E., & Christenson, S.L. (1987a). Evaluating students' instructional environments. *Remedial and Special Education, 8*(3), 17–24.

Ysseldyke, J.E., & Christenson, S.L. (1987b). The Instructional Environment Scale. Austin: PRO-ED.

CHAPTER 13

Accommodating Student Diversity through Adaptive Instruction

Margaret C. Wang

The creation of educational environments that provide equal opportunities for schooling success for every student has been a priority throughout the history of school reform efforts. Recent years have witnessed stepped-up activity in the development of innovative programs and practices to improve schools' capabilities to meet the educational and related service support needs of an increasingly diverse student population. Program development has been paralleled by the evolution of psychological concepts and educational principles regarding the assessment and description of individual differences in learning (e.g., Brown, Bransford, Ferrara, & Campione, 1983; Corno & Snow, 1986; Wang, 1988). In addition, the implementation and refinement of instructional programs that are adaptive to individual learning needs have been influenced greatly by the wealth of recent research on effective teaching (cf. Wittrock, 1986) and on the provision of effective schooling for diverse populations (cf. Wang, Reynolds, & Walberg, 1987–1988; Wang & Walberg, 1985).

This chapter briefly discusses the rationale and design of an educational approach known as *adaptive instruction.* Specific objectives and design features of selected adaptive instruction models are highlighted, as well as key implementation considerations in the effective establishment and maintenance of the adaptive instruction approach in schools.

ADAPTIVE INSTRUCTION DEFINED

Adaptive instruction has a dual focus. It modifies the learning environment to accommodate the unique learning characteristics and needs of individual students, and it provides direct or focused interventions to improve each student's capabilities to successfully acquire subject-matter knowledge and higher-order reasoning and problem-solving skills, to work independently and cooperatively with peers, and to meet the overall intellectual and social demands of schooling. The adaptive instruction approach has a number of distinguishing features, including: a) instruction based on the assessed characteristics and capabilities of each student, b) the availability of a variety of materials and alternative learning sequences, c) instructional procedures that permit mastery of subject-matter content at a pace suited to individual abilities and interests, d) students taking on increasing responsibility for planning and monitoring their own learning (cf. Glaser, 1976; Walberg & Wang, 1987; Wang, 1980).

Adaptive instruction is grounded in the assumption that every class contains students with different interests, needs, and talents, and that whole-class instruction geared to the "average" student is bound to be too difficult for some learners and too easy for others. An important premise in the design of adaptive instruction programs is that the teacher's major task is to identify and provide the diverse instructional supports that are needed by individual students to efficiently master intended learning objectives.

The adaptive instruction approach is not the direct opposite of conventional group-paced, teacher-directed approaches (Brophy, 1979; Rosenshine, 1979), nor is it strictly synonymous with "open education" or the individualized instruction approaches popularized in the late 1960s (e.g., Bangert, Kulik, & Kulik, 1983; Peterson, 1979). Although adaptive instruction calls for individualized instructional planning, teachers work with students individually, in small groups, and in whole-class settings. Similarly, students do not necessarily work alone. Cooperative learning and other group tasks are often prescribed because of their suitability for achieving desirable student outcomes (i.e., group discussion, collaborative planning, social skills, responsibility for learning) and their efficiency for instructional management purposes. One of the basic premises of effective adaptive instruction programs is that a variety of educational objectives, instructional materials, and learning tasks is needed; furthermore, success in achieving instructional objectives requires a wide selection of teaching and learning strategies (Wang, 1980).

RATIONALE FOR IMPLEMENTING ADAPTIVE INSTRUCTION

In recent years, successful implementation of various adaptive instruction programs has reinforced the case for widespread use of this instructional approach. Adaptive instruction furnishes a timely response to current school improvement needs. Further, there is a growing body of research on its features and positive outcomes.

Current School Improvement Needs

There is a growing need for schools to demonstrate greater "adaptability" and responsiveness toward diverse student learning characteristics. Evidence of this need can be seen in demographic trends in the makeup of student populations, in public interest in educational improvement, and in legislative mandates for school reform. Increased educational productivity for all students has become the centerpiece of recent reports and policy statements by governmental officials, advocacy organizations, and special commissions or study groups (e.g., Bennett, 1986; Carnegie Forum, 1986; National Coalition of Advocates for Students, 1985; National Governors' Association, 1987; U.S. Department of Education, 1986, 1987; Youth and America's Future: William T. Grant Foundation Commission, 1988).

Many demographic changes projected for the next decade will greatly expand the diversity of the student population that schools must gear up to serve. These changes include growing enrollments of students from economically disadvantaged and culturally diverse families (U.S. Bureau of the Census, 1983); such students have often been identified as requiring special or compensatory educational services (cf. Brantlinger & Guskin, 1987). One alarming statistic is an increase in the percentage of students under 18 years of age who live in poverty and, consequently, face the likelihood of being singled out for remedial or other special services (Child Trends, 1985; U.S. Bureau of the Census, 1985). Another is an epidemic rise in teenage pregnancies, which often produce low-birthweight babies who tend to develop lifelong health problems and learning difficulties (Hughes, Johnson, Rosenbaum, Simons, & Butler, 1987).

Research on Adaptive Instruction

Evidence is accumulating that supports the prospect of accommodating student diversity effectively through adaptive instructional approaches. During the past decade, the development and implementation of instructional programs to provide for student differences have generated a substantial body of research on the educational effects of these programs. The findings from two recent, large-scale studies of adaptive instruction programs are briefly described here.

Waxman, Wang, Anderson, and Walberg (1985) synthesized the findings from 38 studies of adaptive instruction programs reported in the research literature between 1973 and 1982. All of the studies in the Waxman et al. meta-analysis met three criteria: they were conducted in regular elementary or secondary school classrooms; they produced either contrasted-group or correlational results; and they produced sufficient quantitative data on the sample populations for calculating effect sizes.

From the statistical data on approximately 7,200 students, Waxman et al. (1985) calculated 309 effect sizes to estimate the extent of positive student learning outcomes under the adaptive instruction programs. Results from the study suggest that the adaptive instruction programs had overall positive effects in terms of a variety of cognitive, affective, and behavioral outcomes. (The mean of the study-weighted effect sizes for these outcomes was 0.45; the average score of students under the adaptive instruction programs was at the 67th percentile for all three categories of outcomes, compared to an average score at the 50th percentile for the control group. Furthermore, these positive findings seemed constant when adjusted for grade, socioeconomic status, race, private or public school, and type of community. (See the complete report of statistical findings in Waxman et al., 1985.)

The objectives of a recently completed large-scale observational study by Wang and Walberg (1986) were to : 1) characterize the design features of eight demonstrably effective instructional models, and 2) increase understanding of how different combinations of program features are integrated to produce classroom processes and student learning outcomes considered effective in providing for student diversity. The instructional models included in the Wang and Walberg study were the Adaptive Learning Environments Model (Wang, 1980; Wang, Gennari, & Waxman, 1985), the Bank Street Model (Gilkeson, Smithberg, Bowman, & Rhine, 1981), the Behavior Analysis Model (Ramp & Rhine, 1981), the Direct Instruction Model (Becker, Engelmann, Carnine, & Rhine, 1981), Individually Guided Education (Klausmeier, 1972), the Mastery Learning approach (Bloom, 1968), Team-Assisted Individualization (Slavin, 1983), and the Utah System Approach to Individualized Learning (Jeter, 1980). Wang and Walberg collected data on seven categories of outcomes in a total of 65 second through fourth grade classrooms. The categories of outcomes were program features, classroom processes, classroom climate, students' perceptions of self-responsibility, student achievement, teacher attitudes, and socioeconomic status.

Overall, the results from the Wang and Walberg (1986) study suggest that programs with adaptive instruction features can be effectively implemented in regular classrooms in a variety of school settings. Further, these features can lead to positive learning outcomes for students with diverse characteristics and needs. Findings from this study suggest relationships between specific program features and certain classroom processes and student outcomes. Well-implemented features were found to produce process and achievement results similar to the ideal attainments of traditional, teacher-directed, group-paced instruction. Examples of such well-implemented features are the allocation of available class time for curriculum-related activities and the use of a variety of materials, activities, and learning tasks that are appropriate to the learning needs and achievement levels of individual students. Moreover, program features such as student choice, which is suggested in the effective teaching literature to be an ineffective feature of adaptive instruction programs, were actually found to facilitate student learning. In addition to raising student achievement and self-responsibility, the adaptive instruction programs in the Wang and Walberg study produced other classroom process outcomes that are greatly valued by students, parents, and educators. These outcomes include constructive student interactions, independent work, individual diagnosis and prescription, cooperative learning, and student exploration.

EXAMPLES OF ADAPTIVE INSTRUCTION MODELS

In this section, six different instructional models or programs are briefly described. Each of the models has been implemented in regular classrooms as a core general education program, and each has been designed with the explicit goal of providing for student diversity. The six models/programs are the Adaptive Learning Environments Model, the Bank Street Model, the Behavior Analysis Model, Individually Guided Education, the Mastery Learning approach, and Team-Assisted Individualization.

Adaptive Learning Environments Model

The Adaptive Learning Environments Model (ALEM) is a comprehensive educational system designed with the overall goal of enhancing schools' capabilities for creating environments that provide for student differences (Wang, 1980; Wang et al., 1985). The ALEM's design is based on the premise that students learn in different ways and at different rates, and that adapting instruction to individual differences is a feasible and effective alternative for maximizing learning. The ALEM's approach to accommodating student differences involves a variety of instructional methods and learning experiences that are matched to the learning characteristics and needs of individual students, as well as explicit interventions that increase each student's ability to profit from available instructional and learning alternatives. To these ends, the curriculum in ALEM classrooms combines prescriptive or teacher-directed, instruction that has been shown to be effective in ensuring mastery of basic academic skills (Bloom, 1976; Glaser, 1977; Rosenshine, 1979) with aspects of informal, or open, education that are conducive to generating attitudes and processes of inquiry, self-management, responsibility for learning, and social cooperation (Johnson, Maruyama, Johnson, Nelson, & Skon, 1981; Marshall, 1981; Peterson, 1979; Wang et al., 1985; Wang & Stiles, 1976). Implementation of the ALEM in schools is supported by a systematically developed classroom management system, a teacher collaboration model for instructional planning and implementation, a data-based staff development program, and an adaptive family involvement program (Wang & Walberg, 1985).

Bank Street Model

The Bank Street Model (Gilkeson et al., 1981) is designed to create classroom environments that support students' achievement in four types of competencies: affective, intellectual, physical, and social. Teachers use information from diagnostic tests and from profiles of student interests, learning styles, motivation, and social skills (Bowman, Gilkeson, Mayer, & Thatcher, 1977), to prescribe and provide instruction that is appropriate for each student. The expected outcomes for students under the Bank Street Model are development of a positive self-concept, self-control over learning (self-initiative), and positive relations with peers and adults. The Behavior Rating and Analysis of Communication in Education (BRACE) (Bowman et al., 1976) is designed to assess the achievement of these goals under the model. Information from the BRACE also provides feedback for teachers on the extent to which their interactions with students support learning and the development of self-control over learning activities.

Behavior Analysis Model

The Behavior Analysis Model (Ramp & Rhine, 1981) uses positive reinforcement techniques in conjunction with individualized instructional materials, team teaching, and parent involvement. The critical feature of the Behavior Analysis approach to adaptive instruction is the use of contingency contracts that are developed jointly by teachers and students. The contracts include specific performance goals for individual students in all subject-matter areas. Students are taught the contingent relationship between completing work specified in their contracts, earning points or tokens for completing the work, and exchanging the earned points or tokens for student-selected enrichment activities. The objective of the contingency contracts is "to provide positive consequences for children's appropriate classroom behavior in order to increase the rate at which they acquire academic skills" (Beckwith & Stivers, 1982, p. 30).

Individually Guided Education

Individually Guided Education (IGE) is conceptualized by its developers as a comprehensive alternative system of schooling (Klausmeier, 1972; 1975). Under this program, teams of teachers with differentiated roles are responsible for multi-graded groups of students. Individualized Instructional Program Models (IPMs) are used to accommodate individual differences in students' rates of learning, learning styles, and other characteristics (Klausmeier, Rossmiller, & Sailly, 1977). IPMs are developed jointly by teachers and students based on information from teachers' classroom observations and results from pretests that assess students' learning needs and match them with specific instructional goals. Instructional strategies include teacher presentations and independent student learning activities, as well as periodic testing to monitor students' progress toward the objectives in the IPMs.

Mastery Learning

As conceptualized by Bloom (1968), mastery learning is a theory of instruction and learning based on the contention that every student can be successful in learning, so long as he or she is provided with sufficient help when learning difficulties are first encountered. Two of the critical design features of mastery learning are the setting of criteria or mastery levels for meeting identified learning objectives, and the provision of corrective feedback. Teachers base the criteria for mastery levels on the hierarchical nature of particular skills and the importance of each for mastering higher-order skills. Using corrective feedback, periodic criterion tests are administered to monitor and ensure students' mastery of prescribed skills at appropriate proficiency levels. If students do not meet the criteria for specific skills, they are given task-specific feedback and additional instruction to improve their capabilities for achieving mastery. Because mastery learning requires only minimal changes in the physical and organizational structures of schools (Anderson, 1985), it can be assimilated easily into regular classrooms. In fact, it forms the basis for several existing instructional programs (Block, 1971).

Team-Assisted Individualization

Team-Assisted Individualization (TAI) is designed to realize both the social benefits of cooperation among students at various achievement levels and the academic benefits of instruction geared to each student's level and rate of learning. To these ends, TAI incorporates features of cooperative learning and individualized instruction. Students of heterogeneous ability are grouped in small learning teams; they are encouraged to assist each other by explaining concepts or processes and helping each other to review work prior to unit tests. Teachers present new materials directly and in small steps; they guide students through initial practice; and they check students' understanding of materials before the students move on to independent practice. One of the unique features of TAI is its use of timed exercises and tests on fact sequences to develop automaticity or rudimentary skills for application to more complex tasks.

CRITICAL IMPLEMENTATION CONSIDERATIONS

The implementation of adaptive instruction tends to be more complicated and challenging than that of traditional, whole-class teaching (cf. Brophy, 1987; Walberg & Wang, 1987). Findings from the Wang and Walberg (1986) study, discussed in a preceding section of this chapter, suggest that it is not the inclusion of single, specific instructional features that distinguishes effective from ineffective adaptive instruction programs. Instead, it is the combination and coordination of multiple features in *well-implemented* programs that produce positive classroom processes and a wide range of positive student outcomes. Well-implemented adaptive instruction programs that can accommodate the increasingly diverse student populations of today's schools are based on three major considerations: the importance of effective classroom management systems; the need to provide a continuum of instruction and related services; and the supportive function of school-based, program delivery systems.

Point to Ponder

If some children fail in the mainstream, whose fault is it—the children's or the system's? After a series of in-depth field studies of both successful and unsuccessful mainstreaming programs, Bogdan (1983) concluded:

> We have come to understand them [mainstreaming failures] not as indications that disabled children are inherently incapable of success in mainstream classrooms. Rather, these supposed failures of mainstreaming are problems of organizational arrangements, internecine politics, and a lack of will and skill of school personnel. (p. 428)

Effective Classroom Management Systems

Because they tailor instruction to the characteristics and needs of individual students, adaptive instruction programs are complex to implement and require careful attention to classroom management. The continued success of contemporary models of adaptive instruction depends on management procedures and systems that allow for efficient monitoring of program implementation. Success also depends on having relevant information available so that teachers and students can make effective instructional decisions and provide corrective feedback to students.

Students themselves are an important resource for the management of time and tasks in the classroom. Students can contribute to classroom management in several ways, including helping with routine tasks, acting as peer tutors, and scheduling and monitoring their own activities and accomplishments. As students become increasingly proficient in managing and monitoring their own learning and classroom behavior, teachers are freed from many routine management duties and they are able to devote more time to instruction. From the students' perspective, self-management and self-monitoring skills can lead to a greater sense of personal control over their learning and behavior and foster self-competence and self-responsibility.

Continuum of Instructional and Related Service Supports

To effectively provide for the increasingly diverse student population in regular schools and classrooms, schools need to develop a broadened range of learning options. They also need to provide a continuum of instructional and related services. These services must be made available on an ongoing basis to all students at the time when each student can most benefit from them. The flexibility of adaptive instruction programs for incorporating a variety of instructional strategies and learning activities (Wang & Lindvall, 1984) makes this approach especially suitable for integrating and coordinating a multitude of services. Currently, these various services tend to be implemented in a rather disjointed fashion in an attempt to accommodate the diverse instructional and related service needs of individual students (Reynolds, Wang, & Walberg, 1987; Wang, Reynolds, & Walberg, 1986).

Findings from recent research, combined with knowledge of the state of practice in schools, contribute in significant ways to current understanding of the types of instructional strategies and services that make learning productive for all students (e.g., Brophy, 1987; Good, 1983; Wang, Reynolds, & Walberg, 1987–1988; Wittrock, 1986). Drawing from this knowledge base, it is possible to identify numerous arrangements for coordinating and providing in regular classrooms the greater-than-usual services required by some students. These efforts should be designed to "bring the program to the child," rather than bring "the child to the program" (Will, 1986, p. 23).

An example of one effort to "bring the program to the child" is instructional teaming—coordinated work of classroom teachers and specialized resource personnel. The learning needs of students requiring more than the usual instructional and related services are generally provided by a cadre of resource professionals (i.e., reading specialists, speech therapists, English-as-a-second-language teachers, school psychologists, counselors, and others with expertise in special fields). In traditional educational settings, these staff members tend to function relatively independently of regular classroom teachers. In adaptive instruction programs, a mechanism is established for enhancing and reinforcing collaboration among such groups of professionals. They work together in and out of the classroom to plan and deliver instructional and related services under a coordinated, inclusive program.

The role of resource personnel working in adaptive instruction programs includes both provision of support services to classroom teachers and direct instruction. For example, such personnel can provide additional materials related to their area of expertise, offer advice on teaching methods to meet individual student needs, and help solve instructional problems when they arise. When students require direct services from resource personnel, such services can usually be provided in the classroom. Since the mode of operation in adaptive instruction classrooms includes a variety of group and individual activities occurring concurrently, a resource person meeting with a small group or with an individual student is neither unusual nor disruptive.

School-Based Program Delivery Models

If adaptive instruction is to be effectively implemented as an alternative for accommodating student differences in regular classrooms, the organization and culture of the entire school must be considered. Like other efforts to bring change into the schools, introduction and support of adaptive instruction require innovation and collegiality, collaborative planning on the part of all stakeholders, and an environment that is conducive to exploration and self-evaluation (Goodlad, 1983; Little, 1981; Purkey & Smith, 1983; Rutter, Maughan, Mortimore, & Ouston, 1979).

In school-based models for the delivery of adaptive instruction, the entire school staff, students, and all available resources are channeled toward effective instruction and student learning success. In this process, the specific roles individuals play (e.g., general education teachers, school psychologists, principals) are renegotiated and coordinated. The classroom teacher is the central figure in the instructional process. He or she provides instruction for all students, receiving assistance from resource personnel in the areas of instructional diagnosis, planning, and delivery, and in identifying individual learning difficulties. As schools build strong supportive organizational and administrative systems for service delivery (including consultation, teaching assistance, staff development programs), general education teachers are likely to become increasingly effective in working collaboratively with specialists in serving diverse student populations.

The school principal is a critical member of the instructional team for providing adaptive instruction. In their role as instructional and administrative leaders, principals can design and implement an ongoing staff development delivery system geared to the training support needs of individuals in their day-to-day operations; they can identify and reassign the resource supports needed to serve all students; they can assume increased responsibility for representing their school's instructional approach to parents and other stakeholders; and they can conduct, monitor, and evaluate program implementation and impact.

In addition to the establishment of schoolwide support teams of personnel who share responsibility for serving all students, an effective program delivery model for adaptive instruction contains a number of other important elements, described next.

Awareness and Implementation Planning The first step in the design and operation of delivery systems for adaptive instruction is to conduct a series of preliminary activities aimed at providing adequate information to all stakeholders, identifying necessary resources, and developing school-specific implementation plans (Wang & Vaughan, 1987b). Awareness presentations are conducted for all groups of major stakeholders—teachers, administrators, and parents. In these sessions, the following topics are covered briefly or in depth, depending on the group: a) history and background of adaptive instruction; b) the program's rationale, design, major goals, components, and staff roles; c) the program's outcomes in terms of student achievement, classroom processes, and affective outcomes; and d) the program's cost. Implementation planning involves designing a school-specific delivery system for implementing the program (Wang & Vaughan, 1987b). Decisions need to be made about identifying program classes; staffing; student placements; scheduling; space, facilities, and materials; program monitoring and evaluation; and communication and dissemination of information. The implementation planning process results in the development of a formal document called an "Implementation Plan," which serves as a systematic guide for carrying out required activities.

Needs Assessment A key criterion for successful implementation of an innovative educational program in schools is the optimal matching of local resources with program requirements. A first step in the development of a site-specific program delivery system is a careful and thorough assessment of the resources available at the school site (Wang & Vaughan, 1987a). The information obtained through this process is then used to develop an implementation plan. A comprehensive assessment of needs consists of several stages: a) discussions among central and building administrators leading to a decision to implement an adaptive instruction program to meet the school's improvement needs; b) discussions of the program and its implementation requirements with relevant school staff; and c) collection of site-specific information at the school. Information is sought in the following areas: nature of the student population to be served; staffing resources and patterns; current school goals, policies, and practices; classroom teaching practices; basic skills curricula; physical facilities; school records and documents; and family involvement. A battery of instruments called the Needs Assessment Forms has been developed for the systematic collection of information in each of these areas (Wang & Vaughan, 1987a). It includes a

Principal Interview Form, Observation Notes, and a Records Checklist.

Curriculum Development Adapting classroom instruction to individual differences requires a purposefully structured curriculum that incorporates hierarchically sequenced and clearly delineated objectives for specific subject matter and academic skills. The school district's curriculum, or basal series used by the school, forms the basis of the program's curriculum. Available curriculum resources and materials are inventoried and assembled; a variety of materials and activities is important for accommodating diverse student interests and needs. The program includes systematic diagnosis of learning needs and prescription of appropriate learning tasks (Wang & Vaughan, 1987c). For each student, prescription sheets are prepared that outline lesson topics or objectives and learning activities and tests relevant to each lesson. The sheets provide a systematic and efficient way for teachers to make assignments and track student progress. Procedures are established for recording students' progress through the curriculum on an ongoing basis. Recordkeeping forms (or computerized record-keeping systems) are used that show specific objectives and tests that have been mastered by each student, with dates of mastery.

Management of Resources and Instruction Effective management has been noted already as one of the key considerations in the implementation of adaptive instruction. At the classroom level, the effective delivery of adaptive instruction requires efficient systems and procedures for managing space, facilities, and materials; managing classroom time and task completion; coordinating the work of various staff; and developing students' capabilities for managing their own learning. An example of a student self-management system is the Self-Schedule System of the ALEM (Wang & Vaughan, 1987d). In this model, students are asked to decide the order in which they will do assigned and selected tasks, and they learn to complete all the tasks within the allotted time. The skills involved in achieving self-management are consciously taught as a sequence from the simplest (i.e., deciding on the order of completion of two teacher-prescribed tasks and completing them within the time limit) to more complex skill levels (i.e., deciding the order of completion of a range of teacher-prescribed and self-selected activities in all subjects and completing all within one school day).

Organizational Patterns Successful implementation of educational programs and practices based on the adaptive instruction approach depends, in large part, on a high degree of flexibility in organizational patterns. One example is the organization of students and classrooms in multi-age, as well as the conventional single-grade, patterns. Multi-age grouping results in frequent opportunities for spontaneous and planned peer modeling and tutoring (Allen, 1976; Wang & Weisstein, 1980). Cross-age peer tutoring situations contribute to the school achievement and motivation of tutors and tutees alike (Fogarty & Wang, 1982; Lohman, 1970; Peifer, 1972). A related example of organizational flexibility is variation in the use of individualized, small-group, and whole-class settings for instruction and learning. Group and individual activities are provided for each student. Instructional staff plan and organize schedules and student assignments to groups in ways that accommodate all levels of basic skills competency, while also balancing group and individual work for all students. Finally, organizational flexibility is enhanced by defining staff roles in ways that capitalize on the expertise of all school personnel, as in the instructional teaming discussed earlier.

Data-Based Staff Development Effective educational delivery systems place great emphasis on staff development activities that communicate adequate information on program features and staff roles, and adapt to the learning styles and expertise levels of individual school staff. Staff development begins with preimplementation training, which usually occurs just before a new school year and includes in-depth information on program components, training differentiated according to staff roles, individualized preimplementation support, and development of classroom implementation plans (Wang & Vaughan, 1988a). After the program has begun, staff development activities occur on an ongoing basis and focus on the day-to-day needs of staff for solving both immediate and long-range problems. The level of implementation attained by school staff members and the school as a whole is monitored and assessed through collecting data on program features being implemented, classroom processes, and teacher roles and interactions (Wang & Vaughan, 1988b). An instrument designed for this purpose is the Implementation Assessment Battery for Adaptive Instruction (Wang, Catalano, & Gromoll, 1983). A data-based staff development program systematically draws from the data on program implementation and student outcomes to determine areas for further training and support. Training needs are identified and placed in order of priority, and staff development plans are prepared that specify topics to be addressed, training methods to be used, dates of training sessions, and session facilitators. Consultation with individual teachers is also part of ongoing staff development.

Program Evaluation Decisions by educators and policymakers to improve the delivery and/or to continue the implementation of adaptive instruction programs should be based on information from ongoing program assessment. Areas examined include the degree to which expected program outcomes are being achieved, the degree to which aspects of the program and its implementation are working well, and the degree to which certain aspects need to be refined (Wang & Vaughan, 1987e). Instruments need to be identified, evaluated, and selected for use in program assessment. Decisions about which tests are the most suitable or desirable should be based on their validity, practicality, and interpretability. Where existing instruments are not available or are inadequate for meeting program needs, new tests may have to be constructed that will assess the desired program outcomes. Data collected are analyzed and summarized; and written reports of program effects are prepared, tailored to various stakeholder audiences. Finally, the assessment results are used to pinpoint aspects of program delivery that need to be changed or strengthened and to design strategies for bringing about the desired changes.

CONCLUSION

Adaptive instruction is an instructional approach that incorporates practical wisdom and research-based practices for effective accommodation of the diverse learning needs of individual students so that their chances of learning success are maximized. Many models of adaptive instruction have been established and maintained with high degrees of implementation in regular classrooms in a variety of schools (e.g., Wang & Walberg, 1985, 1986; Waxman et al., 1985).

Moreover, there is a close resemblance between the classroom processes and student outcomes associated with adaptive instruction and those highlighted as effective practices in the research literature on effective teaching and learning.

Based on the wealth of research findings and practical experience that has been amassed over the past decade, several adaptive instruction programs, including those described in this chapter, could be replicated in school sites as alternative programs for accommodating increasingly diverse student populations. Students in well-implemented adaptive instruction programs with appropriately individualized instruction can be expected to experience continuity in daily learning activities and improved chances for schooling success. They are likely to gain academic and social competence, which, in turn, can result in attitudinal and personal growth. Students can be expected to have increased ability and motivation to serve as social and academic resources for their peers, to accept individual differences as the norm rather than the exception, and to gain perceptions of self-competence.

REFERENCES

Allen, V.L. (Ed.). (1976). Operation co-teaching. Dateline: Oceano, California. *Elementary School Journal, 62,* 203–212.

Anderson, L.W. (1985). A retrospective and prospective view of Bloom's "Learning for Mastery." In M.C. Wang & H.J. Walberg (Eds.), *Adapting instruction to individual differences* (pp. 254–269). Berkeley, CA: McCutchan.

Bangert, R.L., Kulik, J.A., & Kulik, C.C. (1983). Individualized systems of instruction in secondary schools. *Review of Educational Research, 59,* 149–158.

Becker, W.C., Engelmann, S., Carnine, D., & Rhine, W.R. (1981). Direct Instruction Model. In W.R. Rhine (Ed.), *Making schools more effective: New directions from Follow Through* (pp. 95–154). New York: Academic Press.

Beckwith, G., & Stivers, M. (Eds.). (1982). *A guide to classroom training: A manual for classroom trainers.* Waukegan, IL: Waukegan Behavior Analysis Follow Through Project.

Bennett, W.J. (1986). *First lessons: A report on elementary education in America.* Washington, DC: U.S. Department of Education.

Block, J.H. (Ed.). (1971). *Mastery learning: Theory and practice.* New York: Holt, Rinehart & Winston.

Bloom, B.S. (1968). Learning for mastery. *Evaluation Comment, 1*(2), 74–86.

Bloom, B.S. (1976). *Human characteristics and school learning.* New York: McGraw-Hill.

Bogdan, R. (1983). A closer look at mainstreaming. *Educational Forum, 47,* 425–434.

Bowman, G.W., Gilkeson, E.C., Mayer, R.S., & Thatcher, S. (1977, April). *Program analysis system in Bank Street Follow Through: Focus on productive language and expression of thoughts and feelings.* Paper presented at annual meeting of American Educational Research Association, New York.

Bowman, G.W., Mayer, R.S., Wolotsky, H., Gilkeson, E.C., Williams, J.H., & Pecheone, R. (1976). *The BRACE program for systematic observation.* New York: Bank Street Publications.

Brantlinger, E.A., & Guskin, S.L. (1987). Ethnocultural and social psychological effects on learning characteristics of handicapped children. In M.C. Wang, M.C. Reynolds, & H.J. Walberg (Eds.), *Handbook of special education: Research and practice, Vol. 1. Learner characteristics and adaptive education* (pp. 213–218). Oxford, England: Pergamon.

Brophy, J.B. (1979). Teacher behavior and its effects. *Journal of Educational Psychology, 71* (6), 733–750.

Brophy, J.B. (1987, October). Remarks made at the Wingspread Conference, Racine, WI.

Brown, A.L., Bransford, J.D., Ferrara, R., & Campione, J. (1983). Learning, remembering, and understanding. In J.H. Flavell & E. Markman (Eds.), *Mussen handbook of child psychology,*

Vol. 3. Cognitive development (4th ed.), (pp. 77–166). New York: John Wiley & Sons.

Carnegie Forum on Education and the Economy. (1986). *A nation prepared: Teachers for the 21st century.* (Report of the Task Force on Teaching as a Profession). New York: Author.

Child Trends, Inc. (1985). *The school-age handicapped* (NCES 85-400). Washington, DC: U.S. Government Printing Office.

Corno, L., & Snow, R.E. (1986). Adapting teaching to individual differences among learners. In M.C. Wittrock (Ed.), *Handbook of research on teaching* (3rd ed., pp. 605–629). New York: Macmillan.

Fogarty, J., & Wang, M.C. (1982). An investigation of the class-age peer tutoring process: Some implications for instructional design and motivation. *Elementary School Journal, 82,* 451–469.

Gilkeson, E.C., Smithberg, L.M., Bowman, G.W., & Rhine, W.R. (1981). Bank Street Model: A developmental-interaction approach. In W.R. Rhine (Ed.), *Making schools more effective: New directions from Follow Through* (pp. 249–288). New York: Academic Press.

Glaser, R. (1976). Components of a psychology of instruction: Toward a science of design. *Review of Educational Research, 46,* 1–24.

Glaser, R. (1977). *Adaptive education: Individual diversity and learning.* New York: Holt, Rinehart & Winston.

Good, T.L. (1983, April). *Classroom research: A decade of progress.* Paper presented at annual meeting of American Educational Research Association, Montreal.

Goodlad, J.I. (1983). *A place called school.* New York: McGraw-Hill.

Hughes, D., Johnson, K., Rosenbaum, S., Simons, J., & Butler, E. (1987). *The health of America's children: Maternal and child health data book.* Washington, DC: Children's Defense Fund.

Jeter, J. (Ed.). (1980). *Approaches to individualized education.* Alexandria, VA: Association for Supervision and Curriculum Development.

Johnson, E.W., Maruyama, G., Johnson, R., Nelson, D., & Skon, L. (1981). Effects of cooperative, competitive, and individualistic goal structures on achievement: A meta-analysis. *Psychological Bulletin, 89,* 47–62.

Klausmeier, H.J. (1972). *Individually Guided Education: An alternative system of elementary schooling* (Hamlin E. Anderson Lecture). New Haven, CT: Yale University, Center for the Study of Education.

Klausmeier, H.J. (1975). IGE: An alternative form of schooling. In H. Talmage (Ed.), *Systems of individualized education* (pp. 48–83). Berkeley, CA: McCutchan.

Klausmeier, H. J., Rossmiller, R. A., & Sailly, M. (1977). *Individually guided elementary education: Concepts and practices.* New York: Academic Press.

Little, J.W. (1981, April). *School success and staff development in urban desegregated schools: A summary of recently completed research.* Paper presented at the annual meeting of American Educational Research Association, Los Angeles.

Lohman, J.E. (1970). Age, sex, socioeconomic status, and youth's relationships with older and younger peers. *Dissertation Abstracts International, 31* (5–A), 2497.

Marshall, H.H. (1981). Open classrooms: Has the term outlived its usefulness? *Review of Educational Research, 51*(2), 181–192.

National Coalition of Advocates for Students. (1985). *Barriers to excellence: Our children at risk.* Boston: Author.

National Governors' Association. (1987). *Making America work: Productive people, productive policies. Bringing down the barriers.* Washington, DC: Author.

Peifer, M.R. (1972). The effects of varying age-grade status of models on the imitative behavior of six-year-old boys. *Dissertation Abstracts International, 32,* (11-A), 6216.

Peterson, P.L. (1979). Direct instruction reconsidered. In P.L. Peterson & H.J. Walberg (Eds.), *Research on teaching: Concepts, findings, and implications* (pp. 57–69). Berkeley, CA: McCutchan.

Purkey, S.C., & Smith, M.S. (1983). Effective schools: A review. *Elementary School Journal, 83,* 427–452.

Ramp, E.A., & Rhine, W.R. (1981). Behavior Analysis Model. In W.R. Rhine (Ed.), *Making schools more effective: New directions for Follow Through.* New York: Academic Press.

Reynolds, M.C., Wang, M.C., & Walberg, H.J. (1987). The necessary restructuring of special and regular education. *Exceptional Children, 53*(5), 391–398.

Rosenshine, B.V. (1979). Content, time, and direct instruction. In P.L. Peterson & H.J. Walberg (Eds.), *Research on teaching: Concepts, find-*

ings, and implications (pp. 28–56). Berkeley, CA: McCutchan.

Rutter, M., Maughan, B., Mortimore, P., & Ouston, J. (1979). *Fifteen thousand hours: Secondary schools and their effects on children.* Cambridge, MA: Harvard University Press.

Slavin, R.E. (1983). *Cooperative learning.* New York: Longman.

Slavin, R.E., Leavey, M., & Madden, N.A. (1982, March). *Effects of student teams and individualized instruction on student mathematics achievement, attitudes, and behaviors.* Paper presented at annual meeting of the American Educational Research Association, New York.

U.S. Bureau of the Census. (1983). Projections of the population of the United States: 1982 to 2050. *Current Population Reports* (Series P25, no. 922). Washington, DC: Author.

U.S. Bureau of the Census. (1985). *Statistical Abstract of the United States, 1986* (106th ed.). Washington, DC: U.S. Government Printing Office.

U.S. Department of Education. (1986). *Effective compensatory education sourcebook, Vol. 1. A review of effective educational practices.* Washington, DC: Author.

U.S. Department of Education. (1987). *Schools that work.* Washington, DC: U.S. Government Printing Office.

Walberg, H.J., & Wang, M.C. (1987). Effective educational practices and provisions for individual differences. In M.C. Wang, M.C. Reynolds, & H.J. Walberg (Eds.), *Handbook of special education: Research and practice, Vol. 1. Learner characteristics and adaptive education* (pp. 113–128). Oxford, England: Pergamon.

Wang, M.C. (1980). Adaptive instruction: Building on diversity. *Theory into Practice, 19*(2), 122–127.

Wang, M.C. (1988). The wedding of instruction and assessment in the classroom. In H. J. Walberg (Ed.), *Assessment in the service of learning* (Proceedings of the 1987 ETS Invitational Conference) (pp. 63–79). Princeton, NJ: Educational Testing Service.

Wang, M.C., Catalano, R., & Gromoll, E. (1983). *Training manual for the Implementation Assessment Battery for Adaptive Instruction* (Vols. 1, 2). Philadelphia: Temple University Center for Research in Human Development and Education.

Wang, M.C., Gennari, P., & Waxman, H.C. (1985). The Adaptive Learning Environments Model: Design, implementation, and effects. In M.C. Wang & H.J. Walberg (Eds.), *Adapting instruction to individual differences* (pp. 191–235). Berkeley, CA: McCutchan.

Wang, M.C., & Lindvall, C.M. (1984). Individual differences and school learning environments. In E. W. Gordon (Ed.), *Review of research in education* (pp. 161–225). Washington, DC: American Educational Research Association.

Wang, M.C., Reynolds, M.C., & Walberg, H.J. (1986). Rethinking special education. *Educational Leadership, 44*(1), 26–31.

Wang, M.C., Reynolds, M.C., & Walberg, H.J. (Eds.). (1987–1988). *Handbook of special education: Research and practice* (Vols. 1–3). Oxford, England: Pergamon.

Wang, M.C., & Stiles, B. (1976). *Effects of the Self-Schedule System for instructional learning management in adaptive school learning environments.* (LRDC Publications Series 1976/9). Pittsburgh: University of Pittsburgh, Learning Research and Development Center.

Wang, M.C., & Vaughan, E.D. (1987a). *Handbook for the implementation of adaptive instruction programs* (8 modules). Philadelphia: Temple University Center for Research in Human Development and Education.

Wang, M.C., & Vaughan, E.D. (1987b). *Handbook for the implementation of adaptive instruction programs, Module 2. Needs assessment and implementation planning.* Philadelphia: Temple University Center for Research in Human Development and Education.

Wang, M.C., & Vaughan, E.D. (1987c). *Handbook for the implementation of adaptive instruction programs, Module 3. Awareness presentations.* Philadelphia: Temple University Center for Research in Human Development and Education.

Wang, M.C., & Vaughan, E.D. (1987d). *Handbook for the implementation of adaptive instruction programs, Module 4. Curriculum resources for individualizing instruction.* Philadelphia: Temple University Center for Research in Human Development and Education.

Wang, M.C., & Vaughan, E.D. (1987e). *Handbook for the implementation of adaptive instruction programs, Module 5. Instructional management.* Philadelphia: Temple University Center for Research in Human Development and Education.

Wang, M.C., & Vaughan, E.D. (1987f). *Handbook for the implementation of adaptive instruction programs, Module 8. Evaluation of program effects*. Philadelphia: Temple University Center for Research in Human Development and Education.

Wang, M.C., & Vaughan, E.D. (1988a). *Handbook for the implementation of adaptive instruction programs, Module 6. Pre-implementation training of staff*. Philadelphia: Temple University Center for Research in Human Development and Education.

Wang, M.C., & Vaughan, E.D. (1988b). *Handbook for the implementation of adaptive instruction programs, Module 7. Implementation assessment and staff development*. Philadelphia: Temple University Center for Research in Human Development and Education.

Wang, M.C., & Walberg, H.J. (Eds.). (1985). *Adapting instruction to individual differences*. Berkeley, CA: McCutchan.

Wang, M.C., & Walberg, H.J. (1986). Classroom climate as mediator of educational inputs and outputs. In B.J. Fraser (Ed.), *The study of learning environments 1985* (pp. 47–58). Salem, OR: Assessment Research.

Wang, M.C., & Weisstein, W.J. (1980). Teacher expectation and student learning. In L.J. Fyans (Ed.), *Achievement motivation: Recent trends in theory and research*. New York: Plenum.

Waxman, H.C., Wang, M.C., Anderson, K.A., & Walberg, H.J. (1985). *Adaptive education and student outcomes: A quantitative synthesis*. Pittsburgh: University of Pittsburgh, Learning Research and Development Center.

Will, M.C. (1986). Educating children with learning problems: A shared responsibility. *Exceptional Children, 52*(5), 411–416.

Wittrock, M.C. (Ed.). (1986). *Handbook of research on teaching* (3d ed.). A Project of the American Educational Research Association. New York: Macmillan.

Youth and America's Future: William T. Grant Foundation Commission on Work, Family, and Citizenship. (1988). *The forgotten half: Non-college youth in America*. Washington, DC: Author.

CHAPTER 14

A Classroom Is Where Differences Are Valued

Peter Knoblock and Berj Harootunian

In some respects, society's view of education has come full circle: from a time when opportunities for schooling were restricted to the few—usually the privileged—to the present when serious thought is being given the notion that everyone "belongs" in the regular classroom. This regular education initiative (Will, 1986) offers teachers, administrators, students, families, and communities a challenge, that of reconceptualizing diversity in classrooms. Meeting this challenge hinges on determining what teachers need to know to teach students with varying needs (Jackson, 1986).

This chapter contends that a broader view of the teaching and learning processes is needed. The perspective these authors advocate, the ecological perspective, emphasizes the interactive process between students and teachers, including the impact that families and communities have on classroom functioning. Use of this perspective will enable educators to find ways to understand students' behaviors in the context of the classroom environments they create, but it is also necessary to incorporate diverse sources of information about students. What teachers learn about their students can then be used to facilitate learning as students' needs are matched with educational goals. This means, therefore, that teachers must function as problem solvers and decision makers; relying on conventional teaching wisdom is not sufficient in view of the need to incorporate firsthand information about learners themselves.

For example, many teachers argue for setting clear rules and regulations at the start of the school year, as a way to establish the classroom management tone for the school year. They maintain it is easier to be firm with students initially and to relax controls later. Well-intentioned as this approach may be, it is not the classroom climate the authors recommend. Whereas clear rules and regulations may need to be laid down for some students, the learning styles of other students may call for a less directive approach that involves students' participation in setting classroom ground rules.

All teachers at one time or another have implicitly acknowledged that the students in their classes are individuals and are different from one another in characteristic ways. The ways in which their teaching has reflected this uniqueness, however, often have remained murky. Many are left with a feeling that they should have done something, but they are not quite sure what.

A major purpose of this chapter is to suggest ways for teachers to make better decisions that will enable them to grapple more effectively with the increasing heterogeneity of talent in their classrooms. The issue of managing and instructing diverse students is even more complicated by the fact that the concept of educational management is itself somewhat murky. Duke (1979) defined educational management in terms of those activities teachers engage in to establish and maintain an environment conducive to instruction and learning. Doyle (1986) has commented about the intertwining of learning tasks with those structured to bring about order. Learning reflects the instructional function of teaching, while order manifests the managerial function. Both may occur simultaneously, but there is a tension between them. Learning forces a focus on the individual; order is concerned with the social system of the class and group processes.

How, then, can a teacher begin to cope with this complex set of circumstances? What decisions are involved and how does one make them? One way to formulate an answer to these and similar questions may be found by considering the introductory statement in Kluckhohn and Murray's (1949) book *Personality:* "Every person is like *every* other person in some ways. Every person is like *some* other person in some ways. Every person is like *no* other person in some ways" (p. 1). These three sentences capture the essence of most of the decisions confronting the classroom teacher. They tell teachers that their students are alike and different at the same time and that it is their task to determine in what ways these likenesses and differences reveal themselves.

David Hunt (1976) has described the three critical components of the educational process as: 1) a student, 2) undergoing an educational experience, with 3) some type of consequence. Essentially, Hunt has translated into educational terms Kurt Lewin's formulation B = f(P,E); which reads as Behavior (B) is a function (f) of the interaction of the Person (P) and Environment (E).

But it should be understood that the B-P-E formulation is not an automatic process by which the teaching-learning process can be mechanically implemented. The teacher's decisions necessitate a vision of the classroom involving more than listing outcomes (B), student characteristics (P), and educational approaches (E). The manner in which these three different aspects are arranged and fit with one another is what the teacher must decide.

According to Hunt (1976), there are at least four necessary features of the B-P-E approach: 1) Teachers should be aware of the *interaction* not only between the person and the environment but in accommodating differential behavioral effects; 2) Teachers need to have a *developmental* perspective so that the effects of the environment may be viewed over time as well as concurrently; 3) Teachers have to see the person-environment interaction in *reciprocal* terms so that the effect of the person on the environment can be considered and vice versa; 4) Finally, the teacher should be aware of the *practical* implications of B-P-E interactions.

A study by Heil, Powell, & Feifer (1960) makes concrete Hunt's conceptualizations. They studied the interactions of approximately 50 elementary teachers and their students. The teachers (E) were identified as either "spontaneous," "orderly," or "fearful" in the way they managed their classes. The teachers were then further subdivided as "superior" or "inferior," with the former being warmer and more democratic. The students (P) had been previously classified as "strivers," "docile conformers," or "opposers." Heil's findings confirmed variations in student achievement (B), as a consequence of different combinations of teachers (E) and students (P).

The "strivers" achieved well across all teachers (Heil et al., 1960), but did particularly well with "orderly" or "spontaneous superior" teachers. The students who had the poorest achievement across all the teachers were the "opposers," who did well with "orderly teachers" but extremely poorly with "spontaneous teachers." The "docile conformers" almost matched the lead of the "strivers" in achievement across all teachers. With "spontaneous superior" or "orderly superior" teachers, the "docile conformers" excelled in achievement; with the "fearful" teachers, they were average; and with the "spontaneous inferior" teachers they did very poorly.

Studies like Heil's are not common in the research literature. His study confirms in a different way the point made earlier in this chapter, that no single approach to teaching will suffice. Given the diversity of individuals even in "regular" classes such as Heil's, such an approach can result in considerable harm to some students. When all the definitions of teacher effectiveness have been considered, the most reasonable one may be the teacher who has

> the capacity to present the same lesson in a variety of instructional forms (environments), to select and use that form (E) most appropriate to produce a desired outcome (B) with a particular student or group of students (P), and to shift to a new form when necessary. (Hunt, 1971, p. 52)

To do what Hunt has described, the teacher needs to be able to "read" students and "flex" to them. Students are not constant or static, but dynamic. For example, as students learn to read, they read more, which in turn makes them better readers, and so on. If teachers do not "read" these readers and "flex" to them appropriately, the teacher/student relationship suffers and learning problems may ensue.

Bereiter (1985) makes an important point in his discussion of children considered educationally disadvantaged:

> For any sort of learning, from swimming to reading, some children learn with almost no help and other children need a great deal of help. . . . Why they need such help is open to all sorts of explanation. But suppose that, instead of reopening that issue, we simply accept the fact that youngsters vary greatly in how much help they need and why. (p. 54)

Edward Fiske (1988), the education editor of the *New York Times*, more recently posed the issue in a different way. Citing both John Dewey and John Goodlad as sources who have recognized that students learn in different ways, Fiske noted that "the problem with teachers . . . is that too many of them have one arrow in their quiver of techniques. They give a lesson and hope that a student gets it. If not, that is too bad." (p. B4). Fiske goes on to say that the potentially negative consequence of this scenario for the child who does not "get it" is to hold him or her back a year, or label him or her as a student with a learning disability, or attribute to the child a character flaw. The tone of Fiske's article reminds us again of the need to appreciate the similarities and yet honor the differences of each student in relation to the other (Kluckhohn and Murray's [1949] earlier-mentioned three-part statement). The remainder of this chapter examines the implications of this approach in detail.

INITIATING CHANGE

The notion that teacher responses must match student needs implies that everyone belongs in the regular classroom. To make classrooms inclusionary rather than exclusionary, it is necessary for teachers and students to build a life together. This effort can be aided if the school district or school building has a statement of philosophy that serves as a living document supporting diversity in classrooms and programs. Increasingly, such position statements are being used as markers to guide educators and parents as they move toward maintaining all students in regular classrooms. Jowonio School in Syracuse, NY, provides an example. Jowonio's administrators and staff believe in affording preschool students such opportunities. Their program developed from a set of assumptions that informed school personnel and the community of the nature of this integrated preschool:

> (1) All children, regardless of severity of handicap, are capable of growth and change and demonstrate normal developmental characteristics; (2) The structure of the learning environment exerts a powerful influence on the rate and direction of a child's growth; (3) Receptiveness to instruction is initiated and maintained through warm, positive, and accepting responses by the school staff.

Jowonio School's assumptions, advocating complete or full integration, address the major points outlined in the opening section of this chapter: that students, regardless of their designation are in some ways more alike than different; that learning environments can be orchestrated for the success of each student; and that learning takes place in the context of relationships between teachers and students.

To offer another example, also in Syracuse, the fourth-grade teaching team of regular and special educators at the Edward Smith School made a presentation to the board of education requesting approval for that team of teachers to integrate one student with severe special needs into each of the fourth grade classrooms. The principal began by discussing the program's progress in the first 6 years of its existence; then the teachers presented a slide show of the students and teachers interacting. No mention was made of student disabilities, only comments on what activities they were engaging in and the adaptations made for a number of students to support their learning goals. Parents of typical students and students with special needs also provided testimonials to the benefits their son or daughter had received in the integrated classroom. The following statement by a fourth grade teacher, however, offered a set of principles that became an inspirational guide similar to a position statement for other teachers as they considered including all students in their classrooms:

> I am here to speak on behalf of the three regular education teachers on the fourth grade team. And yet I am uncomfortable making this distinction. One huge advantage of the fourth grade pilot program is that we all see ourselves as educators of very special children, regardless of whether these children are labeled special education or so-called typical.
>
> We each have had the opportunity to have taught many children with special needs over the years—students labeled hearing impaired, visually impaired, learning disabled, emotionally disturbed, and autistic children, through cross-age grouping in reading and math. Because of these successful experiences, we eagerly sought to become involved in this pilot program.
>
> The children with autism we have in our classrooms are high functioning and not that different from some typical children in certain need areas. Since we have had the experience of teaching the fourth grade curriculum for a few years now, it is not that difficult to identify the essential objectives to be learned and to choose appropriate activities and materials to accomplish this. The "special" children's presence in the classroom does not change the typical students' curriculum or program. Each child—whether labeled autistic, resource, gifted—gets the curriculum presented at his or her level.
>
> If a child requires more support to learn by listening rather than by reading, these oppor-

tunities are seized. Every child benefits from each child's varying learning style. There is a lot of sharing among the students.

Not every team could do this. We feel a tremendous sense of support from one another. Our team works well together. We do not always agree, but we respect the professional expertise of our teammates and are committed to work together for the good of our students. We feel supported by the parents and their testimonies that the children are happy and are enjoying learning. Just the expressions on their faces when they see 20–21 desks rather than the usual wall-to-wall desks speaks volumes. One example is that there are 20 students in my reading class plus 1 child with special needs. This same reading group had 33 children in the class last year. Need I say more about the effect of this on students, parents, and teachers!

Last of all, I would like to comment on the behaviors of children and stress that many times typical children (nonlabeled students) exhibit more bizarre behaviors than do the children with autism. This was made evident when Jeff, the "special" child in my room, asked me the second week of school why "x" didn't behave himself and had to sit in the timeout desk?

Surely we all have our weak areas, and we believe this program best integrates students, teachers, and parents and calls us to share our strengths and strive to acknowledge out teammates' innumerable contributions to our students' educational program and to their progress.

The existence of a statement of principles can be the first step toward developing what is referred to as complete, or full, integration. This implies that students with disabilities are not "placed" into regular classes but are integral parts of them. The authors see a need to move away from a placement focus and toward the design of classrooms and programs to respond to the diversity within each group. School districts can move from a placement orientation to a program structure approach. A current example is found in the planning process developed by the La Grange Area Department of Special Education in Illinois. Comprised of 16 member school districts, their special education program is guided by a mission statement that addresses the importance of enhancing the educational experiences of all students; building learning environments that empower handicapped youth for work and friendships; creating opportunities in schools for meaningful relationships between handicapped and nonhandicapped students; and expanding the knowledge and skills of educators, parents, and the community. The mission statement concludes: "By stating these goals the Directing Board affirms the right of handicapped students to attend programs within neighborhood schools and as close as possible to their home to the maximum extent possible." The La Grange cooperative is now considering extending its programmatic efforts to structure regular classrooms to include all students. Building on its mission statement, the group submitted a grant proposal to the Illinois State Department of Education titled, "Fostering Accepting Environments to Promote Integration." They indicated that all of their students with special needs (including those classified as moderate and severe special needs) are educated in regular school buildings, but that they are now interested in taking the next step—that of structuring regular classrooms to address the needs of all students.

PSYCHOLOGICAL SENSE OF COMMUNITY

Recognizing the heterogeneity among students is a value deeply rooted in America's educational rhetoric. Today's educators have the opportunity to create classrooms in which differences are valued and capitalized upon to enhance the learning of *all*

Point to Ponder

As one classroom teacher recently stated:

> When we create integration programs we open up educational possibilities. How better to teach a student who is blind to get to the cafeteria than to practice with her seeing classmates in the hubbub of everyday school life? How better for a student with severe retardation to learn when to laugh, how to dress, and how to walk, than to observe his so-called nondisabled peers? (Massachusetts Advocacy Center, 1987, p. 6)

participants. This can only be accomplished, however, by building a psychological sense of community in which each class member feels a sense of responsibility to achieve group and individual goals. In the following description, Sarason (1974) anticipates the day when special classes have been eliminated:

> To engender and maintain a psychological sense of community in this classroom would involve everyone, teachers and pupils, in problem-solving behavior around issues of learning, resources, rules, mutuality, and goals. The concept of the psychological sense of community is not ritual or empty rhetoric. It is no less than a basis for confronting the realities of social living, and the fact that we are discussing it in terms of a particular kind of classroom should not make for an arbitrary and misleading distinction between the learning process and the social context in which it is taking place. Classroom learning is always social. The question is the value basis on which the social organization rests and the degree to which both enlarge the range of conceptual experience. (p. 170)

The "range of experiences" referred to by Sarason can be addressed in a regular classroom if one applies the B-P-E approach, which connotes the value of active participation by all students and adults. In contrast to the notion that one can put students in front of a computer and have the machine program for them, teachers are having students learn to write their own programs, or they are finding more interactive programs for students to use. This notion of high activity levels is carried over into classroom life and management as well as in the instructional example just cited. To foster a sense of ownership, rules for the classroom life together must be jointly determined by teachers and students. Active participation is sought and valued, and no one's activity level automatically excludes others from offering their contribution.

The E, the environment, can be supportive in a variety of ways. Regular classrooms can provide opportunities for diagnostic teaching by encouraging the student's involvement in a variety of interpersonal and academic encounters, thus providing the teachers many opportunities to assess student needs and performances. There are opportunities to individualize instruction because curriculum is built on individual needs, styles, and the developmental and functional needs of the students. Embedded within opportunities for individualized instruction are unlimited ways to group students for academic and social purposes: students tutoring other students; one-to-one time with resource persons within the classroom (often referred to as "push-in models"); small groupings based on interests and skill needs; and large-group experiences in which everyone can participate on some level.

In such an environment, appropriate role models are available. In the broadest sense, students with disabilities and many other students experience difficulty communicating. For all students, spending their days in communication environments in which a premium is placed on normal language development and on communication for social purposes can enhance a sense of community, because all of the members have opportunities to communicate and to use communication systems that are understood by others. Having a usable communication system provides more opportunities for developing social skills because students have ways to approach one another. And when there is an instructional balance in the classroom between affective and cognitive development, students will be able to practice their communication skills and social skills throughout the day.

To foster a sense of psychological community, it is necessary to change teaching's emphasis from managing students to helping them. The use of positive practices that are supportive of students' learning needs, that convey teachers' empathy for students' social and emotional needs, and that include students in classroom decision making can contribute to a sense of ownership in the classroom.

The following example, provided by a preschool teacher, illustrates readiness to address student needs:

> Sally is a warm, social, enthusiastic, and busy child. She has made some wonderful gains over the course of the school year, especially in her ability to attend during more structured activities. Recently, through a specific behavior, Sally communicated some of her needs, as recorded in the following activity:
>
> *Activity Taking Place* — Music / Language Circle
> *Where*—Classroom
> *When*—Wednesday, 4/13, 10:10 A.M.
> *Who*—Helen (TA), Mark (TA), myself, Ken, Colleen, Bob, Susan.
> *Preceding Situation*—Kids and teachers are seated in a circle; I am reading a book.
> *Teacher/Child Behaviors*—Sally flops down on the floor, kicking her feet and vocalizing. Linda prompts her, "Sally, sit up so we can hear the rest of the story. We're almost ready to sing some songs." Sally continues to vocalize and kick and does not sit up. I tell her it looks like she's having trouble listening and that she needs to play in another part of the room so the other children can hear the story. Sally promptly gets up and runs to the water table where she starts to splash and pour the water.
> *Consequences*—Sally is allowed to play, and circle continues. I am feeling my actions are inadequate and rather negative in sending Sally from the activity.

Point to Ponder

A parent recently stated:

> My child can talk. And there's one reason why he can. It's because of the other children. The typical children kept coming up to him and demanding that he talk. They knew how to get an answer from him, and they wouldn't let him get away with a single-syllable response. Now I ask you, what teacher or teachers could do that for my son, much less for a whole class of kids with autism? That's just not realistic. (Massachusetts Advocacy Center, 1987, p. 6)

Why?—I think Sally was telling us she wanted to be playing (choosing her own activity), and was unable to attend to the book.
Options for Prevention—Books have just recently become a regular part of the circle, as most of the children are now better able to attend and listen. Sally has increased her ability to attend at circle, but in more musical and movement activities. Books are still very difficult. We decided to plan some open-ended activities for Sally and one of her teachers to do for the first half of our circle time. We included activities of Sally's choice, as well as some simple books in hopes of increasing her interest in books on a one-to-one basis. Sally then joins us for the second half of circle to give her some success in participating with the group. We hope to increase the time Sally spends in circle after she has had more successful experiences. Sally is participating in circle activities that involve more music, movement, and simple flannel board stories.

The preceding example illustrates a teacher's problem-solving approach as she moved from insisting on Sally's complying to an effort to understand the communicative intent of the child's vocalizing and kicking at reading time. By focusing on the behavior within the social context, the teacher is assuming that the environment or what she has been doing as a teacher can be modified to maximize her responsivenes to the child. She is also assuming that the problematic behavior is not necessarily "part of the child."

UTILIZING POSITIVE PRACTICES TO FOSTER COMMUNITY

The application of B = f(P, E) allows teachers to problem solve their way toward the development of a meaningful program for each student. If one believes that learning outcomes (Behaviors) are the result of student characteristics (Person) and approaches to teaching (Environment), then one can begin to study each student by investigating his or her characteristics and needs. The problem-solving process will by necessity have to include an equally diligent effort to study the impact that teacher behavior has on the student. This section of the chapter therefore begins with a recommendation to utilize a communication model in fostering a sense of community.

The reliance on a communication model does not necessitate using disability categories or any of the many descriptors used to classify students as disabled or nondisabled. The assumption made here is that such classifications are not educationally relevant and usually imply that the problem resides within the student—a notion that these authors are eager to dispel.

According to Donnellan, Mirenda, Mesaros, and Fassbender (1984), pragmatically oriented interventions—that is, those approaches to understanding students' behaviors within the social context in which they occur—can be accomplished in three ways: "(a) those designed to teach new communicative behaviors to replace aberrant responses; (b) those designed to teach other functionally related behaviors to replace aberrant responses; and (c) those involving antecedent manipulations" (p. 202).

In each of these three interventions, the role of the teacher is central. Teaching new skills and/or modifying the environment are behaviors within the repertoires of skilled teachers. Hunt (1971) maintains that an effective teacher (Hunt refers to any of the helping professions as agents) can understand the needs of the client, generate appropriate interventions to respond to those needs, and shift from one approach to another when necessary.

The three interventions just cited are often put into practice by classroom teachers in one or more combinations. Conflicts between students and teachers frequently occur around issues of compliance, power relations, and control issues. The teacher may want a student to do something and he or she refuses. The three interventions may be implemented by combining them. For example, in the situation just described, the first question the teacher can ask himself or herself is, "Why is it important for the student to comply?" Put another way, does the request, or demand, as the case may be, foster an outcome that helps the student become more independent, or is compliance the goal? There are several other questions a teacher can ask himself or herself: By insisting on adherence to the teacher's goal, is a power struggle created, and is it worth the battle? Is there a relationship basis for the request, or is it merely a matter of seeing the adult in control? And, does the student understand what to do and why the request or task is important?

These questions and others can be organized into a problem-solving framework to guide teachers and others as they struggle to match adult behaviors to student needs. In the authors' workshops with teachers, parents, institutional and community residence staffs, and the general public, the following "W" questions have proved helpful as the initial step in analyzing a problem behavior:

1. Who is involved in the episode? Who is present? Identify their roles or functions (e.g., friend, parent, wealthy relative, and so on).
2. What is happening? Describe as objectively and precisely as possible what has occurred.
3. When does the behavior occur? Note the time of day, activity that is taking place, and so forth.
4. Where does the behavior occur? What is the setting? Is it environment specific or does it occur across environments?
5. What is the function of the behavior? Does it serve any purpose from the student's perspective? Can you ascertain the communicative intent? The assumption is that students have reasons for behaving the way they do. What they do is not done solely to make a teacher's life miserable!

Using the formula, B = f(P,E), one can generate positive programming approaches that involve the students, teachers, and the environment. Ideally, one strives toward Hunt's goal of enlarging one's repertoire of responses so as to modulate what one does to match student needs. For example, teachers can:

Analyze the problem behavior by focusing on the "W" questions just described.

Determine the communicative intent of the student's behaviors.

Learn to engage in "backing-off" behaviors while they are studying the student's needs.

Provide time for the student to respond before acting or reacting.

Examine their own feelings and thoughts in a particular situation.

Teach students a communication system that is usable for them and understandable to others.

Treat students with respect by actively listening to them; respecting their wishes; and never talking about them in a derogatory fashion when they are present or when discussing them with others.

CONCLUSION

In the preceding sections of this chapter, these authors have attempted to present a picture of teaching that reflects a more expansive view of the various roles teachers must fulfill, a view that comes closer to the real world than some idealized or limited perspectives variously advocated. Joyce (1973) noted that in the typical classroom there are at least five teacher roles that are important in the life of the student: 1) the counselor, 2) the skill builder, 3) the academician, 4) the divergent thinker, and 5) the community builder. These authors wish to point out that although Joyce was describing the *typical* classroom, the teacher roles he specifies apply to *all* classrooms. These roles often work together and are not conceptualized as mutually exclusive. Can one teacher alone assume all of them? Before answering this question, these roles need to be briefly defined. In the role of a counselor, the teacher is a facilitator who helps students negotiate goals, find the means to attain these goals, and identify the criteria to determine their attainment. The skill-builder role requires that teachers diagnose the needs of the learners and prescribe interventions likely to contribute to their development. In the academician role, the teacher helps students identify the important concepts and methods of inquiry of the academic disciplines. The teacher as divergent thinker helps students to express their creativity by discovering problems, by generating different solutions, and by providing alternative means of expression. Finally, in the role of community builder, the teacher organizes the social system of the class or helps the students organize it for themselves.

While these roles and the teacher skills to fulfill them overlap, each requires that the teacher implement a different approach to learners. For one teacher to perform all of these roles within a classroom setting is a difficult, if not complex, task. However, the classroom as conceptualized by the B-P-E approach outlined in this chapter defines the more competent teacher as the one who can fill most or all of these roles; and the less competent teacher as the one who can fill few or none. More important, the priority issue is that these roles so crucial in the lives of learners must be fulfilled by one or several teachers. The examples described in this chapter of teachers working together with colleagues and other support personnel all provide evidence of students experiencing environments fostering differential teacher roles.

The teacher's world continues to change. The diversity of learners in a teacher's classroom today is but one manifestation of the pluralism in our society. To pretend that teaching is a simple activity is misleading because it reinforces a monolithic concept of teaching. The B-P-E paradigm that has served as the heuristic for this chapter is not the sole method for increasing this diversity, but it does offer more relevant and alternative ways than have traditional models for addressing the range of differences that students bring to the classroom. No one claims that the task outlined here will be easy, but the authors believe it will result in a greater number of happier teachers and students.

REFERENCES

Bereiter, C. (1985). The changing face of educational disadvantage. *Phi Delta Kappan, 66*(8), 5389–5554.

Donnellan, A.M., Mirenda, P.L., Mesaros, R.A., & Fassbender, L.L. (1984). Analyzing the communicative functions of aberrant behavior. *Journal of The Association for the Severely Handicapped, 9*, 201–212.

Doyle, W. (1986). Classroom organization and Management. In M.C. Wittrock (Ed.), *Handbook of research on teaching* (3d. ed., pp. 392–431). New York: Macmillan.

Duke, D.L. (Ed.). (1979). *Classroom management.* (78th yearbook of National Society for the Study of Education, Part 2). Chicago: University of Chicago Press.

Fiske, E.B. (1988, June 8). Lessons. *New York Times*, p. B4.

Heil, L.M., Powell, M., & Feifer, I. (1960). *Characteristics of teacher behavior related to achievement of children in several elementary grades.* Unpublished report, Brooklyn College, NY. ED 002843.

Hunt, D.E. (1971). *Matching models in education.* Toronto: Ontario Institute for Studies in Education.

Hunt, D.E. (1976). Teachers' adaptation: "Reading" and "flexing" to students. *Journal of Teacher Education, 27,* 268–275.

Jackson, P.W. (1986) *The practice of teaching.* New York: Teachers College Press.

Joyce, B.R. (1973). *Building the model teacher.* Paper presented at annual meeting of the American Educational Research Association, New Orleans.

Kluckhohn C., & Murray, H. (Eds.). (1949). *Personality in nature, society, and culture.* New York: Alfred A. Knopf.

Massachusetts Advocacy Center. (1987). *Out of the mainstream.* Boston: Author.

Sarason, S.B. (1974). *The psychological sense of community: Prospects for a community psychology.* San Francisco: Jossey-Bass.

Will, M.C. (1986). Educating children with learning problems: A shared responsibility. *Exceptional Children,* 411–415.

PART V

Family and Community Support

CHAPTER 15

Family Support to Promote Integration

Jeffrey L. Strully and Cindy F. Strully

This chapter explores what parents can do to ensure that their children have an opportunity to become integrated, accepted members of their school and community. Attention is focused particularly on the family support children need when they are new to a school or classroom or when for other reasons they have failed to develop natural friendships and supports from their peers and other community members. To illustrate the suggestions presented, personal examples from our own family are included.

OUR DAUGHTER SHAWNTELL

We have a daughter, Shawntell, who is 15½ years old and in the eighth grade. Shawntell is adopted and has been labeled by some professional educators as severely/profoundly handicapped. As do nearly all children, Shawntell has required family support to become an integrated, accepted member of her school and community. This was highlighted to us when we moved from Kentucky to Colorado.

Moving from Louisville, KY, to Littleton, CO, was hard for all of us. But, as in Shawntell's case, when you are 14 years old and must leave the friends, school, and community you have enjoyed for the past 7 years, a move may be particularly traumatic. You may be convinced that you will not like your new home, that it will be terribly hard to make new friendships, and that people will not appreciate you for who and what you are. Shawntell was placed into new settings and had to develop new out-of-family friendships and supports in the school and community.

FAMILIES: DEFINITION AND IMPORTANCE TO EDUCATION

The most important need of any child is to have a family of his or her own. Families are the foundation for the social, emotional, and physical health of all youngsters.

There is much discussion today about what constitutes a family. Although these discussions are intellectually interesting, for our purposes, families can be considered as falling into one of three categories: biological, adoptive, and alternative living. Biological families normally have as their nucleus one or two adults living together with the children they have given birth to. Adoptive (whether shared, open, traditional, one-person, or a couple) families are those that make a legal commitment to raising a child as though he or she were their biological offspring. Alternative living families are those families that have not secured a "legal" arrangement, but have an emotional, moral, and personal commitment to the child in question. This term is used here instead of the traditional term, *foster-care*, which has many negative implications.

Whatever the "type" of family a child may have, the family's functions are basically the same. Whether a child is "normal" or has been identified as having developmental disabilities of one type or another, families provide security and protection from vulnerability; they pick up the pieces when things go wrong; and they have the potential to ensure that their members' most fundamental needs of love and caring are met. Indeed, families are the anchors that many of us need to survive in the world.

While no family is perfect and there is no such thing as the "ideal" family, the large majority of families we have observed do have staying power. Families are the "keepers of the record." It is a sad situation when an individual lives with no one who remembers him or her "when," or can reminisce about what the person was like when he or she was younger. For children placed in institutions, residential child care centers, or long-term hospital care, these basic, daily family supports are generally not a reality.

Thus, families are needed to provide children a sense of support, stability, acceptance, and caring. These fundamental needs are required for the development of self-confidence and the assurance necessary to promote both learning and social success in school. Families provide the foundation for children to become involved, to be accepted, and to survive in challenging new environments in the school and community. It is from such involvement and acceptance that out of family, natural community and friendship supports can evolve.

In addition to providing basic emotional, social, and physical support to children, there are a variety of other things parents can do to promote the development and maintenance of out-of-family friendships and support networks in integrated school and community settings.

WHAT FAMILIES CAN DO—SCHOOL INVOLVEMENT

Following are some important points we have learned through our own experience with our daughter and that of neighbors and friends. Regarding school involvement, the most important structure outside of the family for a child is the school. Schools provide not only academic opportunities to learn things and to enhance one's capacity to learn and grow, but the opportunity for friendships and social life to develop. Recognizing the importance of the school, there are a number of things parents can do to facilitate the integration of their children into school settings:

1. For our children to be included in neighborhood play and learning activities or on the playgrounds, they *need to attend their neighborhood schools and classes with their age-appropriate peers*. Regardless of any differences our children may have, we should not consent for them to be separated from their neighborhood peers by taking special transportation to special schools or even to be isolated in special wings, buildings, or classes in neighborhood schools, if we want them to grow and develop and become accepted, supported members of the neighborhood school and community.
2. To shape the future, it is critical first and foremost to have expectations and to

Point to Ponder

Writing about their experience with Chicago-area schools, which identified their young son as being in need of "special" education, Lori and Bill Granger concluded:

> The trap of Special Education was now open and waiting for the little boy. It is a beguiling trap. Children of Special Education are children of Small Expectations, not great ones. Little is expected and little is demanded. Gradually, these children—no matter their I.Q. level—learn to be cozy in the category of being "special." They learn to be less than they are. (Granger & Granger, 1986, pp. 26–27)

dream about that future; and then to share that dream with other people and work to make the dream a reality. For example, before moving to Colorado, we interviewed a number of school districts. We settled on the Littleton Public Schools for a variety of different reasons, including their receptivity to having Shawntell attend her neighborhood school, Powell Middle School. This meant, among other things, that Shawntell would ride the regular school bus and attend regular education classes. We shared with the district our desire for our daughter to have a group of friends and to be active with them both in school and after school. We told them we knew all of this would be difficult, but we believed together we could make it a reality.

The important issue to remember from a parent's perspective is to establish a focus and goals to work toward. This does not ensure that everything will always go smoothly, but at least it guarantees that people are working on the "right" goals and issues.

3. All parents must understand that they are indeed "teaching" their children things that they need to know. As parents, we are teachers whether we acknowledge it or not, and can provide much worthwhile learning. However, many school personnel do not hear what parents would like their sons/daughters to learn. Rather, educators teach what *they* believe children should learn. For instance, when issues of friendships, community involvement, and the like are raised, sometimes teachers (as well as parents) do not think the child has the skills/competencies yet or is even "worthy" of having friends and relationships or an active community life.

4. Parents should not view their children according to their problems or shortcomings. Seeing a child as "handicapped, shy, overweight, lazy, or poor learners" does not capitalize on a child's potential. Instead, parents should think of their children as having unique gifts, talents, strengths, and needs, and should share this view with educators and classmates. The way in which we regard our children and impart this view to others is as important as anything we do. (See Chapter 5 for more detailed information.)

5. Parents need to make time just to be parents. Some school programs attempt to make families into miniteachers/professionals to carry out programs in their home. This starts with very young children and continues throughout their school years. There is nothing wrong with helping your son/daughter to learn. In fact, this is one of the responsibilities of parenthood. However, parents should take care not to become too preoccupied with keeping charts and data, to the point that such activities distract from the parents' role simply as parents. It is important for children to fit into family life.

Point to Ponder

Unfortunately, many children live in group homes and other places that are not really homes but training centers, schools, and miniaturized institutions. It is important that we become more sensitive to people's basic human need for a home—a place where they can relax and have a sense of peace and security: where they can escape from the stresses and demands of the world outside; where they belong simply because it is home. We should not find ourselves surrounded by our teachers, trainers, or other people called "staff" in our home. Home is where people accept us and value us because of who we are, not because of how we perform. Perhaps we are trying to do too many things for people under the same roof. That was always the case in institutions. The result is that we lose that sacred space called home, where relationships are held more important than anything else (Durner, 1985).

Parents therefore need to find ways to balance their efforts and energy to allow meaningful times together for the entire family, that is, for building relationships. Although some of us are happy to be actively involved in our children's education, we prefer not to be asked to read manuals and textbooks or collect data for a baseline project being conducted by a group of school officials.

WHAT FAMILIES CAN DO—COMMUNITY INVOLVEMENT

The need to be involved in family and community life is another crucial aspect of promoting integration. This entails a child's participating in activities outside of school for fun as well as for education.

The community is not just a place to learn. It is also a place to "hang out," a place where people know your name, where people say "hi," where people invite you to join them in an activity, and so forth. Community involvement is important for our children to develop a strong network of friendships and support to help them in later life.

Some things parents can do to promote community involvement and acceptance of their children include:

1. Families must be involved not only in their child's school life, but must provide chances for their sons/daughters to meet people outside of school. This may mean inviting people over to the house, making telephone calls to arrange get-togethers, setting up situations that are of high interest in order to "grab" the attention of these potential friends. If this sounds either strange or "phony" there is an element of truth in that, at least in the beginning. Clearly gimmicks will not keep a person as a friend, but, on the other hand, some people do need some prodding, and if some "rigging" of the environment is necessary to provide opportunities for children to meet and to motivate friendships, it is worth it.
2. We need to guarantee that each of our children has the opportunity to do the ordinary things that many other children do in their neighborhoods. This includes such things as joining Girl Scouts or Boy Scouts, going to church, joining the Little League, and going to the YMCA after-school program.
3. Another thing parents can do to encourage and facilitate neighborhood peer relationships and support is to ensure to the maximum extent possible that their children have play equipment that can draw the

interest of other children. By purchasing the swing sets, basketball hoops, plastic swimming pools, toys, games, records, and all the other "stuff" that help children get to know and interact with each other, parents can provide opportunities for their children to become one of the "gang."

4. To promote community involvement, parents must help ensure that their children are actively involved in all phases of community life, and that the family does things together such as going out to malls, fast food restaurants, movies, concerts, and the like.

There are far too many situations where a child, particularly one with characteristics unfamiliar to the general public (i.e., a child in a wheelchair, who cannot talk, see, hear, etc.) never participates in the family life outside of the home. If parents do not include their "children" on typical and nontypical outings, how can we expect community members to accept them with equanimity?

5. Family supports for all children should be provided by "natural" means, rather than by paid human service options, whenever possible. For example, if a sitter is needed, most parents of a 7-year-old would hire the 16-year-old down the street. However, if a child is labeled as handicapped, the parents may turn to the human service system, whose first response would be to develop a respite care program. The concept of natural support before "artificial" support means that we consider first the 16-year-old down the street and determine if he or she would be able to provide the support that is needed. Only when we do not have natural school and community support networks available to meet a need should we resort to paid human services, and then only until we have connected with the natural support systems in the community.

6. When moving into a new community, the first thing our family did was "tour" the neighborhood. We wanted to find out where the stores were located and also where the kids "hung out." We quickly found the answers by asking kids we saw while walking around, as well as by asking the "old timers," the people in the "welcome wagon," members of the local church, shopkeepers, and so forth. In short, we asked people where others "hung out."

This provided us and Shawntell with a familiar "map" of the community, a framework in which to operate. This familiarity helped Shawntell to understand and feel more secure about the new community and helped us to match her needs and interests to the people and organizations in the community. (Whether moving into a new community or simply having a child move into a new classroom of peers, learning the "lay of the land" can assist both you and your child to adjust and become integrated into the setting.)

7. One successful way to integrate a child into a club or other group is to find someone to "sponsor" that person in the new group. The old member of the group can thus "smooth" the way for the new member. For instance, our daughter Shawntell was brought into the Girl Scouts by Karen. Since Karen had been a long-time Girl Scout member, her "sponsorship" of Shawntell meant immediate acceptance for her. It is always better to have someone usher you in than for you to try to become a member from the outside.

8. When helping a child to become an integrated member of his or her peer group, it helps to think about the normal routines of a person of your child's age in a certain place during specific times of the year. One reason that age-appropriate peers are important is that they provide one's child with a sense of belonging, in addition to being a barometer to what aspects of life-style are "in" or not "in."

9. It does no good for your child to join things in which he or she has no in-

terest. Parents need to ask their children directly what they like to do. The answer may be "listen to music," "ride horses," "play golf," or whatever. If the child cannot communicate very effectively, then the people closest to the child will need to think about what interests that person. This is another reason why friends who are same-age peers are so important. They can help adults problem-solve and develop creative solutions. For instance, Shawntell's friends, Lori and Judy, felt that Shawntell (who does not communicate verbally) would like to hear the performer Tiffany. (Whether Shawntell really wanted to go to a concert to hear Tiffany is unknown to us, but her friends felt that she would like it. And she appeared to enjoy the concert.)

10. One final suggestion for helping your children get to know people and become involved in the community is to volunteer in organizations that afford lots of opportunities to meet people. Shawntell has volunteered for Jump Rope for Heart, to help feed people in Africa, and for other social causes. It is important to give of yourself as much as to receive.

IMPORTANCE OF INTEGRATION—A PARENT'S PERSPECTIVE

After reading these suggestions for integrating your children and recognizing the work involved, some parents and teachers may ask themselves, "why is it so important that each of my children become an accepted, involved member of his or her school and community?" Although this book and others have cited many benefits of integrating all children into the regular school and society, one often neglected but critical reason in terms of a child's future is that of protection from vulnerability.

Protecting children from vulnerability may sound a little overprotective or limiting, but what is meant here is a kind of protection that our laws and statutes or the "paid advocates" will never be able to perform. By *protection* we mean surrounding the individual with friends and other acquaintances who know the individual and want to stand up for him or her. Each of us is different and potentially vulnerable to dangers in society. The protection that can be provided by friends is illustrated by the following incident. One day, Shawntell was going from class to class and got separated from her girl friends. She was in the middle of a large crowd near the stairwell. A young man came up to her and started to touch her in "inappropriate" places. Shawntell's girl friends saw what took place and went to the principal to tell him.

Peer pressure on young teenagers is great. However, what Shawntell's girl friends saw was wrong, and they knew that Shawntell was unable to stand up for herself. Therefore, they did the only thing they could think of; namely, they stood up for Shawntell. If the girls had not known Shawntell personally, would they have done the same thing? Maybe and maybe not. It is clear that every day people who do not know one another allow acts of violence to take place without raising a finger. However, these girls had formed a bond with Shawntell, and they knew that it was their responsibility to stand up and protect her.

It is this form of protection from vulnerability that cannot be paid for or ensured through legislation or litigation. It is these bonds that will protect all our children as well as adults. This is the only true security and advocacy that will exist for us all.

CONCLUSION

For all children, having a caring family and a community to be involved with are critical components of being active citizens. The number of clubs and organizations you belong to and how active one's social calendar is is not the issue. What is important is being involved in ordinary activities with ordinary people, doing your utmost to arrange opportunities for your children to be involved. It means doing things with others who have similar interests. It means trying out some new things, but also enjoying the "old reliable" pastimes too.

It is important for the entire family, not just the children, to be involved in community life. Such participation will provide the proper diversion, as well as a cushion of support and assistance, that is needed over time. Being involved in the community, including the school, is not a one-way street. Communities are not just places for new or isolated people to learn things. They are places that allow *all* people to learn, enjoy, and flourish.

For lots of reasons, we need communities that include all people. Indeed, a community that does not actively seek and accept difference and diversity among its members is not a community in the highest sense of the word. Of course, communities are not perfect, but neither are human beings. All human beings, however, deserve the dignity that community acceptance brings. Community inclusion is not just a nice thing to work on; it is at the heart of our work as human beings. It is this "work" that will ultimately protect and ensure quality of life for us all.

REFERENCES

Durner, G. (1985). On becoming a member of the community. *The Canadian Journal of Mental Retardation, 35*, 28–30.

Granger, L., & Granger, B. (1986). *The magic feather*. New York: E.P. Dutton.

CHAPTER 16

Systems of Support

A New Vision

Judith A. Snow

PROLOGUE

I was born in 1949 to a middle-class family in southern Ontario, Canada. I am the third child of four. One of my personal attributes has shaped my life to such an extent that it overshadows the impact of every other characteristic of my self. When I was 7 months of age, I was diagnosed as having spinal muscular atrophy, a form of muscular dystrophy. I was labeled as "severely physically disabled."

From this perspective and as an advocate for human rights, I have had the opportunity to observe and study firsthand support systems for families and for individuals themselves in need of support.

This chapter challenges the traditional professional approach most commonly used for families and individuals and presents an alternative approach to support that has been found to be more successful and effective. Family and individual support systems are critical, if children are to be prepared to take full advantage of an integrated, quality education in the mainstream of schools. Teachers and other school personnel must understand this in order to be prepared to help families and individuals form appropriate support systems.

The chapter first describes support that occurs naturally for most people within families and outside of families. It then discusses how this natural support sometimes breaks down and how current professional support systems often do not fill the void and can even have negative effects. Finally, it outlines how to stimulate positive, natural support relationships and friendship circles around families and individuals needing support.

NATURAL SUPPORT SYSTEM

Natural Family Support

In general, one tends to see a family as primarily a two-generational group of people, sharing one dwelling place and related closely both legally and through "blood." One's picture of a "normal" family often includes Mom, Dad, Dick, Jane, Baby Sally on the way, and Spot tied up in the yard. During special occasions, legal events (such as settling estates), and for the purposes of photograph albums, the definition of "family" includes other persons, tied more loosely together legally and genetically over more generations and living in other places. These may include aunts, cousins, in-laws, and so on. When such occasions or events are over, the "extended" family generally reverts to the two-generational, isolated "nuclear family."

The family is our society's model of a close-knit, sustaining, diverse, and gifted relationship network, capable of meeting a variety of needs and crises, as well as of generating hospitality, health, and joy. Within the family context, members are expected to receive their basic emotional nurturance and identity. The parents are supposed to provide security to the family, taking care of the physical, social, and emotional needs of the members. In addition, they are expected to inculcate social values and procedures in their children, as well as love them and keep them happy.

However, to varying degrees and at varying times, both children and adults require support and assistance beyond what the immediate family can provide. They may need support only occasionally, or they may require long-term intensive medical, educational, social, and/or emotional assistance.

Natural Support Outside of the Family

Generally, individuals participate in a network of friends, school or work companions, neighbors, and relatives, along with other multivaried associations. Some of these connections are intimate, many are friendly, most are sustaining.

Relationships and associations between people are based at least in part on what people have to share with each other in terms of abilities, dreams, interests, values, and the like. The capacity to be together and do things together comes from a common, often unspoken, understanding that each person has gifts to bring to the common interactions of daily life. These gifts may be ordinary indeed, but plenty of ordinary gifts are needed in daily life.

Relationships vary for each person, but typically each individual has a small number of close, intimate, potentially lifelong relationships; a somewhat larger group of not-so-close friends who vary widely in interests; and then a modest to extensive group of people who meet one need or another in exchange-based interactions. An individual participates in all aspects of life through these relationships, developing talents, gaining competence, being challenged and affirmed, making more relationships.

Interestingly, a person gains access to a multitude of activities simply on the basis of whom he or she knows. In very few of these activities is prior competence a serious prerequisite. Competence comes with participation, not the other way around.

A BREAKDOWN IN SUPPORTS

Unfortunately, in our society, some individuals are viewed negatively, as bringing not gifts but problems to daily life. As a consequence, some of these people (e.g., disabled people, poor people, minority group members) are rejected by others as friends, so that they lose the potential of such supportive relationships. Often such individuals who are denied naturally occurring friendship supports must resort to a support network populated primarily by people who are paid caregivers rather than friends. This altered network of relationships signals in a powerful way that this person is regarded as less than or as simply not a worthwhile human being.

Denial of social and emotional support relationships in all their rich variety outside of the family puts a strain on family relationships and also often causes the excluded individual to become inactive and a nonparticipator in life. This state in turn leads to a lessening of competence and an increase of unmet needs in the person; in other words, to dramatically increased disadvantage. If in turn, the family sees the child or adult as having no future, having a problem, or as needing to be *fixed*, then the whole dynamic around the person can become a cycle of relationship-destroying and disability-intensifying processes among all the family members. This breakdown of support outside of the family for one member can lead to a situation in which the family itself becomes isolated and needy.

PROBLEMS WITH CURRENT SUPPORT SYSTEMS

Most support services typically offered to such a family have the potential for being very destructive of each individual's giftedness and potential for developing relationships. For example, when a child needs extensive support, adults are often encouraged to engage themselves intensively in therapeutic activities for the child. Thus, Mom or Dad may be trained to become a live-in physiotherapist, behavior modifier, and so forth. The parents' relationship with their child then tends to lose its parent-child focus and to gain a helper-client characteristic. In addition, adults may be required to put endless hours into filling out forms, reporting events, and cutting red tape, limiting already-limited "togetherness" time and relationships with people outside of the family. Also, many services remove the child from the home for respite care, to a medical center for speech skills, and so on.

By their very nature, such services tend to teach the philosophy that what family and neighbors have to offer cannot develop the rejected individual's potential to the extent that the services can. For example, parents may be encouraged to use the respite services of the trained babysitter who can only come from far away and on Tuesday mornings. Because the service is "professional," perhaps even subsidized, the family is discouraged from asking the neighbor kids to come share pizza for lunch that day. Soon the neighbor kids stopped visiting! After all, the professional babysitter has taken a government-funded course and is insured!

Even the label of the sitting service, "respite," implies a temporary removal of the burden of the rejected, needy family member. Consequently, the apparent value of support services can subtly, yet dramatically, lead to the erosion of the number and strength of all the relationships in a person's life.

Moreover, as previously noted, all family members are sometimes in need of support, but positive support is not achievable through creating more disability-focused services. If the individuals and the family are to achieve welcome in the community, all individuals, regardless of their differences, must be regarded as an unusual gift, not a burden, to the broader social structure. People must see that differences do not have to be fixed or cured. Instead, each individual's gifts must be discovered, accepted and shaped. Every person must be welcomed, celebrated, listened to, challenged, and supported in every environment to develop all of his or her potential talents. The individual's contributions must be facilitated and used for the betterment of the wider group.

The potential of any person is not a fixed, unitary quantity. Experience shows that the number of possible ways to support a person to participate, to be a dynamic part of a living, growing relationship network, and to become more competent is vastly greater than the number of ways to cure a disability. In other words, participation in the community, in the final analysis, is much easier to achieve than the elimination of disability.

BUILDING POSITIVE SUPPORT RELATIONSHIPS

True family support is an activity that focuses on discovering the giftedness in every family member and that helps each member to build and maintain a broad range of relationships with peers and other community members. It involves experimenting with a new range of relationships and activities made possible by "differences." In other words, differences must be respected and treated as unusual gifts to be offered to the whole community. It should be remembered that all of us are different in some ways from other people. Thus, this new attitude and approach will help us all.

If society is to provide for the participation of all people, and if all people are to exploit their gifts completely, then many groups and environments in society must be places where dreams are heard, gifts are discovered, and interactions are renewed. Consequently, members of every sort of social group and structure must be invited to directly encounter a person in need of support and to experience the power of that person's dreams and gifts. In this way a community's competence to capitalize upon differences increases.

In this process, valuable meaning is found in differences. This meaning must conform to beliefs that the group already cherishes and must be explicitly interpreted to every member of the group. This allows all members to participate in the new group interactions. For example, one member of a group may have an unquenchable desire to touch every other member of the group one or more times a day. The group can be helped to realize that the individual is being "friendly," and that this group values friendliness and needs friendly members. It then becomes possible to create or use an existing valued role such as "greeter"—someone who touches every member present at least once a day as a sign of welcome and belonging. Then everyone will want to interact with this individual because he or she wants to be welcomed as a means of strengthening his or her own membership in the group.

Consequently, the problem becomes an opportunity. This process is both revolutionary and conservative. At its heart, it conserves the structure of the group interactions, along with the presence and participation of all community members. It does this by expanding the status quo through providing a new range of options to all members. Thus, the community gains a new capacity to meet needs and helps itself to become more adaptive and healthy, rather than stultifying in old, rigid ways that begin to lose their meanings for all.

Not just any new interpretation of a difference will create a stable set of new interactions. The new process must have value for each member, relating to his or her real needs. Consequently, the new interpretation must be grounded in the actual dream, intention, or goal of the person, providing him or her with a genuine opportunity to achieve greater fulfillment. In other words, if our friend's desire to touch does not arise from a desire to be friendly, the role of "greeter" will not be satisfying for long, and the new interactions will not be stable. More than one new set of activities may need to be tried. People must listen to the dream many times to find the best new roles for the person.

BUILDING SUPPORT CIRCLES

One means of engaging ordinary citizens in providing support to others is through building support circles. These family/community-oriented support circles are similar in operation to the friendship circles used in schools described in Chapter 4 of this book by Forest and Lusthaus.

To realize the value of relationships for a person in need of support, some relationship-generating process must be made available. Support circles provide a means to unite people both in an immediate sense and in a community restructuring action. That is, a support circle galvanizes a small number of people into a new and more active commitment to an individual and furthermore creates opportunities for the individual to build new interactions in the wider community.

The support circle has two basic functions that are highly interrelated. On the one side, support circle members must come into a relationship with the person in need of support; they must be prepared to spend the time necessary to get to know the individual—to understand, value, and enjoy him or her. On the other side, the real purpose of the sharing is to empower the person to meet his or her needs, while expressing her or his gifts. This area of activity includes supporting, teaching, and challenging the person, as well as initiating changes in society that will break down obstacles and create opportunities for one's friend.

Support Circle Principles

No two support circles are the same. (This author suggests that each group have its own name.) However, the following general principles are applicable to all circles:

1. Circles often form around two people who are in a strong relationship, where the advocate speaks for the person in need of support. This is particularly evident when parents speak for a young child or when the person cannot easily communicate with others (e.g., the child is nonverbal, speaks a different language, stutters, is shy). For children, it is often necessary to build a double circle: one around the parents and one around the child and his or her new friends. This allows the child to develop independence from his or her family. Later, in adulthood, a single circle around the person will remain, with or without his or her parents, depending on the circumstances.

2. Strong circles usually form around a person who wants to change. Such people make phenomenal changes in their own lives once they have the required relationship support. On the other hand, one cannot force a circle on someone who is content with life or afraid of change. Meetings will always be boring and the group will eventually fall apart.

3. The purpose and direction of the circle are defined by the dream or goal of the person needing support. The key question must constantly be: "What do you really want?" When a circle loses touch with the dream of the "circled" individual, the individual will subvert or stall the agenda by getting sick, behaving badly, or otherwise holding up the process until real listening happens again.

4. The person who is the "focus" of the circle will grow in direct relationship to the honesty and commitment of the circle membership. His or her vision is shaped and brought into reality by a combination of deep listening, caring, challenge, and committed effort on the part of each circle member.

5. If a circle is too small, everyone will feel under pressure. Invite more people to join! If a circle is too big, however, people will quit because they do not have enough to do. The size of the circle is dependent on

how much the "circled" person wants to change and how fast. Small circles form around little dreams; big ones are needed for big changes.

6. Circles often first come into being during a crisis, when the "circled" person (and possibly his or her advocate) discovers that what he or she really needs is to give up tolerating and adjusting to things as they have been. A circle can form without a crisis if the central person is prepared to ask for what he or she really needs. Often people ask for what they think they can get, not what they want, because they have become accustomed to negotiating for whatever appears to be available. This process often causes other people to feel manipulated, and they back off or reject the requests for help. When a person asks for what he or she really needs, other people feel needed and empowered to commit energy and time.

This reality explains why circles usually comprise people that the circled person has known for a long time. They may be old social friends, neighbors, relatives, or former service workers who have listened sympathetically before and offered to help but have also stayed at a distance. With a sincere invitation to listen and act, their commitment is liberated.

7. A facilitator may be called in to help a circle. Because it is often difficult for a person or his or her advocate to tell the dream, or ask for what is really needed, a support circle often is started under the guidance of a facilitator. His or her role is to help people talk about what they really want. Using a list generated by the parents, advocate, and/or person needing support, the first step is to help call together a group of supportive people who are willing to commit themselves to hearing the story and the dream. By the second or third meeting, some will drop out, but several will commit themselves to action, perhaps even suggesting potential new members.

The facilitator may be a member of another support circle; a "broker" or "coordinator" who is paid to form such groups; or someone comfortable with the process. To maintain everyone's trust, he or she must be clear about the amount of time and the number of meetings he or she can spend with each circle. Within a short period of time (two to six meetings approximately), the circle must develop its own process of deciding when and how to get together. (The role of the facilitator is discussed in more detail in an upcoming section of this chapter.)

8. Mature circles often are very informal, with relationships resembling those of a close-knit extended family. The person in need of support will have achieved valued social interactions and identities, and thus will be able to provide the same kind of supports to other circle members as are provided to him or her. Thus, a mature circle does not focus on the support needs of one person only but on the needs of all; as all have equal membership. Should a crisis or special need arise for any member, the circle can meet in a structured manner again.

Potential Circle Problems

Circles are vulnerable to at least two types of distortion. First, they may be established without developing a sense of the need to always be listening for the growing edge of the focus person's giftedness. Circle members may feel that they have heard the person's story or dream, and may lose touch with the need to "check back" for changes resulting from new growth and experience.

Second, the circle members may want only to be friendly to the person needing support, but may be unwilling either to confront the social and political barriers blocking that individual's goals or to challenge their "friend" as a true colleague when he or she strays from his or her own path. This is an indication that circle members do not really believe in the giftedness or dream of the circled person or of society's need to embrace the power of this dream.

To some extent, these problems can be addressed directly by the person needing support. Also, as more and more circles are formed, they can act as a stimulus to each other through sharing stories, celebrating together, or exchanging information. Those involved in relationship building must be aware that strong pressures work against them, and they must take steps to keep their vision clear.

Role of the Circle Facilitator

Typically, the circle-building process is implemented by a person who is not a family member of the circled person. This factor is perfectly natural, as only an external person can get a clear sense of the identities, meanings, and roles that are interacting in any particular situation. An individual who is a "regular" member of the family or group may be feeling enough threat or insecurity to be unable to perceive creative possibilities.

The facilitator must be able to observe, analyse, interpret, and act on three levels at once. On one level, and of primary importance, he or she must be totally allied with the person requiring support, and intimately familiar with the sorts of problems the person is facing. He or she must be able to look and listen past violent or disruptive behavior; or the silence, passivity, and confusion born from fear and self-doubt. There must be absolute trust that this circled person is gifted, has a truly human vocation, can be in a relationship with many others, and can grow and learn to offer and express these valuable contributions.

The facilitator listens for problems and for insight into the efforts the circled person is making to solve these problems. These efforts, as diverse as they may be, express the strengths, needs, and potential of this person. Because of this, if for any reason the facilitator feels uncomfortable with or distrusts the vulnerable person, another facilitator should be found.

The second aspect of the facilitator's work is that of managing a group process and organizing a new set of commitments. One element is helping circle members learn to decide when and where meetings are held, who should be present, and so forth. This work also involves helping people to relax, listen, and contribute during meetings. The facilitator must know the relationship-building process well enough to keep a group on track but also recognize helpful distractions should they occur. Value statements and creative suggestions must be highlighted and positively interpreted. Negative contributions must be respectfully contradicted, or otherwise handled so as to forestall further rejection of the circled individual. Basically, the facilitator strives to reinforce efforts that others make to value, form relationships with, and design actions around the person needing support.

For the facilitator to perform well, the group must accept the authority of the facilitator and of his or her "manipulations." Consequently, the facilitator must not only be totally familiar with the circling process and external to the group but also comfortable with the values and practices of the family.

The third function performed by the facilitator is that of being a visionary and a teacher. This role must permeate all activities, as it protects the person needing support from future rejection and causes the group to tolerate this interference with their beliefs and ways. The facilitator must communicate concretely the vision, building a sense of community in which differences are valued and beneficial for everyone. Not only is the facilitator attempting to resolve problems and support one person, but he or she is working to revolutionize the values of the group to the point where the members can value differences before rejection occurs.

Because of this visionary role, the facilitator must endeavor to limit the number of his or her commitments. In the same way, different facilitators should not stand in for each other too often. A practical commitment to the circled individual and to his or her family or personal community is required to nurture this potential new life.

This three-fold action is both delicate and powerful. Circle facilitators must be mature, growth-oriented people who strive to be loving and caring. They must be open to learning from each other and from the people needing support. In this way, their capacity to help others will remain strong.

STORIES OF CIRCLE BUILDING

Once a person has decided that he or she wants a circle, how does the process start? The next several pages present case examples of circle building (all names are fictionalized).

Parent's Circle

Marie, a single parent, has two daughters, one of whom, named Joan, has been rejected because people feel she cannot be educated in a regular class in a real school (as opposed to a "retarded" school). Marie has just lost a year-long battle with her local school board to have her daughter Joan integrated. The fight has been messy, and Marie is emotionally, physically, and financially drained. She has also been spending every afternoon and weekend with her daughter because Joan has no friends and no supports to meet her social and physical needs. Marie finds herself thinking about placing Joan in a group home for "handicapped" children and wonders why things have gotten so out of hand.

Joan was in a regular first grade class last year, but her teacher kept her on a separate program and often sent the aide and Joan away from the class to do entirely different things from the other first grade students. Joan made no friends because the students soon learned from the teacher's modeling that Joan was not really one of the kids. Now the school board says they have nothing to offer Joan. Marie is wondering, "If this is integration, I don't want it! Inte-

Point to Ponder

Children classified as disabled (and/or their advocates) often must provide extensive justification for why they should be permitted to attend their regular neighborhood public school. In addition, they often must pass certain checklists or tests before being allowed into the mainstream of the school's programs and activities. But so-called normal children do not have to provide any justification or pass any such tests. Is not this blatant discrimination against children that society classifies as having disabilities?

gration doesn't work. She's better off in a segregated school."

Sandy is another parent. She knows that Marie needs help, and has reached out to her through telephone calls and visits. She invites another friend, Judith, who is experienced at building support circles, to get to know Marie and to offer her help. Sandy also invites along another parent who has a child in a good integrated situation. Together they visit Marie and Joan at their own home.

Judith listens to Marie and encourages her over and over again to say what she really needs and wants. She encourages her to direct her anger, not at Joan, but at the professionals who have failed to see her daughter as a gifted addition to a classroom. Judith explains what circles are all about; how people would support her in her dreams or goals to build friends around Joan, find a better job, and get her other daughter a better summer program.

At first Marie says she has no friends, but with some encouragement she is able to come up with a list of 15 neighbors, friends, and professionals who have been supportive over the last few years.

Sandy and the others offer their support, and agree to help Marie invite everyone to a night of storytelling and dreaming. When the evening arrives everyone shows up, and Marie starts to tell everybody how grateful she is for their concern. At first her story reveals no big problems, but Judith helps her to tell the real story, to trust that people will listen and support her. With much anger, frustration, and tears the story unfolds, and then the dream of a real education and real friends for Joan, and of an important new job for Marie plus a chance to start life again.

Several people immediately offer to pressure the school board through personal contact, a petition, and a new appeal. Neighborhood parents invite Joan and her sister to spend time with their kids, at parties, weekends of fun, and the local girl's club. Someone knows of a job coming up and someone else has heard of a retraining program at the local community college. Another has a teenage niece who would love to babysit. Three or four people have nothing to say, but they offer to come again to another circle meeting.

Judith helps Marie to accept these offers and not to put herself down. Everyone agrees that Marie does not have to bake for the next meeting, but they will bring their own potluck supper. The circle has begun!

This story of Marie's difficulties is not unusual. Marie has allowed herself to fall into the handicapping "trap" of taking on all the work and doing all the fighting herself, allowing herself and her daughters to become isolated and victimized by the system. She wants to protect her family from rejection and hurt. She also has some fears about exposing Joan to the real world.

Marie's example demonstrates that no one can change the system by himself or herself, that without help burnout results and that everyone loses without a support system. The pattern is common. A parent starts to believe all the negative messages sent through the years by the medical and educational establishments. The parent begins to see the child as a problem, rather than perceiving that the system is failing the child. Afraid to burden others, the parent becomes more and more isolated, fragmented, and frustrated. Believing that nobody else cares, can understand, believe in, or love her child, she never reaches out for the help that neighbors and friends can provide. Rather, she becomes the recipient of the wrong kind of service—once-a-month respite in a group home, waiting lists and assessments, and so forth.

The mystique is powerful. This child who has medical-sounding labels seems to need experts, pills, treatment. In fact, this child really needs friends, activities, and common-sense guidance to support her life. Marie needs the help of others to ask and to speak about her real experience. She needs to discover that people will care about and believe in her dreams for herself and her daughters. Many circles are started by a facilitator like Judith who will hang in there long enough to support Marie in learning to ask.

This and other similar stories this author has been involved in underscores that ordinary citizens and neighbors do care but are rarely asked. Once asked, they will respond with a multitude of ordinary resources and lots of energy.

Dual Parent and Child Circle

Helen, who is 14 years old, had been educationally segregated all her life. Her parents loved her, but had lost all sense of purpose, direction, and hope for her. During the week, Helen attended a residential behavior management program intended to curb her more disturbing activities, and she came home on weekends. With no friends and a weakening family tie, the future looked monotonous and dim for her.

At an Education for Integration course, Helen's parents joined with other families in sharing dreams and stories. When asked what they really wanted, Helen's parents dared admit that they wanted Helen to go to a regular high school.

The course leader, Marsha, helped Helen's parents hold a small meeting at their home, including a few relatives and some people from the course. After some painful sharing, they were able to create a very short list of Helen's strengths and gifts, as well as think about ordinary solutions to her needs. One glaring aspect of Helen's life was her complete isolation from friends her own age. Their view of her was reflected in her bedroom, the room of a 3-year-old, filled with Teddy Bears, Mickey Mouse toys, and so forth.

With the support of their new friends, Helen's parents decided to approach the school system and ask for Helen to be registered at the local high school. Their request was denied, and school officials turned nasty during appeal procedures. At the human rights board, a compromise was accepted where Helen was registered in a regular high school in another school system.

The circle helped the family find a grant to hire a young woman who began to build a circle of friends around Helen. She and Helen went horseback riding, shopping, and later to a summer program with kids that attended Helen's future high school. The young woman encouraged and allowed the kids to be with Helen, occasionally modeling appropriate interactions for them. Soon the kids were helping to redesign Helen's bedroom into a teenager's room, and going with her, often without her facilitator, to shops, movies, and so on. Helen came home to stay as her behavior became more and more like that of her new friends.

When the school year began, Helen was no stranger to the high school students, and soon an in-school circle was formed. The facilitator invited this group of teenagers to help design and then implement a program at school. They built her curriculum around strengths she had shown during the summer, drawing from the parents' growing respect for their child. The teenagers advocated on Helen's behalf with school authorities to allow Helen to have all of her new program in regular classes where circle members attended. Helen was soon participating fully in gym, religion, computer, and drama classes, the latter being a favourite. Both in school and after school, she became more and more supported by her friends.

At this point two circles existed: one for the parents and one for Helen. As Helen's opportunities opened up, the family, with the encouragement of their circle, began to see new possibilities and to share the work of bringing these ideas to birth. Early on, Helen's parents actually took off for a week's vacation by themselves, allowing Helen to stay with friends. Overwhelmed by the number of friends who were beginning to surround Helen, they were enjoying a new vision for themselves and their daughter. They learned to let go of her, to let her take real risks, and to let her participate in teenage life. During the summer of 1988, Helen was to be a counselor-in-training with three other students at an integrated summer program at York University. The future holds nothing but promise for Helen.

This story reveals the importance of a positive vision in the life of a person with challenging needs. For 14 years, Helen's parents had believed that her life could go nowhere, and so, indeed it was going nowhere. As soon as they knew that she had gifts to share with her community and especially with friends her own age, they began to change, and soon Helen revealed that she, too, was ready for a change.

It took great courage and enormous support, but this family made incredible changes in 1 year. Helen herself has unmasked the ignorance of her former educators who labeled her at the bottom of their imaginary scale of abilities. She has revealed that she is a gifted member of her teenage crowd.

This story demonstrates the importance of two circles or two support systems. Teenagers naturally must lead a life of activity partly separate from their parents' needs and routines. This is a normal part of gaining an adult life of interdependence in the community. A double support group allows this separateness to happen.

We also can see that other teenagers consider Helen to be important. A wide variety of teenagers were attracted to the idea of the circle and ultimately to Helen herself as a real friend in their world.

CONCLUSION

While paid support personnel (doctors, teachers, therapists) may be needed by any person at some points in his or her life, more attention needs to be focused on building natural support networks. This chapter has discussed building such networks for families and individuals who lack adequate support to achieve their goals. This activity calls upon us to determine the goals, dreams, gifts, and strengths of people in need of assistance. It calls for us to see strength in all of our differences, and to interpret differences as an opportunity for community members to grow and meet each other's needs. Such support involves structuring opportunities for all types of people to build and maintain relationships with others.

This author firmly believes that relationship building and community strengthening are threatened by any increase in services that specialize and focus on disabilities or problems. These negatively oriented services blind some people to the giftedness in others. Therefore, family and individual support should not be structured as a professional service activity but should be accomplished through bringing people together in ways that make sense to the people involved and that appreciate the value of the gifts that these people bring to each other. Paid services should never be used as a substitute for what citizens can do with and for each other.

PART VI

Final Considerations

CHAPTER 17

Making Difference Ordinary

Douglas Biklen

Culture defines disability. As with gender, race, social class, and certain other conditions or characteristics, the ways in which society explicitly and implicitly defines disability profoundly influences people's lives. Two examples help illustrate some of these effects. The first concerns the Canadian poet Alden Nowlan's poem, "He's lived there all his life" (1977). Nowlan writes of a blind man who receives differential treatment from the "locals" of the small town and its "newcomers." The "newcomers" treat the man with a measure of charity, even patronizingly. The manager of the local movie theatre gives the man a ride to the movies when a new show opens. Others read him the newspapers. Some listen patiently to the man's boring stories "for the tenth, fifteenth, or twentieth time" (p. 22, 4th verse, lines 4–7). Newcomer's feel sorry for the "poor old man" whom they say the locals treat badly. Nowlan sides with the locals, observing that in a small town people can come to know each other so well that a person's lack of sight does not cloud people's appreciation or disdain for each others' behavior.

The lessons this poem communicates for education are twofold. First, disability often obstructs people's views of each other. A person's blindness, for example, is rarely simply an observable fact (e.g., an inability to see); it usually evokes a social interpretation, in this case "the poor old man." Second, there is nothing inherent in disability that justifies stereotyped responses. Nowlan advocates a more humanistic alternative: evaluating people for qualities over which they have some control, like being humorous or boring, captivating and original, or ordinary and repetitive.

The second example derives from this author's notes of a recent visit to an elementary school:

> I arrived at the school early in the morning, 20 minutes before students were to gather in their homerooms. I wanted to speak with one of the teachers before classes convened. At the entrance of the school, I stopped to hold the door for a student who was blind and who had her hands full; she was carrying a cane in one hand and a brailler in the other. She greeted me and asked me my name. We introduced ourselves (her name was J. P.), and then I asked if she could tell me where I might find Ms. Smith's

Preparation of this chapter was partially supported by the U.S. Department of Education, Office of Special Education and Rehabilitation Services, National Institute on Disability and Rehabilitation Research (NIDRR), under Cooperative Agreement No. G0085C03503 awarded to the Center on Human Policy, Division of Special Education and Rehabilitation, Syracuse University, Syracuse NY. The opinions expressed herein are solely those of the authors, and no official endorsement of the U.S. Department of Education should be inferred.

> class. She volunteered to show me the way, which she did, charging through doorways, angling left, up two flight of stairs, and around the corner to a second floor classroom. I stood by while the student handed her brailler to the teacher and then said goodbye to her as she headed back downstairs to join her classmates at breakfast. Then I met with the teacher. It was wonderful to see how very independent this student is.

When this author recounted the incident to Adrienne Asch, a disability studies scholar, she responded to my interpretation of the student's "independence" this way: "It's interesting that you would call her very independent. I suspect she thinks of herself as ordinary." Adrienne herself does not relish having to constantly combat people's limiting perceptions of her and of people with disabilities in general. She admits to enjoying the humor in observing people's reactions to her when, after she has given them directions for using the New York subway system, they realize that she is blind.

Of course Nowlan's small town street corner, J. P.'s school, and Adrienne Asch's New York subway siding are not the only places we might encounter disability-based stereotyping. It is everywhere. It pervades culture, literature (Biklen, 1987a; Zola, 1987), public policy (Johnson & Lambrinos, 1987), personal interaction (Bogdan & Taylor, 1982; Brightman, 1985), film (Longmore, 1987), the news media (Biklen, 1985), and social institutions such as schools (Gartner & Lipsky, 1987). And as with race, gender, or other social bases of stereotyping, prejudice, and discrimination, negative social definitions of disability do not disappear easily. Even when they are the targets of concerted social reform movements, they may persist. Also, wishing them away does not make them disappear. If we say, for example, "They (children with disabilities) are really no different than anybody else" and/or, "I treat them just the same as I treat anybody else," we deny the disability experience. As Nowlan implies and as Adrienne Asch reminds us, our culture often attributes disability master status. That is, disability has a series of meanings that extend far beyond its observable or objective reality.

Knowledge of how the culture defines disability suggests two broad strategies for school reform. First, educators, parents, and students can attempt to better understand and eradicate handicapism in schools. Second, a consistent effort is needed to accommodate needs arising from disabilities, as with any differences among students that might affect learning.

CHANGES IN SCHOOLS

In the book *Achieving the Complete School* (Biklen, 1985), this author noted a number of examples of how schools communicate social or cultural definitions of disability. For instance, a school principal is seen raising his voice to and being overly solicitous of a young man labeled as moderately retarded, telling him how nice his shop project looks and slapping him on the back in an unusually friendly way. There would not have been anything particularly wrong with this display of affection had it not been totally unlike the way the principal relates to the other junior high students. In addition, we learned from a high school principal that his school has a "total" school population of 952, "not counting the special ed kids." His remark confirms that students with disabilities and the staff and programs to support their presence in school are not taken for granted and are not fully accepted. They were considered an "add-on." We learned that some other administrators tended to see children with disabilities as a burden or unwanted "extra" expense. And we described how a teacher unintentionally seemed to hover over one mainstreamed student, showering her with assistance beyond what she functionally required to participate in regular classroom routines, and in the process drawing special attention to her and her disability.

These events were not isolated ones. They formed patterns of behavior in schools that acted as barriers to the acceptance and mutuality that one envisions for the ideal schools that serve all children. They suggest why it is not enough for schools to simply declare the intent to serve all students. They must do more.

Specifically, schools that are finding a greater measure of success in educating students of differing abilities are those that directly address society's negative interpretations of disability. This section of the chapter examines some of the more apparent of these interpretations. But instead of merely identifying them, the text restates them as positive actions that schools can take to transform the negative interpretations to ones that reflect a valuing and accepting attitude toward differences and, therefore, toward individual students.

Schools without Labels

It is difficult to "see the person" and not a category of person when the individual is surrounded by others who share similar disabilities. The way we group students, and sometimes talk about them, produces an image that denies individuality. Students are labeled as disabled, emotionally disturbed, mentally retarded, multihandicapped, slow learners, the gifted, regular, and so on. The underlying assumption is that students in these categories have similarities that justify their congregation. Yet there is no evidence that such amalgamation helps them. In fact, many parents and teachers complain that the very existence of even the most prestigious category (gifted) diminishes schooling in general. They do not object that gifted education provides opportunities for students to engage in creative evaluation of subjects usually not covered in public school curricula, such as logic, philosophy, economics, and linguistics, but that such opportunities are not part of every student's education. Similarly, parents and teachers want students with severe disabilities to be challenged, to learn to interact with nondisabled peers, and, most of all, to be seen as people. This can begin to happen when students are recognized for their personal qualities, and not simply as "LDs," "MRs" and "EDs," for example. It can also begin when we start speaking about all programs and services in ordinary educational terms so that some students are not singled out to receive "training" or "treatment" instead of education.

One easily finds reasons for not labeling people as "disabled" or programs and teachers as "for the disabled" by listening to the advice given by people labeled as disabled. Autobiographical accounts are nearly unanimous on this question: "Don't label me handicapped or disabled." In fact, a number of authors announce: "I am not disabled" (Bogdan, 1982; Karuth, 1985; Peters, 1986; Saxton, 1985). One might wonder why a person considered by most people to be disabled or handicapped might claim otherwise. But as disability studies scholar Robert Bogdan (1982) has pointed out, when a person says "I am not retarded," that person is saying that he or she does not accept the social meaning of the term. The person who is labeled by others knows that for many people, indeed for society at large, *retarded* means incompetent, less valuable, unequal, even bad or evil. It is a dirty word, an epithet (e.g., a "retard," a "dummy").

A word or two more about labels is important here, for it is easy to misinterpret the central point about them. Obviously, people labeled as disabled consider themselves to be people, ordinary people. And they wonder why it is so hard for others to see them this way. At the same time, they are not anxious to deny *who* they are. They are not anxious to hide a missing limb, a particular gait, or a needed prosthesis. Indeed, a few disability rights activists and scholars have declared, "I *am* disabled, deal with me." Nancy Mairs, in her wonderfully literary book, *Plaintext* (1986), writes, for example:

> I am a cripple. I choose this word to name me. I choose from among several possibilities, the most common of which are "handicapped" and "disabled." (p. 9)
>
> * *
>
> People—crippled or not— wince at the word "cripple," as they do not at "handicapped" or "disabled." Perhaps I want them to wince. I want them to see me as a tough customer. . . . (p. 9)
>
> * *
>
> Sometimes I don't want to play Tiny Tim. I'd rather be Caliban, a most scurvy monster. (p. 15)

Mairs is saying something that schools, society, and we need to hear. All the changing, adapting, and assimilating cannot be justified if it means that people labeled as disabled, or handicapped, or crippled must give up who they are. Willing away the reality that Nancy Mairs has multiple sclerosis is not what she seeks. Rather, she and other people with disabilities (see for example, Kriegel, 1981) seem to want to say: "Don't make me conform to your image of the good handicapped person, always appreciative of your charity, or forever willing to overlook your stares and even, condescension. Don't expect me to deny who I am and what I need in order to be accepted. Don't expect me never to make demands, never to get angry, and not to be your equal, even your leader."

Schools without labels would be places that take account of the central issues facing people with disabilities (e.g., need for easier access, need for competent and widely available sign language interpretation, education in social skills for all students, sharing of expertise between teachers and specialist consultants, available large-type books for students with visual impairments, cooperative learning groups, and peer tutoring). Such schools would refer to children, programs, and teachers by personal names, subject area of instruction, and other typical names, not as *special, disabled,* or other obfuscating terms.

The lessons of such practices become clear almost as soon as they are tried. This author is reminded of the consequences of such a policy in a school that emphasizes inclusion of all students. Two English children were visiting in an American community and would be attending the neighborhood school in the fall. An American child asked one of the British youngsters, "What grade are you in?" The British child hesitated. Her brother jumped in with an explanation: "She's not in a grade. You see, she's in special education." The American student, who attends a school that has classrooms that educate students with severe disabilities and nondisabled students together, responded, "Oh, well, in my school, you'll have to be in a grade. How old are you?" When she learned the girl was 10, she responded, "You'll be in fourth or fifth grade." The school that was getting away from labels was nurturing students who think in nontraditional but normalizing ways about each other.

Point to Ponder

The Labeling controversy is in actuality a political argument between those who support the current system of special education and psychological diagnosis as a constructive and altruistic arrangement and those who wish to break up that system because they see it as oppressive and destructive. (Guskin, 1974, p. 263)

Making Schools Open and Inviting for All Students Is Not Just a Disability Issue

Following are examples of actual comments made by a group of "regular" educators who gathered recently to discuss the issue of schooling for students with disabilities. One teacher remarked, "I understand how it may be possible to integrate elementary age students, and maybe even junior high students, but how can it be done for high school students? I am a chemistry teacher. I just don't see how it's quite possible."

Another teacher raised a similar question when she said, "Who really decides where it is best to educate a student? If they tell me I have to integrate a child who has severe handicaps, is that right? I have no experience."

And a third teacher, an art teacher, suggested that the idea of putting students of differing abilities in the same classroom, including those with disabilities, may not be for her: "If I have a whole group of students, I have to worry about keeping them on track. And I have things like scissors to worry about. I don't even know if a child with severe cerebral palsy could handle the scissors. He might hurt himself."

Viewed in the most positive light, one might interpret the concerns expressed here as coming from people who have no experience or understanding of how a school and its teaching staff can successfully educate students of widely different abilities together. On the other hand, one might just as easily conclude that these are the comments of people who resist the idea of such reforms.

There are a number of ways to respond to these statements and questions. One might answer with reassurances and offer specific classroom strategies to be used in the classroom. One might also accompany the teachers on visits to schools that are engaged in the reforms about which they are concerned. Or one might address the teachers' nervousness about change and their resistant attitudes. However, none of these interpretations of the teachers' statements or possible responses is adequate, because none speaks to the fundamental issues implicit in their comments or recognizes that the problems posed are *not* basically unique to disability, to students with disabilities, or to methods of educating students with a wide range of differences.

When a teacher says she is not sure that there is room in her chemistry class for a child with severe disabilities, she is suggesting that she thinks of education as occurring in predestined tracks. It suggests that she takes the current form of schools as a given. Yet, the idea of making schools and classrooms open to a broad range of students may indeed call for new or different approaches—for example, use of concepts such as partial participation or cooperative learning—but it also calls upon teachers to open their minds to the transformation that is possible in schools.

When a teacher bridles at the prospect of other people, presumably psychologists and special education administrators, making decisions about student placement without ever involving the teacher or determining if he or she is capable of accommodating the proposed placement, the teacher is rightfully skeptical, even resentful. Yet the logical response should not necessarily be to reject the child but to reject the practice of how schools make decisions and of how schools distribute authority. For school reform to work, teachers need to see themselves and be seen as people who can make decisions and who, together with parents, students, and administrators, create the school's values, goals, and therefore its authority.

In other words, we need to see these three teachers' comments in context. Their statements reflect educational philosophy, conceptions of authority in schools, and attitudes about schools as communities, respectively. Of course, there is nothing particularly new about proposing that educators consider the value of democratic authority or the democratic version of excellence (see, for example, Giroux, 1986, and Greene, 1984). But, typically, debates or discussions over how to educate students with disabilities are conceptualized in compartmental terms, strictly as disability issues. One tends not to think about such reform efforts as being linked to larger, contextual questions, such as the nature of authority in schools, the role of teachers in their own community, definitions of educational goals, and ideas about equity and excellence.

Integrating the Adults So that We Might Be Able to Integrate the Students

A little over a year ago, this author was invited to conduct a workshop on "achieving the complete (integrated) school" to a group of six school principals and a dozen teachers in the Kitikmeot region of the Canadian arctic, in Cambridge Bay. The assistant superintendent for this region felt that the idea of educating all students in classrooms together, irrespective of ability level, made sense for rural communities. The population of the largest towns or settlements in the Kitikmeot was only 1,200, and most settlements were far smaller. Interestingly, the circumstances of the teachers, the style of school organization, and the educators' attitudes about areas of professional expertise in these schools mimic what is found in more urban schools in the United States.

As a workshop activity, this author suggested that the principals interview the resource/specialist teachers. Each principal was asked to develop a description of the resource teacher's role. The principals were to record the words of the teachers verbatim, and part of the interview had to include the teachers' completion of the sentence, "I feel like a ______."

Several teachers described themselves as the recipients of students who were other teachers' rejects. One teacher explained this perspective:

> I teach children in my class who have three different types of problems. Some have average intelligence, but they have not been in school. My job is to give them catch-up. Another group are the students who are not succeeding in regular classes. A third group are the ones with moderate or severe behavior problems, the ones who have been disruptive, refused to work, or were violent (in other words screamed

> and yelled on the floor). I seem to get who they think doesn't fit. I think I'm perceived as someone who takes behavior problem students and goes away and is strict. But I'm not. I feel like a safe haven.

Another teacher described a similar misperception of her role: "Some of the teachers think I can fix anything, but of course it doesn't work that way." While she particularly liked working with other teachers to develop programs for integrated classrooms, she said that her day was not designed to accommodate such collaboration. "There's no time to work with other teachers. I feel like a pulley, pulled in too many directions." Another teacher echoed the time problem. She spoke of cutting corners in the name of efficiency, and developing individualized education plans for students without the help or collaboration of other teachers:

> I worry that this might lead to other teachers saying or believing they are not responsible for these children. But I hesitate to ask teachers to meet with me. There just isn't time. There isn't even time for me to observe the students in the regular classroom. Whatever program support I do has to be after hours. I feel like a Band-Aid.

This image of the teacher as first aid officer is a common one. "I don't want to be seen as a doctor with bandages," a teacher from another school complained. Other teachers characterized themselves as a fix-it-all mechanic, a life preserver, or "like an amoeba that is expected to extend a pseudopod each time a new problem comes up." Such analogies reveal the outsider (specialist), stopgap, public relations roles that these teachers fulfill. The frustrations of these teachers are captured in their belief that they are wrongly characterized: "If I could change one thing, it would be the awareness of the other teachers."

Schools that want to integrate students with and without disabilities need also to integrate teachers. Instead of organizing the teaching staff into insiders (regular teachers) and outsiders (specialists), the school needs to develop teams of teachers that include generalists *and* specialists who collaborate to develop curricula, to share teaching strategies, and to teach lessons where each teaches both "classified" and "nonclassified" children. Responsibilities must not lie entirely with one or the other teacher; rather, they must always be shared.

As suggested by several other chapter authors in this book, many initial steps can narrow the gulf separating the specialist from the generalist, to ensure communication and collaboration between them. This author has observed such concrete strategies in use. In one program, specialists and generalists actually switch roles periodically during each year, and then share their adopted role experiences during scheduled meeting times. Other programs use team teaching and consulting teaching models, which facilitate special programming in the typical classroom setting. Some programs also use staff development strategies that prepare each teacher, including those who have no previous specialist training, to provide specific kinds of instruction and support that previously had been the domain only of specialists. In every case, such collaborative processes have resulted in a shared sense of responsibility among the teachers and consultants such that none feels like the *one* responsible for "fixing" certain children, or like the receptacle for other teachers' rejects.

No More Tests to Get In

In 1984, Victoria, Australia, established a policy of integration for students with disabilities (Ministry of Education, 1984). Specifically, the policy rejected the concept of "least restrictive alternative" as too restrictive. Authors of a government report on integration felt that the American least restrictive environment policy left the door open for segregating students with severe, multiple, and behavioral disabilities. Hence, the report adopted a more clearly integrationist position: every child, no matter the child's disability, would have the right to attend his or her neighborhood school. It would be a responsibility of the school and its "enrollment and support group" made up of teachers, administrators, and parents to fashion an effective, integrated program. School psychologists were specifically prohibited from having any further role in the placement decision. Instead, their skills could henceforth be redirected to the tasks of program development.

The practice of testing students and of using the test results to decide who shall be admitted into the typical school classroom or even into the typical school is common across America. Educators and, to a great extent, the public, assume that there is a best placement for students with disabilities and that it can be discovered scientifically, with tests and observations. An alternative practice, however, would be to view placement as a political, philosophical, or moral decision and to use assessment tests or other measurements as useful tools for determining how best to educate students of diverse ability.

Case Example: Sarah There is no tougher eligibility test than the one faced by a little girl named Sarah several years ago. Her test was to prove that she could benefit from any formal education at all. Her parents could not have imagined that someday they would be trying to convince a school system to educate their child. When Sarah was 3, she was sliding down the backyard slide while wearing a poncho and became asphyxiated when her poncho got caught in the apparatus. She returned from the hospital a child who now required tube feeding, seizure medication, and full assistance to move her body and engage in all daily living activities. Progress was slow but noticeable to family members. Sarah began to recognize voices of familiar people, to stiffen her body in the presence of some people, and to relax in the presence of others. She could also move her head toward noises. It appeared that she had some vision, but it was unclear just what she could see. The growing optimism felt by the family was not shared by school district officials. They believed Sarah to be "uneducable" and attempted to substantiate this view by producing an evaluation by a physician who declared her to be in a "vegetable state." A hearing officer eventually determined her educable. Sarah was entitled to a public school education.

It may be that Sarah's hearing officer was persuaded that she could learn, that her parents had proved she was "educable." It may also be that the hearing officer understood, as did Burton Blatt (1987), that "educability is a two-edged sword." Like the Victoria policy makers' view of integration, Blatt sees the issue of educability as something in which we must believe. If we do not believe in educability or integration, then we must be ready to accept the other side of the sword. Explaining the two-edged sword, Blatt (1987) refers to the experiences of Helen Keller and Anne Sullivan:

> Anne Sullivan accepted the responsibility to teach Helen Keller not because she expected Helen to become a world-famous inspiration to people in every walk of life. The "miracle" of the Anne Sullivan—Helen Keller saga was exactly that no one expected things to turn out so marvelously well. By definition, that's the ingredient required for a miracle. The paradox of the Anne Sullivan—Helen Keller saga, the par-

> adox of any miracle, is that it must be unexpected. Anne Sullivan necessarily had other reasons for assuming responsibility for Helen, or there would have been no miracle, no story, no demonstration of educability. Educability is a two-edged sword: Even if educability cannot be empirically verified, the clinician must behave as if it has been verified. (p. 356)

Why do we require that students pass certain tests of eligibility before they can socialize and learn together? Why do we not do as those in Victoria and simply declare integration a right? Is it really possible in any scientifically objective sense to prove that a student can "make it" in a typical class? Or is it, rather, that the determination of whether or not a student succeeds in being educated with his or her peers depends on how we define success, on what our goals are, and on the kind of support we provide to students? In Blatt's (1987) terms, are we any better able to *prove* the correctness of integrated schooling than we are able to prove the idea of universal educability?

Friends and Allies

Judith A. Snow, a disabled activist and lecturer at Canada's G.Allan Roeher Institute, believes that educators focus excessively on strategies for and tests of academic achievement and far too little on students' relationships with each other and, therefore, on their social and emotional well-being (see also Chapter 16 by Snow, in this volume). She recalls her mother driving her long distances to school and, until high school, of never having a school in which she felt accepted. "High school was the first time we ran into people who really were enthused about my presence in school." Growing up, Judith remembers coming to believe what she felt was expected of her. The message she heard was that she would have "to grow up without friends, without a sexual identity, without any outside life." Because the message came from so many people in her life, and so often, she conformed: "After a while you do what is embedded into you. When I look back on my school years I see how I actively kept kids out of my life, actively discouraged people from being my friends." Instead of learning to make friends, she thought she had to concentrate on learning to escape her disability. She believed that school's purpose was to make this happen: "Special therapy, special education—if we would just do the right thing, if we would learn the right thing, just behave the right way, walk or sit the right way, that somehow we'd manage to become undisabled. But it isn't true. It doesn't work." To believe that it might work was to believe that without a cure, all else had to wait, including making friends (J. Snow, personal communication, 1986).

The alternative, Snow explains, is for schools to create an atmosphere where friendships flourish. This happens when people learn to hear each other. Friendships start in ordinary ways, she tells us, on a playground or walking home from school. But in order for that to happen, "a person has to be able to speak to other people who want to listen." Friendships begin when students come together in pairs and groups. This can develop naturally by self-selection and initiation. Or it can also occur when teachers consciously structure opportunities for interaction: teaming students for school jobs, using cooperative learning, with noncompetitive sports and other extracurricular activities, ensuring similar routines or patterns of the school day for all students, opportunities for students to work together in experiential learning projects, recognizing that a student's involvement in any learning activity may be partial (e.g., a student may be able to prepare a microscope plate with the assistance of other students, but may be unable to describe in words what he or she sees), use of open-ended curricula (e.g., story completion exercises) that allow students of very different abilities to participate, and integration of related services into the regular curricula and daily routines.

Group activities create opportunities for students to become each others' allies. The concept of an ally is especially important to students with disabilities, because they are more likely than most to be vulnerable to stereotyping, stigma, and discrimination. An ally allows students interdependence while at the same time rejecting the debilitating, patronizing control of the charity relationship that is so often imposed on people with disabilities. A teacher of a class that includes students with severe disabilities and those with no disabilities recently explained what happened when the class went on a field trip. The school district sent two buses, one short, accessible bus for the student in the class who used a wheelchair, and another regular bus for the other students. The class protested, speaking loudly about the district's insensitivity and lack of fairness. It was an example of students becoming each others' allies.

Other strategies for promoting friendships and alliances include the following: helping to present all students in the most positive light (e.g., calling attention to successes); speaking to students privately about difficult topics (e.g., problems with a test, disappointments in personal relationships); role playing and other structured activities to enable students to discuss feelings; talking about student behavior (good or bad) as occurring in context (i.e., behavior is usually a reaction to something and is intended to communicate something) and as changeable; avoiding labeling students as bad simply because they display a troubling behavior; modeling caring concern and interest in all students.

Creating the "Complete School" Requires More than a New Curriculum

In his classic novel about the human service worker, *The Case Worker* (1974), George Konrad poses the social worker's dilemma (it could just as easily be the teacher's) as having to choose one of two options: to act as society's policing agent, sweeping away surplus people—those who are old, those with disabilities, and the poor—into nursing homes, prisons, mental hospitals, and other institutions for human refuse; or to care. Caring, he tells us, means feeding, cleaning, listening to the babbling, and observing the tantrums of an orphaned child with severe retardation.

Restated, this important choice is really about whether to acknowledge and accept or to reject and turn away from vulnerable people. Although the choice can be simply stated, it requires deep and complex reflection to make. Konrad seems to know that caring is not enough. Yet he also admits that having decided to care, there is no easy answer to the subsequent choices: What to do? There is no "quick fix." Clearly, he rejects the role of social worker as police officer, an armed buffer between the advantaged and the damaged. Yet he will not inspire us with an optimistic solution. He has no packaged curriculum to show us, no listing of "key principles" for the excellent social worker from which we might extrapolate a set of companion principles for educators. Instead, he proffers a simple, unremarkable plan: see suffering with open eyes, commiserate with it, listen to people's stories and complaints, and create dialogue where others only command and remonstrate.

Konrad's modest plan incorporates many of the activities and approaches fundamental to the integrationist schooling reforms discussed throughout this book. And, like the reforms described in this chapter, it requires a democratic philosophy of education. Learning requires dialogue. Memorization and skill collecting, if practiced in the absence of questioning and reflection, disempower and deskill students and teachers alike. Teaching is not simply control and management, and teachers cannot be masters of ceremonies who read only from a prepared script. Rather, teaching demands that the teacher prod, challenge, and question, and be prodded, challenged, and questioned in return. Information merely fuels the process of exploration. Curricula are not the teacher's guides, they are the teacher's tools. What is important is that the teacher possess a framework of values (e.g., the education of the student with the most severe disabilities is as important as the education of the student with unusual academic skills) and a philosophy of education (e.g., interactive, democratic) into which any curricula or teaching strategy is placed.

Manifestations of this at once expansive and dialogical approach to learning are not new. Sylvia Ashton-Warner (1963) founded her literacy work with Maori children on just such fundamental assumptions. She asked students what word they wanted to learn, helped them develop sentences with their words, and taught them how to write out the words and sentences on cards to take home overnight. If they forgot a word, she chose another of their selections that they might find more memorable. Freire used "dialogical" education, what he called "conscientizao" or consciousness raising, as his approach to adult literacy in Brazil. Manifestations of these approaches in schools today are also common, albeit often in competition with packaged, programmed learning. Activities in the interactive tradition include creative writing assignments, learning scientific concepts through experimentation, art classes in which students have opportunities to apply concepts of perception and color, and language arts that encourage students to discover and examine themes and issues of their own lives. Applied to the goal of educating students with a range of abilities, this classical, pedagogical approach to schooling is conveyed in such practices as maximizing students' opportunities to make choices, seeing students as having futures, looking for ways that all students can make contributions, using unobtrusive strategies to promote the worth of each child, and recognizing that students with disabilities, no matter how severe, have ideas and insights. Table 1 includes a partial list of strategies for achieving this style of education.

CONCLUSION

In some ways, educators about to integrate students with disabilities are analogous to parents who have just given birth to a severely disabled child. They are asked to make a leap of faith, to believe that what they are about to undertake will be good for them and for the students. Like parents, they may envision a profoundly trying existence, one clouded by anxiety. Yet, by working together, however difficult the experience, schools have the chance of discovering, as many parents have, that a commitment to working with and relating to youngsters with disabilities is good both for the person with a disability and for his or her allies and friends.

Such a transformation of schools requires acceptance of the fact that *disability* is defined not by the physical condition of a person but by cultural beliefs and attitudes. Consequently, efforts to change the experience of students with disabilities in schools must attend to the social definitions of disability. Specifically, a change agenda would

Table 1. Suggested practices for normalizing the education of students with disabilities

National/state/provincial policies

A policy and plan to foster education of students in the schools that they would attend if not disabled.

Funding incentives to facilitate integrated schooling.

Monitoring of integration implementation.

Leadership training on integration.

Technical assistance, teacher training, and other development strategies on integration.

District policies and practices

Philosophy of serving, accepting, and welcoming all students; valuing all students; assuming that the education of the student with the most severe disabilities is as important as any other student's education.

Locating students in schools with their age peers.

Locating students with disabilities in schools that they would attend if not disabled (e.g., neighborhood schools).

Continuity of schooling (e.g., students in a particular elementary school can anticipate moving to the next-level secondary school with their peers).

Single administrative hierarchy for all student programs.

Common transportation for all students.

Parent participation policy; school sees parents as having expertise on the child and the child's history, and a vision of the child's future.

Architectural accessibility.

Common faculty meetings for special and regular educators.

Community education about the goals for all students' education.

Clearly stated policies on student performance and expectations, including behavior rules.

No labeling of programs by disability or special education jargon (e.g., option classes, special classes, LD classes, special ed resource) but, rather, identification by subject area of age-appropriate grade level.

Equitable distribution of quality space and resources; methods of financing education that foster a common educational system and real student interaction.

Unified scheduling and other data management for all.

Teacher support services, including consulting teachers.

Methods for evaluating quality of faculty and programs.

Building level planning for integration.

Classroom-level practices

Teaching styles that encourage interaction: e.g., multilevel participation activities, parallel learning, heterogeneous grouping, cooperative learning, partial participation.

Curricula that places students in valued roles: e.g., making choices, expressing themselves, making things, or participating in performances that others appreciate.

Curricula that are functional for the students' futures.

Curricula that place students in helping roles.

Curricula that peak student interests.

Curricula that are reflective of students' abilities and needed skills and that maximize student choices.

Willingness of teachers, students, and administrators to confront negative attitudes about disabilities as they arise. Systematic and constant efforts by teachers to help students present themselves in the most positive light.

(continued)

Table 1. *(continued)*

Use of natural environments, natural methods (e.g., not making the program for students with severe disabilities into a highly structured, laboratorylike behavior modification routine), natural cues and reinforcment, and natural (i.e., nonlaboratory or nonmedical) language.

Opportunities for students to model each other's behavior.

Placement of students with disabilities throughout a school and a class rather than congregating them.

Curricula that maximize independence with minimum supervision, yet recognize natural interdependence.

Teacher support through consulting teacher model, team collaboration, problem-solving groups, curriculum development groups, team teaching, and teaching demonstrations.

Curricula that are reflective of teacher preferences.

Curricula and instruction that are sequenced and achieve continuity.

Teacher involvement in curricula development.

Minimal but necessary application of special accommodations.

Activities, discussions, and dialogue that help students learn about themselves (e.g., their values, beliefs, attitudes, aspirations); what educators sometimes call affective education.

Accommodations (e.g., communication system, physical therapy, speech therapy, adaptive physical education) that are integrated into the curricula.

Revisions of instructional strategies on evaluation.

Parent participation through classroom observations, videos, discussion, classroom participation, communication via teacher/parent notebooks and telephone, planning meetings, parent support groups, parent/teacher study groups, and individual program planning.

The author wishes to thank Marsha Forest and Judith Snow of the G. Allan Roeher Institute, Downsview, Ontario, students in the 1986 Institute's Workshop on Integration, the 1986–87 School Leaders' Institute at Syracuse University, NY, and other colleagues who commented on drafts of this inventory.

include the kinds of strategies discussed in this chapter: 1) an end to labeling students, programs, and teaching staff by disability categories; 2) recognition that some of the barriers to changing perceptions of disabilities and the rights of students with disabilities are rooted in the social organization of schools, authority in schools, and resistance to change in general, particularly where change involves empowering traditionally disenfranchised groups; 3) integration of the adults in schools if we truly expect students to become integrated; 4) abolition of eligibility tests that have historically been used to exclude certain groups from educational benefits; 5) recognition that students' social and emotional well-being is important and that these aspects of students' growth cannot be dissociated from academic achievement; and 6) an approach to integrated schooling that extends beyond a revision in curriculum and pursues equity as a philosophy and model of education.

REFERENCES

Ashton-Warner, S. (1963). *Teacher*. New York: Bantam.

Biklen, D. (1985). *Achieving the complete school: Strategies for effective mainstreaming*. New York: Teachers College Press.

Biklen, D. (1987a). The culture of policy: Disability images and their analogues in public policy. *Policy Studies Journal, 15*(3), 515–536.

Biklen, D. (1987b). Framed: Print journalism's treatment of disability issues. In A. Gartner & T. Joe (Eds.), *Images of the disabled, disabling images* (pp. 79–96). New York: Praeger.

Blatt, B. (1987). *The conquest of mental retardation*. Austin: PRO-ED.

Bogdan, R. (1982). What does it mean when a person says, "I am not retarded?" *Education and Training of the Mentally Retarded*. 15, 74–79.

Bogdan, R., & Taylor, S. (1982). *Inside out*. Toronto: University of Toronto Press.

Brightman, A. (Ed.). (1985). *Ordinary moments*. Syracuse: Human Policy Press.

Freire, P. (1970). *Pedogogy of the oppressed*. New York: Herder & Herder.

Gartner, A., & Lipsky, D. (1987). Beyond special education: Toward a quality system for all students. *Harvard Educational Review, 57*(4), 367–395.

Giroux, H. A. (1986). Authority, intellectuals, and the politics of practical learning. *Teachers College Record, 88*(1), 22–40.

Greene, M. (1984). How do we think about our craft? *Teachers College Record, 86*(1), 55–67.

Guskin, S. (1974). Research on labeling retarded persons. *American Journal of Mental Deficiency, 79*, 262–265.

Johnson, W. G., & Lambrinos, J. (1987). The effect of prejudice on the wages of disabled workers. *Policy Studies Journal, 15*(3), 571–590.

Karuth, D. (1985). If I were a car, I'd be a lemon. In A. Brightman (Ed.), *Ordinary moments* (pp. 9–32). Syracuse, NY: Human Policy Press.

Konrad, G. (1974). *The case worker*. New York: Bantam.

Kriegel, L. (1981). Coming through: Manhood, disease, and the authentic self. In D. Biklen & L. Bailey (Eds.), *Rudely stamp'd: Imaginal disability and prejudice* (pp. 49–64). Washington, DC: University Press of America.

Longmore, P. K. (1987). Screening stereotypes: Images of disabled people in television and motion pictures. In A. Gartner & T. Joe (Eds.), *Images of the disabled, disabling images* (pp. 65–78). New York: Praeger.

Mairs, N. (1986). *Plaintext: Deciphering a woman's life*. New York: Harper & Row.

Ministry of Education. (1984). *Report on integration in Victorian schools*. Melbourne, Australia: Ministry of Education.

Nowlan, A. (1977). He'd lived there all his life. In A. Nowlan (Ed.), *Smoked glass* (22). Toronto: Clark, Irwin.

Peters, A. (1986, November/December). Do we have to be named? *Disability Rag, 7*(6), 31.

Saxton, M. (1985). The something that happened before I was born. In A. Brightman (Ed.), *Ordinary moments* (pp. 127–140). Syracuse, NY: Human Policy Press.

Zola, I. K. (1987). "Any distinguishing features?"—The portrayal of disability in the crime-mystery genre. *Policy Studies Journal, 15*(3), 485–514.

CHAPTER 18

Reflections on a Quality Education for All Students

Jack Pearpoint

In the tale of "The Starfish," a person is walking on a lonely beach. As the tide rolls out, thousands of beautiful starfish are stranded and destined to die. A walker begins picking them up, one at a time and putting them back in the ocean. A skeptic, convinced of the futility of the walker's task, comments: "You are wasting your time. There are thousands of starfish here, and saving a few won't make any difference." The walker replies, "Yes, that's true, but I can save this *one*, and another *one*, and for them it makes all the difference."

The task of providing all students a quality education in the mainstream of the schools may be regarded skeptically by some, who will say, "You are wasting your time. Saving a few won't make any difference." But, if our moral values are to be upheld and educational quality is to flourish, we must recognize and practice the philosophy of the walker. "I can save this *one*, and another *one*, and for them it makes all the difference." There is no quick fix that will undo all wrongs and make the world perfect over night. However, if we wait until it is "possible" to fix it, it will be too late. We must begin now, at home and in our communities. If each of us does what we can, we can make an enormous contribution that will be an inspiration to others.

This chapter departs somewhat from a focus on *how* to provide a quality education to all students in regular education, by attempting to outline what constitutes a quality education for all students, whether labeled as "disabled" or "normal."

PERVASIVE AND LIFELONG LEARNING

Possibly the most important aspect of quality education is that it is woven throughout our lives. This characteristic pervades all other possible attributes of education. Education is not the sole prerogative of the schools. Learning can indeed take place in a classroom, but in terms of one's capacity to learn and the nature of the tasks one masters by the very act of surviving, calculus and modern history pale in complexity.

Likewise, learning is not governed or controlled by teachers. It is something each of us does individually throughout our lives. No teacher can learn for us, although a teacher can show the way. We must do it ourselves. The most complex learning we do includes things like seeing, hearing, speaking, walking, remembering. Thus, "lifelong learning" is something we all are engaged in every moment. All of us can learn. Many of us simply need to reclaim the process.

Also, education is social. We learn "in context" with people. People may not learn what we think we are "teaching," but they do learn. When we demand that a person learn "this list now," they will "learn" a great deal—about us, about pressure, and about choices. They are unlikely to want to or be able to regurgitate our "list." At best, if they memorize it, it will be for a brief period before "forgetting" and "boredom" take over. There is a "learning curve" that is paralleled by a "forgetting curve." When learning is "contrived" for us, it is virtually guaranteed to fail. The brain is equipped with a little switch called "boredom" that it turns on when things do not make sense. In contrast, we all learn things that are meaningful and important to us with little difficulty.

"Lifelong learning" is a concept critical to our future. If we are committed to lifelong learning, it will alter the current design of education, since learning is not a "one-shot" activity. Thus, lifelong learning is a challenge to the present structure of our school systems. Our future will be determined less by our technological expertise than by our excellence in developing our human resources.

To this author, "lifelong learning" means life. The very essence of human beings is thinking and learning. This is not an "incidental" activity; it is life.

INFORMATION MANAGEMENT

Education is, or at least is designed to be, an introduction to culture—it is preparation for living and working. However, the problem of preparing students for living and working is complex, because even the foundation skills are changing so quickly that most of the facts learned yesterday will be obsolete within 2 years. Thus, the priority must be to learn how: 1) to think and manage information; and 2) to constantly upgrade our information. This is essential for all learners.

Until recently, a teacher's major function was to convey information to students. The teacher had the information, the students needed it, and the teacher-student classroom system worked. However, with mass television, on-line computer information bases, videos, radio, and even more books, simply providing information is almost redundant. Most people in North America have more information beamed at them per day than they could absorb in months. Thus, the new role of teachers will be to help students master "information management" skills, to help them discriminate, order, and reorder information. Teachers will be called upon to teach people to be critical, to compare findings, and to research material. These skills are survival skills for students of all ages, whether the issue is to pick the correct item in a grocery store, select the correct bus route, understand the next "retooling" in the workplace, or pick a good movie, concert, or hospital.

In a future that puts priority on building lifelong learners, teachers will need to become "learning facilitators," "coaches," and "information management consultants." It will be exciting, challenging, and prestigious to be teaching in that atmosphere, because the students will be more in command of their own learning. The new generation of students will be demanding consumers, which will work to reinject quality and vitality into our education systems.

ADAPTATION AND DECISION MAKING

Our educational structures are designed to provide youth with answers to the problems that have already been solved. This is an essential function. However, the world's problems are changing so rapidly that new concepts are needed even to understand them. People write about "paradigm shifts," which means that the rules are changing in the ball park, but even more confusing, the location, shape, size, and even concept of the ball park are being reformulated at the same time. It is difficult to get one's bearings. And that is why looking back is not enough. One could fine tune the system to the ball park that was, but by the time one finishes, it won't even be there.

Norman Cousins (1986) writes that

> one of the prime elements of human uniqueness is the ability to create and exercise new options. The ultimate test of education is whether it makes people comfortable in the presence of options; whether it enables them to pursue their possibilities with confidence. Similarly, a society can be judged according to the number and range of options of consequences it makes open to its people. (p. 106)

Given this view, if education can provide students with the decision-making skills to choose viable options and the ability to adapt to these options, education can be considered successful. It should be noted here that decision making is important for all students, regardless of their intellectual, psychological, or physical characteristics and or their abilities and disabilities.

Professors H. Levin and R. Rumberger (1981) at Stanford University make the point clearly: "The changes in technology, work organization, and corporate structure make it more important than ever that future workers be equipped with strong analytic, expressive, communicative and computation skills" (p. 57). They further state that no one can predict the jobs and job skills one will need over a 40-year working life. Thus, it is best to provide students with a strong general education and an ability to adapt to a changing work environment.

VALUES

For quality and equality to exist in education, there must be a clear value base. All school systems have a value base, whether these values are specified or not. A school system's values need to focus on a respect for the dignity of the individual, and build on the individual's capacity to grow in communities (interdependence, not independence). Future education cannot be simply about "skills." It must foster the growth of community—of people learning, working, and living together in supportive relationships that enhance dignity, allow for individuality (differences), and share responsibility.

The "me generation" educational system missed an essential ingredient. Growth and strength come from relationships with others. Life is not lived in isolation; it is shared with people. Thus, we need to enhance our skills for and appreciation of sharing responsibilities and privileges with others. That is the value base. As noted by Margaret Attwood (1972): "We need each others' breathing, warmth: Surviving is the only way we can afford" (p. 13). The current educational system promotes a so-called value-free education, which translates into "anything goes—it's all right with me." However, such a system is untenable. With a "me first" value base, our future survival is at risk.

Martin Neimoeller (1981) summed up this dilemma and the need for action:

> In Germany they came first for the Communists, and I didn't speak up because I wasn't a Communist. Then they came for the Jews, and I didn't speak up because I wasn't a Jew. Then they came for the trade unionist, and I didn't speak up because I wasn't a trade unionist. Then they came for the Catholics, and I didn't speak up because I was a Protestant. Then they came for me, and by that time no one was left to speak up. (p. 79)

INCLUSION AND DIVERSITY

For quality in education, we must insist that *all* people be included in future planning and education. Inclusion, not exclusion, must be the norm. The reason is enlightened self-interest. The "dropouts" like Einstein and Churchill may have been eccentric, but they made major contributions to our world. It is sobering to think how our present-day systems might well have siphoned Christ off to an immigrant technical school. We need the talents and creativity of the very people we so often relegate to the sidelines. We need to liberate our thinking to appreciate and embrace the gifts they offer.

People who have been on the fringes of society are evolving as the leaders—not simply the token leaders—of the next stage of development. Aboriginal Canadians are a case in point. Statistically, they should have given up and collected their treaty money long ago. Objectively, they face tremendous difficulties. A decade ago, who could have imagined that Native Canadian leaders would sit at a meeting with all the first ministers of Canada. These new leaders performed with pride, integrity and an eloquence that was stunning to all Canadians (including the politicians around the table). Against all odds, a new leadership cadre is evolving that will restore the self-esteem of Aboriginal Canadians, and thus build a new and constructive future from the ashes of the welfare sink hole.

There are other examples. "People First" is an organization of people who have been labeled as mentally handicapped. The wisdom this author has witnessed in their leadership puts many of us to shame. Often they do not have time for trivia, so they only remember the important points. They are showing us that labels belong on jars, not on people.

I recently heard a university teacher/researcher speak excitedly about the capacities of a new computer and about how finally she and her colleagues would be able to develop "diagnostic" and "treatment" tools that would solve learning problems for thousands. I shared my enthusiasm for the capacities of the computer, but told her that the language she used was the greatest danger to the goals she espoused. If learning is about life and living, we must beware of disease paradigms like "diagnostic" and "treatment," which imply that a learner is sick and needs to be fixed. Learning is not a sickness; it is something we all can enjoy. We need to shift our attention from disabling to enabling. This is a very different focus.

PARTNERSHIP

Education needs to shift its emphasis from professional problem solving to cooperation. Paternalism, no matter how well intentioned, is unacceptable, and more important, unworkable and uneconomic. The next logical stage is "partnerships." The experts on any problem are the people on the frontline; they have more information than any-

Point to Ponder

Since many school districts—urban, suburban, and rural alike—have shown that they can serve even the most severely disabled students in regular education . . . when accompanied by supplementary aids and services, pleas by other districts to continue segregating their disabled students are no longer credible. Thus, educational leaders can now speak unequivocally for integration as a consummately possible, as well as morally desirable, goal. (Massachusetts Advocacy Center, 1987, p.6)

one else. However, they may need a partner to help organize and manage that information. For example, the individual is the key source of information on his or her own health, but for an attack of appendicitis, one needs to partner with a medical doctor. Thus, partnerships are essential.

Supportive professionals can assist local groups to manage the information they have and need access to. They can help transform this information into the action required to meet their goals. The key is that "consumers" must have genuine involvement and control. It is a touch regime to work in, but it works, which is more than can be said for many of the earlier models. Partnerships build on strengths and can deliver.

SELF-ESTEEM

Self-esteem is a prerequisite for achieving a quality education. Learning is based on complex but simple factors beginning with self-confidence and dignity. People with low self-esteem who are also treated like "nothing" are unlikely to believe they can make a positive contribution in the world. What begins as a downhill skid almost inevitably ends in personal disaster and loss of a happy and productive life.

When we give up on some students, label them, and segregate them from their peers, we damage their self-esteem. As former chief Justice Earl Warren stated in the landmark 1954 *Brown v. Board of Education* decision, separateness in education can "generate a feeling of inferiority as to [children's] status in the community that may affect their hearts and minds in a way unlikely ever to be undone. This sense of inferiority . . . affects the motivation of a child to learn . . . [and] has a tendency to retard . . . educational and mental development" (p. 493).

THE PRODUCT OF A QUALITY EDUCATION

What do we want a quality education to produce? In this author's perception, a quality education should stimulate one's capacity to innovate, to anticipate, to discriminate, and to think critically and clearly. It must develop one's capacity to solve problems that are in flux. It must foster a kind of culture that is founded on respect for life and grounded in a solid understanding of how to manipulate the vast information resources currently available in order to manage diversity and complexity constructively.

ACHIEVING QUALITY EDUCATION: A MATTER OF PRIORITY

It is staggering to this author that at a time when we can pick satellites out of space or put 200 books on a three-inch plastic disk, we have yet to devise the creative responses to give all our citizens an integrated education and a solid grasp of basic skills and problem solving. It comes down to a matter of will. Where will we put our priorities—on people or on widgets? on human learning or on Star Wars? Reflecting on some of his choices, Dr. Albert Schweitzer commented: "If you have something difficult to do, don't expect people to roll stones out of your way."

MOVING MOUNTAINS

In the Chinese fable about "The Old Man Who Moved the Mountain," there was a very poor small village at the base of a mountain. The people were hungry. There was always drought. On the other side of the mountain there was water aplenty, but no land, so the villagers could not think of moving. They exhausted every alternative and were resigned to their fate when an old man suggested that they dig a tunnel through the mountain to bring water to the village. Everyone scoffed. It was impossible. They dismissed the old man, and continued in their poverty and despair.

But the old man took his pick and shovel, and slowly began to dig a tunnel through the mountain. The skeptics jeered. The old man continued. Finally, one of the village elders went to him. He said: "I admire your will, but you will never succeed. Stop now. You have made your point." But the old man would not stop. He said "We will get water. The mountain cannot grow. And if I do not complete the tunnel by my death, then my sons and daughters, and their sons and daughters, will continue to dig. One day, we will have water and green fields in our village."

The elder thought carefully, then went home and got his own pick and shovel and joined the old man digging.

The village got its water.

OUR TASK

We have a mountain of learning to move as well. If we wait for an easy solution, or a giant power shovel to do it for us, it may be too late. But if some of us begin now to unearth a way, our children will also see the way. And whether they use shovels, or giant robotic inventions, we will have set the values and the direction by our example.

REFERENCES

Attwood, M. (1972). *Survival.* Toronto: Anansi Publishers.

Cousins, N. (1986). *Human options.* Berkley, CA: Berkley Publishing.

Levin, H., & Rumberger, R. (1981). *Overeducation in the U.S. labor market.* New York: Praeger.

Massachusetts Advocacy Center. (1987). *Out of the mainstream.* Boston: Author.

Neimoeller, M. (1981). *Concise dictionary of religious quotations.* Toronto: Library Press.

Schwietzer, A. (1968). *Bartlett's quotations* (4th ed.). (p. 939). Boston: Little, Brown.

CHAPTER 19

Common Concerns Regarding Merger

William Stainback and Susan Stainback

In the past few years, a number of issues and concerns have been expressed about merging regular and special education and educating all students in regular education as a normal, standard, and expected practice. This final chapter addresses a number of the most commonly voiced concerns.

CONCERN #1

Regular education does not have the resources or personnel to address the unique educational needs of all students.

RESPONSE

This is, in the authors' view, a valid concern. As currently structured, it is true that regular education has neither the necessary resources nor the personnel to meet the individual needs of all students. Team teachers, support facilitators, small class sizes, time, materials, instructional aides, and equipment needed to address the diverse educational needs demonstrated across the entire student population simply are not available to many regular classroom teachers. For these reasons, attempts to integrate students from special education into regular education without integrating special education resources and personnel—as is currently practiced in many mainstreaming and integration projects—limit the quality of programming that can be offered all students. What is needed is the integration not only of the students but also of the resources and personnel from special education into regular education. These personnel and resources are necessary to broaden the capabilities of regular education to meet the unique educational needs of all students.

However, some people still ask, where in the "real" world are the schools going to get the money and personnel to provide the small class sizes and additional support and services needed? The answer is that, if we do what is advocated above, the billions of dollars and hundreds of thousands of personnel now in special education will be integrated into regular education to help provide support and assistance. Unless this is done, the reality that students with disabilities will be integrated into regular education will be fulfilled, and there will be few, if any, resources to meet the diverse needs of all students in the mainstream. Thus, it is critical that we advocate for the integration of resources and personnel as well as students into regular education. No one wants children in a mainstream that cannot meet their needs. Unfortunately, when billions of dollars are drained and hundreds of thousands of personnel are recruited from the mainstream to support special, segregated programs, the end result is a weak and ineffective mainstream that can meet few, if any, children's needs, whether the children are classified as having disabilities or not.

CONCERN #2

Regular educators are unwilling to individualize or adapt instruction to individual needs.

RESPONSE

After talking with regular educators and working in the schools, these authors have found that, for the most part, this concern is not justified *if regular educators understand and accept the reasons for integration.* However, regular educators, like all educators, want the resources, time, and personnel to enable them to individualize and adapt instruction. This is another reason why it is so important to integrate more than just *students* into regular education. The regular educators these authors have talked with are tired of receiving students from special education, unaccompanied by little, if any, resources from special education.

CONCERN #3

Students with disabilities are sometimes rejected, ridiculed, and/or teased by other students in regular classrooms.

RESPONSE

Unfortunately, for many students, this is a reality. Teasing is experienced not only by students labeled as handicapped but also by those who are obese, thin, short, ugly, and tall, as well as by those who cannot afford to wear fashionable clothes, have an unusual name, and so on.

One option for dealing with such cruelty is to protect students who are rejected or ridiculed by segregating them from their peers. While this protects the students to some degree during the school hours, it simply intensifies the potential for the problem to occur during nonschool hours, in the community, and in later life. Segregation denies all students the opportunity to learn about, gain an understanding of, and grow comfortable with diversity and differences among people. Segregation fosters discomfort and fear and perpetuates intolerance and bigotry.

A second option for dealing with cruelty is to face it directly and work to eliminate it within the educational mainstream. This second approach requires taking direct action to change and eliminate rejecting, ridiculing, and teasing behaviors of students. It focuses on providing all students instruction and guidance about individual differences, along with opportunities to be together in integrated situations, so that a knowledge and understanding of individual differences and similarities among all students can be fostered. It is only through on-going daily experiences with peers having diverse characteristics, along with guidance and instruction from the early school years on, that one can expect students to learn to function as humane, understanding members of their community and society at large. As noted by Vandercook et al. (1988), "In integrated classroooms, all children are enriched by having the opportunity to learn from one another, grow to care for one another and gain the attitudes, skills, and values necessary for our communities to support the inclusion of all citizens" (p. 19).

CONCERN #4

Having students with disabilities in regular classes will interfere with the quality of education offered students considered as "nonhandicapped."

RESPONSE

"Nonhandicapped" students have not been found to suffer academically or socially from being around students considered as disabled, handicapped, or special (Stainback & Stainback, 1981). In fact, students defined as nonhandicapped have been found to actually benefit from integrated school activities by gaining a greater knowledge and understanding of the diversity of individual differences and needs of people in our society (McHale & Simeonsson, 1980; Voeltz, 1982).

With the development of a merged or more comprehensive regular education system, those students labeled as nonhandicapped are likely to profit rather than suffer educationally. With the merger of considerable resources and personnel from special education into regular education, greater individualization, flexibility, and adaptation of educational opportunities to the unique needs of all students, including those currently considered nonhandicapped, should be possible.

Finally, it is inequitable to contend that the mainstream of education should be designed to provide a quality education to nonhandicapped students and that by integrating students with disabilities into regular education one may threaten this quality. Such a notion is inherently unfair and discriminatory. The mainstream does *not* belong only to students labeled as nonhandicapped or to any subgroup of students. It belongs to all students, including those considered to have disabilities. Thus, the mainstream should be organized to provide a quality education to all students.

CONCERN #5

One cannot ensure that all students will receive appropriate educational programs and related services in regular education.

RESPONSE

As personnel from special education are integrated into regular education, they can join many concerned and caring regular educators to help ensure that all students, including those traditionally ill-served and underserved in the past, are served appropriately in regular education. Because of the integration of personnel as well as students, there will be an increased number of con-

Point to Ponder

All children benefit when regular neighborhood schools and classrooms develop a sense of community, that is, when all students are made to feel that they belong and education is sensitive and responsive to individual differences. Issues involved in educating all students in the mainstream of regular education are not disability issues; they are issues that are pertinent to providing a free and appropriate education for *all* students.

cerned and caring adults in regular education. This will help increase, rather than reduce, the probabilities that all students will receive a free and appropriate education.

In addition, it is possible to protect the rights of all students legally, including those labeled as having disabilities, to receive appropriate educational programs and ancillary services in regular classes and regular education. One way to accomplish this would be to modify PL 94-142 to require that every child be provided a free and appropriate educational program and related services in regular education. For instance, the title of the law might be changed from "The Education for All Handicapped Children Act" to "The Appropriate Education for All Students in Regular Education Act." This modified law could require that all students receive a free and appropriate education within the mainstream of regular education. As a consequence, when a team from a state department or a federal agency monitored a school district, if *any* student—classified as disabled or nondisabled—was not receiving an appropriate program or services within regular education, then the school district would be in violation of the law. In this way, the law would ensure that all students, including those with disabilities, received a free and appropriate education in regular education.

Finally, it should be stressed that the authors understand and support the need to protect the rights of students traditionally classified as disabled to receive the programs and services they need to progress in school. But it is also essential not to overlook the need to protect the rights of *all* students to receive the programs and services they need to progress in school. That is, it is not possible to conceive of a single child whose right to a free and appropriate education should not be protected. Such an education can take place in a merged and integrated system by strong and consistent advocacy to guarantee that programs and services are offered in the public schools to meet *all* students needs and to ensure that some students are not unserved or ill-served. As soon as we protect the rights of all students to receive the services and programs they need to progress in school, the needs of students traditionally classified as disabled, handicapped, disadvantaged, or any other classification will be protected, since no student can be denied the services and programs he or she needs.

CONCERN #6

Some students do not have the ability or skills to succeed in the mainstream.

RESPONSE

This is true, if as a society we are unwilling to: a) provide each student the support necessary for him or her to be in the mainstream and b) adapt and adjust, when necessary, the mainstream to accommodate all students. Thus, the critical issue is our willingness to visualize, work for, and achieve a mainstream that is adaptive and supportive and includes everyone. The other option is to be satisfied with a mainstream designed for the majority or so-called normal and continue to do research and design and administer competency tests and checklists to determine who should and should not be in the mainstream. The better and more humane, just, and equitable option is to let everyone into the mainstream and provide the necessary adaptions, support, and assistance so that we can all learn and grow together. As stated by Forest (1988), "If we really want someone to be part of our lives, we will do what it takes to welcome that person and accommodate his or her needs" (p. 3).

Finally, it should be noted that a number of schools throughout the United States, Canada, Italy, and other countries have successfully integrated students classified as having severe, profound, and multiple disabilities into regular classes, while others are struggling with achieving the integration of students labeled as mildly handicapped. This tells us that it is not the level of disability that is the decisive factor; rather, it is the motivation and attitudes of educators, parents, and/or community members (Gerry, 1988).

CONCERN #7

Special education can be offered in regular classes and schools. Thus, there is no real need to integrate or merge special and regular education.

RESPONSE

By continuing to label some educational services and programs as special, even when they are offered in regular education settings, one perpetuates the concept that it is somehow extraordinary or special to provide some students a free and appropriate education. This special approach is analogous to operating a welfare model in the public schools. If students qualify as being truly needy, special, or handicapped, they are then eligible to receive special assistance or a special education. This is similar to the model used to dispense food stamps or housing subsidies to persons deemed truly needy and thus eligible for welfare programs. However, providing some students an appropriate educational opportunity is not, or at least should not be, an altruistic gesture by society. There is *no* student whose unique educational needs should not be met in the public schools. Thus, no child is being done a favor or provided something special when he or she receives an education that meets his or her unique needs. It is a disservice to students classified as having disabilities to set them apart from their peers by making them qualify to receive an appropriate education and subsequently identify the educational services and programs they receive as special.

As noted in Chapter 2, equality suffers when the education of some students is viewed as special and different, as a charity operation. "Until accommodation for the disabled is seen as regular, normal and expected, it will be seen instead as special. As long as it is special, it will be, by definition, unequal" (Biklen, 1985, p. 176). In short, the schools should not operate like the public welfare system, wherein some students must qualify as economically disadvantaged, disabled, or otherwise "needy" in order to receive the assistance and services they need to progress in school. Every child in the public schools deserves a free and appropriate education that meets his or her unique needs as a regular, normal and expected practice.

CONCERN #8

Special education, and thus the dual systems of special and regular education is needed, since "without strong advocacy by well connected special groups, few advances for the handicapped have ever occurred, . . . no strong advocacy group equals no funds for the handicapped" (Messinger, 1985, p. 511).

RESPONSE

While the authors agree with Messinger that strong advocacy for educational funding is critical to the quality of services that can be offered students, the authors do not agree with the contention that we must operate a dual system of education—one for "special" people and one for "regular" people—to have strong advocacy. Contrary to popular opinion in special education, it is possible to have strong advocacy without advocating for or operating a dual system of education.

We all agree that advocacy is important. The critical question is: "What should one advocate for?" As opposed to advocating for special school programs for special categories of students, one could advocate, as noted in Chapter 6, that the schools hire, as needed, support personnel such as support facilitators, physical therapists, speech and language specialists, and/or behavior management specialists. One also could advocate that instruction be offered in basic self-care/community living skills as well as vocational and competitive employment skills, and/or that more instruction be offered in sign language, braille, speech reading, self-control training, or the like. In addition, one could advocate for increased resources for the schools to offer more flexible, individualized, and adaptive educational programs to meet the unique needs of all children, including those unserved or ill-served in the past or present.

More specifically, if it is documented that there is a deficiency of research, personnel preparation, or other resources in an area traditionally covered by special education (e.g., sign language and speech reading), it may be necessary to lobby for monies to be allocated for the particular deficient area(s), as is done when such a lack is identified in mathematics or science. Rather than seeking "child-in-category" funding, advocates could lobby state and federal legislators to earmark funds to facilitate research, training, and the accumulation of resources in the deficient instructional area(s).

In short, it is not necessary to advocate for special school programs designed for the "truly" handicapped to ensure that a wide range of educational programs is available to meet diverse students' needs.

CONCERN #9

While integrating special and regular education and educating all students in regular education might be desirable, the reality is that the public schools are a long way from doing this.

RESPONSE

In response to an earlier proposal to integrate special and regular education, Lieberman (1985) stated that merger was an inappropriate goal based on present day realities, and went on to say that: "Of course they are right, but being right and being real are very different" (p. 513). While the authors agree that reality in education does not always reflect what is perceived as right or desirable, the authors do not see this as an indication that the integration of special and regular education is an inappropriate goal. Rather, the very fact that common practice does not always represent what is desirable or right appears to lend credence to the need to clarify and refine education's goals and practices. If we are to progress, we need to base our goals and objectives for practice on "what should be" rather than on "what presently is." While the authors agree with Lieberman that "being right and being real are very different," the authors believe that a major goal for educators should be to make "what is right, real." The present day reality was made by educators. The authors believe that we educators can and should make a different one.

Thus, if we believe that an integrated, unified system of education is right and desirable, we should not let present day realities keep us from working *toward the goal*. The authors fully realize that based on today's realities, there are likely to be many obstacles, battles, wars, and bloodbaths along the way. But the central question is: Should we give up our ideals and goals because reality dictates that they will be difficult to achieve? In the authors' opinion, it is critical to work toward the goal and make as much progress each day as possible.

Based on the "reality" of today's schools, it is easy to make a long list of very real and serious reasons why successful integration will be difficult to achieve: rigid and standardized curricular and grading practices in regular education; already overworked regular class teachers who do not have the resources and time to meet diverse student needs in heterogeneous classes; and the potential danger that, if not done carefully, students who have been unserved or ill-served in the past will fail to receive the educational programs and related services they need in regular education. In the authors' view, these are not unfounded or merely made-up problems by those who are reluctant to accept the integration of schools.

However, if we desire an integrated society, we must start looking for solutions to such problems rather than accepting them as a reality that must remain with us forever. We cannot just say, "That's the way it is" and do nothing. We must accept the challenge to make the mainstream of our schools a place where the needs of all students, including those with disabilities, are met and they are made to feel comfortable, secure, happy, and challenged to be the best they can be. It will not be easy. But, if we desire an integrated society, we have no other choice.

Finally, we cannot wait until all possible research variations on integration are completed and everything is perfect before integrating our classrooms and schools. If we do, we will never integrate. There always will be those who call for at least one more study before we integrate, and there will never be quite enough research for them to support integration. There are two major flaws in waiting for the research to be completed. First, as explained later in this chapter, integration versus segregation is not a research question. Second, the best way to learn how to make integrated schools and classes work is to establish integrated schools and classrooms and work every day within these "real world" integrated environments to find solutions to problems. Experience has shown repeatedly that you cannot learn how to make integration successful in segregated schools and classrooms.

CONCERN #10

Special education and/or special services may, in fact, be effective and needed for some students.

RESPONSE

When carefully analyzed, the issue is not whether special education is effective and needed. Those techniques, methods, or procedures within special education that have been proven effective, can be integrated into regular education. Inherent in the rationale for merger is the belief that there are people, programs, and procedures within special education that are very effective and needed and thus should be integrated into and become an inherent part of regular education in order to provide quality educational services to all students.

Those effective people, programs, and procedures that have formerly been labeled "special" simply require a label change and integration into regular education. By defining some people and techniques as "special," we have unnecessarily separated personnel, techniques, methods, and students in our schools on a psychological, if not physical, level. This can be rectified by classifying or defining all effective personnel, programs and procedures worthy of inclusion in our schools as regular and accessible to any student who requires them.

Finally, while some researchers advocate for integration because they believe that special education and special services have failed and are ineffective, the authors do not share their belief. The relevant issue is not the effectiveness of special or regular education, but integration versus segregation; throughout history, segregation has been found to be morally and ethically wrong.

CONCERN #11

The scientific evidence related to integrated, regular educational services versus more segregated special services is mixed and inconclusive; thus, we should continue with current practices.

RESPONSE

It is true that the scientific evidence related to integrated versus segregated services is mixed and inclusive. It appears that much of the confusion is due to variations in the ways that researchers have organized and conducted their studies. For example, if researchers compare students in special and regular classes when the regular classes use support personnel; peer tutoring; and adaptive, cooperative, and individualized programs, students almost inevitably do better in regular classes (see Madden & Slavin, 1983; Stainback & Stainback, 1981; Wang & Birch, 1984). But when researchers compare traditional, "nonadaptive," regular classes to special classes (in which individualized and adaptive instruction take place), the students in the special classes do as well or better than those in regular classes (Marston, 1987–88). Thus, it appears that the outcome of research comparing the effectiveness of special classes versus regular classes is dependent upon what is actually offered in "regular" or "special" classes. A major advantage of merger is that it can offer the best from present day "special" and "regular" education within integrated, regular education classrooms and schools.

A more fundamental point that needs to be made here is that although research will likely continue to be conducted on the quality of special and regular classes, whether we integrate our schools is in the final analysis *not* a scientific or research issue. It is one of equality for all society's members. It encompasses such questions as: Do we want to live in an integrated society in which all people are considered of equal worth? Or, do we want to segregate some people? Should we require some people to earn their access to the mainstream by demonstrating various competencies created by professionals, when this access is an inherent right for others? Most integration advocates believe that if we want a democratic, egalitarian society, the answers to these questions are obvious. Throughout history we have focused on such questions repeatedly, specifically in regard to nationality, religion, race, sex, and now in relation to physical and intellectual differences, and in every instance we have reaffirmed a commitment to integration and equality for all.

Point to Ponder

Do we really want a society wherein some children have to prove in carefully designed studies conducted by experimental researchers that they should be included in the mainstream of their communities and attend their neighborhood schools? If some of us have to prove that we belong, who among us will be next? Do not all children who have not broken any laws have a right to live in and be a part of their communities and neighborhood schools simply because they are human beings?

The decision to integrate our schools is a moral or ethical decision based on societal values (Biklen, 1985; Sarason, 1982). Our basic societal values should not be subjected to quantitative (or qualitative) investigations or reviews of scientific research to determine their efficiency or popularity, but, rather, they should be evaluated according to what is right, just, and desirable. The rights to life, privacy, equality, religious choice, marriage, or parenthood are value choices made based on the type of life we wish to live, not on research indicating their popularity or ease of implementation. For instance, should the decision to racially integrate the schools in the *Brown v. Board of Education* ruling have been based on research finding regarding citizens' attitudes about it in the 1950s, its "feasibility," or on the enormous obstacles that would have to be overcome to achieve integration? Should the decision have been delayed until experimental researchers said racial integration was satisfactory? Of course not, since segregation is morally wrong. The court recognized that segregation on the basis of race conflicted with society's values of equality and fair treatment of all people. These same values form the basis for advocating the integration of persons classified as disabled into the mainstream of education and the community.

Thus the premise that the research base for allowing persons with disabilities to become an integral part of our educational and community mainstream is not yet strong enough or foolproof enough is illogical. The decision as to whether integration is right or wrong is fundamentally a moral or ethical decision. As stated by Biklen (1985):

> Some people would have us wait for science, in this case educational researchers, to prove that integration yields faster, more effective learning than does segregation. But . . . to look to science for an answer to the question, "Is integration a good idea?" is like asking, . . . "Is it good and right for people to care for their aging parents?" In other words, the practice of integration . . . is not fundamentally a question that science can answer. From science, we can learn some of the effects of such a policy (e.g., . . . types of education possible, . . .), or how to make it work better, but science cannot tell us that integration is right. . . . We can answer it only by determining what we believe, what we consider important. (pp. 183–184)

While the decision to integrate schools is based on values, research does have a critical part to play, however, in achieving excellence in the education for all students in integrated regular education classes. Quality instruction in schools cannot be expected to occur without well conceived and conducted research. Research can provide the basis of development and refinement of programs, procedures, and techniques that can allow for quality education to occur within groups of students with diverse needs in integrated regular education classes. This type of research is reflected in research on cooperative learning strategies, adaptive learning models, effective teaching, behavior management, support facilitation, peer tutoring, material and procedure adaptation for individual differences, curricular-based assessment, and the vast body of information available on curricular learning areas such as communication and alternative communication skills, classroom computer technology, and parent and professional collaboration.

Research procedures also are necessary to evaluate and monitor the effectiveness of programs implemented in the schools; the effectiveness of schools, classrooms, and teachers; and the progress of students, both collectively and individually. Such evaluation research is needed to ensure accountability in addressing the goal of providing every student an education appropriate to his or her unique needs within a regular, mainstream educational structure.

In summary, whether integration is right or wrong is *not* a scientific or research question. As indicated earlier, should the court in the *Brown* case have based its decision on a review and analysis of research studies on the "feasibility" of racial integration? Of course not, since segregation has no justification. Based on moral values, the only defensible thing to do is integrate and do research to determine how best to provide appropriate instruction for every student within integrated classrooms and schools.

CONCERN #12

The least restrictive environment (LRE) clause of PL 94-142 does not require integration into regular classes or schools.

RESPONSE

The appropriateness of perpetuating the concept of the LRE for students considered as disabled as a policy direction has been questioned (Taylor, 1988). As Taylor points out, while the LRE was forward looking when it was conceived over a decade ago, it is now time to progress beyond it for a number of reasons. These include pitfalls such as:

1. The LRE principle legitimates restrictive environments by implying that restrictive environments are appropriate in some circumstances.
2. It confuses segregation and integration with the intensity of services by assuming that least restrictive, more integrated settings cannot provide specialized intensive services.
3. It is based on the "readiness model" in which people considered as disabled must earn the right to placement in least restrictive settings.
4. It supports the primacy of professional decision making in which professionals are given the power to determine if an integrated setting is appropriate for an individual, rather than recognizing that it should be a basic right of individuals to live and learn in the mainstream of schools and communities.
5. It implies that the decision to be made is one of to what extent students classified as disabled should be restricted, rather than whether they should be restricted, which basically infringes on students' basic rights to live and learn in the mainstream.
6. It assumes change in placement as students demonstrate increasing competencies or skills, which does not allow for development of relationships and a sense of stability with peers and friends in one setting.

7. It focuses on physical placements rather than services and supports needed to assist students to function in integrated classrooms and schools.

For reasons such as these, adherence to the concept of the least restrictive environment as a future policy direction appears neither warranted nor worthwhile to foster the goals of achieving an integrated society.

CONCERN #13

It is important to know a student's specific disability in order to plan an appropriate educational program for him or her.

RESPONSE

It is essential that the individual characteristics of all students be considered when planning educational programs. But, as noted previously in Chapter 2, it is a mistake to design an educational program for a child based on one or two characteristics or a disability label. The problem with the current disabilities approach to education is that there is much more to a child than is described by a label or categorical affiliation (e.g., retarded, autistic, blind).

Educational programs should be designed based on each child's specific interests, needs, and capabilities. When this is done, all individual characteristics are taken into account. In the authors' view, all children should be approached and educated as individuals and as whole persons, each with unique characteristics, rather than according to whether they are classified as disabled or nondisabled, black or white, or male or female. This is as important for those students considered normal or average—who are often grouped together and given standardized instruction—as for any other students.

CONCERN #14

The notions involved in merging regular and special education do not take into account the specific roles of special and regular educators and how they can coordinate their efforts to best serve all children.

RESPONSE

While special and regular educators may need to coordinate or collaborate at the present time, the ultimate goal of merger is not collaboration or coordination, but *integration*. In a merged system, there will not be "special" and "regular" educators. Present day special educators will become regular educators, with expertise in individualized and adaptive instruction, braille, support facilitation, community-referenced instruction, integration, and the like. Many will serve as teachers, support facilitators, or regular education consulting personnel in their areas of expertise. Thus, all educators will be regular educators in an integrated, merged system, and there will be no need for collaboration between "special" and "regular" education. There will, of course, always be a need for *all* educators to work closely together and to coordinate expertise in natural and normal ways.

CONCERN #15

Some people favor various forms of special and/or segregated services.

RESPONSE

Some educators, parents, and students do favor special and/or segregated services. However, people's attitudes are not a stable, static condition. Attitudes change, and al-

Point to Ponder

When some people who are deaf say that they would rather be in isolated, segregated settings (Commission on the Education of the Deaf, 1988) than in the mainstream of neighborhood public schools, it is a sad commentary on how warm, welcoming, adaptive, and flexible the mainstream is for people who are deaf. We must do better. We must make the mainstream of schools a place where the needs of all children are met and they are made to feel welcome and secure. To do otherwise is to chance losing the participation and contributions of many people, including those who are deaf, in the mainstream of society.

though some people still advocate for segregation, growing numbers of educators, parents, and students favor integration. Based on the history of past integration movements, the number of people who favor integration will likely continue to grow and one day constitute the vast majority.

In nearly all equality and integration movements (e.g., blacks, women), the inherent notions that called for change in common practice or the status quo were never initially overwhelmingly popular (not even with many blacks and women for example). But over time, as people recognized the benefits of the change, it became accepted. While there will be ups and downs over the next several decades, the same gradual but steady trend toward acceptance of people defined as disabled into the mainstream of our schools and communities is likely to occur (Bogdan, 1983).

It is important to remember that only 20 years ago very few people believed in the integration of people classified as having and not having disabilities in neighborhood schools and communities. Thus, even if the numbers for agreement with integration were only in the 10%, 20%, or 30% range today, that would be a significant trend toward greater acceptance.

Discussing attitudes here is not meant to imply that the attitudes people have toward integration are what makes it right or wrong. Obviously, this is not the case. As noted earlier in this chapter, in the 1950s, the majority of white and black people in this country were against the integration of the races. Did that make racial segregation right?

CONCERN #16

Recently in the professional literature, there has been some indication that some students would rather be "pulled-out" or separated from their classmates than have a specialist work with them in the regular classroom.

RESPONSE

There is little doubt that students do not want to be targeted as, for example, "mentally retarded," or "disturbed," by having a specialist, recognized as working with "deviant" students, come in to the regular classroom to work with them. This can cause embarrassment and humiliation. Under these circumstances, students would naturally choose to work with the specialist in private rather than in front of their classmates. Few, if any, students want their classmates to have a constant reminder that professional educators think of them as "retarded," "disturbed," or "deviant."

For this reason, it is critical that special education and other specialists blend in and become a natural, inherent part of regular classroom situations. They need to become regular education teachers, consultants, specialists, and support facilitators designated to work with any student as needed, rather than being identified as special education specialists who work only with students classified as "deviant," "disordered," or "different." In addition, and perhaps more important, specialists need to work with classroom teachers to assist them to deal with and adapt to the diverse learning needs of all the students in their classrooms.

CONCERN #17

People like to be with others with whom they share common characteristics and concerns.

RESPONSE

We would all probably agree that the persons with whom an individual associates or forms friendships should be their personal choice. The key word here is *choice*. For example, if a person who is blind happens to associate with and become friends with a sighted person or another person who is blind, that is his or her choice. Also, if people who share a common concern (e.g., deafness) want to band together, that is their personal choice. But we should never *impose* or support at public expense the clustering together of people perceived as having common characteristics in segregated settings such as group homes for the retarded, schools for the blind or deaf, or handicapped scout troops.

In addition, it is stereotyping and misleading to say that people who share one or two characteristics are alike and therefore should be grouped together. As noted repeatedly throughout this book, people are complex, possessing a wide array of psychological, physical, and intellectual characteristics. To say that any two or more people are alike because they happen to possess one or two similar characteristics fails to take into account the complexity of people and fosters stereotyping.

CONCERN #18

"Special" and "regular" educators are inherently different in their views and practice of education, and thus merger is not feasible (Lieberman, 1985; Messinger, 1985).

RESPONSE

In the authors' view, the contention that "special" and "regular" educators are different "breeds" results from educators having aligned themselves with different "camps," and are natural self-preservation reactions rather than valid differences. There is no reason to think that regular and special educators either come from and/or evolve into somehow different "kinds of people." Rather, any differences can generally be attributed to training rather than anything inherent. Thus, if special educators exhibit some traits desirable for but different from regular educators, and/or regular educators exhibit some differences desirable for but different from special educators, training can be modified as needed, rather than continuing to justify two camps.

Point to Ponder

The notion that we need to determine who is truly handicapped in order to provide "special" educational services only to students who deserve to receive them is a hold over from basing what we do in schools on medical and welfare models. It is time to move beyond the notion that some students deserve certain educational services and others do not. There is no need for eligibility criteria for any educational services that are based on a categorical affiliation. The only reason to have such eligibility criteria is if you want to exclude some groups of students, but not others, from a service. In the public schools, we want to help *all* children based on their unique needs, interest, and capabilities, using whatever services are available, regardless of whether they are classified as black/white, male/female, or disabled/nondisabled. That is, there simply are no children in public schools who should not receive whatever assistance is available, based on their unique needs, to help them fulfill their potential.

As noted in Chapter 2, there are no inherently regular versus special students. Likewise, there are no inherently different regular versus special educators. We are all educators, with unique differences among each member of the group, rather than two distinct groups "carved by nature." While all of us require strong basic teaching skills, each has different interests and areas of specialization (e.g., reading, mathematics, self-help skills, sign language, vocational programming and competitive employment, and science). These differences can be capitalized upon to provide maximally beneficial programming opportunities to each of the diverse students within one unified system of education. Thus, to enable educators to work together for the common educational benefit of students, we all will need to take a constructive approach in the future. Rather than seeking out weaknesses in the "other camp" as a reason not to trust each other and not to work together, we should build upon the variety of skills inherent in the unique differences in each of us, while working to enhance the knowledge-based, common skills and practices needed by all educators.

CONCERN #19

Some students are truly handicapped and should be recognized as different and as needing help from the general population.

RESPONSE

If within an educational structure we truly attempt to meet the individual needs of each student, there is no functional reason to label some students and assign them to a subgroup represented as handicapped or deviant for educational purposes. A handicap is relative and there are few, if any, students who could be considered totally free from handicaps across all environments. Some people cannot walk; some cannot button their shirt or toilet themselves; others are clumsy, uncoordinated, short, blind, deaf, or unmotivated, each of which could be considered a handicap when engaging in various sports, games, learning, or daily living activities. However, just as each person can have a handicap in some situation, each person could have a potential advantage in some activity or situation. If each student can be viewed as an individual, particular "strengths" could be capitalized upon and particular "handicaps" minimized. In addition, the extensive resource expenditures involved in unproductive classification and labeling practices could be eliminated.

Why do we persist in advocating for an educational structure that requires the assignment of some students to categories that have negative connotations and that psychologically, if not physically, segregates or sets them apart as "different" from their school (and societal) peers? It has never been shown to be of any major instructional value to do so. While it can be argued that the label does provide some general guidelines or information, once one approaches and assesses children as individuals, "the label is no longer necessary or useful, for instructional purposes, since it has been replaced with far more specific information" (Lilly, 1979, p. 40).

CONCERN #20

Special classes and schools are needed for students who display severe forms of maladaptive behavior.

RESPONSE

Research has found that to promote positive social behavior, the best placement for students who display severe forms of maladaptive behavior is with well-behaved students (e.g., Stainback, Stainback, Etscheidt, & Doud, 1986). The placement most detrimental in fostering positive behavior change is in special classes with other students who also display severe forms of maladaptive behavior. Students tend to model the behaviors of those around them. That is, if other students are acting appropriately, a student is more likely to follow suit. Thus, regular classes are much better for students who display severe forms of maladaptive behavior than special classes for disruptive or "behaviorally disordered" students. It should be noted that the same thing is true for students who are shy or withdrawn. Withdrawn students who are grouped with other such students tend to learn to be more withdrawn. When these students are placed with friendly and outgoing students they tend to become more social and outgoing (Nietupski, Stainback, Gleisner, Stainback, & Hamre-Nietupski, 1983).

It has been argued that it is important not to interrupt the education of nonhandicapped students by integrating with them a child who displays disruptive behaviors. The authors agree that it is essential to control or deal with disruptive behavior regardless of who displays the behavior (whether by students defined as disabled or nondisabled). However, it is inappropriate, in the authors' opinion, to assume that it is acceptable for a disruptive student to interfere with the education of students classified as disabled in a "special" class, but wrong for him or her to interfere with the education of nondisabled students in a regular class. The point is that maladaptive behavior is a problem, whether the child is placed in a regular or special class. And since disruptive behavior can be more effectively controlled in regular classrooms where positive peer behavior models are available, it is best to try to marshall all the resources and expertise available in behavior management to deal with maladaptive behavior in the regular class setting.

CONCERN #21

We must recognize that some students need special consideration, services, and as-

Point to Ponder

Back in the 18th and 19th centuries, Martha's Vineyard was the place in the United States that had the highest concentration of community members who were deaf. However, although many of the residents could not hear, all were active, full participants and held equal membership in the community as workers, friends, neighbors, and family members. None were considered handicapped or disabled people. This experience suggests strongly that the concept of a handicap is an arbitrary social category. And if it is a question of definition, rather than a universal given, perhaps it [the term *handicapped*] can be redefined and many of the cultural preconceptions summarized in the term as it is now used, eliminated. (Groce, 1985, p. 108)

sistance because of their needy, handicapped, or disabled condition.

RESPONSE

As noted by Ted Kennedy, Jr., who has been labeled as disabled: "We are tired of being treated as dependents to be cared for through special and welfare programs" (Kennedy, 1986, p. 4). When students are labeled as disabled, handicapped, or needy in order to receive the services they require to progress in school, they are being told they are being done a favor or being treated specially because they are "pitied" and less able to succeed than their peers. This generally results in poor expectations by others, along with the person suffering a loss of self-esteem and the confidence needed to succeed in school. In addition, when students are not labeled, they are generally denied access to the services and assistance they may require to succeed in school. As a result, the provision of special accommodations for students labeled as disabled is detrimental and counterproductive to the goal of providing an integrated, quality education for all students. In contrast to the stated concern, the authors believe it is essential to provide assistance and adaptive educational accommodations to all students as needed. This should be done as a normal, regular and expected practice within the public schools. By doing so, no student will have to be labeled as needy or disabled to receive the services he or she needs to progress in school.

CONCERN #22

There is a need to care about, protect, and support the rights and needs of students traditionally classified as having disabilities.

RESPONSE

Since the concept of educating all students within a single, comprehensive, regular system of education has emerged, a great deal of concern has focused on the importance of supporting, promoting, protecting, and caring for the needs of students classified as having disabilities within integrated, neighborhood schools without disrupting the quality of education provided nonhandicapped students. The authors believe that this is the wrong approach. It divides students, parents, and educators and sometimes even pits one group against the other (i.e., the needs of the "handicapped" versus those of "nonhandicapped"). Rather than continue in this mode, we need to become concerned about the importance of supporting, promoting, protecting, and caring for the needs of *all* students and ensuring a quality education for each student.

One way to do this is to promote equality among all students. That is, recognize that each student is an equally worthwhile member of a school and have every student become a focus of receiving a free and appropriate education that addresses his or her unique needs, interests, and capabilities. This is not a difficult position to take as soon as one accepts that there are no students in the public schools who should not receive a free and appropriate education geared to their unique needs. But the authors are frequently asked, "Aren't there some truly handicapped or disabled students who require special help and attention?" The authors' response is, "People do not have to be considered disabled or handicapped." We define, by the way we construct our schools and society, who is nonhandicapped and who is handicapped or disabled. For instance, a person who uses a wheelchair is handicapped or disabled if we build a multistory building that has no ramps or elevators. By the same token, a person who walks very well with two legs would also be handicapped if we built a multistory building that had no ramps, elevators, or steps to get from one level to another. (Since people who walk with two legs are in the majority, such a handicapping factor in a building would not be tolerated.) As another example, a person who is blind is disabled or handicapped if we require him or her to drive a car for transportation when there is, at present, no technology or know-how for teaching a person who is blind to drive. A student in a learning situation is handicapped or disabled when we operate an educational system that is insensitive to and nonaccommodating to the student's needs by requiring him or her to learn something that the system does not know how to teach him or her or lacks the resources to do so.

As indicated by these illustrations, handicaps or disabilities are socially imposed conditions. All people have both capabilities and needs, and if society requires performance in a situation but does not provide the resources or accommodations necessary for an individual to succeed, we handicap him or her. As noted by Ted Kennedy, Jr. (1986), in regard to people considered as disabled, "Our handicap is one caused by a society insensitive to the needs of others" (p. 4). Either due to insensitivity, lack of resources, or lack of motivation to accommodate for the needs of all of us, society imposes handicaps. That is, while there are people who are blind, deaf, have cerebral palsy, Down syndrome, and the like, whether they are disabled or handicapped in the mainstream of our schools and society at large depends upon how society chooses to react—whether it is accepting and accommodating or rejecting, rigid, and inflexible.

Generally, as a society we have chosen not to include certain accommodations (e.g., ramps, braille, sign language, community-referenced instruction) in regular, normal, or natural environments, and thus we have created a group of handicapped individuals for living and working in the mainstream. Subsequently, we have constructed different, special, or separate environments or systems to address the needs of those we have handicapped. In education we have developed special education, special class-

Point to Ponder

Equality among students in the schools has been threatened by attempts to define groups of students as negatively different, with terms such as *retarded, disordered, handicapped,* or *disabled.* Likewise, at the other end of the spectrum, some children have been characterized or labeled as being gifted, positively different, or superior to the general student population. Mara Sapon-Shevin (1987) has pointed out that such labeling should be no more tolerated than the negative labeling. She emphasizes that all children need to be recognized as having gifts and talents and challenged to be the best they can be, and that until this happens charges of elitism will be leveled at those who defend concepts like "giftedness." She advises proponents of "giftedness" that

> until such time as our schools meet the needs of all children, efforts to silence the cries of elitism that torment gifted education are likely to be unsuccessful. We must listen to these protestations of unfairness not in an effort to find arguments to counter them, but in order to find ways of supporting those who issue them as they struggle to define social and educational justice. (p. 50)

It should be stressed that Sapon-Shevin is not arguing against nurturing the gifts, talents, and creativity of any child, but she is telling us that we should not discriminate against or shut out some children or leave them behind by defining, categorizing, and labeling only selected children as "gifted" and providing this select group programs that meet their unique needs. To achieve true equality in our schools, all children need educational programs that meet their unique needs and that capitalize on their gifts—not just selected categories of students.

es, special schools, and special residential institutions to address the educational needs of students educators have labeled as disabled.

In education, if we choose to be a caring people and truly support integration and equality for all students, we can achieve it. We already have the technology or "know how." By recognizing strengths that every student has and can offer others, while at the same time recognizing the student's needs *and* choosing to form a sense of community in which everyone is accepted, supported, and belongs, we can virtually do away with handicaps or disabilities in our schools (and in society, if we choose). By capitalizing on strengths and accommodating for needs, we can construct schools and nonschool environments to address the diversity in individual differences among all members. No longer would we need to accept inequality among people by imposing handicaps or disabilities on some and constructing special, separate, or different educational systems or environments for them.

To achieve the desired goal, we will need to construct a school system in which each member is important, cared about, and both facilitated and protected by his or her fellow classmates and school personnel. For this to happen we must develop trust in one another to support and want the best for all students. We must develop a sense of community in our schools. We must accept and practice interdependence.

CONCLUSION

Issues and concerns such as those discussed in this chapter need to be resolved if education and society are to progress toward educating all students in the mainstream of regular education. As noted by Lipsky and Gartner (1987), the establishment of a special system of education is an outgrowth of attitudes toward people classified as disabled. The merging of regular and special education so that all students are educated in the mainstream of regular education will require that educators and the general public change their attitudes. These authors are optimistic. Historical trends indicate that increasing numbers of people are adopting an attitude whereby people classified by society as having disabilities should be accepted into the mainstream of school and community life. Growing numbers of people defined as disabled are beginning to demand this (People First, 1987). As a result, we are beginning to "turn from the effort to perfect a separate special education system to the struggle of changing the educational system to make it both one and special for all students" (Lipsky & Gartner, 1987).

It is hoped that in the not too distant future we will arrive at a point where integration programs or books about integration are no longer needed. When that time comes, all students, from their first day of school onward, will be provided an appropriate education in the regular education mainstream as a natural, expected, and normal practice. Likewise, all personnel and resources will be available within regular education to meet diverse students' needs.

REFERENCES

Biklen, D. (1985). *Achieving the complete school.* New York: Columbia University Press.

Bogdan, R. (1983). A closer look at mainstreaming. *Educational Forum, 47,* 425–434.

Braaten, S., Kauffman, J., Braaten, B., Polsgrove, L., & Nelson, M. (1988). The regular education initiative: Patent medicine for behavioral disorders. *Exceptional Children, 55,* 21–29.

Commission on the Education of the Deaf. (1988). *Toward equality: Education of the deaf.* Washington, DC: U.S. Government Printing Office.

Forest, M. (1988). Full inclusion is possible. *IMPACT, 2,* 3–4.

Gerry, M. (1988). *Meeting the challenge of educational integration: The administrative charge.* Paper presented at "We're getting together: Making integration a reality," Ventura County Conference, Ventura, CA.

Groce, N. E. (1985). *Everyone here spoke sign language: Hereditary deafness on Martha's Vineyard.* Cambridge, MA: Harvard University Press.

Kennedy, T., Jr. (1986, Nov. 23). Our right to independence. *Parade Magazine,* pp. 4–7.

Lieberman, L. (1985). Special and regular education: A merger made in heaven? *Exceptional Children, 51,* 513–517.

Lilly, S. (1979). *Children with exceptional needs.* New York: Holt, Rinehart & Winston.

Lipsky, D., & Gartner, A. (1987). Capable of achievement and worthy of respect: Education of handicapped students as if they were full-fledged human beings. *Exceptional Children,* 1987, *54,* 69–74.

Madden, N., & Slavin, R. (1983). Mainstreaming students with mild handicaps: Academic and social outcomes. *Review of Educational Research, 53,* 519–569.

Marston, D. (1987–88, Winter). The effectiveness of special education. *Journal of Special Education, 21,* 13–27.

McHale, S., & Simeonsson, R. (1980). Effects of interaction on nonhandicapped children's attitudes toward autistic children. *American Journal of Mental Deficiency, 85,* 18–24.

Messinger, J. (1985). A commentary on "A rationale for the merger of special and regular education. *Exceptional Children, 51,* 510–513.

Nietupski, J., Stainback, W., Gleissner, L., Stainback, S., & Hamre-Nietupski, S. (1983). Effects of socially outgoing versus withdrawn peer partners on nonhandicapped-handicapped students' interactions. *Behavioral Disorders, 8,* 244–250.

People First. (1987). *People First* (video). Downsview, Ont.: Canadian Association for Community Living.

Rynders, J., Johnson, R., Johnson, D., & Schmidt, B. (1980). Producing positive interaction among Downs syndrome and nonhandicapped teenagers through cooperative goal structuring. *American Journal of Mental Deficiency, 85,* 268–273.

Sapon-Shevin, M. (1987). Giftedness as a social construct. *Teachers College Record, 89,* 39–53.

Sarason, S. (1982). *The culture of the school and the problem of change.* Boston: Allyn & Bacon.

Stainback, W., & Stainback, S. (1981). A review of research on interactions between severely handicapped and nonhandicapped students. *Journal of the Association for the Severely Handicapped, 6,* 23–29.

Stainback, W., & Stainback, S. (1988). The role of research in the movement to educate all students in regular classes. *Newsletter Impact* (distributed by the University of Minnesota's University Affiliated Programs), *1,* 12–16.

Stainback, W., Stainback, S., Etscheidt, S., & Doud, J. (1986). A nonintrusive intervention for acting out behavior. *Teaching Exceptional Children, 19,* 38–41.

Strain, P. (1983). Generalization of autistic children's social behavior change: Effects of developmentally integrated and segregated settings. *Analysis and Intervention in Developmental Disabilities, 3,* 23–24.

Taylor, S. J. (1988). Caught in the continuum: A critical analysis of the principle of the least restrictive environment. *Journal of the Association for the Severely Handicapped, 13,* 41–53.

Vandercook, T., Fleetham, D., Sinclair, S., & Tettie, R. (1988). Cath, Jess, Jules and Ames . . . A story of friendship. *IMPACT, 2,* 18–19.

Voeltz, L. (1982). Effects of structured interactions with severely handicapped peers on children's attitudes. *American Journal of Mental Deficiency, 86,* 380–390.

Wang, M., & Birch, J. (1984). Effective special education in regular classes. *Exceptional Children, 50,* 391–399.

Index